THE ESSENTIAL STALIN

Major Theoretical Writings 1905-52

Edited and with an Introduction by

BRUCE FRANKLIN

CROOM HELM LONDON

FIRST PUBLISHED IN GREAT BRITAIN 1973

CROOM HELM LTD.
2–10 ST. JOHN'S ROAD, LONDON SW11

ISBN 0–85664–056–5 HARDBACK
ISBN 0–35664–076–X PAPERBACK

PRINTED IN GREAT BRITAIN BY
LOWE AND BRYDONE (PRINTERS) LTD, THETFORD, NORFOLK
BOUND BY G. AND J. KITCAT LTD, LONDON

THE ESSENTIAL
STALIN

CONTENTS

Introduction 1

The Proletarian Class and the Proletarian Party (1905) 39

Armed Insurrection and Our Tactics (1905) 48

From: Marxism and the National Question (1913) 54
- I. The Nation 57
- II. The National Movement 65
- III. Presentation of the Question 72
- VII. The National Question in Russia 78

Two Camps (1919) 85

The Foundations of Leninism (1924) 89
- I. The Historical Roots of Leninism 92
- II. Method 98
- III. Theory 105
- IV. The Dictatorship of the Proletariat 120
- V. The Peasant Question 132
- VI. The National Question 145
- VII. Strategy and Tactics 154
- VIII. The Party 170
- IX. Style in Work 184

Concerning the Question of the Proletariat and the Peasantry (1925) 187

Notes on Contemporary Themes: China (1927) 194

Organise Mass Criticism from Below (1928) 220

Report to the Seventeenth Congress of the Communist Party of the Soviet Union (Bolshevik) on the Work of the Central Committee (1934) 224

I. The Continuing Crisis of World Capitalism and the External Situation of the Soviet Union 224
1. The Course of the Economic Crisis in the Capitalist Countries 226
2. The Growing Tension in the Political Situation in the Capitalist Countries 231
3. The Relations Between the U.S.S.R and the Capitalist States 238
II. The Continuing Progress of the National Economy and the Internal Situation in the U.S.S.R. 243
1. The Progress of Industry 246
2. The Progress of Agriculture 252
3. The Rise in the Material and Cultural Standard of the Working People 264
4. The Progress of Trade Turnover, and Transport 269
III. The Party 274
1. Questions of Ideological and Political Leadership 275
2. Questions of Organisational Leadership 287

Dialectical and Historical Materialism (1938) 300

Report to the Eighteenth Congress of the Communist Party of the Soviet Union (Bolshevik) on the Work of the Central Committee (1939) 334
I. The Soviet Union and International Affairs 334
1. New Economic Crisis in the Capitalist Countries. Intensification of the Struggle for Markets and Sources of Raw Material, and for a New Redivision of the World. 335
2. Increasing Acuteness of the International Political Situation. Collapse of the Post-war System of Peace Treaties. Beginning of a New Imperialist War. 339
3. The Soviet Union and the Capitalist Countries 344

II. Internal Affairs of the Soviet Union 346
1. Further Progress of Industry and Agriculture 349
2. Further Rise in the Material and Cultural Standard of the People 363
3. Further Consolidation of the Soviet System 367
III. Further Strengthening of the C.P.S.U.(B.) 370
1. Measures to Improve the Composition of The Party. Division of Organisations. Closer Contact between the Leading Party Bodies and the Work of the Lower Bodies. 371
2. Selection, Promotion and Allocation of Cadres 373
3. Party Propaganda. Marxist-Leninist Training of Party Members and Party Cadres. 376
4. Some Questions of Theory 379

The Twenty-sixth Anniversary of the October Revolution (1943) 393
I. A Year of Radical Turn in the Course of the War 394
II. Nationwide Assistance to the Front 398
III. Consolidation of the Anti-Hitler Coalition. Disintegration of the Fascist Bloc. 402

Marxism and Linguistics (1950) 407
I. Concerning Marxism in Linguistics 407
II. Reply to Krasheninnikova 430
III. Reply to Sanzheyev 436
IV. Reply to D. Belkin and S. Furer 437
V. Reply to A. Kholopov 439

Economic Problems of Socialism in the U.S.S.R. (1952) 445
I. Remarks on Economic Questions Connected with the November 1951 Discussion 445
1. Character of Economic Laws Under Socialism 445
2. Commodity Production Under Socialism 451
3. The Law of Value Under Socialism 458

4. Abolition of the Antithesis Between Town and Country, and Between Mental Labour and Physical Labour, and Elimination of Distinctions Between Them 463
5. Disintegration of the Single World Market and Deepening of the Crisis of the World Capitalist System 467
6. Inevitability of Wars Between Capitalist Countries 469
7. The Basic Economic Laws of Modern Capitalism and of Socialism 473
8. Other Questions 477
9. International Importance of a Marxist Textbook on Political Economy 479
10. Ways of Improving the Draft Textbook on Political Economy 481

Reply to Comrade Alexander Ilyich Notkin 482

From: Concerning the Errors of Comrade L. D. Yaroshenko 490

I. Comrade Yaroshenko's Chief Error 490
II. Other Errors of Comrade Yaroshenko 500

Speech to the Nineteenth Congress of the Communist Party of the Soviet Union (1952) 508

INTRODUCTION

I used to think of Joseph Stalin as a tyrant and butcher who jailed and killed millions, betrayed the Russian revolution, sold out liberation struggles around the world, and ended up a solitary madman, hated and feared by the people of the Soviet Union and the world. Even today I have trouble saying the name "Stalin" without feeling a bit sinister.

But, to about a billion people today, Stalin is the opposite of what we in the capitalist world have been programmed to believe. The people of China, Vietnam, Korea, and Albania consider Stalin one of the great heroes of modern history, a man who personally helped win their liberation. This belief could be dismissed as the product of an equally effective brainwashing from the other side, except that the workers and peasants of the Soviet Union, who knew Stalin best, share this view. For almost two decades the Soviet rulers have systematically attempted to make the Soviet people accept the capitalist world's view of Stalin, or at least to forget him. They expunged him from the history books, wiped out his memorials, and even removed his body from his tomb. Yet, according to all accounts, the great majority of the Soviet people still revere the memory of Stalin, and bit by bit they have forced concessions. First it was granted that Stalin had been a great military leader and the main anti-fascist strategist of World War II. Then it was conceded that he had made important contributions to the material progress of the Soviet people. Now a recent Soviet film shows Stalin, several years before his death, as a calm, rational, wise leader.

But the rulers of the Soviet Union still try to keep the people actually from reading Stalin. When they took over, one of their first acts was to ban his writings. They stopped the publication of his collected works, of which thirteen volumes had already appeared, covering the period only through 1934. This has made it difficult throughout the world to obtain Stalin's writings in the last two decades of his life. Recently the Hoover Institute of Stanford University, whose purpose, as stated by its founder, Herbert Hoover, is to "demonstrate the evils of the doctrines of Karl Marx," completed the final volumes in Russian so that they would be available to Stanford's team of émigré anti-Communists. (In preparing this volume, I was able to use the Hoover collection of writings by and about Stalin only by risking jail, directly violating my banishment by court injunction from this citadel of the Free World.)

The situation in the U.S. is not much different from that in the U.S.S.R. In fact the present volume represents the first time since 1955 that a major publishing house in either country has authorized the publication of Stalin's works. U.S. capitalist publishers have printed only Stalin's wartime diplomatic correspondence and occasional essays, usually much abridged, in anthologies. Meanwhile his enemies and critics are widely published. Since the early 1920s there have been basically two opposing lines claiming to represent Marxism-Leninism, one being Stalin's and the other Trotsky's. The works of Trotsky are readily available in many inexpensive editions. And hostile memoirs, such as those of Khrushchev and Svetlana Stalin, are actually serialized in popular magazines.

The suppression of Stalin's writings spreads the notion that he did not write anything worth reading. Yet Stalin is clearly one of the three most important historical figures of our century, his thought and deeds still affecting our daily lives, considered by hundreds of millions today as one of the leading political theorists of any time, his very name a strongly emotional household word throughout the world. Anyone familiar with the development of Marxist-Leninist theory in the past half century knows that Stalin was not merely a man of action. Mao names him "the greatest genius of our time," calls himself Stalin's disciple, and argues that Stalin's theoretical works are still the core of world Communist revolutionary strategy.

Gaining access to Stalin's works is not the hardest part of coming to terms with him. First we must recognize that there can be no "objective" or "neutral" appraisal of Stalin, any more than there can be of any major historical figure during the epochs of class struggle. From the point of view of some classes, George Washington was an arrogant scoundrel and traitor to his country, king, and God, a renegade who brought slaughter and chaos to a continent; Abraham Lincoln was responsible for the deaths of millions and the destruction of a civilized, cultured, harmonious society based on the biblically sanctioned relationship with the black descendants of Ham; Sitting Bull was a murderous savage who stood in the way of the progress of a superior civilization; Eldridge Cleaver, George and Jonathan Jackson, Ruchell Magee, and Angela Davis are vicious murderers, while Harry Truman, Nelson Rockefeller, Mayor Daley, John F. Kennedy, and Richard Nixon are rational and patriotic men who use force only when necessary to protect the treasured values of the Free World.

Any historical figure must be evaluated from the interests of one class or another. Take J. Edgar Hoover, for example. Anti-Communists may disagree about his performance, but they start from the assumption that the better he did his job of preserving "law and order" as defined by our present rulers, the better he was. We Communists, on the other hand, certainly would not think Hoover "better" if he had been more efficient in running the secret police and protecting capitalism. And so the opposite with Stalin, whose job was not to preserve capitalism but to destroy it, not to suppress communism but to advance it. The better he did his job, the worse he is likely to seem to all those who profit from this economic system and the more he will be appreciated by the victims of that system. The Stalin question is quite different for those who share his goals and for those who oppose them. For the revolutionary people of the world it is literally a life-and-death matter to have a scientific estimate of Stalin, because he was, after all, the principal leader of the world revolution for thirty crucial years.

I myself have seen Stalin from both sides. Deeply embedded in my consciousness and feelings was that vision of Stalin as tyrant and butcher. This was part of my over-all view of communism as a slave system, an idea that I was taught in capitalist society. Communist society was not red but a dull-gray world. It was ruled by a secret clique of powerful men. Everybody else worked for these few and kept their mouths shut. Propaganda poured from all the media. The secret police were everywhere, tapping phones, following people on the street, making midnight raids. Anyone who spoke out would lose his job, get thrown in jail, or even get shot by the police. One of the main aims of the government was international aggression, starting wars to conquer other countries. When I began to discover that this entire vision point by point described my own society, a number of questions arose in my mind.

For me, as for millions of others in the United States, it was the Vietnamese who forced a change in perception. How could we fail to admire the Vietnamese people and to see Ho Chi Minh as one of the great heroes of our times? What stood out most about Ho was his vast love for the people and his dedication to serving them. (In 1965, before I became a Communist, I spoke at a rally soliciting blood for the Vietnamese victims of U.S. bombing. When I naively said that Ho was a nationalist above being a Communist, and a human being above being a nationalist, I was pelted with garbage and, much to my surprise, called a "dirty Commie.") But we were supposed to believe that Ho was a "tyrant and butcher." Later, it dawned on me that Fidel Castro was also supposed to be a "tyrant and butcher," although earlier he had been portrayed as a freedom fighter against the Batista dictatorship. Still later, I began to study the Chinese revolution, and found in Mao's theory and practice the guide for my own thinking and action. But, again, we were supposed to see Mao as a "tyrant and butcher," and also a "madman." The more I looked into it, the more I found that these "tyrants and butchers"—Ho, Fidel, and Mao—were all dedicated servants of the people, inspired by a deep and self-sacrificing love for them. At some point, I began to wonder if perhaps even Stalin was not a "tyrant and butcher." With this thought came intense feelings that must resemble what someone in a tribe experiences when violating a taboo. But if we want to understand the world we live in, we must face Stalin.

Joseph Stalin personifies a major aspect of three decades of twentieth-century history. If we seek answers to any of the crucial questions about the course of our century, at some point we find Stalin standing directly in our path. Is it possible for poor and working people to make a revolution and then wield political power? Can an undeveloped, backward nation whose people are illiterate, impoverished, diseased, starving, and lacking in all the skills and tools needed to develop their productive forces possibly achieve both material and cultural well-being? Can this be done under a condition of encirclement by hostile powers, greedy for conquest, far more advanced industrially and militarily, and fanatical in their opposition to any people's revolutionary government? What price must be paid for the success of revolutionary development? Can national unity be achieved in a vast land inhabited by many peoples of diverse races, religions, culture, language, and levels of economic development? Is it possible to attain international unity among the exploited and oppressed peoples of many different nations whose governments depend upon intense nationalism and the constant threat of war? Then, later, can the people of any modern, highly industrialized society also have a high degree of freedom, or must the state be their enemy? Can any society flourish without some form of ruling elite?

These questions are all peculiarly modern, arising in the epoch of capitalism as it reaches its highest form, modern imperialism, and becoming critical in our own time, the era of global revolution. Each of these questions leads us inevitably to Stalin. In my opinion, it is not going too far to say that Stalin is the key figure of our era.

All the achievements and all the failures, all the strengths and all the weaknesses, of the Soviet revolution and indeed of the world revolution in the period 1922–53 are summed up in Stalin. This is not to say that he is personally responsible for all that was and was not accomplished, or that nobody else could have done what he did. We are not dealing with a "great man" theory of history. In fact, quite the opposite. If we are to understand Stalin at all, and evaluate him from the point of view of either of the two major opposing classes, we must see him, like all historical figures, as a being created by his times and containing the contradictions of those times.

Every idea of Stalin's, as he would be the first to admit,

came to him from his historical existence, which also fixed limits to the ideas available to him. He could study history in order to learn from the experience of the Paris Commune, but he could not look into a crystal ball to benefit from the lessons of the Chinese Cultural Revolution. And the decisions he made also had fixed and determined limits on either side, as we shall see.

To appraise Stalin, the best way to begin is to compare the condition of the Soviet Union and the rest of the world at two times: when he came into leadership and when he died. Without such a comparison, it is impossible to measure what he may have contributed or taken away from human progress. If the condition of the Soviet people was much better when he died than when he took power, he cannot have made their lives worse. The worst that can be said is that they would have progressed more without him. The same is true for the world revolution. Was it set back during the decades of his leadership, or did it advance? Once we put the questions this way, the burden of proof falls on those who deny Stalin's positive role as a revolutionary leader.

As World War I began, the Russian Empire consisted primarily of vast undeveloped lands inhabited by many different peoples speaking a variety of languages with a very low level of literacy, productivity, technology, and health. Feudal social relations still prevailed throughout many of these lands. Czarist secret police, officially organized bands of military terrorists, and a vast bureaucracy were deployed to keep the hungry masses of workers and peasants in line. The war brought these problems to a crisis. Millions went to their deaths wearing rags, with empty stomachs, often waiting for those in front of them to fall so they could have a rifle and a few rounds of ammunition. When the Bolsheviks seized power in 1917, the entire vast empire, including the great cities of Russia itself, was in chaos.

Before the new government could begin to govern, it was immediately set upon by the landlords, capitalists, and generals of the old regime, with all the forces they could buy and muster, together with combined military forces of Britain, France, Japan, and Poland, and additional military contingents from the U.S. and other capitalist countries. A vicious civil war raged for three years, from Siberia through European Russia, from the White Sea to the Ukraine. At the end of the Civil War, in 1920, agricultural output was less than half that of the prewar poverty-stricken countryside. Even worse was the situation in industry. Many mines and factories had been destroyed. Transport had been torn up. Stocks of raw materials and semifinished products had been exhausted. The output of large-scale industry was about one seventh of what it had been before the war. And the fighting against foreign military intervention had to go on for two more years. Japanese and U.S. troops still held a portion of Siberia, including the key port city of Vladivostok, which was not recaptured until late 1922.

Lenin suffered his first stroke in 1922. From this point on, Stalin, who was the General Secretary of the Central Committee, began to emerge as the principal leader of the Party. Stalin's policies were being implemented at least as early as 1924, the year of Lenin's death, and by 1927 the various opposing factions had been defeated and expelled from the Party. It is the period of the early and mid-1920s that we must compare to 1953.

The Soviet Union of the early 1920s was a land of deprivation. Hunger was everywhere, and actual mass famines swept across much of the countryside. Industrial production was extremely low, and the technological level of industry was so backward that there seemed little possibility of mechanizing agriculture. Serious rebellions in the armed forces were breaking out, most notably at the Kronstadt garrison in 1921. By 1924 large-scale peasant revolts were erupting, particularly in Georgia. There was virtually no electricity outside the large cities. Agriculture was based on tiny peasant holdings and medium-sized farms seized by rural capitalists (the kulaks) who forced the peasants back into wage labor and tenant farming. Health care was almost non-existent in much of the country. The technical knowledge and skills needed to develop modern industry, agriculture, health, and education were concentrated in the hands of a few, mostly opposed to socialism, while the vast majority of the population were illiterate and could hardly think about education while barely managing to subsist. The Soviet Union was isolated in a world controlled by powerful capitalist countries, physically surrounding it, setting up economic blockades, and officially refusing to recognize its existence while outdoing each other in their pledges to wipe out this Red menace.

The counterrevolution was riding high throughout Europe, Great Britain, and even in the U.S.A., where the Red threat was used as an excuse to smash labor unions. Fascism was emerging in several parts of the capitalist world, particularly in Japan and in Italy, where Mussolini took dictatorial power in 1924. Most of the world consisted of colonies and neo-colonies of the European powers.

When Stalin died in 1953, the Soviet Union was the second greatest industrial, scientific, and military power in the world, and showed clear signs of moving to overtake the U.S. in all these areas. This was despite the devastating losses it suffered while defeating the fascist powers of Germany, Romania, Hungary, and Bulgaria. The various peoples of the U.S.S.R. were unified. Starvation and illiteracy were unknown throughout the country. Agriculture was completely collectivized and extremely productive. Preventive health care was the finest in the world, and medical treatment of exceptionally high quality was available free to all citizens. Education at all levels was free. More books were published in the U.S.S.R. than in any other country. There was no unemployment.

Meanwhile, in the rest of the world, not only had the main fascist powers of 1922–45 been defeated, but the forces of revolution were on the rise everywhere. The Chinese Communist Party had just led one fourth of the world's population to victory over foreign imperialism and domestic feudalism and capitalism. Half of Korea was socialist, and the U.S.-British imperialist army, having rushed to intervene in the civil war under the banner of the United Nations, was on the defensive and hopelessly demoralized. In Vietnam, a strong socialist power, which had already defeated Japanese imperialism, was administering the final blows to the beaten army of the French empire. The monarchies and fascist military dictatorships of Eastern Europe had been destroyed by a combination of partisan forces, led by local Communists, and the Soviet Army; everywhere except for Greece there were now governments that supported the world revolution and at least claimed to be governments of the workers and peasants. The largest political party in both France and Italy was the Communist Party. The national liberation movement among the European colonies and neocolonies was surging forward. Between 1946 and 1949 alone, at least nominal national independence was achieved by Burma, Indonesia, India, Pakistan, Laos, Libya, Ceylon, Jordan, and the Philippines, countries comprising about one third of the world's population. The entire continent of Africa was stirring.

Everybody but the Trotskyites, and even some of them, would have to admit that the situation for the Communist world revolution was incomparably advanced in 1953 over what it had been in the early or mid 1920s. Of course, that does not settle the Stalin question. We still have to ask whether Stalin contributed to this tremendous advance, or slowed it down, or had negligible influence on it. And we must not duck the question as to whether Stalin's theory and practice built such serious faults into revolutionary communism that its later failures, particularly in the Soviet Union, can be pinned on him. So let us look through Stalin's career, focusing particularly on its most controversial aspects.

"Stalin," which means "steel-man," was the code name for a young Georgian revolutionary born as Joseph Vissarionovich Djugashvili in 1879 in the town of Gori. His class origins combine the main forces of the Russian revolution. His father, formerly a village cobbler of peasant background, became a worker in a shoe factory. His mother was the daughter of peasant serfs. So Stalin was no stranger to either workers or peasants, and being from Georgia, he had first-hand knowledge of how czarist Russia oppressed the non-Russian peoples of its empire.

While studying at the seminary for a career as a priest, he made his first contact with the Marxist underground at the age of fifteen, and at eighteen he formally joined the Russian Social-Democratic Labor Party, which was to evolve into the Communist Party. Shortly after joining the party in 1898, he became convinced that Lenin was the main theoretical leader of the revolution, particularly when Lenin's newspaper *Iskra* began to appear in 1900. After being thrown out of his seminary, Stalin concentrated on organizing workers in the area of Tiflis, capital of Georgia, and the Georgian industrial city of Batum. After one of his many arrests by the czarist secret police, he began to correspond with Lenin from exile.

Escaping from Siberian exile in 1904, Stalin returned to organizing workers in the cities of Georgia, where mass strikes were beginning to assume a decidedly political and revolutionary character. Here he began to become one of the main spokesmen for Lenin's theory, as we see in the first two selections in this volume. In December 1904 he led a huge strike of the Baku workers, which helped precipitate the abortive Russian revolution of 1905. During the revolution, and after it was suppressed, Stalin was one of the main Bolshevik underground and military organizers, and was frequently arrested by the secret police. At the Prague Conference of 1912, in which the Bolsheviks completed the split with the Mensheviks and established themselves as a separate party, Stalin was elected in absentia to the Central Committee, a position he was to maintain for over four decades. Then, on the eve of World War I, he published what may properly be considered his first major contribution to Marxist-Leninist theory, *Marxism and the National Question.* (See footnote 1, p. 54–55.)

Prior to World War I, the various social-democratic parties of Europe were loosely united in the Second International. All pledged themselves to international proletarian solidarity. But when the war broke out, the theory Stalin had developed in *Marxism and the National Question* proved to be crucial and correct. As Stalin had foreseen, every party that had compromised with bourgeois nationalism ended up leading the workers of its nation to support their "own" bourgeois rulers by going out to kill and be killed by the workers of the other nations.

Lenin, Stalin, and the other Bolsheviks took a quite different position. They put forward the slogan "Turn the imperialist war into a civil war." Alone of all the parties of the Second International, they came out for actual armed revolution.

In February 1917 the workers, peasants, and soldiers of Russia, in alliance with the liberal bourgeoisie, overthrew the czarist autocracy, which had bled the country dry and brought it to ruin in a war fought to extend the empire. The liberal bourgeoisie established a new government. The next few months led to a key moment in history. Most of the parties that claimed to be revolutionary now took the position that the Russian proletariat was too weak and backward to assume political power. They advocated that the proletariat should support the new bourgeois government and enter a long period of capitalist development until someday in the future when they could begin to think about socialism. This view even penetrated the Bolsheviks. So when Stalin was released from his prison exile in March and the Central Committee brought him back to help lead the work in St. Petersburg, he found a heavy internal struggle. He took Lenin's position, and, being placed in charge of the Bolshevik newspaper *Pravda,* was able to put it forward vigorously to the masses. When the Central Committee finally decided, in October, to lead the workers and soldiers of St. Petersburg to seize the Winter Palace and establish a proletarian government, it was over the violent objections of many of the aristocratic intellectuals who, much to their own surprise and discomfort, had found themselves in an actual revolutionary situation. Two of them, Zinoviev and Kamenev, even went so far as to inform the bourgeois newspapers that the Bolsheviks had a secret plan to seize power. After the virtually bloodless seizure by the workers and soldiers took place, a third member of the Central Committee, Rykov, joined Zinoviev and Kamenev in a secret deal made with the bourgeois parties whereby the Bolsheviks would resign from power, the press would be returned to the bourgeoisie, and Lenin would be permanently barred from holding public office. (All this is described in John Reed's *Ten Days That Shook the World,* which was first published in 1919. I mention this because Zinoviev, Kamenev, and Rykov were three of the central figures of the purge trials of the 1930s, and it is they who have been portrayed as stanch Bolsheviks in such works as Arthur Koestler's *Darkness at Noon.*)

During the Civil War, which followed the seizure of power, Stalin began to emerge as an important military leader. Trotsky was nominally the head of the Red Army. Believing, as he always did, in the primacy of technique, Trotsky took as one of his main tasks winning over the high officers of the former czarist army and turning them into the general command of the revolutionary army. The result was defeat after defeat for the Red forces, either through outright betrayal by their aristocratic officers or because these officers tried to apply military theories appropriate to a conscript or mercenary army to the leadership of a people's army made up of workers and peasants. Stalin, on the other hand, understood the military situation from the point of view of the workers and peasants, and with a knowledge of their capabilities and limitations.

In 1919 Stalin was sent as a special plenipotentiary to the key Volga city of Tsaritsyn. His mission was simply to assure the delivery of food supplies from this entire region. What he found was a disastrous military situation, with the city not only surrounded by the White Army but heavily infiltrated by counterrevolutionary forces. He saw that the food supply could not be safeguarded unless the military and political situations were dealt with. He instituted an uncompromising purge of counterrevolutionary elements within both the officer corps and the political infrastructure, took personal command of the military forces over the heads of both the local authorities and Trotsky, and then proceeded to save the city, the region, and the food supply. Trotsky, furious, demanded his recall. As for the citizens of Tsaritsyn, their opinion became known six years later, when they renamed their city Stalingrad.

After this episode, rather than being recalled, Stalin was dispatched far and wide to every major front in the Civil War. In each and every place, he was able to win the immediate respect of the revolutionary people and to lead the way to military victory, even in the most desperate circumstances. Certain qualities emerged more and more clearly, acknowledged by both friends and enemies. These were his enormous practicality and efficiency, his worker-peasant outlook, and the unswerving way he proceeded to the heart of every problem. By the end of the war, Stalin was widely recognized as a man who knew how to run things, a quality sorely lacking among most of the aristocratic intellectuals who then saw themselves as great proletarian leaders. In April 1922 he was made General Secretary of the Central Committee of the Communist Party. It was in this position that Stalin was quickly to become the de facto leader of the Party and the nation.

Stalin's career up to this point is relatively uncontroversial in comparison with everything that follows. But nothing at all about Stalin is beyond controversy. Most of his biographers in the capitalist world minimize his revolutionary activities prior to 1922. At least two influential biographies, Boris Souvarine's *Stalin* (1939) and Edward Ellis Smith's *The Young Stalin* (1967), even argue that during most of this period Stalin was actually an agent for the czarist secret police. Trotsky's mammoth biography *Stalin* (1940) not only belittles Stalin's revolutionary activities but actually sees his life and "moral stature" predetermined by his racially defined genetic composition; after discussing whether or not Stalin had "an admixture of Mongolian blood," Trotsky decides that in any case he was one perfect type of the national character of southern countries such as Georgia, where, "in addition to the so-called Southern type, which is characterized by a combination of lazy shiftlessness and explosive irascibility, one meets cold natures, in whom phlegm is combined with stubbornness and slyness." The most influential biographer of all, Trotsky's disciple Isaac Deutscher, is a bit more subtle, blaming Stalin's crude and vicious character not on his race but on his low social class:

> The revolutionaries from the upper classes (such as Trotsky, Zinoviev, Kamenev, Bukharin, Rakovsky, Radek, Lunacharsky, Chicherin) came into the Socialist movement with inherited cultural traditions. They . . . brought into the milieu of the revolution some of the values and qualities of their own milieu—not only knowledge, but also refinement of thought, speech, and manners. Indeed, their Socialist rebellion was itself the product of moral sensitiveness and intellectual refinement. These were precisely the qualities that life had not been kind enough to cultivate in Djugashvili [Stalin]. On the contrary, it had heaped enough physical and moral squalor in his path to blunt his sensitiveness and his taste. (*Stalin, A Political Biography*, p. 26)

Although there are vastly different views of Stalin's career up to this point, his activities are relatively less controversial, because they are relatively less important. Whatever Stalin's contribution, there is still a good chance that even without him Lenin could have led the revolution and the Red forces would have won the Civil War. But, from this point on, there are at least two widely divergent, in fact wildly contradictory, versions of Stalin's activities and their significance. Most readers of this book have heard only one side of this debate, the side of Trotsky and the capitalist world. I shall not pretend to make a "balanced presentation," but instead give a summary of the unfamiliar other side of the argument.

Everyone, friend and foe alike, would agree that at the heart of the question of Stalin lies the theory and practice of "socialism in one country." All of Stalin's major ideological opponents in one way or another took issue with this theory.

Actually, the theory did not originate with Stalin but with Lenin. In 1915, in his article "On the Slogan for a United States of Europe," Lenin argued that "the victory of socialism is possible first in several or even in one capitalist country alone." He foresaw "a more or less prolonged and stubborn struggle" internationally that could begin like this in one country: "After expropriating the capitalists and organizing their own socialist production, the victorious proletariat of that country will arise *against* the rest of the world—the capitalist world—attracting to its cause the oppressed classes of other countries, stirring uprisings in those countries against the capitalists, and in case of need using even armed force against the exploiting classes and their states."

Of course, at the end of World War I most Bolsheviks (and many capitalists) expected revolution to break out in many of the European capitalist countries. In fact, many of the returning soldiers did turn their guns around. A revolutionary government was established in Hungary and Slovakia. Germany and Bulgaria for a while were covered by soviets of workers, peasants, and soldiers. But counterrevolution swept all these away.

Trotsky and his supporters continued to believe that the proletariat of Europe was ready to make socialist revolution.

They also believed that unless this happened, the proletariat would be unable to maintain power in the Soviet Union. They belittled the role of the peasantry as an ally of the Russian proletariat and saw very little potential in the national liberation movements of the predominantly peasant countries of Asia, Africa, and Latin America. Their so-called "Left opposition" put forward the theory of "permanent revolution," which pinned its hopes on an imminent uprising of the industrial proletariat of Europe. They saw the world revolution then spreading outward from these "civilized" countries to the "backward" regions of Asia, Africa, and Latin America.

Meanwhile there also developed what was later to be called the "Right opposition," spearheaded by Bukharin, Zinoviev, and Kamenev. They were realistic enough to recognize that the revolutionary tide was definitely ebbing in Europe, but they concluded from this that the Soviet Union would have to be content to remain for a long time a basically agricultural country without pretending to be a proletarian socialist state.

Stalin was not about to give up on socialism in the Soviet Union simply because history was not turning out exactly the way theorists had wanted, with revolution winning out quickly in the most advanced capitalist countries. He saw that the Soviet revolution had indeed been able to maintain itself against very powerful enemies at home and abroad. Besides, the Soviet Union was a vast country whose rich natural resources gave it an enormous potential for industrial and social development. He stood for building socialism in this one country and turning it into an inspiration and base area for the oppressed classes and nations throughout the world. He believed that, helped by both the example and material support of a socialist Soviet Union, the tide of revolution would eventually begin rising again, and that, in turn, proletarian revolution in Europe and national liberation struggles in the rest of the world would eventually break the Soviet isolation.

There are two parts to the concept of socialism in one country. Emphasis is usually placed only on the part that says "one country." Equally important is the idea that only socialism, and not communism, can be achieved prior to the time when the victory of the world revolution has been won. A Communist society would have no classes, no money, no scarcity, and no state, that is, no army, police force, prisons, and courts. There is no such society in the world, and no society claims to be Communist. A socialist society, according to Marxism-Leninism, is the transitional form on the road to communism. Classes and class struggle still exist, all the material needs of the people have not as yet been met, and there is indeed a state, a government of the working class known as the dictatorship of the proletariat (as opposed to the government of capitalist nations, the dictatorship of the bourgeoisie).

Neither Lenin nor Stalin ever had any illusion that any single country, even one as vast and potentially rich as the Soviet Union, would ever be able to establish a stateless, classless society while capitalism still had power in the rest of the world. But Stalin, like Lenin, did believe that the Soviet Union could eliminate capitalism, industrialize, extend the power of the working class, and wipe out real material privation all during the period of capitalist encirclement.

To do this, Stalin held, the proletariat would have to rely on the peasantry. He rejected Trotsky's scorn for the Russian peasants and saw them, rather than the European proletariat, as the only ally that could come to the immediate aid of the Russian workers.

When the Civil War ended, in 1921, with most of the Soviet Union in chaotic ruin, Lenin won a struggle against Trotsky within the Party to institute what was called the New Economic Policy (NEP), under which a limited amount of private enterprise based on trade was allowed to develop in both the cities and the countryside. NEP was successful in averting an immediate total catastrophe, but by 1925 it was becoming clear that this policy was also creating problems for the development of socialism. This brings us to the first great crux of the Stalin question.

We have been led to believe that in order to industrialize at any price, Stalin pursued a ruthless policy of forced collectivization, deliberately murdering several million peasants known as kulaks during the process. The truth is quite different.

When the Bolsheviks seized power, one of their first acts was to allow the poor peasants to seize the huge landed estates. The slogan was "Land to the tiller." This, however, left most land in the form of tiny holdings, unsuited for large-scale agriculture, particularly the production of the vital grain crops. Under NEP, capitalism and a new form of landlordism began to flourish in the countryside. The class known as kulaks (literally "tight-fists"), consisting of usurers and other small capitalists including village merchants and rich peasants, were cornering the market in the available grain, grabbing more and more small holdings of land, and, through their debt holdings, forcing peasants back into tenant farming and wage labor. Somehow, the small peasant holdings had to be consolidated so that modern agriculture could begin. There were basically two ways this could take place: either through capitalist accumulation, as the kulaks were then doing, or through the development of large-scale socialist farms. If the latter, there was then a further choice: a rapid forced collectivization, or a more gradual process in which co-operative farms would emerge first, followed by collectives, and both would be on a voluntary basis, winning out by example and persuasion. What did Stalin choose? Here, in his own words, is the policy he advocated and that was adopted at the Fifteenth Party Congress, in 1927:

> What is the way out? The way out is to turn the small and scattered peasant farms into large united farms based on cultivation of the land in common, to go over to collective cultivation of the land on the basis of a new and higher technique.
>
> The way out is to unite the small and dwarf peasant farms gradually but surely, not by pressure, but by example and persuasion, into large farms based on common, co-operative, collective cultivation of the land with the use of agricultural machines and tractors and scientific methods of intensive agriculture.
>
> There is no other way out.

To implement this policy, the capitalist privileges allowed under NEP were revoked. This was known as the restriction of the kulaks. The kulaks, whose very existence as a class was thus menaced, struck back. They organized terrorist bands who attacked the co-operatives and collectives, burning down barns when they were filled with grain, devastating the fields, and even murdering Communist peasant leaders. Even more serious than these raids, the kulaks held back their own large supplies of grain from the market in an effort to create hunger and chaos in the cities. The poor and middle peasants struck back. Virtual open civil war began to rage throughout the countryside. As the collective farm movement spread rapidly, pressure mounted among the poor and middle peasants to put an end to landlordism and usury in the countryside for good. In 1929 Stalin agreed that the time had come to eliminate the kulaks as a class. He led the fight to repeal the laws that allowed the renting of land and the hiring of labor, thus depriving the kulaks both of land and of hired workers. The ban on expropriation of the large private holdings was lifted, and the peasants promptly expropriated the kulak class. The expropriation of the rural capitalists in the late 1920s was just as decisive as the expropriation of the urban capitalists a decade earlier. Landlords and village usurers were eliminated as completely as private factory owners. It is undoubtedly true that in many areas there was needless violence and suffering. But this did not originate with Stalin. It was the hour of Russia's peasant masses, who had been degraded and brutalized for centuries and who had countless blood debts to settle with their oppressors. Stalin may have unleashed their fury, but he was not the one who had caused it to build up for centuries. In fact it was Stalin who checked the excesses generated by the enthusiasm of the collective movement. In early 1930 he published in *Pravda* "Dizzy with Success," reiterating that "the voluntary principle" of the collective farm movement must under no circumstances be violated and that anybody who engages in forced collectivization objectively aids the enemies of socialism. Furthermore, he argues, the correct form for the present time is the co-operative (known as the *artel*), in which "the household plots (small vegetable gardens, small orchards), the dwelling houses, a part of the dairy cattle, small livestock, poultry, etc., are *not socialized.*" Again, overzealous attempts to push beyond this objectively aid the enemy. The movement must be based on the needs and desires of the masses of peasants.

Stalin's decision about the kulaks perfectly exemplifies the limits under which he operated. He could decide, as he did, to end the kulaks as a class by allowing the poor and middle peasants to expropriate their land. Or he could decide to let the kulaks continue withholding their grain from the starving peasants and workers, with whatever result. He might have continued bribing the kulaks. But it is highly doubtful, to say the least, that he had the option of persuading the kulaks into becoming good socialists.

There can be no question that, whatever may be said about its cost, Stalin's policy in the countryside resulted in a vast, modern agricultural system, capable, for the first time in history, of feeding all the peoples of the Soviet lands. Gone were the famines that seemed as inevitable and were as vicious as those of China before the revolution or of India today.

Meanwhile, Stalin's policy of massive industrialization was going full speed ahead. His great plan for a modern, highly industrialized Soviet Union has been so overwhelmingly successful that we forget that it was adopted only over the bitter opposition of most of the Party leaders, who thought it a utopian and therefore suicidal dream. Having overcome this opposition on both the right and "left," Stalin in 1929 instituted the first five-year plan in the history of the world. It was quickly overfulfilled. By the early 1930s the Soviet Union had clearly become both the inspiration and the main material base area for the world revolution. And it was soon to prove much more than a match for the next military onslaught from the capitalist powers, which Stalin had predicted and armed against.

This brings us to the second great crux of the Stalin question, the "left" criticism, originating with Trotsky and then widely disseminated by the theorists of what used to be called "the New Left." This criticism holds that Stalin was just a nationalist who sold out revolution throughout the rest of the world. The debate ranges over all the key events of twentieth-century history and can be only touched on in an essay.

Stalin's difference with Trotsky on the peasantry was not confined to the role of the peasantry within the Soviet Union. Trotsky saw very little potential in the national liberation movements in those parts of the world that were still basically peasant societies. He argued that revolution would come first to the advanced capitalist countries of Europe and North America and would then spread to the "uncivilized" areas of the world. Stalin, on the other hand, saw that the national liberation movements of Asia, Africa, and Latin America were key to the development of the world revolution because objectively they were leading the fight against imperialism. We see this argument developed clearly as early as 1924, in "The Foundations of Leninism," where he argues that "the struggle that the Egyptian merchants and bourgeois intellectuals are waging for the independence of Egypt is objectively a revolutionary struggle, despite the bourgeois origin and bourgeois title of the leaders of the Egyptian national movement, despite the fact that they are opposed to socialism; whereas the struggle that the British 'Labour' Government is waging to preserve Egypt's dependent position is for the same reasons a *reactionary* struggle, despite the proletarian origins and the proletarian title of the members of that government, despite the fact that they are 'for' socialism." To most European Marxists, this was some kind of barbarian heresy. But Ho Chi Minh expressed the view of many Communists from the colonies in that same year, 1924, when he recognized that Stalin was the leader of the only Party that stood with the national liberation struggles and when he agreed with Stalin that the viewpoint of most other so-called Marxists on the national question was nothing short of "counterrevolutionary" (Ho Chi Minh, *Report on the National and Colonial Questions at the Fifth Congress of the Communist International*).

The difference between Stalin's line and Trotsky's line, and the falsification of what Stalin's line was, can be seen most clearly on the question of the Chinese revolution. The typical "left" view prevalent today is represented in David

Horowitz's *The Free World Colossus* (1965), which asserts "Stalin's continued blindness to the character and potential of the Chinese Revolution." Using as his main source a Yugoslav biography of Tito, Horowitz blandly declares: "Even after the war, when it was clear to most observers that Chiang was finished, Stalin did not think much of the prospects of Chinese Communism" (p. 111). Mao's opinion of Stalin is a little different:

> Rallied around him, we constantly received advice from him, constantly drew ideological strength from his works. . . . It is common knowledge that Comrade Stalin ardently loved the Chinese people and considered that the forces of the Chinese revolution were immeasurable. He displayed the greatest wisdom in matters pertaining to the Chinese revolution. . . . Sacredly preserving the memory of our great teacher Stalin, the Communist Party of China and the Chinese people . . . will even more perseveringly study Stalin's teaching. . . .
>
> ("A Great Friendship," 1953)

It is possible that this statement can be viewed as a formal tribute made shortly after Stalin's death and before it was safe to criticize Stalin within the international Communist movement. But years later, after the Russian attack on Stalin and after it was unsafe *not* to spit on Stalin's memory, the Chinese still consistently maintained their position. In 1961, after listening to Khrushchev's rabid denunciations of Stalin at the Twenty-second Party Congress, Chou En-lai ostentatiously laid a wreath on Stalin's tomb. Khrushchev and his supporters then disinterred Stalin's body, but the Chinese responded to this in 1963 by saying that Khrushchev "can never succeed in removing the great image of Stalin from the minds of the Soviet people and of the people throughout the world." ("On the Question of Stalin")

In fact, as his 1927 essay on China included in this collection shows, Stalin very early outlined the basic theory of the Chinese revolution. Trotsky attacks this theory, which he sneers at as "guerrilla adventure," because it is not based on the cities as the revolutionary centers, because it relies on class allies of the proletariat, particularly the peasantry, and because it is primarily anti-feudal and anti-imperialist rather than focused primarily against Chinese capitalism. After 1927, when the first liberated base areas were established in the countryside, Trotsky claimed that this revolution could no longer be seen as proletarian but as a mere peasant rebellion, and soon he began to refer to its guiding theory as the Stalin-Mao line. To this day, Trotskyites around the world deride the Chinese revolution as a mere "Stalinist bureaucracy." The Chinese themselves do acknowledge that at certain points Stalin gave some incorrect tactical advice, but they are quick to add that he always recognized and corrected these errors and was self-critical about them. They are very firm in their belief that they could not have made their revolution without his general theory, his over-all leadership of the world revolutionary movement, and the firm rear area and base of material support he provided. Thus the only really valid major criticism comes from anti-Communists, because without Stalin, at least according to the Chinese, the Communists would not have won.

Stalin's role in the Spanish Civil War likewise comes under fire from the "left." Again taking their cue from Trotsky and such professional anti-Communist ideologues as George Orwell, many "socialists" claim that Stalin sold out the Loyalists. A similar criticism is made about Stalin's policies in relation to the Greek partisans in the late 1940s, which we will discuss later. According to these "left" criticisms, Stalin didn't "care" about either of these struggles, because of his preoccupation with internal development and "Great Russian power." The simple fact of the matter is that in both cases Stalin was the only national leader anyplace in the world to support the popular forces, and he did this in the face of stubborn opposition within his own camp and the dangers of military attack from the leading aggressive powers in the world (Germany and Italy in the late 1930s, the U.S. ten years later).

Because the U.S.S.R., following Stalin's policies, had become a modern industrial nation by the mid-1930s, it was able to ship to the Spanish Loyalists Soviet tanks and planes that were every bit as advanced as the Nazi models. Because the U.S.S.R. was the leader of the world revolutionary forces, Communists from many nations were able to organize the International Brigades, which went to resist Mussolini's fascist divisions and the crack Nazi forces, such as the Condor Legion, that were invading the Spanish Republic. The capitalist powers, alarmed by this international support for the Loyalists, planned joint action to stop it. In March 1937, warships of Germany, Italy, France, and Great Britain began jointly policing the Spanish coast. Acting on a British initiative, these same countries formed a bloc in late 1937 to isolate the Soviet Union by implementing a policy they called "non-intervention," which Lloyd George, as leader of the British Opposition, labeled a clear policy of support for the fascists. Mussolini supported the British plan and called for a campaign "to drive Bolshevism from Europe." Stalin's own foreign ministry, which was still dominated by aristocrats masquerading as proletarian revolutionaries, sided with the capitalist powers. The New York *Times* of October 29, 1937, describes how the "unyielding" Stalin, representing "Russian stubbornness," refused to go along: "A struggle has been going on all this week between Joseph Stalin and Foreign Commissar Maxim Litvinoff," who wished to accept the British plan. Stalin stuck to his guns, and the Soviet Union refused to grant Franco international status as a combatant, insisting that it had every right in the world to continue aiding the duly elected government of Spain, which it did until the bitter end.

The Spanish Civil War was just one part of the world-wide imperialist aims of the Axis powers. Japan was pushing ahead in its conquest of Asia. Japanese forces overran Manchuria in 1931, only nine years after the Red Army had driven them out of Siberia, and then invaded China on a full scale. Ethiopia fell to Italy in 1936. A few months later, Germany and Japan signed an anti-Comintern pact, which was joined by Italy in 1937. In 1938, Germany invaded Austria. Hitler, who had come to power on a promise to rid Germany and the world of the Red menace, was now almost prepared to launch his decisive strike against the Soviet Union.

The other major capitalist powers surveyed the scene with

mixed feelings. On one hand, they would have liked nothing better than to see the Communist threat ended once and for all, particularly with the dirty work being done by the fascist nations. On the other hand, they had to recognize that fascism was then the ideology of the have-not imperialists, upstarts whose global aims included a challenge to the hegemony of France, Britain, and the United States. Should they move now to check these expansionist aims, or should they let them develop unchecked, hoping that they would move against the Soviet Union rather than Western Europe and the European colonies in Asia and Africa?

In 1938 they found the answer, a better course than either of these two alternatives. They would appease Hitler by giving him the Sudetenland of Czechoslovakia. This would not only dissuade the Nazis from attacking their fellow capitalists to the west, but it would also remove the last physical barriers to the east, the mountains of the Czech Sudetenland. All logic indicated to them that they had thus gently but firmly turned the Nazis eastward, and even given them a little shove in that direction. Now all they had to do was wait, and, after the fascist powers and the Soviet Union had devastated each other, they might even be able to pick up the pieces. So they hailed the Munich agreement of September 30, 1938, as the guarantee of "Peace in our time"—for them.

Stalin had offered to defend Czechoslovakia militarily against the Nazis if any one of the European capitalist countries would unite with the Soviet Union in this effort. The British and the French had evaded what they considered this trap, refusing to allow the Soviet Union even to participate at Munich. They now stepped back and waited, self-satisfied, to watch the Reds destroyed.

It seemed they didn't have long to wait. Within a few months, Germany seized all of Czechoslovakia, giving some pieces of the fallen republic to its allies Poland and Hungary. By mid-March 1939 the Nazis had occupied Bohemia and Moravia, the Hungarians had seized Carpatho-Ukraine, and Germany had formally annexed Memel. At the end of that month, Madrid fell and all of Spain surrendered to the fascists. On May 7, Germany and Italy announced a formal military and political alliance. The stage was set for the destruction of the Soviet Union.

Four days later, on May 11, 1939, the first attack came. The crack Japanese army that had invaded Manchuria struck into the Soviet Union. The Soviet-Japanese war of 1939 is conveniently omitted from our history books, but this war, together with the Anglo-French collaboration with the Nazis and fascists in the west, form the context for another of Stalin's great "crimes," the Soviet-German non-aggression pact of August 1939. Stalin recognized that the main aim of the Axis was to destroy the Soviet Union, and that the other capitalist nations were conniving with this scheme. He also knew that sooner or later the main Axis attack would come on the U.S.S.R.'s western front. Meanwhile, Soviet forces were being diverted to the east, to fend off the Japanese invaders. The non-aggression pact with Nazi Germany, which horrified and disillusioned Communist sympathizers, particularly intellectuals, in the capitalist nations, was actually one of the most brilliant strategic moves of Stalin's life, and perhaps of diplomatic history. From the Soviet point of view it accomplished five things: (1) it brought needed time to prepare for the Nazi attack, which was thus delayed two years; (2) it allowed the Red Army to concentrate on smashing the Japanese invasion, without having to fight on two fronts; they decisively defeated the Japanese within three months; (3) it allowed the Soviet Union to retake the sections of White Russia and the Ukraine that had been invaded by Poland during the Russian Civil War and were presently occupied by the Polish military dictatorship; this meant that the forthcoming Nazi invasion would have to pass through a much larger area defended by the Red Army; (4) it also allowed Estonia, Latvia, and Lithuania, which also had been part of Russia before the Civil War, to become part of the U.S.S.R. as Soviet Republics; this meant that the forthcoming Nazi attack could not immediately outflank Leningrad; (5) most important of all, it destroyed the Anglo-French strategy of encouraging a war between the Axis powers and the Soviet Union while they enjoyed neutrality; World War II was to begin as a war between the Axis powers and the other capitalist nations, and the Soviet Union, if forced into it, was not going to have to fight alone against the combined fascist powers. The world-wide defeat of the fascist Axis was in part a product of Stalin's diplomatic strategy, as well as his later military strategy.

But before we get to that, we have to go back in time to the events for which Stalin has been most damned—the purge trials. Most readers of this book have been taught that the major defendants in these trials were innocent, and that here we see most clearly Stalin's vicious cruelty and paranoia. This is certainly not the place to sift through all the evidence and retry the major defendants, but we must recognize that there is a directly contradictory view of the trials and that there is plenty of evidence to support that view.

It is almost undeniable that many of the best-known defendants had indeed organized clandestine groups whose aim was to overthrow the existing government. It is also a fact that Kirov, one of the leaders of that government, was murdered by a secret group on December 1, 1934. And it is almost beyond dispute that there were systematic, very widespread, and partly successful attempts, involving party officials, to sabotage the development of Soviet industry. Anyone who doubts this should read an article entitled "Red Wreckers in Russia" in the *Saturday Evening Post*, January 1, 1938, in which John Littlepage, an anti-Communist American engineer, describes in detail what he saw of this sabotage while he was working in the Soviet Union. In fact, Littlepage gives this judgment:

> For ten years I have worked alongside some of the many recently shot, imprisoned or exiled in Russia as wreckers. Some of my friends have asked me whether or not I believe these men and women are guilty as charged. I have not hesitated a moment in replying that I believe most of them are guilty.

To those who hold the orthodox U.S. view of the purge trials, perhaps the most startling account is the book *Mission to Moscow*, by Joseph E. Davies, U. S. Ambassador to the Soviet Union from 1936 to 1938. Davies is a vigorous defender of capitalism and a former head of the U. S. Chamber of Commerce. An experienced trial lawyer, he points out that, "I had myself prosecuted and defended men charged with crime in many cases." He personally attended the purge trials on a regular basis. Most of his accounts and judgments are contained in official secret correspondence to the State Department; the sole purpose of these dispatches was to provide as realistic an assessment as possible of what was actually going on. His summary judgment in his confidential report to the Secretary of State on March 17, 1938, is:

> . . . it is my opinion so far as the political defendants are concerned sufficient crimes under Soviet law, among those charged in the indictment, were established by the proof and beyond a reasonable doubt to justify the verdict of guilty of treason and the adjudication of the punishment provided by Soviet criminal statutes. The opinion of those diplomats who attended the trial most regularly was general that the case had established the fact that there was a formidable political opposition and an exceedingly serious plot, which explained to the diplomats many of the hitherto unexplained developments of the last six months in the Soviet Union. The only difference of opinion that seemed to exist was the degree to which the plot had been implemented by different defendants and the degree to which the conspiracy had become centralized. (p. 272)

But Davies himself admits to being puzzled and confused at the time because of the vast scope of the conspiracy and its penetration high into the Soviet government. It is only later, after the Nazi invasion of the Soviet Union, in the summer of 1941, that Davies feels he understands what he actually observed.

> Thinking over these things, there came a flash in my mind of a possible new significance to some of the things that happened in Russia when I was there. . . .
>
> None of us in Russia in 1937 and 1938 were thinking in terms of "Fifth Column" activities. The phrase was not current. It is comparatively recent that we have found in

our language phrases descriptive of Nazi technique such as "Fifth Column" and "internal aggression." . . .

As I ruminated over this situation, I suddenly saw the picture as I should have seen it at the time. The story had been told in the so-called treason or purge trials of 1937 and 1938 which I had attended and listened to. In reexamining the record of these cases and also what I had written at the time from this new angle, I found that practically every device of German Fifth Columnist activity, as we now know it, was disclosed and laid bare by the confessions and testimony elicited at these trials of self-confessed "Quislings" in Russia.

It was clear that the Soviet government believed that these activities existed, was thoroughly alarmed, and had proceeded to crush them vigorously. By 1941, when the German invasion came, they had wiped out any Fifth Column which had been organized.

(pp. 273–74)

All of these trials, purges, and liquidations, which seemed so violent at the time and shocked the world, are now quite clearly a part of a vigorous and determined effort of the Stalin government to protect itself from not only revolution from within but from attack from without. They went to work thoroughly to clean up and clean out all treasonable elements within the country. All doubts were resolved in favor of the government.

(p. 280)

In 1956, at the Twentieth Party Congress, when Khrushchev launched his famous attack on Stalin, he dredged up all the denunciations of the purge trials circulated for two decades by the Trotskyite and capitalist press. He called Stalin a "murderer," a "criminal," a "bandit," a "despot," etc. He asserted the innocence of many who had been imprisoned, exiled, or shot during the purge trials. But in doing so, he conveniently forgot two things: what he had said at the time about those trials, and what Stalin had said. On June 6, 1937, at the Fifth Party Conference of Moscow Province, Khrushchev had declared:

> Our Party will mercilessly crush the band of traitors and betrayers, and wipe out all the Trotskyist-Right dregs. . . . We shall totally annihilate the enemies—to the last man—and scatter their ashes to the winds.

On June 8, 1938, at the Fourth Party Conference of Kiev Province, Khrushchev avowed:

> We have annihilated a considerable number of enemies, but still not all. Therefore, it is necessary to keep our eyes open. We should bear firmly in mind the words of Comrade Stalin, that as long as capitalist encirclement exists, spies and saboteurs will be smuggled into our country.

Earlier, at a mass rally in Moscow, in January 1937, Khrushchev had condemned all those who had attacked Stalin in these words: "In lifting their hand against Comrade Stalin, they lifted it against all of us, against the working class and the working people!"

As for Stalin himself, on the other hand, he had publicly admitted, not in 1956, but at least as early as 1939, that innocent people had been convicted and punished in the purge: "It cannot be said that the purge was not accompanied by grave mistakes. There were unfortunately more mistakes than might have been expected." (Report to the Eighteenth Congress.) That is one reason why many of those tried and convicted in the last trials were high officials from the secret police, the very people guilty of forcing false confessions.

There are certainly good grounds for criticizing both the conduct and the extent of the purge. But that criticism must begin by facing the facts that an anti-Soviet conspiracy did exist within the Party, that it had some ties with the Nazis, who were indeed preparing to invade the country, and that one result of the purge was that the Soviet Union was the only country in all of Europe that, when invaded by the Nazis, did not have an active Fifth Column. It must also recognize that capitalism has since been restored in the Soviet Union, on the initiative of leading members of the Party bureaucracy, and so it is hardly fantastical or merely paranoid to think that such a thing was possible. The key question about the purges is whether there was a better way to prevent either a Nazi victory or the restoration of capitalism. And the answer to that question probably lies in the Chinese Cultural Revolution of 1966–67. Instead of relying on courts and police, exiles and executions, the Chinese mobilized hundreds of millions of people to expose and defeat the emerging Party bureaucracy that was quietly restoring capitalism and actively collaborating with the great imperialist power to the north. But while doing this, they carefully studied Stalin, both for his achievements and for what he was unable to do. For Stalin himself had seen as early as 1928 the need to mobilize mass criticism from below to overcome the rapidly developing Soviet bureaucracy. It is also possible that the two goals the purges tried to meet were mutually exclusive. That is, the emergency measures necessary to secure the country against foreign invasion may actually have helped the bureaucracy to consolidate its power.

In any event, when the Nazis and their allies did invade, they met the most united and fierce resistance encountered by the fascist forces anyplace in the world. Everywhere the people were dedicated to socialism. Even in the Ukraine, where the Nazis tried to foment old grievances and anti-Russian nationalism, they never dared meddle with the collective farms. In fact, Stalin's military strategy in World War II, like his strategy during the Russian Civil War, was based firmly on the loyalty of the masses of workers, peasants, and soldiers. Everybody, except for Khrushchev and his friends, who in 1956 tried to paint Stalin as a military incompetent and meddler, recognizes him as a great strategist.

Nazi military strategy was based on the *blitzkrieg* (lightning war). Spearheaded by highly mobile armor, their way paved by massive air assaults, the Nazi army would break through any static line at a single point, and then spread out rapidly behind that line, cutting off its supplies and then encircling the troops at the front. On April 9, 1940, the Nazis, vastly outnumbered, opened their assault on the combined forces of Denmark, Norway, Belgium, the Netherlands, France, and

Great Britain. By June 4, virtually the last of these fighting forces had been evacuated in panic from Dunkirk and each of the continental countries lay under a fascist power, the victim of blitzkrieg combined with internal betrayal. Having secured his entire western front, and then with air power alone having put the great maritime power Britain into a purely defensive position, Hitler could now move his crack armies and his entire air force into position to annihilate the Soviet Union.

The first step was to consolidate Axis control in Eastern Europe and the Balkans. Hungary, Bulgaria, and Romania were already fascist allies. Italy had overrun Albania. By early April 1941 Greece and Yugoslavia were occupied. Crete was seized in May. On June 22, the greatest invasion of all time was hurled at the Soviet heartland.

One hundred seventy-nine German divisions, twenty-two Romanian divisions, fourteen Finnish divisions, thirteen Hungarian divisions, ten Italian divisions, one Slovak division, and one Spanish division, a total of well over three million troops, the best armed and most experienced in the world, attacked along a 2,000-mile front, aiming their spearheads directly at Leningrad, Moscow, and Stalingrad. Instead of holding a line, the Red Army beat an orderly retreat, giving up space for time. Behind them they left nothing but scorched earth and bands of guerrilla fighters, constantly harassing the lengthening fascist supply lines. Before the invaders reached industrial centers such as Kharkov and Smolensk, the workers of these cities disassembled their machines and carried them beyond the Ural Mountains, where production of advanced Soviet tanks, planes, and artillery was to continue throughout the war.

The main blow was aimed directly at the capital, Moscow, whose outskirts were reached by late fall. Almost all the government offices had been evacuated to the east. But Stalin remained in the capital, where he assumed personal command of the war. On December 2, 1941, the Nazis were stopped in the suburbs of Moscow. On December 6, Stalin ordered the first major counterattack to occur in World War II. The following day, Japan, which had wisely decided against renewing their invasion of the Soviet Union, attacked Pearl Harbor.

From December until May the Red Army moved forward,

using a strategy devised by Stalin. Instead of confronting the elite Nazi corps head on, the Red forces would divide into smaller units and then move to cut off the fascist supply lines, thus encircling and capturing the spearheads of the blitzkrieg. This was the ideal counterstrategy, but it depended on a high level of political loyalty, consciousness, and independence on the part of these small units. No capitalist army could implement this strategy. By the end of May 1942 Moscow was safe and the fascist forces had given ground in the Ukraine.

In the early summer, the Nazi forces, heavily reinforced, moved to seize Stalingrad and the Caucasus, thus cutting the Soviet Union in two. The greatest and perhaps the most decisive battle in history was now to take place. The siege of Stalingrad lasted from August 1942 until February 1943. As early as September, the Nazi forces, which were almost as large as the entire U.S. force at its peak in Vietnam, penetrated the city and were stopped only by house-to-house fighting. But unknown to the Germans, because Soviet security was perfect, they were actually in a vast trap, personally designed by Stalin. A gigantic pincers movement had begun as soon as the fascist forces reached the city. In late November the two Soviet forces met and the trap snapped shut. From this trap 330,000 elite Nazi troops were never to emerge. In February 1943 the remnants, about 100,000 troops, surrendered. The back of Nazi military power had been broken. The Red Army now moved onto a vast offensive, which was not to stop before it had liberated all of Eastern and Central Europe and seized Berlin, the capital of the Nazi empire, in the spring of 1945.

It was the Soviet Union that had beaten the fascist army. The second front, which Great Britain and the U.S. had promised as early as 1942, was not to materialize until June 1944, after it was clear that the Nazis had already been decisively defeated. In fact, the Anglo-American invasion was aimed more at stopping communism than defeating fascism. (This invasion took place during the same period that the British Army "liberated" Greece, which had already been liberated by the Communist-led Resistance.) For under Communist leadership, underground resistance movements, based primarily on the working class, had developed throughout

Europe. Because the Communists, both from the Soviet Union and within the other European nations, were the leaders of the entire anti-fascist struggle, by the end of the war they had by far the largest parties in all the nations of Eastern and Central Europe, as well as Italy and France, where the fascists' power had been broken more by internal resistance than by the much-heralded Allied invasion. In fact, it is likely that if the Anglo-American forces had not invaded and occupied Italy and France, within a relatively short time the Communists would have been in power in both countries.

As soon as victory in Germany was assured, in May 1945, much of the Soviet Army began to make the 5,000-mile journey to face the Japanese Army. At Potsdam, July 17 to August 2, Stalin formally agreed to begin combat operations against Japan by August 8. On August 6, the U.S. dropped the first atomic bomb on Japan, in what is now widely considered the opening shot of the so-called "Cold War" against the U.S.S.R. On August 8, the Red Army engaged the main Japanese force, which was occupying Manchuria. The Soviet Army swept forward, capturing Manchuria, the southern half of Sakhalin Island, and the Kuriles, and liberating, by agreement, the northern half of Korea. Except for the Chinese Communist battles with the Japanese, these Soviet victories were probably the largest land engagements in the entire war against Japan.

The Soviet Union had also suffered tremendously while taking the brunt of the fascist onslaught. Between twenty and twenty-five million Soviet citizens gave their lives in defense of their country and socialism. The industrial heartland lay in ruins. The richest agricultural regions had been devastated. In addition to the seizure of many cities and the destruction of much of Moscow and Stalingrad, there was the desperate condition of Leningrad, which had withstood a massive, two-year Nazi siege.

Once again, the Soviet Union was to perform economic miracles. Between 1945 and 1950 they were to rebuild not only everything destroyed in the war, but vast new industries and agricultural resources. And all this was conducted under the threat of a new attack by the capitalist powers, led by the nuclear blackmail of the U.S., which opened up a world-wide "Cold War" against communism.

Spearheaded by British and rearmed Japanese troops, the French restored their empire in Indochina. U.S. troops occupied the southern half of Korea and established military bases throughout the Pacific. Europe itself became a vast base area for the rapidly expanding U.S. empire, which, despite its very minimal role in the war (or perhaps because of it), was to gain the greatest profit from it. One European showdown against the popular forces occurred in Greece.

Here we meet another "left" criticism of Stalin, similar to that made about his role in Spain but even further removed from the facts of the matter. As in the rest of Eastern Europe and the Balkans, the Communists had led and armed the heroic Greek underground and partisan fighters. In 1944 the British sent an expeditionary force commanded by General Scobie to land in Greece, ostensibly to aid in the disarming of the defeated Nazi and Italian troops. As unsuspecting as their comrades in Vietnam and Korea, who were to be likewise "assisted," the Greek partisans were slaughtered by their British "allies," who used tanks and planes in an all-out offensive, which ended in February 1945 with the establishment of a right-wing dictatorship under a restored monarchy. The British even rearmed and used the defeated Nazi "Security Battalions." After partially recovering from this treachery, the partisan forces rebuilt their guerrilla apparatus and prepared to resist the combined forces of Greek fascism and Anglo-American imperialism. By late 1948 full-scale civil war raged, with the right-wing forces backed up by the intervention of U.S. planes, artillery, and troops. The Greek resistance had its back broken by another betrayal, not at all by Stalin, but by Tito, who closed the Yugoslav borders to the Soviet military supplies that were already hard put to reach the land-locked popular forces. This was one of the two main reasons why Stalin, together with the Chinese, led the successful fight to have the Yugoslav "Communist" Party officially thrown out of the international Communist movement.

Stalin understood very early the danger to the world revolution posed by Tito's ideology, which served as a Trojan horse for U.S. imperialism. He also saw that Tito's revisionist ideas, including the development of a new bureaucratic ruling elite, were making serious headway inside the Soviet Union. In 1950, the miraculous postwar reconstruction was virtually complete, and the victorious Chinese revolution had decisively broken through the global anti-Communist encirclement and suppression campaign. At this point Stalin began to turn his attention to the most serious threat to the world revolution, the bureaucratic-technocratic class that had not only emerged inside the Soviet Union but had begun to pose a serious challenge to the leadership of the working class. In the last few years of his life, Joseph Stalin, whom the present rulers of the U.S.S.R. would like to paint as a mad recluse, began to open up a vigorous cultural offensive against the power of this new elite. "Marxism and Linguistics" and "Economic Problems of Socialism in the U.S.S.R." are milestones in this offensive, major theoretical works aimed at the new bourgeois authorities beginning to dominate various areas of Soviet thought.

In "Economic Problems of Socialism in the U.S.S.R.," published a few months before his death and intended to serve as a basis for discussion in the Nineteenth Party Congress of 1952, Stalin seeks to measure scientifically how far the Soviet Union had come in the development of socialism and how far it had to go to achieve communism. He criticizes two extreme tendencies in Soviet political economy: mechanical determinism and voluntarism. He sets this criticism within an international context where, he explains, the sharpening of contradictions among the capitalist nations is inevitable.

Stalin points out that those who think that objective laws, whether of socialist or capitalist political economy, can be abolished by will are dreamers. But he reserves his real scorn for those who make the opposite error, the technocrats who assert that socialism is merely a mechanical achievement of a certain level of technology and productivity, forgetting both the needs and the power of the people. He shows that when these technocrats cause "the disappearance of man as the aim of socialist production," they arrive at the triumph of bourgeois ideology. These proved to be prophetic words.

In his final public speech, made to that Nineteenth Party Congress in 1952, Stalin explains a correct revolutionary line for the parties that have not yet led their revolutions. The victories of the world revolution have constricted the capitalist world, causing the decay of the imperialist powers. Therefore the bourgeoisie of the Western democracies inherit the banners of the defeated fascist powers, with whom they establish a world-wide alliance while turning to fascism at home, and the would-be bourgeoisie of the neocolonial nations become merely their puppets. Communists then become the main defenders of the freedoms and progressive principles established by the bourgeoisie when they were a revolutionary class and defended by them until the era of their decay. Communists will lead the majority of people in their respective nations only when they raise and defend the very banners thrown overboard by the bourgeoisie—national independence and democratic freedoms. It is no surprise that these final words of Stalin have been known only to the Cold War "experts," and have been expunged throughout the Soviet Union and the nations of Eastern Europe.

A few months after this speech, Stalin died. Very abruptly, the tide of revolution was temporarily reversed. Stalin's death came in early March 1953. By that July, the new leaders of the Soviet Union had forced the Korean people to accept a division of their nation and a permanent occupation of the southern half by U.S. forces. A year later, they forced the victorious Viet Minh liberation army, which had thoroughly defeated the French despite massive U.S. aid, to withdraw from the entire southern half of that country, while the U.S. proclaimed that its faithful puppet, Ngo Dinh Diem, was now president of the fictitious nation of South Vietnam. When the Chinese resisted their global sellouts of the revolution, these new Soviet leaders first tried to destroy the Chinese economy, then tried to overthrow the government from within, and, when that failed, actually began armed incursions by Russian troops under a policy of nuclear blackmail copied from the U.S. In Indonesia, the Soviet Union poured ammunition and spare parts into the right-wing military forces while they were massacring half a million Communists, workers, and peasants. And so on, around the world. Meanwhile, internally, they restored capitalism as rapidly as they could. By the mid-1960s, unemployment had appeared in the Soviet Union for the first time since the first Five Year Plan. By the end of the 1960s, deals had been made with German, Italian, and Japanese capitalism for the exploitation of Soviet labor and vast Soviet resources.

From an anti-Communist point of view, Stalin was certainly one of the great villains of history. While he lived, the Red forces consolidated their power in one country and then led what seemed to be an irresistible world-wide revolutionary upsurge. By the time he died, near hysteria reigned in the citadels of capitalism. In Washington, frenzied witch hunts tried to ferret out the Red menace that was supposedly about to seize control of the last great bastion of capitalism. All this changed, for the time being, after Stalin's death, when the counterrevolutionary forces were able to seize control even within the Soviet Union.

From a Communist point of view, Stalin was certainly one of the greatest of revolutionary leaders. But still we must ask why it was that the Soviet Union could fall so quickly to a new capitalist class. For Communists, it is as vital to understand Stalin's weaknesses and errors as it is to understand his historic achievements.

Stalin's main theoretical and practical error lay in underestimating the bourgeois forces within the superstructure of Soviet society. It is ridiculous to pose the problem the way we customarily hear it posed: that the seeds of capitalist restoration were sown under Stalin. This assumes that the Soviet garden was a Communist paradise, totally free of weeds, which then somehow dropped in from the skies. Socialism, as Stalin saw more keenly than anybody before, is merely a transitional stage on the way to communism. It begins with the conquest of *political* power by the working class, but that is only a bare beginning. Next comes the much more difficult task of establishing socialist *economic* forms, including a high level of productivity based on collective labor. Most difficult of all is the *cultural* revolution, in which socialist ideas and attitudes, based on collective labor and the political power of the working people, overthrow the bourgeois world view, based on competition, ambition, and the quest for personal profit and power and portraying "human nature" as corrupt, vicious, and selfish, that is, as the mirror image of bourgeois man.

Stalin succeeded brilliantly in carrying through the political and economic revolutions. That he failed in consolidating the cultural revolution under the existing internal and external conditions can hardly be blamed entirely on him. He certainly saw the need for it, particularly when the time seemed most ripe to make it a primary goal, in the 1950s. But it must be admitted that he underestimated the threat posed by the new intelligentsia, as we see most strikingly in the "Report to the Eighteenth Party Congress," where he unstintingly praises them and denies that they could constitute a new social class. This error in theory led to an error in practice in which, despite his earlier calls for organizing mass criticism from below, he tended to rely on one section of the bureaucracy to check or defeat another. He was unwilling to unleash a real mass movement like the Chinese Cultural Revolution, and, as a result, the masses were made increasingly less capable of carrying out such a gigantic task. All this is easy to say in hindsight, now that we have the advantage of having witnessed the Chinese success, which may prove to be the most important single event in human history. But who would have had the audacity to recommend such a course in the face of the Nazi threat of the late 1930s or the U.S. threat after World War II, when the Soviet Union lay in ruins? In 1967, when the Chinese Cultural Revolution was at its height and the country was apparently in chaos, many revolutionaries around the world were dismayed. Certainly, they acknowledged, China had to have a cultural revolution. But not at that moment, when the Vietnamese absolutely needed that firm rear base area and when U.S. imperialism was apparently looking for any opening to smash China. And so it must have looked to Stalin, who postponed the Soviet cultural revolution until it was too late.

It is true that socialism in the Soviet Union has been reversed. But Stalin must be held primarily responsible not for its failure to achieve communism but rather for its getting as far along the road as it did. It went much further than the "left" and the right Opposition, the capitalists, and almost everybody in the world thought possible. It went far enough to pass the baton to a fresher runner, the workers and peasants of China, who, studying and emulating Stalin, have already gone even further, as we are beginning to see.

THE PROLETARIAN CLASS AND THE PROLETARIAN PARTY[1]

(*Concerning Paragraph One of the Party Rules*)

The time when people boldly proclaimed "Russia, one and indivisible," has gone. Today even a child knows that there is no such thing as Russia "one and indivisible," that Russia long ago split up into two opposite classes, the bourgeoisie and the proletariat. Today it is no secret to anyone that the struggle

[1] Published in Stalin's native language, Georgian, on January 1, 1905. In this article and throughout the volume, footnotes marked with an asterisk are Stalin's, while those marked with numbers are the editor's.

On the eve of the 1905 revolution, intense struggle raged inside the main revolutionary party of Russia, the Russian Social-Democratic Labor Party (RSDLP). Two distinct camps had formed, and they were disagreeing about almost every major political, strategic, and tactical question. But when the actual split came, a few months after this article appeared, it was precisely over the organizational question Stalin here addresses. The group that was to become known as the Mensheviks (literally "minority"), led by Martov, Trotsky, and others, held that the revolutionary party should be a broad organization with a loosely defined membership. Quite opposed to this stood the group that was to become known as the Bolsheviks (literally "majority"). They followed the theory developed by Lenin, who saw the party as an organization of highly trained professional revolutionaries equipped with both theory and practice and capable of providing political and military leadership, whether legal or illegal, under all circumstances. Lenin's theory was to prove one of the main formative ideas of twentieth-century history, and Stalin was to be one of its main practitioners. This theory of course is lambasted not only by the ruling classes throughout the world but also by many groups and individuals claiming to be revolutionary. Whatever its weaknesses and dangers, however, one thing must be admitted: no twentieth-century social revolution has been accomplished without such a party.

between these two classes has become the axis around which our contemporary life revolves.

Nevertheless, until recently it was difficult to notice all this, the reason being that hitherto we saw only individual groups in the arena of the struggle, for it was only individual groups in individual towns and parts of the country that waged the struggle, while the proletariat and the bourgeoisie, as classes, were not easily discernible. But now towns and districts have united, various groups of the proletariat have joined hands, joint strikes and demonstrations have broken out—and before us has unfolded the magnificent picture of the struggle between the two Russias—bourgeois Russia and proletarian Russia. Two big armies have entered the arena—the army of proletarians and the army of the bourgeoisie—and the struggle between these two armies embraces the whole of our social life.

Since an army cannot operate without leaders, and since every army has a vanguard which marches at its head and lights up its path, it is obvious that with these armies there had to appear corresponding groups of leaders, corresponding parties, as they are usually called.

Thus, the picture presents the following scene: on one side there is the bourgeois army, headed by the liberal party; on the other, there is the proletarian army, headed by the Social-Democratic Party; each army, in its class struggle, is led by its own party.*

We have mentioned all this in order to compare the proletarian party with the proletarian class and thus briefly to bring out the general features of the Party.

The foregoing makes it sufficiently clear that the proletarian party, being a fighting group of leaders, must, firstly, be considerably smaller than the proletarian class with respect to membership; secondly, it must be superior to the proletarian class with respect to its understanding and its experience; and, thirdly, it must be a compact organization.

In our opinion, what has been said needs no proof, for it is self-evident that, so long as the capitalist system exists, with

* We do not mention the other parties in Russia, because there is no need to deal with them in examining the questions under discussion.

its inevitably attendant poverty and backwardness of the masses, the proletariat as a whole cannot rise to the desired level of class consciousness, and, consequently, there must be a group of class-conscious leaders to enlighten the proletarian army in the spirit of socialism, to unite and lead it in its struggle. It is also clear that a party which has set out to lead the *fighting* proletariat must not be a chance conglomeration of individuals, but a compact, centralized *organization,* so that its activities can be directed according to a single plan.

Such, in brief, are the general features of our Party.

Bearing all this in mind, let us pass to the main question: Whom can we call a Party member? Paragraph One of the Party Rules, which is the subject of the present article, deals with precisely this question.

And so, let us examine this question.

Whom, then, can we call a member of the Russian Social-Democratic Labour Party—i.e., what are the duties of a Party member?

Our Party is a Social-Democratic Party. This means that it has its own program (the immediate and the ultimate aims of the movement), its own tactics (methods of struggle), and its own organizational principle (form of association). *Unity* of program, tactical and organizational views is the basis on which our Party is built. Only the *unity* of these views can unite the Party members in *one* centralized party. If unity of views collapses, the Party collapses. Consequently, only one who fully accepts the Party's program, tactics and organizational principle can be called a Party member. Only one who has adequately studied and has fully accepted our Party's program, tactical and organizational views can be in the ranks of our Party and, thereby, in the ranks of the leaders of the proletarian army.

But is it enough for a Party member merely to *accept* the Party's program, tactics and organizational views? Can a person like that be regarded as a true leader of the proletarian army? Of course not! In the first place, everybody knows that there are plenty of windbags in the world who would readily "accept" the Party's program, tactics and organizational views, but who are incapable of being anything else than windbags. It would be a desecration of the Party's Holy of Holies to call a windbag like that a Party member (i.e., a leader of the proletarian army)! Moreover, our Party is not a school of philosophy or a religious sect. Is not our Party a *fighting* party? Since it is, is it not self-evident that our Party will not be satisfied with a platonic *acceptance* of its program, tactics and organizational views, that it will undoubtedly demand that its members should *apply* the views they have accepted? Hence, whoever wants to be a member of our Party cannot rest content with merely accepting our Party's program, tactical and organizational views, but must set about applying these views, putting them into effect.

But what does applying the Party's views mean for a Party member? When can he apply these views? Only when he is fighting, when he is marching with the whole Party at the head of the proletarian army. Can the struggle be waged by solitary, scattered individuals? Certainly not! On the contrary, people first unite, first they organize, and only then do they go into battle. If that is not done, all struggle is fruitless. Clearly, then, the Party members too will be able to fight and, consequently, apply the Party's views, only if they unite in a compact *organization*. It is also clear that the more compact the organization in which the Party members unite, the better will they be able to fight, and, consequently, the more fully will they apply the Party's program, tactics and organizational views. It is not for nothing that our Party is called an *organization* of leaders and not a conglomeration of individuals. And, since the Party is an *organization* of leaders, it is obvious that only those can be regarded as members of this Party, of this organization, who work in this organization and, therefore, deem it their duty to merge their wishes with the wishes of the Party and to act in unison with the Party.

Hence, to be a Party member one must apply the Party's program, tactics and organizational views; to apply the Party's views one must fight for them; and to fight for these views one must work in a Party organization, work in unison with the Party. Clearly, to be a Party member one must belong to one of the Party organizations.* Only when we join one of

* Just as every complex organism is made up of an incalculable number of the simplest organisms, so our Party, being a complex and

the Party organizations and thus merge our personal interests with the Party's interests can we become Party members, and, consequently, real leaders of the proletarian army.

If our Party is not a conglomeration of individual windbags, but an *organization* of leaders which, through its Central Committee, is worthily leading the proletarian army forward, then all that has been said above is self-evident.

The following must also be noted.

Up till now our Party has resembled a hospitable patriarchal family, ready to take in all who sympathize. But now that our Party has become a centralized *organization,* it has thrown off its patriarchal aspect and has become in all respects like a *fortress,* the gates of which are opened only to those who are worthy. And that is of great importance to us. At a time when the autocracy is trying to corrupt the class consciousness of the proletariat with "trade unionism," nationalism, clericalism and the like, and when, on the other hand, the liberal intelligentsia is persistently striving to kill the political independence of the proletariat and to impose its tutelage upon it—at such a time we must be extremely vigilant and never forget that our Party is a *fortress,* the gates of which are opened only to those who have been tested.

We have ascertained two essential conditions of Party membership (acceptance of the program and work in a Party organization). If to these we add a third condition, namely, that a Party member must render the Party financial support, then we shall have all the conditions that give one right to the title of Party member.

Hence, a member of the Russian Social-Democratic Labour Party is one who accepts the program of this Party, renders the Party financial support, and *works in one of the Party organizations.*

---

general organization, is made up of numerous district and local bodies called Party organizations, provided they have been endorsed by the Party Congress or the Central Committee. As you see, not only Committees are called Party organizations. To direct the activities of these organizations according to a single plan there is a Central Committee, through which these local Party organizations constitute one, large, centralized organization.

That is how Paragraph One of the Party Rules, drafted by Comrade Lenin,* was formulated.

The formula, as you see, springs entirely from the view that our Party is a centralized *organization* and not a *conglomeration* of individuals.

Therein lies the supreme merit of this formula.

But it appears that some comrades reject Lenin's formula on the grounds that it is "narrow" and "inconvenient," and propose their own formula, which, it must be supposed, is neither "narrow" nor "inconvenient." We are referring to Martov's** formula, which we shall now analyze.

Martov's formula is: "A member of the R.S.D.L.P. is one who accepts its program, supports the Party financially and renders it regular personal assistance under the direction of one of its organizations." As you see, this formula omits the third essential condition of Party membership, namely, the duty of Party members *to work* in one of the Party *organizations*. It appears that Martov regards this definite and essential condition as superfluous, and in his formula he has substituted for it the nebulous and dubious "personal assistance under the direction of one of the Party organizations." It appears, then, that one can be a member of the Party without belonging to any Party organization (a fine "party," to be sure!) and without feeling obliged to submit to the Party's will (fine "party discipline," to be sure!). Well, and how can the Party "regularly" direct persons who do not belong to any Party organization and, consequently, do not feel absolutely obliged to submit to Party discipline?

That is the question that shatters Martov's formula of Paragraph One of the Party Rules, and it is answered in masterly fashion in Lenin's formula, inasmuch as the latter definitely stipulates that a third and indispensable condition of Party membership is *that one must work in a Party organization.*

All we have to do is to throw out of Martov's formula the nebulous and meaningless "personal assistance under the direction of one of the Party organizations." With this con-

* Lenin is an outstanding theoretician and practical leader of revolutionary Social-Democracy.

** Martov is one of the editors of *Iskra.*

dition eliminated, there remain only two conditions in Martov's formula (acceptance of the program and financial support), which, by themselves, are utterly worthless, since every windbag can "accept" the Party program and support the Party financially—but that does not in the least entitle him to Party membership.

A "convenient" formula, we must say!

We say that real Party members cannot possibly rest content with merely accepting the Party program, but must without fail strive to apply the program they have accepted. Martov answers: You are too strict, for it is not so very necessary for a Party member to apply the program he has accepted, once he is willing to render the Party financial support, and so forth. It looks as though Martov is sorry for certain windbag "Social-Democrats" and does not want to close the Party's doors to them.

We say, further, that inasmuch as the application of the program entails fighting, and that it is impossible to fight without unity, it is the duty of every prospective Party member to join one of the Party organizations, merge his wishes with those of the Party and, in unison with the Party, lead the fighting proletarian army, i.e., he must organize in the well-formed detachments of a centralized party. To this Martov answers: It is not so very necessary for Party members to organize in well-formed detachments, to unite in organizations; fighting singlehanded is good enough.

What, then, is our Party? we ask. A chance conglomeration of individuals, or a compact organization of leaders? And if it is an organization of leaders, can we regard as a member one who does not belong to it and, consequently, does not consider it his bounden duty to submit to its discipline? Martov answers that the Party is not an organization, or, rather, that the Party is an *unorganized* organization (fine "centralism," to be sure!)!

Evidently, in Martov's opinion, our Party is not a centralized organization, but a conglomeration of local organizations and individual "Social-Democrats" who have accepted our Party program, etc. But if our Party is not a centralized organization it will not be a fortress, the gates of which can be opened only for those who have been tested. And, indeed, to

Martov, as is evident from his formula, the Party is not a fortress but a banquet, which every sympathizer can freely attend. A little knowledge, an equal amount of sympathy, a little financial support and there you are—you have full right to count as a Party member. Don't listen—cries Martov to cheer up the frightened "Party members"—don't listen to those people who maintain that a Party member must belong to one of the Party organizations and thus subordinate his wishes to the wishes of the Party. In the first place, it is hard for a man to accept these conditions; it is no joke to subordinate one's wishes to those of the Party! And, secondly, as I have already pointed out in my explanation, the opinion of those people is mistaken. And so, gentlemen, you are welcome to . . . the banquet!

It looks as though Martov is sorry for certain professors and high-school students who are both to subordinate their wishes to the wishes of the Party, and so he is forcing a breach in our Party fortress through which these estimable gentlemen may smuggle into our Party. He is opening the door to opportunism, and this at a time when thousands of enemies are assailing the class consciousness of the proletariat!

But that is not all. The point is that Martov's dubious formula makes it possible for opportunism to arise in our Party from another side.

Martov's formula, as we know, refers only to the acceptance of the program; about tactics and organization it contains not a word; and yet, unity of organizational and tactical views is no less essential for Party unity than unity of program views. We may be told that nothing is said about this even in Comrade Lenin's formula. True, but there is no need to say anything about it in Comrade Lenin's formula. Is it not self-evident that one who works in a Party organization and, consequently, fights in unison with the Party and submits to Party discipline, cannot pursue tactics and organizational principles other than the Party's tactics and the Party's organizational principles? But what would you say of a "Party member" who has accepted the Party program, but does not belong to any Party organization? What guarantee is there that such a "member's" tactics and organizational views will be those of the Party and not some other? That is what

Martov's formula fails to explain! As a result of Martov's formula we would have a queer "party," whose "members" subscribe to the same program (and that is questionable!), but differ in their tactical and organizational views! What ideal variety! In what way will our Party differ from a banquet?

There is just one question we should like to ask: What are we to do with the ideological and practical centralism that was handed down to us by the Second Party Congress and which is radically contradicted by Martov's formula? Throw it overboard? If it comes to making a choice, it will undoubtedly be more correct to throw Martov's formula overboard.

Such is the absurd formula Martov presents to us in opposition to Comrade Lenin's formula!

We are of the opinion that the decision of the Second Party Congress, which adopted Martov's formula, was a blunder, and we hope that the Third Party Congress will not fail to rectify the blunder of the Second Congress and adopt Comrade Lenin's formula.

We shall briefly recapitulate: The proletarian army entered the arena. Since every army must have a vanguard, this army also had to have such a vanguard. Hence the appearance of a group of proletarian leaders—the Russian Social-Democratic Labour Party. As the vanguard of a definite army, this Party must, firstly, be armed with its own program, tactics and organizational principle; and, secondly, it must be a compact organization. To the question—who can be called a member of the Russian Social-Democratic Labour Party?—this Party can have only one answer: one who accepts the Party program, supports the Party financially and works in one of the Party organizations.

It is this obvious truth that Comrade Lenin has expressed in his splendid formula.

1905

ARMED INSURRECTION AND OUR TACTICS[1]

The revolutionary movement "has already brought about the necessity for an armed insurrection"—this idea, expressed by the Third Congress of our Party, finds increasing confirmation day after day. The flames of revolution are flaring up with ever-increasing intensity, now here and now there calling forth local uprisings. The three days' barricade and street fighting in Lodz, the strike of many tens of thousands of workers in Ivanovo-Voznesensk with the inevitable bloody collisions with the troops, the uprising in Odessa, the "mutiny" in the Black Sea Fleet and in the Libau naval depot, and the "week" in Tiflis—are all harbingers of the approaching storm. It is approaching, approaching irresistibly, it will break over Russia any day and, in a mighty, cleansing flood, sweep

[1] The abortive Russian revolution of 1905 was a prelude to the successful revolution of 1917. Growing out of the defeat of the czarist armies in the Russo-Japanese War, massive workers' strikes erupted in late 1904. On January 9, 1905, 140,000 workers in St. Petersburg, singing hymns and carrying portraits of the Czar, peacefully marched to the Winter Palace to petition their divine Sovereign, who proceeded to have them butchered in the streets. After this, strikes and revolts soon spread to the peasants and soldiers. In June 1905 the crew of the battleship Potemkin seized control of the ship and ran up the red flag of revolution. By December of that year the major cities of Russia saw intense barricade fighting and the creation of the first revolutionary soviets (literally "councils") of workers and soldiers.

In April 1905 the Social-Democratic Party essentially split in two. The Mensheviks held that the proletariat was not yet historically ready to seize state power and therefore should support the liberal bourgeoisie against the autocracy. The Bolsheviks, led by Lenin, maintained that the proletariat could win power if they developed allies in the form of the other exploited classes, particularly the peasants and the urban poor. But, to do this, the proletariat would

away all that is antiquated and rotten; it will wipe out the disgrace called the autocracy, under which the Russian people have suffered for ages. The last convulsive efforts of tsarism —the intensification of repression of every kind, the proclamation of martial law over half the country and the multiplication of gallows, all accompanied by alluring speeches addressed to the liberals and by false promises of reform—these things will not save it from the fate history has in store for it. The days of the autocracy are numbered; the storm is inevitable. A new social order is already being born, welcomed by the entire people, who are expecting renovation and regeneration from it.

What new questions is this approaching storm raising before our Party? How must we adjust our organization and tactics to the new requirements of life so that we may take a more active and organized part in the insurrection, which is the only necessary beginning of the revolution? To guide the insurrection, should we—the leading unit of the class which is not only the vanguard, but also the main driving force of the revolution—set up special bodies, or is the existing Party machinery enough?

These questions have been confronting the Party and demanding immediate solution for several months already. For those who worship "spontaneity," who degrade the Party's ob-

---

have to arm itself and physically, as well as politically, lead the revolution.

In this period Stalin became one of the main Bolshevik spokesmen to the workers on the need for serious military preparation. This article, published in Georgian on July 15, 1905, develops the key Marxist-Leninist position on the role of the revolutionary party in military affairs. On one hand Stalin rejects the line of no military preparation, whether based on the belief that it is not feasible (the proletariat can't win) or that it is not necessary (the proletariat can arm spontaneously). On the other hand, he repudiates the ultraleft idea that the party serves as the military arm of the masses and does their fighting for them, as propounded by the nineteenth-century Russian terrorists and some recent theorists of elite revolutionary guerrilla bands. Stalin, like Lenin, saw that the party must concretely help arm the masses and must lead them militarily. Hence his famous declaration a few months later, in October, to a mass meeting of workers in Tiflis, the capital of his native Georgia: "What do we need in order to really win? We need three things: first—arms, second—arms, third—arms and arms again!"

jects to the level of simply following in the wake of life, who drag at the tail and do not march at the head as the leading class-conscious unit should do, such questions do not exist. Insurrection is spontaneous, they say, it is impossible to organize and prepare it, every prearranged plan of action is a utopia (they are opposed to any sort of "plan"—why, that is "consciousness" and not a "spontaneous phenomenon"!), a waste of effort—social life follows its own, unknown paths and will shatter all our projects. Hence, they say, we must confine ourselves to conducting propaganda and agitation in favour of the idea of insurrection, the idea of the "self-arming" of the masses; we must only exercise "political guidance"; as regards "technical" guidance of the insurgent people, let anybody who likes undertake that.

But we have always exercised such guidance up to now!—the opponents of the "khvostist policy" reply. Wide agitation and propaganda, political guidance of the proletariat, are absolutely essential. That goes without saying. But to confine ourselves to such general tasks means either evading an answer to the question which life bluntly puts to us, or revealing utter inability to adjust our tactics to the requirements of the rapidly growing revolutionary struggle. We must, of course, now intensify political agitation tenfold, we must try to establish our influence not only over the proletariat, but also over those numerous strata of the "people" who are gradually joining the revolution; we must try to popularize among all classes of the population the idea that an insurrection is necessary. But we cannot confine ourselves solely to this! To enable the proletariat to utilize the impending revolution for the purposes of its own class struggle, to enable it to establish a democratic system that will provide the greatest guarantees for the subsequent struggle for socialism—it, the proletariat, around which the opposition is rallying, must not only serve as the centre of the struggle, but become the leader and guide of the insurrection. It is *the technical guidance and organizational preparation of the all-Russian insurrection* that constitute the new tasks with which life has confronted the proletariat. And if our Party wishes to be the real political leader of the working class it cannot and must not repudiate these new tasks.

And so, what must we do to achieve this object? What must our first steps be?

Many of our organizations have already answered this question in a practical way by directing part of their forces and resources to the purpose of arming the proletariat. Our struggle against the autocracy has entered the stage when the necessity of arming is universally admitted. But mere realization of the necessity of arming is not enough—*the practical task must be bluntly and clearly put before the Party*. Hence, our committees must at once, forthwith, proceed to arm the people locally, to set up special groups to arrange this matter, to organize district groups for the purpose of procuring arms, to organize workshops for the manufacture of different kinds of explosives, to draw up plans for seizing state and private stores of arms and arsenals. We must not only arm the people "with a burning desire to arm themselves," as the new *Iskra* advises us, but also "take the most energetic measures to arm the proletariat," as the Third Party Congress made it incumbent upon us to do. It is easier on this issue than on any other to reach agreement with the section that has split off from the Party (if it is really in earnest about arming and is not merely talking about "a burning desire to arm themselves"), as well as with the national Social-Democratic organizations, such as, for example, the Armenian Federalists and others who have set themselves the same object. Such an attempt has already been made in Baku, where after the February massacre our committee, the Balakhany-Bibi-Eibat group and the Gnchak Committee set up among themselves an organizing committee for procuring arms. It is absolutely essential that this difficult and responsible undertaking be organized by joint efforts, and we believe that factional interests should least of all hinder the amalgamation of all the Social-Democratic forces on this ground.

In addition to increasing stocks of arms and organizing their procurement and manufacture, it is necessary to devote most serious attention to the task of organizing fighting squads of every kind for the purpose of utilizing the arms that are being procured. Under no circumstances should actions such as distributing arms directly to the masses be resorted to. In view of the fact that our resources are limited and that it is extremely difficult to conceal weapons from the vigilant eyes of the police, we shall be unable to arm any considerable section of the population, and all our efforts will be wasted. It will be quite different when we set up a special fighting organization. Our fighting squads will learn to handle their weapons, and during the insurrection—irrespective of whether it breaks out spontaneously or is prepared beforehand—they will come out as the chief and leading units around which the insurgent people will rally, and under whose leadership they will march into battle. Thanks to their experience and organization, and also to the fact that they will be well armed, it will be possible to utilize all the forces of the insurgent people and thereby achieve the immediate object—the arming of the entire people and the execution of the prearranged plan of action. They will quickly capture various stores of arms, government and public offices, the post office, the telephone exchange, and so forth, which will be necessary for the further development of the revolution.

But these fighting squads will be needed not only when the revolutionary uprising has already spread over the whole town; their role will be no less important on the eve of the insurrection. During the past six months it has become convincingly clear to us that the autocracy, which has discredited itself in the eyes of all classes of the population, has concentrated all its energy on mobilizing the dark forces of the country—professional hooligans, or the ignorant and fanatical elements among the Tatars—for the purpose of fighting the revolutionaries. Armed and protected by the police, they are terrorizing the population and creating a tense atmosphere for the liberation movement. Our fighting organizations must always be ready to offer due resistance to all the attempts made by these dark forces, and must try to convert the anger and the resistance called forth by their actions into an anti-government movement. The armed fighting squads, ready to go out into the streets and take their place at the head of the masses of the people at any moment, can easily achieve the object set by the Third Congress—"to organize armed resistance to the actions of the Black Hundreds, and generally, of all reactionary elements led by the government" ("Resolution on Attitude Towards the Government's Tactics on the Eve of the Revolution"—see "Announcement").

One of the main tasks of our fighting squads, and of the military-technical organizations in general, should be to draw up plans of insurrection for their respective districts and coordinate them with the plan drawn up by the Party centre for the whole of Russia. Ascertain the enemy's weakest spots, choose the points from which the attack against him is to be launched, distribute all the forces over the district and thoroughly study the topography of the town—all this must be done beforehand, so that we shall not be taken by surprise under any circumstances. It is totally inappropriate here to go into a detailed analysis of this aspect of our organizations' activity. Strict secrecy in drawing up the plan of action must be accompanied by the widest possible dissemination among the proletariat of military-technical knowledge which is absolutely necessary for conducting street fighting. For this purpose we must utilize the services of the military men in the organization. For this purpose also we must utilize the services of a number of other comrades who will be extremely useful in this matter because of their natural talent and inclinations.

Only such thorough preparation for insurrection can ensure for Social-Democracy the leading role in the forthcoming battles between the people and the autocracy.

Only complete fighting preparedness will enable the proletariat to transform the isolated clashes with the police and the troops into a nation-wide insurrection with the object of setting up a provisional revolutionary government in place of the tsarist government.

The supporters of the "khvostist policy" notwithstanding, the organized proletariat will exert all its efforts to concentrate both the technical and political leadership of the insurrection in its own hands. This leadership is the essential condition which will enable us to utilize the impending revolution in the interests of our class struggle.

1905

MARXISM
AND THE NATIONAL QUESTION[1]

The period of counter-revolution in Russia brought not only "thunder and lightning" in its train, but also disillusionment in the movement and lack of faith in common forces. As long as people believed in "a bright future," they fought side by side irrespective of nationality—common questions first and foremost! But when doubt crept into people's hearts, they began to depart, each to his own national tent—let every man count only upon himself! The "national question" first and foremost!

[1] The present text omits sections IV, V, and VI, which present an intricate and rather scholarly argument about different nationalist tendencies in Russia and Central Europe.

The national question has proved to be the most difficult theoretical problem for revolutionaries throughout the twentieth century. "Marxism and the National Question" is still considered by many Communists throughout the world to be the basic Marxist-Leninist text on the problem. Published in 1913, on the eve of World War I, this treatise was Stalin's first major contribution to Marxist-Leninist theory. As the child of a worker and a peasant from Georgia, thus belonging to both an oppressed class and an oppressed nation, Stalin saw both sides of the question.

Stalin points out that nations arose on one material and historical basis: the economic development toward capitalism. The first modern nation-states were the creation of the bourgeoisie and served as an instrument of their class purposes. Hence the nationalism that forces the exploited masses to support their "own" national bourgeoisie and go out to fight against other exploited and oppressed peoples. Stalin's main attack is leveled against the Austrian school, personified by Springer and Bauer, which he sees as leading to a total breakdown of international class solidarity. The events of the next few years proved the dangers of this Austrian theory, which became dominant in the European social-democratic parties. While Austria-Hungary disintegrated into warring nation-states, and all of Europe was plunged into a war pitting nation against nation, the leaders of each and every

At the same time a profound upheaval was taking place in the economic life of the country. The year 1905 had not been in vain: one more blow had been struck at the survivals of serfdom in the countryside. The series of good harvests which succeeded the famine years, and the industrial boom which followed, furthered the progress of capitalism. Class differentiation in the countryside, the growth of the towns, the development of trade and means of communication all took a big stride forward. This applied particularly to the border regions. And it could not but hasten the process of economic consolidation of the nationalities of Russia. They were bound to be stirred into movement. . . .

The "constitutional regime" established at that time also acted in the same direction of awakening the nationalities. The spread of newspapers and of literature generally, a certain freedom of the press and cultural institutions, an increase in the number of national theatres, and so forth, all unquestionably helped to strengthen "national sentiments." The

---

social-democratic party, except for Lenin in Russia and Connolly in Ireland, helped convince the workers of their own nation to kill and be killed by the workers of the rival nations.

Although Stalin concentrates on attacking this reactionary nationalism, he also sees the other side of the question. Some nations are actually oppressed by others, particularly in the era of modern imperialism, and it is therefore the duty of the proletariat to lead the fight against this national oppression. To do this, it must fully support the right of nations to self-determination, that is, to have a separate government. Stalin, like Lenin (and, earlier, Marx, particularly writing on the Irish question), saw that international or multinational unity could be attained only if the workers of a dominant nation were ready to support this principle for nations oppressed by their own rulers. And it was the duty of the workers of an oppressed nation to lead all other classes in both the fight for national liberation and international class solidarity.

On the national question, Stalin's theory and Trotsky's were to become the main ideological poles in the later history of our century, with Trotsky condemning all nationalism as reactionary while Stalin continually stressed the importance of national liberation movements as a major part of the world revolution. Hence the central question of post-1917 history: Can socialism be built in a single "backward" (that is, oppressed) nation on the basis of a national alliance between the workers and peasants, or must socialism wait until the day of an international revolution by the industrial proletariat of the "advanced" (that is, capitalist) nations?

Duma, with its election campaign and political groups, gave fresh opportunities for greater activity of the nations and provided a new and wide arena for their mobilization.

And the mounting wave of militant nationalism above and the series of repressive measures taken by the "powers that be" in vengeance on the border regions for their "love of freedom," evoked an answering wave of nationalism below, which at times took the form of crude chauvinism. The spread of Zionism among the Jews, the increase of chauvinism in Poland, Pan-Islamism among the Tatars, the spread of nationalism among the Armenians, Georgians and Ukrainians, the general swing of the philistine towards anti-Semitism—all these are generally known facts.

The wave of nationalism swept onwards with increasing force, threatening to engulf the mass of the workers. And the more the movement for emancipation declined, the more plentifully nationalism pushed forth its blossoms.

At this difficult time Social-Democracy had a high mission—to resist nationalism and to protect the masses from the general "epidemic." For Social-Democracy, and Social-Democracy alone, could do this, by countering nationalism with the tried weapon of internationalism, with the unity and indivisibility of the class struggle. And the more powerfully the wave of nationalism advanced, the louder had to be the call of Social-Democracy for fraternity and unity among the proletarians of all the nationalities of Russia. And in this connection particular firmness was demanded of the Social-Democrats of the border regions, who came into direct contact with the nationalist movement.

But not all Social-Democrats proved equal to the task—and this applies particularly to the Social-Democrats of the border regions. The Bund,[2] which had previously laid stress on the common tasks, now began to give prominence to its own specific, purely nationalist aims: it went to the length of declaring "observance of the Sabbath" and "recognition of Yid-

[2] The Bund: the General Jewish Workers' Union of Lithuania, Poland, and Russia. It joined the Social-Democrats as an autonomous group in 1898 and went with the Mensheviks in the split. Its leadership was mostly petty bourgeois and its main base was among artisans.

dish" a fighting issue in its election campaign. The Bund was followed by the Caucasus; one section of the Caucasian Social-Democrats, which, like the rest of the Caucasian Social-Democrats, had formerly rejected "cultural-national autonomy," are now making it an immediate demand. This is without mentioning the conference of the Liquidators,[3] which in a diplomatic way gave its sanction to nationalist vacillations.

But from this it follows that the views of Russian Social-Democracy on the national question are not yet clear to all Social-Democrats.

It is evident that a serious and comprehensive discussion of the national question is required. Consistent Social-Democrats must work solidly and indefatigably against the fog of nationalism, no matter from what quarter it proceeds.

I. THE NATION

What is a nation?

A nation is primarily a community, a definite community of people.

This community is not racial, nor is it tribal. The modern Italian nation was formed from Romans, Teutons, Etruscans, Greeks, Arabs, and so forth. The French nation was formed from Gauls, Romans, Britons, Teutons, and so on. The same must be said of the British, the Germans and others, who were formed into nations from people of diverse races and tribes.

Thus, a nation is not a racial or tribal, but a historically constituted community of people.

On the other hand, it is unquestionable that the great empires of Cyrus and Alexander could not be called nations, although they came to be constituted historically and were

[3] The Liquidators were Mensheviks who in the period of savage repression following the 1905 revolution tried to liquidate the illegal, underground party apparatus. They gave up overt revolutionary aims and advocated working entirely within the system. The conference to which Stalin refers took place in August 1912 in Vienna. There all the Menshevik groups united on their common opposition to the Bolsheviks into the August Bloc, headed by Trotsky.

formed out of different tribes and races. They were not nations, but casual and loosely-connected conglomerations of groups, which fell apart or joined together according to the victories or defeats of this or that conqueror.

Thus, a nation is not a casual or ephemeral conglomeration, but a stable community of people.

But not every stable community constitutes a nation. Austria and Russia are also stable communities, but nobody calls them nations. What distinguishes a national community from a state community? The fact, among others, that a national community is inconceivable without a common language, while a state need not have a common language. The Czech nation in Austria and the Polish in Russia would be impossible if each did not have a common language, whereas the integrity of Russia and Austria is not affected by the fact that there are a number of different languages within their borders. We are referring, of course, to the spoken languages of the people and not to the official governmental languages.

Thus, *a common language* is one of the characteristic features of a nation.

This, of course, does not mean that different nations always and everywhere speak different languages, or that all who speak one language necessarily constitute one nation. A *common* language for every nation, but not necessarily different languages for different nations! There is no nation which at one and the same time speaks several languages, but this does not mean that there cannot be two nations speaking the same language! Englishmen and Americans speak one language, but they do not constitute one nation. The same is true of the Norwegians and the Danes, the English and the Irish.

But why, for instance, do the English and the Americans not constitute one nation in spite of their common language?

Firstly, because they do not live together, but inhabit different territories. A nation is formed only as a result of lengthy and systematic intercourse, as a result of people living together generation after generation. But people cannot live together for lengthy periods unless they have a common territory. Englishmen and Americans originally inhabited the same territory, England, and constituted one nation. Later, one section of the English emigrated from England to a new territory, America, and there, in the new territory, in the course of time, came to form the new American nation. Difference of territory led to the formation of different nations.

Thus, *a common territory* is one of the characteristic features of a nation.

But this is not all. Common territory does not by itself create a nation. This requires, in addition, an internal economic bond to weld the various parts of the nation into a single whole. There is no such bond between England and America, and so they constitute two different nations. But the Americans themselves would not deserve to be called a nation were not the different parts of America bound together into an economic whole, as a result of division of labour between them, the development of means of communication, and so forth.

Take the Georgians, for instance. The Georgians before the Reform[4] inhabited a common territory and spoke one language. Nevertheless, they did not, strictly speaking, constitute one nation, for, being split up into a number of disconnected principalities, they could not share a common economic life; for centuries they waged war against each other and pillaged each other, each inciting the Persians and Turks against the other. The ephemeral and casual union of the principalities which some successful king sometimes managed to bring about embraced at best a superficial administrative sphere, and rapidly disintegrated owing to the caprices of the princes and the indifference of the peasants. Nor could it be otherwise in economically disunited Georgia. . . . Georgia came on the scene as a nation only in the latter half of the nineteenth century, when the fall of serfdom and the growth of the economic life of the country, the development of means of communication and the rise of capitalism, introduced division of labour between the various districts of Georgia, completely shattered the economic isolation of the principalities and bound them together into a single whole.

The same must be said of the other nations which have passed through the stage of feudalism and have developed capitalism.

[4] The abolition of serfdom in Georgia (1863–67).

Thus, *a common economic life, economic cohesion,* is one of the characteristic features of a nation.

But even this is not all. Apart from the foregoing, one must take into consideration the specific spiritual complexion of the people constituting a nation. Nations differ not only in their conditions of life, but also in spiritual complexion, which manifests itself in peculiarities of national culture. If England, America and Ireland, which speak one language, nevertheless constitute three distinct nations, it is in no small measure due to the peculiar psychological make-up which they developed from generation to generation as a result of dissimilar conditions of existence.

Of course, by itself, psychological make-up or, as it is otherwise called, "national character," is something intangible for the observer, but in so far as it manifests itself in a distinctive culture common to the nation it is something tangible and cannot be ignored.

Needless to say, "national character" is not a thing that is fixed once and for all, but is modified by changes in the conditions of life; but since it exists at every given moment, it leaves its impress on the physiognomy of the nation.

Thus, *a common psychological make-up,* which manifests itself in a common culture, is one of the characteristic features of a nation.

We have now exhausted the characteristic features of a nation.

A nation is a historically constituted, stable community of people, formed on the basis of a common language, territory, economic life, and psychological make-up manifested in a common culture.

It goes without saying that a nation, like every historical phenomenon, is subject to the law of change, has its history, its beginning and end.

It must be emphasized that none of the above characteristics taken separately is sufficient to define a nation. More than that, it is sufficient for a single one of these characteristics to be lacking and the nation ceases to be a nation.

It is possible to conceive of people possessing a common "national character" who, nevertheless, cannot be said to constitute a single nation if they are economically disunited, inhabit different territories, speak different languages, and so forth. Such, for instance, are the Russian, Galician, American, Georgian and Caucasian Highland *Jews*, who, in our opinion, do not constitute a single nation.

It is possible to conceive of people with a common territory and economic life who nevertheless would not constitute a single nation because they have no common language and no common "national character." Such, for instance, are the Germans and Letts in the Baltic region.

Finally, the Norwegians and the Danes speak one language, but they do not constitute a single nation owing to the absence of the other characteristics.

It is only when all these characteristics are present together that we have a nation.

It might appear that "national character" is not one of the characteristics but the *sole* essential characteristic of a nation, and that all the other characteristics are, properly speaking, only *conditions* for the development of a nation, rather than its characteristics. Such, for instance, is the view held by R. Springer, and more particularly by O. Bauer, who are Social-Democratic theoreticians on the national question well known in Austria.

Let us examine their theory of the nation.

> According to Springer, "a nation is a union of similarly thinking and similarly speaking persons." It is "a cultural community of modern people *no longer tied to the 'soil'* "* (our italics).

Thus, a "union" of similarly thinking and similarly speaking people, no matter how disconnected they may be, no matter where they live, is a nation.

Bauer goes even further.

> "What is a nation?" he asks. "Is it a common language which makes people a nation? But the English and the Irish . . . speak the same language without, however,

* R. Springer, *The National Problem,* Obshchestvennaya Polza Publishing House, 1909.

being one people; the Jews have no common language and yet are a nation."*

What, then, is a nation?

"A nation is a relative community of character."

But what is character, in this case national character?

National character is "the sum total of characteristics which distinguish the people of one nationality from the people of another nationality—the complex of physical and spiritual characteristics which distinguish one nation from another."

Bauer knows, of course, that national character does not drop from the skies, and he therefore adds:

"The character of people is determined by nothing so much as by their destiny. . . . A nation is nothing but a community with a common destiny" which, in turn, is determined "by the conditions under which people produce their means of subsistence and distribute the products of their labour."

We thus arrive at the most "complete," as Bauer calls it, definition of a nation:

"*A nation is an aggregate of people bound into a community of character by a common destiny.*"

We thus have common national character based on a common destiny, but not necessarily connected with a common territory, language or economic life.

But what in that case remains of the nation? What common nationality can there be among people who are economically disconnected, inhabit different territories and from generation to generation speak different languages?

* O. Bauer, *The National Question and Social-Democracy*, Serp Publishing House, 1909.

Bauer speaks of the Jews as a nation, although they "have no common language"; but what "common destiny" and national cohesion is there, for instance, between the Georgian, Daghestanian, Russian and American Jews, who are completely separated from one another, inhabit different territories and speak different languages?

The above-mentioned Jews undoubtedly lead their economic and political life in common with the Georgians, Daghestanians, Russians and Americans respectively, and they live in the same cultural atmosphere as these; this is bound to leave a definite impress on their national character; if there is anything common to them left, it is their religion, their common origin and certain relics of the national character. All this is beyond question. But how can it be seriously maintained that petrified religious rites and fading psychological relics affect the "destiny" of these Jews more powerfully than the living social, economic and cultural environment that surrounds them? And it is only on this assumption that it is possible to speak of the Jews as a single nation at all.

What, then, distinguishes Bauer's nation from the mystical and self-sufficient "national spirit" of the spiritualists?

Bauer sets up an impassable barrier between the "distinctive feature" of nations (national character) and the "conditions" of their life, divorcing the one from the other. But what is national character if not a reflection of the conditions of life, a coagulation of impressions derived from environment? How can one limit the matter to national character alone, isolating and divorcing it from the soil that gave rise to it?

Further, what indeed distinguished the English nation from the American nation at the end of the eighteenth and the beginning of the nineteenth centuries, when America was still known as New England? Not national character, of course; for the Americans had originated from England and had brought with them to America not only the English language, but also the English national character, which, of course, they could not lose so soon; although, under the influence of the new conditions, they would naturally be developing their own specific character. Yet, despite their more or less common character, they at that time already constituted a nation distinct from England! Obviously, New England as a nation differed then from England as a nation not by its specific national character, or not so much by its national character, as by its environment and conditions of life, which were distinct from those of England.

It is therefore clear that there is in fact no *single* distinguishing characteristic of a nation. There is only a sum total of characteristics, of which, when nations are compared, sometimes one characteristic (national character), sometimes another (language), or sometimes a third (territory, economic conditions), stands out in sharper relief. A nation constitutes the combination of all these characteristics taken together.

Bauer's point of view, which identifies a nation with its national character, divorces the nation from its soil and converts it into an invisible, self-contained force. The result is not a living and active nation, but something mystical, intangible and supernatural. For, I repeat, what sort of nation, for instance, is a Jewish nation which consists of Georgian, Daghestanian, Russian, American and other Jews, the members of which do not understand each other (since they speak different languages), inhabit different parts of the globe, will never see each other, and will never act together, whether in time of peace or in time of war?!

No, it is not for such paper "nations" that Social-Democracy draws up its national programme. It can reckon only with real nations, which act and move, and therefore insist on being reckoned with.

Bauer is obviously confusing *nation*, which is a historical category, with *tribe*, which is an ethnographical category.

However, Bauer himself apparently feels the weakness of his position. While in the beginning of his book he definitely declares the Jews to be a nation, he corrects himself at the end of the book and states that "in general capitalist society makes it impossible for them (the Jews) to continue as a nation," by causing them to assimilate with other nations. The reason, it appears, is that "the Jews have no closed territory of settlement," whereas the Czechs, for instance, have such a territory and, according to Bauer, will survive as a nation. In short, the reason lies in the absence of a territory.

By arguing thus, Bauer wanted to prove that the Jewish workers cannot demand national autonomy, but he thereby inadvertently refuted his own theory, which denies that a common territory is one of the characteristics of a nation.

But Bauer goes further. In the beginning of his book he definitely declares that "the Jews have no *common* language, and yet are a nation." But hardly has he reached p. 130 than he effects a change of front and just as definitely declares that "*unquestionably, no nation is possible without a common language*" (our italics).

Bauer wanted to prove that "language is the most important instrument of human intercourse," but at the same time he inadvertently proved something he did not mean to prove, namely, the unsoundness of his own theory of nations, which denies the significance of a common language.

Thus this theory, stitched together by idealistic threads, refutes itself.

II. THE NATIONAL MOVEMENT

A nation is not merely a historical category but a historical category belonging to a definite epoch, the epoch of rising capitalism. The process of elimination of feudalism and development of capitalism is at the same time a process of the constitution of people into nations. Such, for instance, was the case in Western Europe. The British, French, Germans, Italians and others were formed into nations at the time of the victorious advance of capitalism and its triumph over feudal disunity.

But the formation of nations in those instances at the same time signified their conversion into independent national states. The British, French and other nations are at the same time British, etc., states. Ireland, which did not participate in this process, does not alter the general picture.

Matters proceeded somewhat differently in Eastern Europe. Whereas in the West nations developed into states, in the East multi-national states were formed, states consisting of several nationalities. Such are Austria-Hungary and Russia. In Austria, the Germans proved to be politically the most developed, and they took it upon themselves to unite the Austrian nationalities into a state. In Hungary, the most adapted for state organization were the Magyars—the core of the Hungarian nationalities—and it was they who united Hungary. In Russia, the uniting of the nationalities was undertaken by the Great Russians, who were headed by a historically formed, powerful and well-organized aristocratic military bureaucracy.

That was how matters proceeded in the East.

This special method of formation of states could take place only where feudalism had not yet been eliminated, where capitalism was feebly developed, where the nationalities which had been forced into the background had not yet been able to consolidate themselves economically into integral nations.

But capitalism also began to develop in the Eastern states. Trade and means of communication were developing. Large towns were springing up. The nations were becoming economically consolidated. Capitalism, erupting into the tranquil life of the nationalities which had been pushed into the background, was arousing them and stirring them into action. The development of the press and the theatre, the activity of the Reichsrat (Austria) and of the Duma (Russia) were helping to strengthen "national sentiments." The intelligentsia that had arisen was being imbued with "the national idea" and was acting in the same direction. . . .

But the nations which had been pushed into the background and had now awakened to independent life, could no longer form themselves into independent national states; they encountered on their path the very powerful resistence of the ruling strata of the dominant nations, which had long ago assumed the control of the state. They were too late! . . .

In this way the Czechs, Poles, etc., formed themselves into nations in Austria; the Croats, etc., in Hungary; the Letts, Lithuanians, Ukrainians, Georgians, Armenians, etc., in Russia. What had been an exception in Western Europe (Ireland) became the rule in the East.

In the West, Ireland responded to its exceptional position by a national movement. In the East, the awakened nations were bound to respond in the same fashion.

Thus arose the circumstances which impelled the young nations of Eastern Europe on to the path of struggle.

The struggle began and flared up, to be sure, not between nations as a whole, but between the ruling classes of the dominant nations and of those that had been pushed into the background. The struggle is usually conducted by the urban petty bourgeoisie of the oppressed nation against the big bourgeoisie of the dominant nation (Czechs and Germans), or by the rural bourgeoisie of the oppressed nation against the landlords of the dominant nation (Ukrainians in Poland), or by the whole "national" bourgeoisie of the oppressed nations against the ruling nobility of the dominant nation (Poland, Lithuania and the Ukraine in Russia).

The bourgeoisie plays the leading role.

The chief problem for the young bourgeoisie is the problem of the market. Its aim is to sell its goods and to emerge victorious from competition with the bourgeoisie of a different nationality. Hence its desire to secure its "own," its "home" market. The market is the first school in which the bourgeoisie learns its nationalism.

But matters are usually not confined to the market. The semi-feudal, semi-bourgeois bureaucracy of the dominant nation intervenes in the struggle with its own methods of "arresting and preventing." The bourgeoisie—whether big or small—of the dominant nation is able to deal more "swiftly" and "decisively" with its competitor. "Forces" are united and a series of restrictive measures is put into operation against the "alien" bourgeoisie, measures passing into acts of repression. The struggle spreads from the economic sphere to the political sphere. Restriction of freedom of movement, repression of language, restriction of franchise, closing of schools, religious restrictions, and so on, are piled upon the head of the "competitor." Of course, such measures are designed not only in the interest of the bourgeois classes of the dominant nation, but also in furtherance of the specifically caste aims, so to speak, of the ruling bureaucracy. But from the point of view of the results achieved this is quite immaterial; the bourgeois classes and the bureaucracy in this matter go hand in hand—whether it be in Austria-Hungary or in Russia.

The bourgeoisie of the oppressed nation, repressed on every hand, is naturally stirred into movement. It appeals to its "native folk" and begins to shout about the "fatherland," claiming that its own cause is the cause of the nation as a whole. It recruits itself and army from among its "countrymen" in the interests of . . . the "fatherland." Nor do the "folk" always remain unresponsive to its appeals; they rally around its banner: the repression from above affects them too and provokes their discontent.

Thus the national movement begins.

The strength of the national movement is determined by the degree to which the wide strata of the nation, the proletariat and peasantry, participate in it.

Whether the proletariat rallies to the banner of bourgeois nationalism depends on the degree of development of class antagonisms, on the class consciousness and degree of organization of the proletariat. The class-conscious proletariat has its own tried banner, and has no need to rally to the banner of the bourgeoisie.

As far as the peasants are concerned, their participation in the national movement depends primarily on the character of the repressions. If the repressions affect the "land," as was the case in Ireland, then the mass of the peasants immediately rally to the banner of the national movement.

On the other hand, if, for example, there is no serious *anti-Russian* nationalism in Georgia, it is primarily because there are neither Russian landlords nor a Russian big bourgeoisie there to supply the fuel for such nationalism among the masses. In Georgia there is *anti-Armenian* nationalism; but this is because there is still an Armenian big bourgeoisie there which, by getting the better of the small and still unconsolidated Georgian bourgeoisie, drives the latter to anti-Armenian nationalism.

Depending on these factors, the national movement either assumes a mass character and steadily grows (as in Ireland and Galicia), or is converted into a series of petty collisions, degenerating into squabbles and "fights" over signboards (as in some of the small towns of Bohemia).

The content of the national movement, of course, cannot everywhere be the same: it is wholly determined by the diverse demands made by the movement. In Ireland the movement bears an agrarian character; in Bohemia it bears a "language" character; in one place the demand is for civil equality and religious freedom, in another for the nation's "own" officials, or its own Diet. The diversity of demands not infrequently reveals the diverse features which characterize a nation in general (language, territory, etc.). It is worthy of note that we never meet with a demand based on Bauer's all-embracing "national character." And this is natural: "national character" *in itself* is something intangible, and, as was correctly remarked by J. Strasser, "a politician can't do anything with it."

Such, in general, are the forms and character of the national movement.

From what has been said it will be clear that the national struggle under the conditions of *rising* capitalism is a struggle of the bourgeois classes among themselves. Sometimes the bourgeoisie succeeds in drawing the proletariat into the national movement, and then the national struggle *externally* assumes a "nation-wide" character. But this is so only externally. *In its essence* it is always a bourgeois struggle, one that is to the advantage and profit mainly of the bourgeoisie.

But it does not by any means follow that the proletariat should not put up a fight against the policy of national oppression.

Restriction of freedom of movement, disfranchisement, repression of language, closing of schools, and other forms of persecution affect the workers no less, if not more, than the bourgeoisie. Such a state of affairs can only serve to retard the free development of the intellectual forces of the proletariat of subject nations. One cannot speak seriously of a full development of the intellectual faculties of the Tatar or Jewish worker if he is not allowed to use his native language at meetings and lectures, and if his schools are closed down.

But the policy of nationalist persecution is dangerous to the cause of the proletariat also on another account. It diverts the attention of large strata from social questions, questions of the class struggle, to national questions, questions "common" to the proletariat and the bourgeoisie. And this creates a favourable soil for lying propaganda about "harmony of interests," for glossing over the class interests of the proletariat and for the intellectual enslavement of the workers. This creates a serious obstacle to the cause of uniting the workers of all nationalities. If a considerable proportion of the Polish workers are still in intellectual bondage to the bourgeois nationalists, if they still stand aloof from the international labour movement, it is chiefly because the age-old anti-Polish policy of the "powers that be" creates the soil for this bondage and hinders the emancipation of the workers from it.

But the policy of persecution does not stop there. It not infrequently passes from a "system" of *oppression* to a "system" of *inciting* nations against each other, to a "system" of massacres and pogroms. Of course, the latter system is not everywhere and always possible, but where it is possible—in the absence of elementary civil rights—it frequently assumes horrifying proportions and threatens to drown the cause of unity of the workers in blood and tears. The Caucasus and south Russia furnish numerous examples. "Divide and rule" —such is the purpose of the policy of incitement. And where such a policy succeeds, it is a tremendous evil for the proletariat and a serious obstacle to the cause of uniting the workers of all the nationalities in the state.

But the workers are interested in the complete amalgamation of all their fellow-workers into a single international army, in their speedy and final emancipation from intellectual bondage to the bourgeoisie, and in the full and free development of the intellectual forces of their brothers, whatever nation they may belong to.

The workers therefore combat and will continue to combat the policy of national oppression in all its forms, from the most subtle to the most crude, as well as the policy of inciting nations against each other in all its forms.

Social-Democracy in all countries therefore proclaims the right of nations to self-determination.

The right of self-determination means that only the nation itself has the right to determine its destiny, that no one has the right *forcibly* to interfere in the life of the nation, to *destroy* its schools and other institutions, to *violate* its habits and customs, to *repress* its language, or *curtail* its rights.

This, of course, does not mean that Social-Democracy will support every custom and institution of a nation. While combating the coercion of any nation, it will uphold only the right of the *nation* itself to determine its own destiny, at the same time agitating against harmful customs and institutions of that nation in order to enable the toiling strata of the nation to emancipate themselves from them.

The right of self-determination means that a nation may arrange its life in the way it wishes. It has the right to arrange its life on the basis of autonomy. It has the right to enter into federal relations with other nations. It has the right to complete secession. Nations are sovereign, and all nations have equal rights.

This, of course, does not mean that Social-Democracy will support every demand of a nation. A nation has the right even to return to the old order of things; but this does not mean that Social-Democracy will subscribe to such a decision if taken by some institution of a particular nation. The obligations of Social-Democracy, which defends the interests of the proletariat, and the rights of a nation, which consists of various classes, are two different things.

In fighting for the right of nations to self-determination, the aim of Social-Democracy is to put an end to the policy of national oppression, to render it impossible, and thereby to remove the grounds of strife between nations, to take the edge off that strife and reduce it to a minimum.

This is what essentially distinguishes the policy of the class-conscious proletariat from the policy of the bourgeoisie, which attempts to aggravate and fan the national struggle and to prolong and sharpen the national movement.

And that is why the class-conscious proletariat cannot rally under the "national" flag of the bourgeoisie.

That is why the so-called "evolutionary national" policy advocated by Bauer cannot become the policy of the proletariat. Bauer's attempt to identify his "evolutionary national" policy with the policy of the "modern working class" is an attempt to adapt the class struggle of the workers to the struggle of the nations.

The fate of a national movement, which is essentially a bourgeois movement, is naturally bound up with the fate of the bourgeoisie. The final disappearance of a national movement is possible only with the downfall of the bourgeoisie. Only under the reign of socialism can peace be fully established. But even within the framework of capitalism it is possible to reduce the national struggle to a minimum, to undermine it at the root, to render it as harmless as possible to the proletariat. This is borne out, for example, by Switzerland and America. It requires that the country should be democratized and the nations be given the opportunity of free development.

III. PRESENTATION OF THE QUESTION

A nation has the right freely to determine its own destiny. It has the right to arrange its life as it sees fit, without, of course, trampling on the rights of other nations. That is beyond dispute.

But *how* exactly should it arrange its own life, *what forms* should its future constitution take, if the interests of the majority of the nation and, above all, of the proletariat are to be borne in mind?

A nation has the right to arrange its life on autonomous lines. It even has the right to secede. But this does not mean that it should do so under all circumstances, that autonomy, or separation, will everywhere and always be advantageous for a nation, i.e., for its majority, i.e., for the toiling strata. The Transcaucasian Tatars as a nation may assemble, let us say, in their Diet and, succumbing to the influence of their beys and mullahs, decide to restore the old order of things and to secede from the state. According to the meaning of the clause on self-determination they are fully entitled to do so. But will this be in the interest of the toiling strata of the Tatar nation? Can Social-Democracy look on indifferently when the beys and mullahs assume the leadership of the masses in the solution of the national question? Should not Social-Democracy interfere in the matter and influence the will of the nation in a definite way? Should it not come forward with a definite plan for the solution of the question, a plan which would be most advantageous for the Tatar masses?

But what solution would be most compatible with the interests of the toiling masses? Autonomy, federation or separation?

All these are problems the solution of which will depend on the concrete historical conditions in which the given nation finds itself.

More than that; conditions, like everything else, change, and a decision which is correct at one particular time may prove to be entirely unsuitable at another.

In the middle of the nineteenth century Marx was in favour of the secession of Russian Poland; and he was right, for it was then a question of emancipating a higher culture from a lower culture that was destroying it. And the question at that time was not only a theoretical one, an academic question, but a practical one, a question of actual reality. . . .

At the end of the nineteenth century the Polish Marxists were already declaring against the secession of Poland; and they too were right, for during the fifty years that had elapsed profound changes had taken place, bringing Russia and Poland closer economically and culturally. Moreover, during that period the question of secession had been converted from a practical matter into a matter of academic dispute, which excited nobody except perhaps intellectuals abroad.

This, of course, by no means precludes the possibility that certain internal and external conditions may arise in which the question of the secession of Poland may again come on the order of the day.

The solution of the national question is possible only in connection with the historical conditions taken in their development.

The economic, political and cultural conditions of a given nation constitute the only key to the question *how* a particular nation ought to arrange its life and *what forms* its future constitution ought to take. It is possible that a specific solution of the question will be required for each nation. If the dialectical approach to a question is required anywhere it is required here, in the national question.

In view of this we must declare our decided opposition to a certain very widespread, but very summary manner of "solving" the national question, which owes its inception to the Bund. We have in mind the easy method of referring to Austrian and South-Slav* Social-Democracy, which has supposedly already solved the national question and whose solution the

* South-Slav Social-Democracy operates in the Southern part of Austria.

Russian Social-Democrats should simply borrow. It is assumed that whatever, say, is right for Austria is also right for Russia. The most important and decisive factor is lost sight of here, namely, the concrete historical conditions in Russia as a whole and in the life of each of the nations inhabiting Russia in particular.

Listen, for example, to what the well-known Bundist, V. Kossovsky, says:

> "When at the Fourth Congress of the Bund the principles of the question (i.e., the national question—*J. St.*) were discussed, the proposal made by one of the members of the congress to settle the question in the spirit of the resolution of the South-Slav Social-Democratic Party met with general approval."

And the result was that "the congress unanimously adopted" . . . national autonomy.

And that was all! No analysis of the actual conditions in Russia, no investigation of the condition of the Jews in Russia. They first borrowed the solution of the South-Slav Social-Democratic Party, then they "approved" it, and finally they "unanimously adopted" it! This is the way the Bundists present and "solve" the national question in Russia. . . .

As a matter of fact, Austria and Russia represent entirely different conditions. This explains why the Social-Democrats in Austria, when they adopted their national programme at Brünn (1899) in the spirit of the resolution of the South-Slav Social-Democratic Party (with certain insignificant amendments, it is true), approached the question in an entirely non-Russian way, so to speak, and, of course, solved it in a non-Russian way.

First, as to the presentation of the question. How is the question presented by the Austrian theoreticians of cultural-national autonomy, the interpreters of the Brünn national programme and the resolution of the South-Slav Social-Democratic Party, Springer and Bauer?

> "Whether a multi-national state is possible," says Springer, "and whether, in particular, the Austrian nation-

alities are obliged to form a single political entity, is a question we shall not answer here but shall assume to be settled. For anyone who will not concede this possibility and necessity, our investigation will, of course, be purposeless. Our theme is as follows: inasmuch as these nations are *obliged* to live together, what *legal forms* will enable them *to live together in the best possible way?*" (Springer's italics).

Thus, the starting point is the state integrity of Austria. Bauer says the same thing:

> "We therefore start from the assumption that the Austrian nations will remain in the same state union in which they exist at present and inquire how the nations within this union will arrange their relations among themselves and to the state."

Here again the first thing is the integrity of Austria.

Can Russian Social-Democracy present the question *in this way?* No, it cannot. And it cannot because from the very outset it holds the view of the right of nations to self-determination, by virtue of which a nation has the right of secession.

Even the Bundist Goldblatt admitted at the Second Congress of Russian Social-Democracy that the latter could not abandon the standpoint of self-determination. Here is what Goldblatt said on that occasion:

> "Nothing can be said against the right of self-determination. If any nation is striving for independence, we must not oppose it. If Poland does not wish to enter into 'lawful wedlock' with Russia, it is not for us to interfere with her."

All this is true. But it follows that the starting points of the Austrian and Russian Social-Democrats, far from being identical, are diametrically opposite. After this, can there be any question of borrowing the national programme of the Austrians?

Furthermore, the Austrians hope to achieve the "freedom of nationalities" by means of petty reforms, by slow steps. While they propose cultural-national autonomy as a practical measure, they do not count on any radical change, on a democratic movement for liberation, which they do not even contemplate. The Russian Marxists, on the other hand, associate the "freedom of nationalities" with a probable radical change, with a democratic movement for liberation, having no grounds for counting on reforms. And this essentially alters matters in regard to the probable fate of the nations of Russia.

> "Of course," says Bauer, "there is little probability that national autonomy will be the result of a great decision, of a bold action. Austria will develop towards national autonomy step by step, by a slow process of development, in the course of a severe struggle, as a consequence of which legislation and administration will be in a state of chronic paralysis. The new constitution will not be created by a great legislative act, but by a multitude of separate enactments for individual provinces and individual communities."

Springer says the same thing.

> "I am very well aware," he writes, "that institutions of this kind (i.e., organs of national autonomy—*J. St.*) are not created in a single year or a single decade. The reorganization of the Prussian administration alone took considerable time. . . . It took the Prussians two decades finally to establish their basic administrative institutions. Let nobody think that I harbour any illusions as to the time required and the difficulties to be overcome in Austria."

All this is very definite. But can the Russian Marxists avoid associating the national question with "bold actions"? Can they count on partial reforms, on "a multitude of separate enactments" as a means for achieving the "freedom of nationalities"? But if they cannot and must not do so, is it not clear that the methods of struggle of the Austrians and the

Russians and their prospects must be entirely different? How in such a state of affairs can they confine themselves to the one-sided, milk-and-water cultural-national autonomy of the Austrians? One or the other: either those who are in favour of borrowing do not count on "bold actions" in Russia, or they do count on such actions but "know not what they do."

Finally, the immediate tasks facing Russia and Austria are entirely different and consequently dictate different methods of solving the national question. In Austria parliamentarism prevails, and under present conditions no development in Austria is possible without parliament. But parliamentary life and legislation in Austria are frequently brought to a complete standstill by severe conflicts between the national parties. That explains the chronic political crisis from which Austria has for a long time been suffering. Hence, in Austria the national question is the very hub of political life; it is the vital question. It is therefore not surprising that the Austrian Social-Democratic politicians should first of all try in one way or another to find a solution for the national conflicts—of course on the basis of the existing parliamentary system, by parliamentary methods. . . .

Not so with Russia. In the first place, in Russia "there is no parliament, thank God."[5] In the second place—and this is the main point—the hub of the political life of Russia is not the national but the agrarian question. Consequently, the fate of the Russian problem, and, accordingly, the "liberation" of the nations too, is bound up in Russia with the solution of the agrarian question, i.e., with the destruction of the relics of feudalism, i.e., with the democratization of the country. That explains why in Russia the national question is not an independent and decisive one, but a part of the general and more important question of the emancipation of the country.

> "The barrenness of the Austrian parliament," writes Springer, "is due precisely to the fact that every reform gives rise to antagonisms within the national parties which may affect their unity. The leaders of the parties, there-

[5] A public remark made by the czarist Minister of Finance in 1908.

fore, avoid everything that smacks of reform. Progress in Austria is generally conceivable only if the nations are granted indefeasible legal rights which will relieve them of the necessity of constantly maintaining national militant groups in parliament and will enable them to turn their attention to the solution of economic and social problems."

Bauer says the same thing.

"National peace is indispensable first of all for the state. The state cannot permit legislation to be brought to a standstill by the very stupid question of language or by every quarrel between excited people on a linguistic frontier, or over every new school."

All this is clear. But it is no less clear that the national question in Russia is on an entirely different plane. It is not the national, but the agrarian question that decides the fate of progress in Russia. The national question is a subordinate one.

And so we have different presentations of the question, different prospects and methods of struggle, different immediate tasks. Is it not clear that, such being the state of affairs, only pedants who "solve" the national question without reference to space and time can think of adopting examples from Austria and of borrowing a programme?

To repeat: the concrete historical conditions as the starting point, and the dialectical presentation of the question as the only correct way of presenting it—such is the key to solving the national question.

VII. THE NATIONAL QUESTION IN RUSSIA

It remains for us to suggest a positive solution of the national question.

We take as our starting point that the question can be solved only in intimate connection with the present situation in Russia.

Russia is in a transitional period, when "normal," "constitutional" life has not yet been established and when the political crisis has not yet been settled. Days of storm and "complications" are ahead. And this gives rise to the movement, the present and the future movement, the aim of which is to achieve complete democratization.

It is in connection with this movement that the national question must be examined.

Thus the complete democratization of the country is the *basis* and condition for the solution of the national question.

When seeking a solution of the question we must take into account not only the situation at home but also the situation abroad. Russia is situated between Europe and Asia, between Austria and China. The growth of democracy in Asia is inevitable. The growth of imperialism in Europe is not fortuitous. In Europe, capital is beginning to feel cramped, and it is reaching out towards foreign countries in search of new markets, cheap labour and new fields of investment. But this leads to external complications and to war. No one can assert that the Balkan War[6] is the end and not the beginning of the complications. It is quite possible, therefore, that a combination of internal and external conditions may arise in which one or another nationality in Russia may find it necessary to raise and settle the question of its independence. And, of course, it is not for Marxists to create obstacles in such cases.

But it follows that Russian Marxists cannot dispense with the right of nations to self-determination.

Thus, *the right of self-determination is an essential element* in the solution of the national question.

Further. What must be our attitude towards nations which for one reason or another will prefer to remain within the framework of the whole?

We have seen that cultural-national autonomy is unsuitable. Firstly, it is artificial and impracticable, for it proposes artificially to draw into a single nation people whom the march of events, real events, is disuniting and dispersing to every corner of the country. Secondly, it stimulates nationalism, because it leads to the viewpoint in favour of the "de-

[6] The first Balkan War, which broke out in 1912 between Bulgaria, Serbia, Montenegro, and Greece, on the one hand, and Turkey on the other.

marcation" of people according to national curiae, the "organization" of nations, the "preservation" and cultivation of "national peculiarities"—all of which are entirely incompatible with Social-Democracy. It is not fortuitous that the Moravian separatists in the Reichsrat, having severed themselves from the German Social-Democratic deputies, have united with the Moravian bourgeois deputies to form a single, so to speak, Moravian "kolo." Nor is it fortuitous that the separatists of the Bund have got themselves involved in nationalism by acclaiming the "Sabbath" and "Yiddish." There are no Bundist deputies yet in the Duma, but in the Bund area there is a clerical-reactionary Jewish community, in the "controlling institutions" of which the Bund is arranging, for a beginning, a "get-together" of the Jewish workers and bourgeois. Such is the logic of cultural-national autonomy.

Thus, *national* autonomy does not solve the problem.

What, then, is the way out?

The only correct solution is *regional* autonomy, autonomy for such crystallized units as Poland, Lithuania, the Ukraine, the Caucasus, etc.

The advantage of regional autonomy consists, first of all, in the fact that it does not deal with a fiction bereft of territory, but with a definite population inhabiting a definite territory. Next, it does not divide people according to nations, it does not strengthen national barriers; on the contrary, it breaks down these barriers and unites the population in such a manner as to open the way for division of a different kind, division according to classes. Finally, it makes it possible to utilize the natural wealth of the region and to develop its productive forces in the best possible way without awaiting the decisions of a common centre—functions which are not inherent features of cultural-national autonomy.

Thus, *regional autonomy is an essential element* in the solution of the national question.

Of course, not one of the regions constitutes a compact, homogeneous nation, for each is interspersed with national minorities. Such are the Jews in Poland, the Letts in Lithuania, the Russians in the Caucasus, the Poles in the Ukraine, and so on. It may be feared, therefore, that the minorities will be oppressed by the national majorities. But there will be grounds for fear only if the old order continues to prevail in the country. Give the country complete democracy and all grounds for fear will vanish.

It is proposed to bind the dispersed minorities into a single national union. But what the minorities want is not an artificial union, but real rights in the localities they inhabit. What can such a union give them *without* complete democratization? On the other hand, what need is there for a national union *when there is* complete democratization?

What is it that particularly agitates a national minority?

A minority is discontented not because there is no national union but because it does not enjoy the right to use its native language. Permit it to use its native language and the discontent will pass of itself.

A minority is discontented not because there is no artificial union but because it does not possess its own schools. Give it its own schools and all grounds for discontent will disappear.

A minority is discontented not because there is no national union, but because it does not enjoy liberty of conscience (religious liberty), liberty of movement, etc. Give it these liberties and it will cease to be discontented.

Thus, *equal rights of nations in all forms (language, schools, etc.) is an essential element* in the solution of the national question. Consequently, a state law based on complete democratization of the country is required, prohibiting all national privileges without exception and every kind of disability or restriction on the rights of national minorities.

That, and that alone, is the real, not a paper guarantee of the rights of a minority.

One may or may not dispute the existence of a logical connection between organizational federalism and cultural-national autonomy. But one cannot dispute the fact that the latter creates an atmosphere favouring unlimited federalism, developing into complete rupture, into separatism. If the Czechs in Austria and the Bundists in Russia began with autonomy, passed to federation and ended in separatism, there can be no doubt that an important part in this was played by the nationalist atmosphere that is naturally generated by cultural-national autonomy. It is not fortuitous that national autonomy and organizational federalism go hand in hand. It is quite understandable. Both demand demarcation according to nationalities. Both presume organization according to nationalities. The similarity is beyond question. The only difference is that in one case the population as a whole is divided, while in the other it is the Social-Democratic workers who are divided.

We know where the demarcation of workers according to nationalities leads to. The disintegration of a united workers' party, the splitting of trade unions according to nationalities, aggravation of national friction, national strikebreaking, complete demoralization within the ranks of Social-Democracy—such are the results of organizational federalism. This is eloquently borne out by the history of Social-Democracy in Austria and the activities of the Bund in Russia.

The only cure for this is organization on the basis of internationalism.

To unite locally the workers of all nationalities of Russia into *single, integral* collective bodies, to unite these collective bodies into a *single* party—such is the task.

It goes without saying that a party structure of this kind does not preclude, but on the contrary presumes, wide autonomy for the *regions* within the single integral party.

The experience of the Caucasus proves the expediency of this type of organization. If the Caucasians have succeeded in overcoming the national friction between the Armenian and Tatar workers; if they have succeeded in safeguarding the population against the possibility of massacres and shooting affrays; if in Baku, that kaleidoscope of national groups, national conflicts are now no longer possible, and if it has been possible to draw the workers there into the single current of a powerful movement, then the international structure of the Caucasian Social-Democracy was not the least factor in bringing this about.

The type of organization influences not only practical work. It stamps an indelible impress on the whole mental life of the worker. The worker lives the life of his organization, which stimulates his intellectual growth and educates him. And thus, acting within his organization and continually meeting there comrades from other nationalities, and side by side with them waging a common struggle under the leadership of a common collective body, he becomes deeply imbued with the idea that workers are *primarily* members of one class family, members of the united army of socialism. And this cannot but have a tremendous educational value for large sections of the working class.

Therefore, the international type of organization serves as a school of fraternal sentiments and is a tremendous agitational factor on behalf of internationalism.

But this is not the case with an organization on the basis of nationalities. When the workers are organized according to nationality they isolate themselves within their national shells, fenced off from each other by organizational barriers. The stress is laid not on what is *common* to the workers but on what distinguishes them from each other. In this type of organization the worker is *primarily* a member of his nation: a Jew, a Pole, and so on. It is not surprising that *national* federalism in organization inculcates in the workers a spirit of national seclusion.

Therefore, the national type of organization is a school of national narrow-mindedness and stagnation.

Thus we are confronted by two *fundamentally* different types of organization: the type based on international solidarity and the type based on the organizational "demarcation" of the workers according to nationalities.

Attempts to reconcile these two types have so far been vain. The compromise rules of the Austrian Social-Democratic Party drawn up in Wimberg in 1897 were left hanging in the air. The Austrian party fell to pieces and dragged the trade unions with it. "Compromise" proved to be not only utopian, but harmful. Strasser is right when he says that "separatism achieved its first triumph at the Wimberg Party Congress."* The same is true in Russia. The "compromise" with the federalism of the Bund which took place at the Stockholm Congress ended in a complete fiasco. The Bund violated the Stockholm compromise. Ever since the Stockholm Congress the Bund has been an obstacle in the way of union of the workers locally in a *single* organization, which would include

* See his *Der Arbeiter und die Nation*, 1912.

workers of all nationalities. And the Bund has obstinately persisted in its separatist tactics in spite of the fact that in 1907 and in 1908 Russian Social-Democracy repeatedly demanded that unity should at last be established from below among the workers of all nationalities. The Bund, which began with organizational national autonomy, in fact passed to federalism, only to end in complete rupture, separatism. And by breaking with the Russian Social-Democratic Party it caused disharmony and disorganization in the ranks of the latter. . . .

The path of "compromise" must therefore be discarded as utopian and harmful.

One thing or the other: *either* the federalism of the Bund, in which case the Russian Social-Democratic Party must re-form itself on a basis of "demarcation" of the workers according to nationalities; *or* an international type of organization, in which case the Bund must re-form itself on a basis of territorial autonomy after the pattern of the Caucasian, Lettish and Polish Social-Democracies, and thus make possible the direct union of the Jewish workers with the workers of the other nationalities of Russia.

There is no middle course: principles triumph, they do not "compromise."

Thus, *the principle of international solidarity of the workers is an essential element* in the solution of the national question.

January 1913

TWO CAMPS[1]

The world has definitely and irrevocably split into two camps: the camp of imperialism and the camp of socialism.

Over there, *in their* camp, are America and Britain, France and Japan, with their capital, armaments, tried agents and experienced administrators.

Here, *in our* camp, are Soviet Russia and the young Soviet republics and the growing proletarian revolution in the countries of Europe, without capital, without tried agents or experienced administrators, but, on the other hand, with experienced agitators capable of firing the hearts of the working people with the spirit of emancipation.

The struggle between these two camps constitutes the hub of present-day affairs, determines the whole substance of the present home and foreign policies of the leaders of the old and the new worlds.

Estland and Lithuania, the Ukraine and the Crimea, Turkestan and Siberia, Poland and the Caucasus, and, finally, Russia itself are not aims in themselves. They are only an arena of struggle, of a mortal struggle between two forces: imperialism, which is striving to strengthen the yoke of slavery, and socialism, which is fighting for emancipation from slavery.

The strength of imperialism lies in the ignorance of the masses, who create wealth for their masters and forge chains of oppression for themselves. But the ignorance of the masses is a transient thing and inevitably tends to be dispelled in the course of time, as the dissatisfaction of the masses grows and the revolutionary movement spreads. The imperialists have capital—but who does not know that capi-

[1] February 22, 1919. In the midst of the Civil War, Stalin here predicts and defines the main struggle of the rest of the century.

tal is powerless in the face of the inevitable? For this reason, the rule of imperialism is impermanent and insecure.

The weakness of imperialism lies in its powerlessness to end the war *without* catastrophe, *without* increasing mass unemployment, *without* further robbery of its own workers and peasants, *without* further seizures of foreign territory. It is a question not of ending the war, nor even of victory over Germany, but of who is to be made to pay the billions spent on the war. Russia emerged from the imperialist war rejuvenated, because she ended the war at the cost of the imperialists, home and foreign, and laid the expense of the war on those who were directly responsible for it by expropriating them. The imperialists cannot do this; they cannot expropriate themselves, otherwise they would not be imperialists. To end the war in imperialist fashion, they are "compelled" to doom the workers to starvation (wholesale unemployment due to the closing down of "unprofitable" plants, additional indirect taxation, a terrific rise in prices of food); they are "compelled" to plunder Germany, Austria-Hungary, Rumania, Bulgaria, the Ukraine, the Caucasus, Turkestan, Siberia.

Need it be said that all this broadens the base of revolution, shakes the foundations of imperialism and hastens the inevitable catastrophe?

Three months ago imperialism, drunk with victory, was rattling the sabre and threatening to overrun Russia with its armed hordes. How could "poverty-stricken" and "savage" Soviet Russia hold out against the "disciplined" army of the British and French, who had smashed "even" the Germans, for all their vaunted technical equipment? So they thought. But they overlooked a "trifle," they failed to realize that peace, even an "indecent" peace, would inevitably undermine the "discipline" of their army and rouse its opposition to another war, while unemployment and high living costs would inevitably strengthen the revolutionary movement of the workers against their imperialists.

And what did we find? The "disciplined" army proved unfit for purposes of intervention: it sickened with an inevitable disease—demoralization. The boasted "civil peace" and "law and order" turned into their opposite, into civil war. The hastily concocted bourgeois "governments" in the border regions of Russia proved to be soap bubbles, unsuitable as a camouflage for intervention, which had been undertaken, of course (of course!), in the name of "humanitarianism" and "civilization." As to Soviet Russia, not only did their hope for a "walk over" fail; they even deemed it necessary to retreat a little and invite her to a "conference," on the Princes' Islands.[2] For the successes of the Red Army, the appearance of new national Soviet republics which were infecting neighbouring countries with the spirit of revolution, the spread of revolution in the West and the appearance of Workers' and Soldiers' Soviets in the Entente countries were arguments that were more than persuasive. What is more, things have reached a point where even Clemenceau the "implacable," who only yesterday refused to issue passports to the Berne Conference[3] and who was preparing to devour "anarchistic" Russia, is today, having been rather mauled by the revolution, not averse to availing himself of the services of that honest "Marxist" broker, the old Kautsky, and wants to send him to Russia to negotiate—that is to say, "investigate."

Truly:

> *"Where are they now, the haughty words,*
> *The lordly strength, the royal mien?"*

All these changes took place in the space of some three months.

We have every ground for affirming that the trend will continue in the same direction, for it has to be admitted that in the present moment of "storm and stress" Russia is the *only* country in which social and economic life is proceeding "normally," without strikes or anti-government demonstrations, that the Soviet Government is the *most stable* of all the

[2] With their military intervention in the Russian Civil War failing, Britain and France tried to arrange a conference between the Soviet government and the various Russian counterrevolutionary "governments" in February 1919 on the Princes' Islands in the Sea of Marmora. The conference never took place.

[3] The Berne Conference of February 3–10, 1919, in which the various European social-democratic parties tried to attain international unity after each had just supported its own government in the war against each other.

existing governments in Europe, and that the strength and prestige of Soviet Russia, both at home and abroad, are growing day by day in direct proportion to the decline of the strength and prestige of the imperialist governments.

The world has split into two irreconcilable camps: the camp of imperialism and the camp of socialism. Imperialism in its death throes is clutching at the last straw, the "League of Nations," trying to save itself by uniting the robbers of all countries into a single alliance. But its efforts are in vain, because time and circumstances are working against it and in favour of socialism. The tide of socialist revolution is irresistibly rising and investing the strongholds of imperialism. Its thunder is re-echoing through the countries of the oppressed East. The soil is beginning to burn under the feet of imperialism. Imperialism is doomed to inevitable destruction.

1919

THE FOUNDATIONS OF LENINISM[1]

(*Lectures Delivered at the Sverdlov University*)

DEDICATED
TO THE LENIN ENROLMENT[2]

J. STALIN

The foundations of Leninism is a big subject. To exhaust it a whole volume would be required. Indeed, a number of volumes would be required. Naturally, therefore, my lectures cannot be an exhaustive exposition of Leninism; at best they can only offer a concise synopsis of the foundations of Leninism. Nevertheless, I consider it useful to give this synopsis, in order to lay down some basic points of departure necessary for the successful study of Leninism.

[1] In 1923 Lenin became gravely ill. Immediately, Trotsky, who had come over to the Bolsheviks at the moment of victory of the 1917 revolution, began to organize opposition groups within the Party. They reopened much of the debate that had led to the 1905 split in the Social-Democratic Party, taking many of the old Menshevik positions. They particularly attacked Lenin's formulations about the leading role of a unified party, the need to build socialism in one country while relying on the peasantry as an ally, and the revolutionary potential of national liberation movements.

Lenin died on January 21, 1924. Stalin, who was Secretary of the Party, assumed leadership, particularly at first theoretical leadership, of those adhering to Lenin's principles. In *The Foundations of Leninism,* first published in April and May 1924, Stalin summarized and developed these principles as they applied to what he saw as the major theoretical and practical problems of the century, both for the Soviet Union and the world revolution. It is the most comprehensive statement of Stalin's theory on all these questions. It can also be read as the most concise statement extant of twentieth-century Marxist-Leninist theory.

The struggle over who was to succeed Lenin as leader of the Party

Expounding the foundations of Leninism still does not mean expounding the basis of Lenin's world outlook. Lenin's world outlook and the foundations of Leninism are not identical in scope. Lenin was a Marxist, and Marxism is, of course, the basis of his world outlook. But from this it does not at all follow that an exposition of Leninism ought to begin with an exposition of the foundations of Marxism. To expound Leninism means to expound the distinctive and new in the works of Lenin that Lenin contributed to the general treasury of Marxism and that is naturally connected with his name. Only in this sense will I speak in my lectures of the foundations of Leninism.

And so, what is Leninism?

Some say that Leninism is the application of Marxism to the conditions that are peculiar to the situation in Russia. This definition contains a particle of truth, but not the whole truth by any means. Lenin, indeed, applied Marxism to Russian conditions, and applied it in a masterly way. But if Leninism were only the application of Marxism to the conditions that are peculiar to Russia it would be a purely national and only a national, a purely Russian and only a Russian, phenomenon. We know, however, that Leninism is not merely a Russian, but an international phenomenon rooted in the whole of international development. That is why I think this definition suffers from one-sidedness.

Others say that Leninism is the revival of the revolutionary elements of Marxism of the forties of the nineteenth century, as distinct from the Marxism of subsequent years, when, it is alleged, it became moderate, non-revolutionary. If we disregard this foolish and vulgar division of the teachings of Marx into two parts, revolutionary and moderate, we must

---

was not, as most of us have been taught, primarily a battle of individuals for personal power. It was a contest among conflicting political ideas, whose outcome was to have enormous historical consequences. *The Foundations of Leninism* marks Stalin's emergence as Lenin's successor, that is, as the main practical and theoretical leader of the world revolution.

[2] When Lenin died, the Party was opened to workers dedicated to carrying on his heritage. In this Lenin Enrolment, almost a quarter of a million joined the Party. Stalin dedicates this work to them so it can serve as their guidebook to the principles of Leninism.

admit that even this totally inadequate and unsatisfactory definition contains a particle of truth. This particle of truth is that Lenin did indeed restore the revolutionary content of Marxism, which had been suppressed by the opportunists of the Second International. Still, that is but a particle of the truth. The whole truth about Leninism is that Leninism not only restored Marxism, but also took a step forward, developing Marxism further under the new conditions of capitalism and of the class struggle of the proletariat.

What, then, in the last analysis, is Leninism?

Leninism is Marxism of the era of imperialism and the proletarian revolution. To be more exact, Leninism is the theory and tactics of the proletarian revolution in general, the theory and tactics of the dictatorship of the proletariat in particular. Marx and Engels pursued their activities in the pre-revolutionary period (we have the proletarian revolution in mind), when developed imperialism did not yet exist, in the period of the proletarians' preparation for revolution, in the period when the proletarian revolution was not yet an immediate practical inevitability. But Lenin, the disciple of Marx and Engels, pursued his activities in the period of developed imperialism, in the period of the unfolding proletarian revolution, when the proletarian revolution had already triumphed in one country, had smashed bourgeois democracy and had ushered in the era of proletarian democracy, the era of the Soviets.

That is why Leninism is the further development of Marxism.

It is usual to point to the exceptionally militant and exceptionally revolutionary character of Leninism. This is quite correct. But this specific feature of Leninism is due to two causes: firstly, to the fact that Leninism emerged from the proletarian revolution, the imprint of which it cannot but bear; secondly, to the fact that it grew and became strong in clashes with the opportunism of the Second International, the fight against which was and remains an essential preliminary condition for a successful fight against capitalism. It must not be forgotten that between Marx and Engels, on the one hand, and Lenin, on the other, there lies a whole period of undivided domination of the opportunism of the Second

International, and the ruthless struggle against this opportunism could not but constitute one of the most important tasks of Leninism.

I. THE HISTORICAL ROOTS OF LENINISM

Leninism grew up and took shape under the conditions of imperialism, when the contradictions of capitalism had reached an extreme point, when the proletarian revolution had become an immediate practical question, when the old period of preparation of the working class for revolution had arrived at and passed into a new period, that of direct assault on capitalism.

Lenin called imperialism "moribund capitalism." Why? Because imperialism carries the contradictions of capitalism to their last bounds, to the extreme limit, beyond which revolution begins. Of these contradictions, there are three which must be regarded as the most important.

The *first contradiction* is the contradiction between labour and capital. Imperialism is the omnipotence of the monopolist trusts and syndicates, of the banks and the financial oligarchy, in the industrial countries. In the fight against this omnipotence, the customary methods of the working class—trade unions and co-operatives, parliamentary parties and the parliamentary struggle—have proved to be totally inadequate. Either place yourself at the mercy of capital, eke out a wretched existence as of old and sink lower and lower, or adopt a new weapon—this is the alternative imperialism puts before the vast masses of the proletariat. Imperialism brings the working class to revolution.

The *second contradiction* is the contradiction among the various financial groups and imperialist Powers in their struggle for sources of raw materials, for foreign territory. Imperialism is the export of capital to the sources of raw materials, the frenzied struggle for monopolist possession of these sources, the struggle for a redivision of the already divided world, a struggle waged with particular fury by new financial groups and Powers seeking a "place in the sun" against the old groups and Powers, which cling tenaciously to what they have seized. This frenzied struggle among the various groups of capitalists is notable in that it includes as an inevitable element imperialist wars, wars for the annexation of foreign territories. This circumstance, in its turn, is notable in that it leads to the mutual weakening of the imperialists, to the weakening of the position of capitalism in general, to the acceleration of the advent of the proletarian revolution and to the practical necessity of this revolution.

The *third contradiction* is the contradiction between the handful of ruling, "civilised" nations and the hundreds of millions of the colonial and dependent peoples of the world. Imperialism is the most barefaced exploitation and the most inhuman oppression of hundreds of millions of people inhabiting vast colonies and dependent countries. The purpose of this exploitation and of this oppression is to squeeze out super-profits. But in exploiting these countries imperialism is compelled to build there railways, factories and mills, industrial and commercial centres. The appearance of a class of proletarians, the emergence of a native intelligentsia, the awakening of national consciousness, the growth of the liberation movement—such are the inevitable results of this "policy." The growth of the revolutionary movement in all colonies and dependent countries without exception clearly testifies to this fact. This circumstance is of importance for the proletariat inasmuch as it saps radically the position of capitalism by converting the colonies and dependent countries from reserves of imperialism into reserves of the proletariat revolution.

Such, in general, are the principal contradictions of imperialism which have converted the old, "flourishing" capitalism into moribund capitalism.

The significance of the imperialist war which broke out ten years ago lies, among other things, in the fact that it gathered all these contradictions into a single knot and threw them on to the scales, thereby accelerating and facilitating the revolutionary battles of the proletariat.

In other words, imperialism was instrumental not only in making the revolution a practical inevitability, but also in creating favourable conditions for a direct assault on the citadels of capitalism.

Such was the international situation which gave birth to Leninism.

Some may say: this is all very well, but what has it to do with Russia, which was not and could not be a classical land of imperialism? What has it to do with Lenin, who worked primarily in Russia and for Russia? Why did Russia, of all countries, become the home of Leninism, the birthplace of the theory and tactics of the proletarian revolution?

Because Russia was the focus of all these contradictions of imperialism.

Because Russia, more than any other country, was pregnant with revolution, and she alone, therefore, was in a position to solve those contradictions in a revolutionary way.

To begin with, tsarist Russia was the home of every kind of oppression—capitalist, colonial and militarist—in its most inhuman and barbarous form. Who does not know that in Russia the omnipotence of capital was combined with the despotism of tsarism, the aggressiveness of Russian nationalism with tsarism's role of executioner in regard to the non-Russian peoples, the exploitation of entire regions—Turkey, Persia, China—with the seizure of these regions by tsarism, with wars of conquest? Lenin was right in saying that tsarism was "military-feudal imperialism." Tsarism was the concentration of the worst features of imperialism, raised to a high pitch.

To proceed. Tsarist Russia was a major reserve of Western imperialism, not only in the sense that it gave free entry to foreign capital, which controlled such basic branches of Russia's national economy as the fuel and metallurgical industries, but also in the sense that it could supply the Western imperialists with millions of soldiers. Remember the Russian army, fourteen million strong, which shed its blood on the imperialist fronts to safeguard the staggering profits of the British and French capitalists.

Further. Tsarism was not only the watchdog of imperialism in the east of Europe, but, in addition, it was the agent of Western imperialism for squeezing out of the population hundreds of millions by way of interest on loans obtained in Paris and London, Berlin and Brussels.

Finally, tsarism was a most faithful ally of Western imperialism in the partition of Turkey, Persia, China, etc. Who does not know that the imperialist war was waged by tsarism in alliance with the imperialists of the Entente, and that Russia was an essential element in that war?

That is why the interests of tsarism and of Western imperialism were interwoven and ultimately became merged in a single skein of imperialist interests.

Could Western imperialism resign itself to the loss of such a powerful support in the East and of such a rich reservoir of manpower and resources as old, tsarist, bourgeois Russia was without exerting all its strength to wage a life-and-death struggle against the revolution in Russia, with the object of defending and preserving tsarism? Of course not.

But from this it follows that whoever wanted to strike at tsarism necessarily raised his hand against imperialism, whoever rose against tsarism had to rise against imperialism as well; for whoever was bent on overthrowing tsarism had to overthrow imperialism too, if he really intended not merely to defeat tsarism, but to make a clean sweep of it. Thus the revolution against tsarism verged on and had to pass into a revolution against imperialism, into a proletarian revolution.

Meanwhile, in Russia a tremendous popular revolution was rising, headed by the most revolutionary proletariat in the world, which possessed such an important ally as the revolutionary peasantry of Russia. Does it need proof that such a revolution could not stop halfway, that in the event of success it was bound to advance further and raise the banner of revolt against imperialism?

That is why Russia was bound to become the focus of the contradictions of imperialism, not only in the sense that it was in Russia that these contradictions were revealed most plainly, in view of their particularly repulsive and particularly intolerable character, and not only because Russia was a highly important prop of Western imperialism, connecting Western finance capital with the colonies in the East, but also because Russia was the only country in which there existed a real force capable of resolving the contradictions of imperialism in a revolutionary way.

From this it follows, however, that the revolution in Russia could not but become a proletarian revolution, that from its very inception it could not but assume an international character, and that, therefore, it could not but shake the very foundations of world imperialism.

Under these circumstances, could the Russian Communists confine their work within the narrow national bounds of the Russian revolution? Of course not. On the contrary, the whole situation, both internal (the profound revolutionary crisis) and external (the war), impelled them to go beyond these bounds in their work, to transfer the struggle to the international arena, to expose the ulcers of imperialism, to prove that the collapse of capitalism was inevitable, to smash social-chauvinism and social-pacifism, and, finally, to overthrow capitalism in their own country and to forge a new fighting weapon for the proletariat—the theory and tactics of the protelarian revolution—in order to facilitate the task of overthrowing capitalism for the proletarians of all countries. Nor could the Russian Communists act otherwise, for only this path offered the chance of producing certain changes in the international situation which could safeguard Russia against the restoration of the bourgeois order.

That is why Russia became the home of Leninism, and why Lenin, the leader of the Russian Communists, became its creator.

The same thing, approximately, "happened" in the case of Russia and Lenin as in the case of Germany and Marx and Engels in the forties of the last century. Germany at that time was pregnant with bourgeois revolution just like Russia at the beginning of the twentieth century. Marx wrote at that time in the *Communist Manifesto:*

> "The Communists turn their attention chiefly to Germany, because that country is on the eve of a bourgeois revolution that is bound to be carried out under more advanced conditions of European civilisation, and with a much more developed proletariat, than that of England was in the seventeenth, and of France in the eighteenth century, and because the bourgeois revolution in Germany will be but the prelude to an immediately following proletarian revolution."

In other words, the centre of the revolutionary movement was shifting to Germany.

There can hardly be any doubt that it was this very circumstance, noted by Marx in the above-quoted passage, that served as the probable reason why it was precisely Germany that became the birthplace of scientific socialism and why the leaders of the German proletariat, Marx and Engels, became its creators.

The same, only to a still greater degree, must be said of Russia at the beginning of the twentieth century. Russia was then on the eve of a bourgeois revolution; she had to accomplish this revolution at a time when conditions in Europe were more advanced, and with a proletariat that was more developed than that of Germany in the forties of the nineteenth century (let alone Britain and France); moreover, all the evidence went to show that this revolution was bound to serve as a ferment and as a prelude to the proletarian revolution.

We cannot regard it as accidental that as early as 1902, when the Russian revolution was still in an embryonic state, Lenin wrote the prophetic words in his pamphlet *What Is To Be Done?*:

> "History has now confronted us (i.e., the Russian Marxists—*J. St.*) with an immediate task which is the *most revolutionary* of all the *immediate* tasks that confront the proletariat of any country. The fulfilment of this task, the destruction of the most powerful bulwark, not only of European, but also (it may now be said) of Asiatic reaction, would make the Russian proletariat the vanguard of the international revolutionary proletariat."

In other words, the centre of the revolutionary movement was bound to shift to Russia.

As we know, the course of the revolution in Russia has more than vindicated Lenin's prediction.

Is it surprising, after all this, that a country which has accomplished such a revolution and possesses such a proletariat should have been the birthplace of the theory and tactics of the proletarian revolution?

It is surprising that Lenin, the leader of Russia's proletariat, became also the creator of this theory and tactics and the leader of the international proletariat?

II. METHOD

I have already said that between Marx and Engels, on the one hand, and Lenin, on the other, there lies a whole period of domination of the opportunism of the Second International. For the sake of exactitude I must add that it is not the formal domination of opportunism I have in mind, but only its actual domination. Formally, the Second International was headed by "faithful" Marxists, by the "orthodox"—Kautsky and others. Actually, however, the main work of the Second International followed the line of opportunism. The opportunists adapted themselves to the bourgeoisie because of their adaptive, petty-bourgeois nature; the "orthodox," in their turn, adapted themselves to the opportunists in order to "preserve unity" with them, in the interests of "peace within the party." Thus the link between the policy of the bourgeoisie and the policy of the "orthodox" was closed, and, as a result, opportunism reigned supreme.

This was the period of the relatively peaceful development of capitalism, the pre-war period, so to speak, when the catastrophic contradictions of imperialism had not yet become so glaringly evident, when workers' economic strikes and trade unions were developing more or less "normally," when election campaigns and parliamentary groups yielded "dizzying" successes, when legal forms of struggle were lauded to the skies, and when it was thought that capitalism would be "killed" by legal means—in short, when the parties of the Second International were living in clover and had no inclination to think seriously about revolution, about the dictatorship of the proletariat, about the revolutionary education of the masses.

Instead of an integral revolutionary theory, there were contradictory theoretical postulates and fragments of theory, which were divorced from the actual revolutionary struggle of the masses and had been turned into threadbare dogmas. For the sake of appearances, Marx's theory was mentioned, of course, but only to rob it of its living, revolutionary spirit.

Instead of a revolutionary policy, there was flabby philistinism and sordid political bargaining, parliamentary diplomacy and parliamentary scheming. For the sake of appearances, of course, "revolutionary" resolutions and slogans were adopted, but only to be pigeonholed.

Instead of the party being trained and taught correct revolutionary tactics on the basis of its own mistakes, there was a studied evasion of vexed questions, which were glossed over and veiled. For the sake of appearances, of course, there was no objection to talking about vexed questions, but only in order to wind up with some sort of "elastic" resolution.

Such was the physiognomy of the Second International, its method of work, its arsenal.

Meanwhile, a new period of imperialist wars and of revolutionary battles of the proletariat was approaching. The old methods of fighting were proving obviously inadequate and impotent in face of the omnipotence of finance capital.

It became necessary to overhaul the entire activity of the Second International, its entire method of work, and to drive out all philistinism, narrow-mindedness, political scheming, renegacy, social-chauvinism and social-pacifism. It became necessary to examine the entire arsenal of the Second International, to throw out all that was rusty and antiquated, to forge new weapons. Without this preliminary work it was useless embarking upon war against capitalism. Without this work the proletariat ran the risk of finding itself inadequately armed, or even completely unarmed, in the future revolutionary battles.

The honour of bringing about this general overhauling and general cleansing of the Augean stables of the Second International fell to Leninism.

Such were the conditions under which the method of Leninism was born and hammered out.

What are the requirements of this method?

Firstly, the *testing* of the theoretical dogmas of the Second International in the crucible of the revolutionary struggle of the masses, in the crucible of living practice—that is to say, the restoration of the broken unity between theory and practice, the healing of the rift between them; for only in this way can a truly proletarian party armed with revolutionary theory be created.

Secondly, the *testing* of the policy of the parties of the Second International, not by their slogans and resolutions (which cannot be trusted), but by their deeds, by their actions; for only in this way can the confidence of the proletarian masses be won and deserved.

Thirdly, the *reorganisation* of all Party work on new revolutionary lines, with a view to training and preparing the masses for the revolutionary struggle; for only in this way can the masses be prepared for the proletarian revolution.

Fourthly, *self-criticism* within the proletarian parties, their education and training on the basis of their own mistakes; for only in this way can genuine cadres and genuine leaders of the Party be trained.

Such is the basis and substance of the method of Leninism.

How was this method applied in practice?

The opportunists of the Second International have a number of theoretical dogmas to which they always revert as their starting point. Let us take a few of these.

First dogma: concerning the conditions for the seizure of power by the proletariat. The opportunists assert that the proletariat cannot and ought not to take power unless it constitutes a majority in the country. No proofs are brought forward, for there are no proofs, either theoretical or practical, that can bear out this absurd thesis. Let us assume that this is so, Lenin replies to the gentlemen of the Second International; but suppose a historical situation has arisen (a war, an agrarian crisis, etc.) in which the proletariat, constituting a minority of the population, has an opportunity to rally around itself the vast majority of the labouring masses; why should it not take power then? Why should the proletariat not take advantage of a favourable international and internal situation to pierce the front of capital and hasten the general denouement? Did not Marx say as far back as the fifties of the last century that things could go "splendidly" with the proletarian revolution in Germany were it possible to back it by, so to speak, a "second edition of the Peasants' War"? Is it not a generally known fact that in those days the number of proletarians in Germany was relatively smaller than, for example, in Russia in 1917? Has not the practical experience of the Russian proletarian revolution shown that this favourite dogma of the heroes of the Second International is devoid of all vital significance for the proletariat? Is it not clear that the practical experience of the revolutionary struggle of the masses refutes and smashes this obsolete dogma?

Second dogma: the proletariat cannot retain power if it lacks an adequate number of trained cultural and administrative cadres capable of organising the administration of the country; these cadres must first be trained under capitalist conditions, and only then can power be taken. Let us assume that this is so, replies Lenin; but why not turn it this way: first take power, create favourable conditions for the development of the proletariat, and then proceed with seven-league strides to raise the cultural level of the labouring masses and train numerous cadres of leaders and administrators from among the workers? Has not Russian experience shown that the cadres of leaders recruited from the ranks of the workers develop a hundred times more rapidly and effectually under the rule of the proletariat than under the rule of capital? Is it not clear that the practical experience of the revolutionary struggle of the masses ruthlessly smashes this theoretical dogma of the opportunists too?

Third dogma: the proletariat cannot accept the method of the *political* general strike because it is unsound in theory (see Engels's criticism) and dangerous in practice (it may disturb the normal course of economic life in the country, it may deplete the coffers of the trade unions), and cannot serve as a substitute for parliamentary forms of struggle, which are the principal form of the class struggle of the proletariat. Very well, reply the Leninists; but, firstly, Engels did not criticise every kind of general strike. He only criticised a certain kind of general strike, namely, the *economic* general strike advocated by the Anarchists *in place of* the political struggle of the proletariat. What has this to do with the method of the *political* general strike? Secondly, where and by whom has it ever been proved that the parliamentary form of struggle is the principal form of struggle of the proletariat? Does not the history of the revolutionary movement show that the parliamentary struggle is only a school for, and an auxiliary in, organising the extra-parliamentary struggle of the proletariat, that under capitalism the fundamental problems of the working-class movement are solved by force, by the direct struggle of the proletarian masses, their general strike, their uprising? Thirdly, who suggested that the method of the political general strike be substituted for the parliamentary struggle? Where and when have the supporters of the political general strike sought to substitute extra-parliamentary forms of struggle for parliamentary forms? Fourthly, has not the revolution in Russia shown that the *political* general strike is a highly important school for the proletarian revolution and an indispensable means of mobilising and organising the vast masses of the proletariat on the eve of storming the citadels of capitalism? Why then the philistine lamentations over the disturbance of the normal course of economic life and over the coffers of the trade unions? Is it not clear that the practical experience of the revolutionary struggle smashes this dogma of the opportunists too?

And so on and so forth.

That is why Lenin said that "revolutionary theory is not a dogma," that it "assumes final shape only in close connection with the practical activity of a truly mass and truly revolutionary movement" (*"Left-Wing" Communism*); for theory must serve practice, for "theory must answer the questions raised by practice" (*What the "Friends of the People" Are*), for it must be tested by practical results.

As to the political slogans and the political resolutions of the parties of the Second International, it is sufficient to recall the history of the slogan "war against war" to realise how utterly false and utterly rotten are the political practices of these parties, which use pompous revolutionary slogans and resolutions to cloak their anti-revolutionary deeds. We all remember the pompous demonstration of the Second International at the Basel Congress,[3] at which it threatened the imperialists with all the horrors of insurrection if they should dare to start a war, and with the menacing slogan "war

[3] The Basel Congress, November 24–25, 1912, convened to deal with the Balkan War and the impending threat of world war.

against war." But who does not remember that some time after, on the very eve of the war, the Basel resolution was pigeonholed and the workers were given a new slogan—to exterminate each other for the glory of their capitalist fatherlands? Is it not clear that revolutionary slogans and resolutions are not worth a farthing unless backed by deeds? One need only contrast the Leninist policy of transforming the imperialist war into civil war with the treacherous policy of the Second International during the war to understand the utter baseness of the opportunist politicians and the full grandeur of the method of Leninism.

I cannot refrain from quoting at this point a passage from Lenin's book *The Proletarian Revolution and the Renegade Kautsky*, in which Lenin severely castigates an opportunist attempt by the leader of the Second International, K. Kautsky, to judge parties not by their deeds, but by their paper slogans and documents:

> "Kautsky is pursuing a typically petty-bourgeois, philistine policy by pretending . . . that *putting forward a slogan* alters the position. The entire history of bourgeois democracy refutes this illusion; the bourgeois democrats have always advanced and still advance all sorts of 'slogans' in order to deceive the people. The point is to *test* their sincerity, to compare their words with their *deeds*, not to be satisfied with idealistic or charlatan *phrases*, but to get down to *class reality*."

There is no need to mention the fear the parties of the Second International have of self-criticism, their habit of concealing their mistakes, of glossing over vexed questions, of covering up their shortcomings by a deceptive show of well-being which blunts living thought and prevents the Party from deriving revolutionary training from its own mistakes—a habit which was ridiculed and pilloried by Lenin. Here is what Lenin wrote about self-criticism in proletarian parties in his pamphlet *"Left-Wing" Communism:*

> "The attitude of a political party towards its own mistakes is one of the most important and surest ways of

judging how earnest the party is and how it *in practice* fulfils its obligations towards its *class* and the toiling *masses.* Frankly admitting a mistake, ascertaining the reasons for it, analysing the circumstances which gave rise to it, and thoroughly discussing the means of correcting it—that is the earmark of a serious party; that is the way it should perform its duties, that is the way it should educate and train the *class,* and then the *masses.*"

Some say that the exposure of its own mistakes and self-criticism are dangerous for the Party because they may be used by the enemy against the party of the proletariat. Lenin regarded such objections as trivial and entirely wrong. Here is what he wrote on this subject as far back as 1904, in his pamphlet *One Step Forward,* when our Party was still weak and small:

"They (i.e., the opponents of the Marxists—*J. St.*) gloat and grimace over our controversies; and, of course, they will try to pick isolated passages from my pamphlet, which deals with the defects and shortcomings of our Party, and to use them for their own ends. The Russian Social-Democrats are already steeled enough in battle not to be perturbed by these pinpricks and to continue, in spite of them, their work of self-criticism and ruthless exposure of their own shortcomings, which will unquestionably and inevitably be overcome as the working-class movement grows."

Such, in general, are the characteristic features of the method of Leninism.

What is contained in Lenin's method was in the main already contained in the teachings of Marx, which, according to Marx himself, were "in essence critical and revolutionary." It is precisely this critical and revolutionary spirit that pervades Lenin's method from beginning to end. But it would be wrong to suppose that Lenin's method is merely the restoration of the method of Marx. As a matter of fact, Lenin's method is not only the restoration, but also the concretisation and further development of the critical and revolutionary method of Marx, of his materialist dialectics.

III. THEORY

From this theme I take three questions:

a) the importance of theory for the proletarian movement;
b) criticism of the "theory" of spontaneity;
c) the theory of the proletarian revolution.

1) *The importance of theory.* Some think that Leninism is the precedence of practice over theory in the sense that its main point is the translation of the Marxist theses into deeds, their "execution"; as for theory, it is alleged that Leninism is rather unconcerned about it. We know that Plekhanov time and again chaffed Lenin about his "unconcern" for theory, and particularly for philosophy. We also know that theory is not held in great favour by many present-day Leninist practical workers, particularly in view of the immense amount of practical work imposed upon them by the situation. I must declare that this more than odd opinion about Lenin and Leninism is quite wrong and bears no relation whatever to the truth; that the attempt of practical workers to brush theory aside runs counter to the whole spirit of Leninism and is fraught with serious dangers to the work.

Theory is the experience of the working-class movement in all countries taken in its general aspect. Of course, theory becomes purposeless if it is not connected with revolutionary practice, just as practice gropes in the dark if its path is not illumined by revolutionary theory. But theory can become a tremendous force in the working-class movement if it is built up in indissoluble connection with revolutionary practice; for theory, and theory alone, can give the movement confidence, the power of orientation, and an understanding of the inner relation of surrounding events; for it, and it alone, can help practice to realise not only how and in which direction classes are moving at the present time, but also how and in which direction they will move in the near future. None other than Lenin uttered and repeated scores of times the well-known thesis that:

*"Without a revolutionary theory there can be no revolutionary movement."**

Lenin, better than anyone else, understood the great importance of theory, particularly for a party such as ours, in view of the role of vanguard fighter of the international proletariat which has fallen to its lot, and in view of the complicated internal and international situation in which it finds itself. Foreseeing this special role of our Party as far back as 1902, he thought it necessary even then to point out that:

"The role of vanguard fighter can be fulfilled only by a party that is guided by the most advanced theory."

It scarcely needs proof that now, when Lenin's prediction about the role of our Party has come true, this thesis of Lenin's acquires special force and special importance.

Perhaps the most striking expression of the great importance which Lenin attached to theory is the fact that none other than Lenin undertook the very serious task of generalising, on the basis of materialist philosophy, the most important achievements of science from the time of Engels down to his own time, as well as of subjecting to comprehensive criticism the anti-materialistic trends among Marxists. Engels said that materialism has to change its form with each epoch-making discovery. It is well known that none other than Lenin accomplished this task for his own time in his remarkable work *Materialism and Empirio-Criticism.* It is well known that Plekhanov, who loved to chaff Lenin about his "unconcern" for philosophy, did not even dare to make a serious attempt to undertake such a task.

2) *Criticism of the "theory" of spontaneity, or the role of the vanguard in the movement.* The "theory" of spontaneity is a theory of opportunism, a theory of worshipping the spontaneity of the labour movement, a theory which actually repudiates the leading role of the vanguard of the working class, of the party of the working class.

The theory of worshipping spontaneity is decidedly opposed to the revolutionary character of the working-class movement; it is opposed to the movement taking the line of struggle against the foundations of capitalism; it is in favour

* My italics.—*J. St.*

of the movement proceeding exclusively along the line of "realisable" demands, of demands "acceptable" to capitalism; it is wholly in favour of the "line of least resistance." The theory of spontaneity is the ideology of trade unionism.

The theory of worshipping spontaneity is decidedly opposed to giving the spontaneous movement a politically conscious, planned character. It is opposed to the Party marching at the head of the working class, to the Party raising the masses to the level of political consciousness, to the Party leading the movement; it is in favour of the politically conscious elements of the movement not hindering the movement from taking its own course; it is in favour of the Party only heeding the spontaneous movement and dragging at the tail of it. The theory of spontaneity is the theory of belittling the role of the conscious element in the movement, the ideology of "khvostism," the logical basis of *all* opportunism.

In practice this theory, which appeared on the scene even before the first revolution in Russia, led its adherents, the so-called "Economists," to deny the need for an independent workers' party in Russia, to oppose the revolutionary struggle of the working class for the overthrow of tsarism, to preach a purely trade-unionist policy in the movement, and, in general, to surrender the labour movement to the hegemony of the liberal bourgeoisie.

The fight of the old *Iskra* and the brilliant criticism of the theory of "khvostism" in Lenin's pamphlet *What Is To Be Done?* not only smashed so-called "Economism," but also created the theoretical foundations for a truly revolutionary movement of the Russian working class.

Without this fight it would have been quite useless even to think of creating an independent workers' party in Russia and of its playing a leading part in the revolution.

But the theory of worshipping spontaneity is not an exclusively Russian phenomenon. It is extremely widespread—in a somewhat different form, it is true—in all the parties of the Second International, without exception. I have in mind the so-called "productive forces" theory as debased by the leaders of the Second International, which justifies everything and conciliates everybody, which records facts and explains them after everyone has become sick and tired of them, and, having recorded them, rests content. Marx said that the materialist theory could not confine itself to explaining the world, that it must also change it. But Kautsky and Co. are not concerned with this; they prefer to rest content with the first part of Marx's formula.

Here is one of the numerous examples of the application of this "theory." It is said that before the imperialist war the parties of the Second International threatened to declare "war against war" if the imperialists should start a war. It is said that on the very eve of the war these parties pigeonholed the "war against war" slogan and applied an opposite one, viz., "war for the imperialist fatherland." It is said that as a result of this change of slogans millions of workers were sent to their death. But it would be a mistake to think that there were some people to blame for this, that someone was unfaithful to the working class or betrayed it. Not at all! Everything happened as it should have happened. Firstly, because the International, it seems, is "an instrument of peace," and not of war. Secondly, because, in view of the "level of the productive forces" which then prevailed, nothing else could be done. The "productive forces" are "to blame." That is the precise explanation vouchsafed to "us" by Mr. Kautsky's "theory of the productive forces." And whoever does not believe in that "theory" is not a Marxist. The role of the parties? Their importance for the movement? But what can a party do against so decisive a factor as the "level of the productive forces"? . . .

One could cite a host of similar examples of the falsification of Marxism.

It scarcely needs proof that this spurious "Marxism," designed to hide the nakedness of opportunism, is merely a European variety of the selfsame theory of "khvostism" which Lenin fought even before the first Russian revolution.

It scarcely needs proof that the demolition of this theoretical falsification is a preliminary condition for the creation of truly revolutionary parties in the West.

3) *The theory of the proletarian revolution.* Lenin's theory of the proletarian revolution proceeds from three fundamental theses.

First thesis: The domination of finance capital in the

advanced capitalist countries; the issue of stocks and bonds as one of the principal operations of finance capital; the export of capital to the sources of raw materials, which is one of the foundations of imperialism; the omnipotence of a financial oligarchy, which is the result of the domination of finance capital—all this reveals the grossly parasitic character of monopolist capitalism, makes the yoke of the capitalist trusts and syndicates a hundred times more burdensome, intensifies the indignation of the working class with the foundations of capitalism, and brings the masses to the proletarian revolution as their only salvation. (See Lenin, *Imperialism.*)

Hence the first conclusion: intensification of the revolutionary crisis within the capitalist countries and growth of the elements of an explosion on the internal, proletarian front in the "metropolises."

Second thesis: The increase in the export of capital to the colonies and dependent countries; the expansion of "spheres of influence" and colonial possessions until they cover the whole globe; the transformation of capitalism into a *world system* of financial enslavement and colonial oppression of the vast majority of the population of the world by a handful of "advanced" countries—all this has, on the one hand, converted the separate national economies and national territories into links in a single chain called world economy, and, on the other hand, split the population of the globe into two camps: a handful of "advanced" capitalist countries which exploit and oppress vast colonies and dependencies, and the huge majority consisting of colonial and dependent countries which are compelled to wage a struggle for liberation from the imperialist yoke (see *Imperialism*).

Hence the second conclusion: intensification of the revolutionary crisis in the colonial countries and growth of the elements of revolt against imperialism on the external, colonial front.

Third thesis: The monopolistic possession of "spheres of influence" and colonies; the uneven development of the capitalist countries, leading to a frenzied struggle for the redivision of the world between the countries which have already seized territories and those claiming their "share"; imperialist wars as the only means of restoring the disturbed "equilibrium"—all this leads to the intensification of the struggle on the third front, the inter-capitalist front, which weakens imperialism and facilitates the union of the first two fronts against imperialism: the front of the revolutionary proletariat and the front of colonial emancipation (see *Imperialism*).

Hence the third conclusion: that under imperialism wars cannot be averted, and that a coalition between the proletarian revolution in Europe and the colonial revolution in the East in a united world front of revolution against the world front of imperialism is inevitable.

Lenin combines all these conclusions into one general conclusion that "*imperialism is the eve of the socialist revolution.*"*

The very approach to the question of the proletarian revolution, of the character of the revolution, of its scope, of its depth, the scheme of the revolution in general, changes accordingly.

Formerly, the analysis of the pre-requisites for the proletarian revolution was usually approached from the point of view of the economic state of individual countries. Now, this approach is no longer adequate. Now the matter must be approached from the point of view of the economic state of all or the majority of countries, from the point of view of the state of world economy; for individual countries and individual national economies have ceased to be self-sufficient units, have become links in a single chain called world economy; for the old "cultured" capitalism has evolved into imperialism, and imperialism is a world system of financial enslavement and colonial oppression of the vast majority of the population of the world by a handful of "advanced" countries.

Formerly it was the accepted thing to speak of the existence or absence of objective conditions for the proletarian revolution in individual countries, or, to be more precise, in one or another developed country. Now this point of view is no longer adequate. Now we must speak of the existence of objective conditions for the revolution in the entire system

* My italics.—*J. St.*

of world imperialist economy as an integral whole; the existence within this system of some countries that are not sufficiently developed industrially cannot serve as an insuperable obstacle to the revolution, *if* the system as a whole or, more correctly, *because* the system as a whole is already ripe for revolution.

Formerly it was the accepted thing to speak of the proletarian revolution in one or another developed country as of a separate and self-sufficient entity opposing a separate national front of capital as its antipode. Now, this point of view is no longer adequate. Now we must speak of the world proletarian revolution; for the separate national fronts of capital have become links in a single chain called the world front of imperialism, which must be opposed by a common front of the revolutionary movement in all countries.

Formerly the proletarian revolution was regarded exclusively as the result of the internal development of a given country. Now, this point of view is no longer adequate. Now the proletarian revolution must be regarded primarily as the result of the development of the contradictions within the world system of imperialism, as the result of the breaking of the chain of the world imperialist front in one country or another.

Where will the revolution begin? Where, in what country, can the front of capital be pierced first?

Where industry is more developed, where the proletariat constitutes the majority, where there is more culture, where there is more democracy—that was the reply usually given formerly.

No, objects the Leninist theory of revolution, *not necessarily where industry is more developed,* and so forth. The front of capital will be pierced where the chain of imperialism is weakest, for the proletarian revolution is the result of the breaking of the chain of the world imperialist front at its weakest link; and it may turn out that the country which has started the revolution, which has made a breach in the front of capital, is less developed in a capitalist sense than other, more developed, countries, which have, however, remained within the framework of capitalism.

In 1917 the chain of the imperialist world front proved to

be weaker in Russia than in the other countries. It was there that the chain broke and provided an outlet for the proletarian revolution. Why? Because in Russia a great popular revolution was unfolding, and at its head marched the revolutionary proletariat, which had such an important ally as the vast mass of the peasantry, which was oppressed and exploited by the landlords. Because the revolution there was opposed by such a hideous representative of imperialism as tsarism, which lacked all moral prestige and was deservedly hated by the whole population. The chain proved to be weaker in Russia, although Russia was less developed in a capitalist sense than, say, France or Germany, Britain or America.

Where will the chain break in the near future? Again, where it is weakest. It is not precluded that the chain may break, say, in India. Why? Because that country has a young, militant, revolutionary proletariat, which has such an ally as the national liberation movement—an undoubtedly powerful and undoubtedly important ally. Because there the revolution is confronted by such a well-known foe as foreign imperialism, which has no moral credit and is deservedly hated by all the oppressed and exploited masses of India.

It is also quite possible that the chain will break in Germany. Why? Because the factors which are operating, say, in India are beginning to operate in Germany as well; but, of course, the enormous difference in the level of development between India and Germany cannot but stamp its imprint on the progress and outcome of a revolution in Germany.

That is why Lenin said that:

> "The West-European capitalist countries will consummate their development towards socialism . . . not by the even 'maturing' of socialism in them, but by the exploitation of some countries by others, by the exploitation of the first of the countries to be vanquished in the imperialist war combined with the exploitation of the whole of the East. On the other hand, precisely as a result of the first imperialist war, the East has definitely come into revolutionary movement, has been definitely drawn into the general maelstrom of the world revolutionary movement."

Briefly: the chain of the imperialist front must, as a rule, break where the links are weaker and, at all events, not necessarily where capitalism is more developed, where there is such and such a percentage of proletarians and such and such a percentage of peasants, and so on.

That is why in deciding the question of proletarian revolution statistical estimates of the percentage of the proletarian population in a given country lose the exceptional importance so eagerly attached to them by the doctrinaires of the Second International, who have not understood imperialism and who fear revolution like the plague.

To proceed. The heroes of the Second International asserted (and continue to assert) that between the bourgeois-democratic revolution and the proletarian revolution there is a chasm, or at any rate a Chinese Wall, separating one from the other by a more or less protracted interval of time, during which the bourgeoisie having come into power, develops capitalism, while the proletariat accumulates strength and prepares for the "decisive struggle" against capitalism. This interval is usually calculated to extend over many decades, if not longer. It scarcely needs proof that this Chinese Wall "theory" is totally devoid of scientific meaning under the conditions of imperialism, that it is and can be only a means of concealing and camouflaging the counter-revolutionary aspirations of the bourgeoisie. It scarcely needs proof that under the conditions of imperialism, fraught as it is with collisions and wars; under the conditions of the "eve of the socialist revolution," when "flourishing" capitalism becomes "moribund" capitalism (*Lenin*) and the revolutionary movement is growing in all countries of the world; when imperialism is allying itself with all reactionary forces without exception, down to and including tsarism and serfdom, thus making imperative the coalition of all revolutionary forces, from the proletarian movement of the West to the national liberation movement of the East; when the overthrow of the survivals of the regime of feudal serfdom becomes impossible without a revolutionary struggle against imperialism—it scarcely needs proof that the bourgeois-democratic revolution, in a more or less developed country, must under such circumstances verge upon the proletarian revolution, that the former must pass into the latter. The history of the revolution in Russia has provided palpable proof that this thesis is correct and incontrovertible. It was not without reason that Lenin, as far back as 1905, on the eve of the first Russian revolution, in his pamphlet *Two Tactics* depicted the bourgeois-democratic revolution and the socialist revolution as two links in the same chain, as a single and integral picture of the sweep of the Russian revolution:

> *"The proletariat must carry to completion the democratic revolution, by allying to itself the mass of the peasantry in order to crush by force the resistance of the autocracy and to paralyse the instability of the bourgeoisie. The proletariat must accomplish the socialist revolution, by allying to itself the mass of the semi-proletarian elements of the population in order to crush by force the resistance of the bourgeoisie and to paralyse the instability of the peasantry and the petty bourgeoisie.* Such are the tasks of the proletariat, which the new *Iskra*-ists present so narrowly in all their arguments and resolutions about the sweep of the revolution."

There is no need to mention other, later works of Lenin's, in which the idea of the bourgeois revolution passing into the proletarian revolution stands out in greater relief than in *Two Tactics* as one of the cornerstones of the Leninist theory of revolution.

Some comrades believe, it seems, that Lenin arrived at this idea only in 1916, that up to that time he had thought that the revolution in Russia would remain within the bourgeois framework, that power, consequently, would pass from the hands of the organ of the dictatorship of the proletariat and peasantry into the hands of the bourgeoisie and not of the proletariat. It is said that this assertion has even penetrated into our communist press. I must say that this assertion is absolutely wrong, that it is totally at variance with the facts.

I might refer to Lenin's well-known speech at the Third Congress of the Party (1905), in which he defined the dictatorship of the proletariat and peasantry, i.e., the victory of the democratic revolution, not as the "organisation of 'order'" but as the "organisation of war".

Further, I might refer to Lenin's well-known articles "On a Provisional Government" (1905), where, outlining the prospects of the unfolding Russian revolution, he assigns to the Party the task of "ensuring that the Russian revolution is not a movement of a few months, but a movement of many years, that it leads, not merely to slight concessions on the part of the powers that be, but to the complete overthrow of those powers"; where, enlarging further on these prospects and linking them with the revolution in Europe, he goes on to say:

> "And if we succeed in doing that, then . . . then the revolutionary conflagration will spread all over Europe; the European worker, languishing under bourgeois reaction, will rise in his turn and will show us 'how it is done'; then the revolutionary wave in Europe will sweep back again into Russia and will convert an epoch of a few revolutionary years into an epoch of several revolutionary decades. . . ."

I might further refer to a well-known article by Lenin published in November 1915, in which he writes:

> "The proletariat is fighting, and will fight valiantly, to capture power, for a republic, for the confiscation of the land . . . for the participation of the '*non*-proletarian masses of the people' in liberating *bourgeois* Russia from *military-feudal* 'imperialism' (=tsarism). And the proletariat will *immediately** take advantage of this liberation of bourgeois Russia from tsarism, from the agrarian power of the landlords, not to aid the rich peasants in their struggle against the rural worker, but to bring about the socialist revolution in alliance with the proletarians of Europe."

Finally, I might refer to the well-known passage in Lenin's pamphlet *The Proletarian Revolution and the Renegade*

* My italics.—*J. St.*

Kautsky, where, referring to the above-quoted passage in *Two Tactics* on the sweep of the Russian revolution, he arrives at the following conclusion:

> "Things turned out just as we said they would. The course taken by the revolution confirmed the correctness of our reasoning. *First*, with the 'whole' of the peasantry against the monarchy, against the landlords, against the medieval regime (and to that extent the revolution remains bourgeois, bourgeois-democratic). *Then*, with the poor peasants, with the semi-proletarians, with all the exploited, *against capitalism*, including the rural rich, the kulaks, the profiteers, and to that extent the revolution becomes a *socialist* one. To attempt to raise an artificial Chinese Wall between the first and second, to separate them by anything else *than* the degree of preparedness of the proletariat and the degree of its unity with the poor peasants, means monstrously to distort Marxism, to vulgarise it, to replace it by liberalism."

That is sufficient, I think.

Very well, we may be told; but if that is the case, why did Lenin combat the idea of "permanent (uninterrupted) revolution"?

Because Lenin proposed that the revolutionary capacities of the peasantry be "exhausted" and that the fullest use be made of their revolutionary energy for the complete liquidation of tsarism and for the transition to the proletarian revolution, whereas the adherents of "permanent revolution" did not understand the important role of the peasantry in the Russian revolution, underestimated the strength of the revolutionary energy of the peasantry, underestimated the strength and ability of the Russian proletariat to lead the peasantry, and thereby hampered the work of emancipating the peasantry from the influence of the bourgeoisie, the work of rallying the peasantry around the proletariat.

Because Lenin proposed that the revolution *be crowned* with the transfer of power to the proletariat, whereas the adherents of "permanent" revolution wanted *to begin* at once with the establishment of the power of the proletariat, failing to realise that in so doing they were closing their eyes to such a "minor detail" as the survivals of serfdom and were leaving out of account so important a force as the Russian peasantry, failing to understand that such a policy could only retard the winning of the peasantry over to the side of the proletariat.

Consequently, Lenin fought the adherents of "permanent" revolution, not over the question of uninterruptedness, for Lenin himself maintained the point of view of uninterrupted revolution, but because they underestimated the role of the peasantry, which is an enormous reserve of the proletariat, because they failed to understand the idea of the hegemony of the proletariat.

The idea of "permanent" revolution should not be regarded as a new idea. It was first advanced by Marx at the end of the forties in his well-known *Address to the Communist League* (1850). It is from this document that our "permanentists" took the idea of uninterrupted revolution. It should be noted that in taking it from Marx our "permanentists" altered it somewhat, and in altering it "spoilt" it and made it unfit for practical use. The experienced hand of Lenin was needed to rectify this mistake, to take Marx's idea of uninterrupted revolution in its pure form and make it a cornerstone of his theory of revolution.

Here is what Marx says in his *Address* about uninterrupted (permanent) revolution, after enumerating a number of revolutionary-democratic demands which he calls upon the Communists to win:

> "While the democratic petty bourgeois wish to bring the revolution to a conclusion as quickly as possible, and with the achievement, at most, of the above demands, it is our interest and our task to make the revolution permanent, until all more or less possessing classes have been forced out of their position of dominance, until the proletariat has conquered state power, and the association of proletarians, not only in one country but in all the dominant countries of the world, has advanced so far that competition among the proletarians of these countries has ceased and that at least the decisive productive forces are concentrated in the hands of the proletarians."

In other words:

a) Marx did not at all propose *to begin* the revolution in the Germany of the fifties with the immediate establishment of proletarian power—*contrary* to the plans of our Russian "permanentists."

b) Marx proposed only that the revolution *be crowned* with the establishment of proletarian state power, by hurling, step by step, one section of the bourgeoisie after another from the heights of power, in order, after the attainment of power by the proletariat, to kindle the fire of revolution in every country—and everything that Lenin taught and carried out in the course of our revolution in pursuit of his theory of the proletarian revolution under the conditions of imperialism was *fully in line* with that proposition.

It follows, then, that our Russian "permanentists" have not only underestimated the role of the peasantry in the Russian revolution and the importance of the idea of the hegemony of the proletariat, but have altered (for the worse) Marx's idea of "permanent" revolution and made it unfit for practical use.

That is why Lenin ridiculed the theory of our "permanentists," calling it "original" and "fine," and accusing them of refusing to "think why, for ten whole years, life has passed by this fine theory." (Lenin's article was written in 1915, ten years after the appearance of the theory of the "permanentists" in Russia.

That is why Lenin regarded this theory as a semi-Menshevik theory and said that it "borrows from the Bolsheviks their call for a resolute revolutionary struggle by the proletariat and the conquest of political power by the latter, and from the Mensheviks the 'repudiation' of the role of the peasantry." (See Lenin's article "Two Lines of the Revolution.")

This, then, is the position in regard to Lenin's idea of the bourgeois-democratic revolution passing into the proletarian revolution, of utilising the bourgeois revolution for the "immediate" transition to the proletarian revolution.

To proceed. Formerly, the victory of the revolution in one country was considered impossible, on the assumption that it would require the combined action of the proletarians of all or at least of a majority of the advanced countries to achieve victory over the bourgeoisie. Now this point of view no longer fits in with the facts. Now we must proceed from the possibility of such a victory, for the uneven and spasmodic character of the development of the various capitalist countries under the conditions of imperialism, the development within imperialism of catastrophic contradictions leading to inevitable wars, the growth of the revolutionary movement in all countries of the world—all this leads, not only to the possibility, but also to the necessity of the victory of the proletariat in individual countries. The history of the revolution in Russia is direct proof of this. At the same time, however, it must be borne in mind that the overthrow of the bourgeoisie can be successfully accomplished only when certain absolutely necessary conditions exist, in the absence of which there can be even no question of the proletariat taking power.

Here is what Lenin says about these conditions in his pamphlet *"Left-Wing" Communism:*

> "The fundamental law of revolution, which has been confirmed by all revolutions, and particularly by all three Russian revolutions in the twentieth century, is as follows: it is not enough for revolution that the exploited and oppressed masses should understand the impossibility of living in the old way and demand changes; it is essential for revolution that the exploiters should not be able to live and rule in the old way. Only when the *'lower classes' do not want* the old way, and when the 'upper classes' *cannot carry on in the old way*—only then can revolution triumph. This truth may be expressed in other words: *revolution is impossible without a nation-wide crisis* (*affecting both the exploited and the exploiters*).* It follows that for revolution it is essential, first, that a majority of the workers (or at least a majority of the class conscious, thinking, politically active workers) should fully understand that revolution is necessary and be ready to sacrifice their lives for it; secondly, that the ruling classes should be passing through a governmental crisis, which draws even the most backward masses into

* My italics.—*J. St.*

politics . . . weakens the government and makes it possible for the revolutionaries to overthrow it rapidly."

But the overthrow of the power of the bourgeoisie and establishment of the power of the proletariat in one country does not yet mean that the complete victory of socialism has been ensured. After consolidating its power and leading the peasantry in its wake the proletariat of the victorious country can and must build a socialist society. But does this mean that it will thereby achieve the complete and final victory of socialism, i.e., does it mean that with the forces of only one country it can finally consolidate socialism and fully guarantee that country against intervention and, consequently, also against restoration? No, it does not. For this the victory of the revolution in at least several countries is needed. Therefore, the development and support of revolution in other countries is an essential task of the victorious revolution. Therefore, the revolution which has been victorious in one country must regard itself not as a self-sufficient entity, but as an aid, as a means for hastening the victory of the proletariat in other countries.

Lenin expressed this thought succinctly when he said that the task of the victorious revolution is to do "the utmost possible in one country *for* the development, support and awakening of the revolution *in all countries*."

These, in general, are the characteristic features of Lenin's theory of proletarian revolution.

IV. THE DICTATORSHIP OF THE PROLETARIAT

From this theme I take three fundamental questions:

a) the dictatorship of the proletariat as the instrument of the proletarian revolution;

b) the dictatorship of the proletariat as the rule of the proletariat over the bourgeoisie;

c) Soviet power as the state form of the dictatorship of the proletariat.

1) *The dictatorship of the proletariat as the instrument of the proletarian revolution.* The question of the proletar-

ian dictatorship is above all a question of the main content of the proletarian revolution. The proletarian revolution, its movement, its sweep and its achievements acquire flesh and blood only through the dictatorship of the proletariat. The dictatorship of the proletariat is the instrument of the proletarian revolution, its organ, its most important mainstay, brought into being for the purpose of, firstly, crushing the resistance of the overthrown exploiters and consolidating the achievements of the proletarian revolution, and, secondly, carrying the proletarian revolution to its completion, carrying the revolution to the complete victory of socialism. The revolution can defeat the bourgeoisie, can overthrow its power, even without the dictatorship of the proletariat. But the revolution will be unable to crush the resistance of the bourgeoisie, to maintain its victory and to push forward to the final victory of socialism unless, at a certain stage in its development, it creates a special organ in the form of the dictatorship of the proletariat as its principal mainstay.

"The fundamental question of every revolution is the question of power" (*Lenin*). Does this mean that all that is required is to assume power, to seize it? No, it does not. The seizure of power is only the beginning. For many reasons, the bourgeoisie that is overthrown in one country remains for a long time stronger than the proletariat which has overthrown it. Therefore, the whole point is to retain power, to consolidate it, to make it invincible. What is needed to attain this? To attain this it is necessary to carry out at least three main tasks that confront the dictatorship of the proletariat "on the morrow" of victory:

a) to break the resistance of the landlords and capitalists who have been overthrown and expropriated by the revolution, to liquidate every attempt on their part to restore the power of capital;

b) to organise construction in such a way as to rally all the working people around the proletariat, and to carry on this work along the lines of preparing for the elimination, the abolition of classes;

c) to arm the revolution, to organise the army of the revolution for the struggle against foreign enemies, for the struggle against imperialism.

The dictatorship of the proletariat is needed to carry out, to fulfil these tasks.

> "The transition from capitalism to communism," says Lenin, "represents an entire historical epoch. Until this epoch has terminated, the exploiters inevitably cherish the hope of restoration, and this *hope* is converted into *attempts* at restoration. And after their first serious defeat, the overthrown exploiters—who had not expected their overthrow, never believed it possible, never conceded the thought of it—throw themselves with energy grown tenfold, with furious passion and hatred grown a hundredfold, into the battle for the recovery of the 'paradise' of which they have been deprived, on behalf of their families, who had been leading such a sweet and easy life and whom now the 'common herd' is condemning to ruin and destitution (or to 'common' labour . . .). In the train of the capitalist exploiters follow the broad masses of the petty bourgeoisie, with regard to whom decades of historical experience of all countries testify that they vacillate and hesitate, one day marching behind the proletariat and the next day taking fright at the difficulties of the revolution; that they become panic-stricken at the first defeat or semi-defeat of the workers, grow nervous, rush about, snivel, and run from one camp into the other."

The bourgeoisie has its grounds for making attempts at restoration, because for a long time after its overthrow it remains stronger than the proletariat which has overthrown it.

> "If the exploiters are defeated in one country only," says Lenin, "and this, of course, is the typical case, since a simultaneous revolution in a number of countries is a rare exception, they *still* remain *stronger* than the exploited."

Wherein lies the strength of the overthrown bourgeoisie?

> Firstly, "in the strength of international capital, in the strength and durability of the international connections of the bourgeoisie."

Secondly, in the fact that "for a long time after the revolution the exploiters inevitably retain a number of great practical advantages: they still have money (it is impossible to abolish money all at once); some movable property—often fairly considerable; they still have various connections, habits of organisation and management, knowledge of all the 'secrets' (customs, methods, means and possibilities) of management, superior education, close connections with the higher technical personnel (who live and think like the bourgeoisie), incomparably greater experience in the art of war (this is very important), and so on, and so forth."

Thirdly, "in the *force of habit*, in the strength of *small production*. For, unfortunately, small production is still very, very widespread in the world, and small production *engenders* capitalism and the bourgeoisie continuously, daily, hourly, spontaneously, and on a mass scale" . . . for "the abolition of classes means not only driving out the landlords and capitalists—that we accomplished with comparative ease—it also means *abolishing the small commodity producers*, and they *cannot be driven out*, or crushed; we *must live in harmony* with them, they can (and must) be remoulded and re-educated only by very prolonged, slow, cautious organisational work."

That is why Lenin says that:

> "The dictatorship of the proletariat is a most determined and most ruthless war waged by the new class against a *more powerful* enemy, the bourgeoisie, whose resistance is increased *tenfold* by its overthrow."

and that:

> "The dictatorship of the proletariat is a stubborn struggle—bloody and bloodless, violent and peaceful, military and economic, educational and administrative—against the forces and traditions of the old society."

It scarcely needs proof that there is not the slightest possibility of carrying out these tasks in a short period, of accomplishing all this in a few years. Therefore, the dictatorship of the proletariat, the transition from capitalism to communism, must not be regarded as a fleeting period of "super-revolutionary" acts and decrees, but as an entire historical era, replete with civil wars and external conflicts, with persistent organisational work and economic construction, with advances and retreats, victories and defeats. This historical era is needed not only to create the economic and cultural pre-requisites for the complete victory of socialism, but also to enable the proletariat, firstly, to educate itself and become steeled as a force capable of governing the country, and, secondly, to re-educate and remould the petty-bourgeois strata along such lines as will assure the organisation of socialist production.

> "You will have to go through fifteen, twenty, fifty years of civil wars and international conflicts," Marx said to the workers, "not only to change existing conditions, but also to change yourselves and to make yourselves capable of wielding political power." (See K. Marx and F. Engels, *Works.*)

Continuing and developing Marx's idea still further, Lenin wrote that:

> "It will be necessary under the dictatorship of the proletariat to re-educate millions of peasants and small proprietors, hundreds of thousands of office employees, officials and bourgeois intellectuals, to subordinate them all to the proletarian state and to proletarian leadership, to overcome their bourgeois habits and traditions," just as we must "—in a protracted struggle waged on the basis of the dictatorship of the proletariat—re-educate the proletarians themselves, who do not abandon their petty-bourgeois prejudices at one stroke, by a miracle, at the bidding of the Virgin Mary, at the bidding of a slogan, resolution or decree, but only in the course of a long and difficult mass struggle against mass petty-bourgeois influences."

2) *The dictatorship of the proletariat as the rule of the proletariat over the bourgeoisie.* From the foregoing it is evident that the dictatorship of the proletariat is not a mere

change of personalities in the government, a change of the "cabinet," etc., leaving the old economic and political order intact. The Mensheviks and opportunists of all countries, who fear dictatorship like fire and in their fright substitute the concept "conquest of power" for the concept dictatorship, usually reduce the "conquest of power" to a change of the "cabinet," to the accession to power of a new ministry made up of people like Scheidemann and Noske, MacDonald and Henderson. It is hardly necessary to explain that these and similar cabinet changes have nothing in common with the dictatorship of the proletariat, with the conquest of real power by the real proletariat. With the MacDonalds and Scheidemanns in power, while the old bourgeois order is allowed to remain, their so-called governments cannot be anything else than an apparatus serving the bourgeoisie, a screen to conceal the ulcers of imperialism, a weapon in the hands of the bourgeoisie against the revolutionary movement of the oppressed and exploited masses. Capital needs such governments as a screen when it finds it inconvenient, unprofitable, difficult to oppress and exploit the masses without the aid of a screen. Of course, the appearance of such governments is a symptom that "over there" (i.e., in the capitalist camp) all is not quiet "at the Shipka Pass";[4] nevertheless, governments of this kind inevitably remain governments of capital in disguise. The government of a MacDonald or a Scheidemann is as far removed from the conquest of power by the proletariat as the sky from the earth. The dictatorship of the proletariat is not a change of government, but a new state, with new organs of power, both central and local; it is the state of the proletariat, which has arisen on the ruins of the old state, the state of the bourgeoisie.

The dictatorship of the proletariat arises not on the basis of the bourgeois order, but in the process of the breaking up of this order, after the overthrow of the bourgeoisie, in the process of the expropriation of the landlords and capitalists, in the process of the socialisation of the principal instruments and means of production, in the process of violent proletarian

[4] In the Russo-Turkish War of 1877–78 there was heavy fighting at the Shipka Pass, but czarist headquarters kept reporting: "All quiet at the Shipka Pass."

revolution. The dictatorship of the proletariat is a revolutionary power based on the use of force against the bourgeoisie.

The state is a machine in the hands of the ruling class for suppressing the resistance of its class enemies. *In this respect* the dictatorship of the proletariat does not differ essentially from the dictatorship of any other class, for the proletarian state is a machine for the suppression of the bourgeoisie. But there is one *substantial* difference. This difference consists in the fact that all hitherto existing class states have been dictatorships of an exploiting minority over the exploited majority, whereas the dictatorship of the proletariat is the dictatorship of the exploited majority over the exploiting minority.

Briefly: *the dictatorship of the proletariat is the rule—unrestricted by law and based on force—of the proletariat over the bourgeoisie, a rule enjoying the sympathy and support of the labouring and exploited masses.* (Lenin, *The State and Revolution.*)

From this follow two main conclusions:

First conclusion: The dictatorship of the proletariat cannot be "complete" democracy, democracy for *all*, for the rich as well as for the poor; the dictatorship of the proletariat "must be a state that is democratic *in a new way* (*for** the proletarians and the non-propertied in general) and dictatorial *in a new way* (*against** the bourgeoisie)." The talk of Kautsky and Co. about universal equality, about "pure" democracy, about "perfect" democracy, and the like, is a bourgeois disguise of the indubitable fact that equality between exploited and exploiters is impossible. The theory of "pure" democracy is the theory of the upper stratum of the working class, which has been broken in and is being fed by the imperialist robbers. It was brought into being for the purpose of concealing the ulcers of capitalism, of embellishing imperialism and lending it moral strength in the struggle against the exploited masses. Under capitalism there are no real "liberties" for the exploited, nor can there be, if for no other reason than that the premises, printing plants, paper supplies, etc., indispensable for the enjoyment of "liberties" are the

* My italics.—*J. St.*

privilege of the exploiters. Under capitalism the exploited masses do not, nor can they ever, really participate in governing the country, if for no other reason than that, even under the most democratic regime, under conditions of capitalism, governments are not set up by the people but by the Rothschilds and Stinneses, the Rockefellers and Morgans. Democracy under capitalism is *capitalist* democracy, the democracy of the exploiting minority, based on the restriction of the rights of the exploited majority and directed against this majority. Only under the proletarian dictatorship are real liberties for the exploited and real participation of the proletarians and peasants in governing the country possible. Under the dictatorship of the proletariat, democracy is *proletarian* democracy, the democracy of the exploited majority, based on the restriction of the rights of the exploiting minority and directed against this minority.

Second conclusion: The dictatorship of the proletariat cannot arise as the result of the peaceful development of bourgeois society and of bourgeois democracy; it can arise only as the result of the smashing of the bourgeois state machine, the bourgeois army, the bourgeois bureaucratic apparatus, the bourgeois police.

> "The working class cannot simply lay hold of the ready-made state machinery, and wield it for its own purposes," say Marx and Engels in a preface to the *Communist Manifesto*.
>
> The task of the proletarian revolution is "no longer, as before, to transfer the bureaucratic-military machine from one hand to another, but to *smash* it . . . this is the preliminary condition for every real people's revolution on the continent," says Marx in his letter to Kugelmann in 1871.

Marx's qualifying phrase about the continent gave the opportunists and Mensheviks of all countries a pretext for clamouring that Marx had thus conceded the possibility of the peaceful evolution of bourgeois democracy into a proletarian democracy, at least in certain countries outside the European continent (Britain, America). Marx did in fact concede that possibility, and he had good grounds for conceding it in regard to Britain and America in the seventies of the last century, when monopoly capitalism and imperialism did not yet exist, and when these countries, owing to the particular conditions of their development, had as yet no developed militarism and bureaucracy. That was the situation before the appearance of developed imperialism. But later, after a lapse of thirty or forty years, when the situation in these countries had radically changed, when imperialism had developed and had embraced all capitalist countries without exception, when militarism and bureaucracy had appeared in Britain and America also, when the particular conditions for peaceful development in Britain and America had disappeared—then the qualification in regard to these countries necessarily could no longer hold good.

> "Today," said Lenin, "in 1917, in the epoch of the first great imperialist war, this qualification made by Marx is no longer valid. Both Britain and America, the biggest and the last representatives—in the whole world—of Anglo-Saxon 'liberty' in the sense that they had no militarism and bureaucracy, have completely sunk into the all-European filthy, bloody morass of bureaucratic-military institutions which subordinate everything to themselves and trample everything underfoot. Today, in Britain and in America, too, 'the preliminary condition for every real people's revolution' is the *smashing*, the *destruction* of the 'ready-made state machinery' (perfected in those countries, between 1914 and 1917, up to the 'European' general imperialist standard)."

In other words, the law of violent proletarian revolution, the law of the smashing of the bourgeois state machine as a preliminary condition for such a revolution, is an inevitable law of the revolutionary movement in the imperialist countries of the world.

Of course, in the remote future, if the proletariat is victorious in the principal capitalist countries, and if the present capitalist encirclement is replaced by a socialist encirclement, a "peaceful" path of development is quite possible for certain capitalist countries, whose capitalists, in view of the "unfavourable" international situation, will consider it expedient "voluntarily" to make substantial concessions to the proletariat. But this supposition applies only to a remote and possible future. With regard to the immediate future, there is no ground whatsoever for this supposition.

Therefore, Lenin is right in saying:

> "The proletarian revolution is impossible without the forcible destruction of the bourgeois state machine and the substitution for it of a *new one*."

3) *Soviet power as the state form of the dictatorship of the proletariat.* The victory of the dictatorship of the proletariat signifies the suppression of the bourgeoisie, the smashing of the bourgeois state machine, and the substitution of proletarian democracy for bourgeois democracy. That is clear. But by means of what organisations can this colossal work be carried out? The old forms of organisation of the proletariat, which grew up on the basis of bourgeois parliamentarism, are inadequate for this work—of that there can hardly be any doubt. What, then, are the new forms of organisation of the proletariat that are capable of serving as the gravediggers of the bourgeois state machine, that are capable not only of smashing this machine, not only of substituting proletarian democracy for bourgeois democracy, but also of becoming the foundation of the proletarian state power?

This new form of organisation of the proletariat is the Soviets.

Wherein lies the strength of the Soviets as compared with the old forms of organisation?

In that the Soviets are the most *all-embracing* mass organisations of the proletariat, for they and they alone embrace all workers without exception.

In that the Soviets are the *only* mass organisations which unite all the oppressed and exploited, workers and peasants, soldiers and sailors, and in which the vanguard of the masses, the proletariat, can, for this reason, most easily and most completely exercise its political leadership of the mass struggle.

In that the Soviets are the *most powerful organs* of the revolutionary struggle of the masses, of the political actions of the masses, of the uprising of the masses—organs capable of breaking the omnipotence of finance capital and its political appendages.

In that the Soviets are the *immediate* organisations of the masses themselves, i.e., they are *the most democratic* and therefore the most authoritative organisations of the masses, which facilitate to the utmost their participation in the work of building up the new state and in its administration, and which bring into full play the revolutionary energy, initiative and creative abilities of the masses in the struggle for the destruction of the old order, in the struggle for the new, proletarian order.

Soviet power is the union and constitution of the local Soviets into one common state organisation, into the state organisation of the proletariat as the vanguard of the oppressed and exploited masses and as the ruling class—their union in the Republic of Soviets.

The essence of Soviet power consists in the fact that these most all-embracing and most revolutionary mass organisations of precisely those classes that were oppressed by the capitalists and landlords are now the "*permanent and sole* basis of the whole power of the state, of the whole state apparatus"; that "precisely those masses which even in the most democratic bourgeois republics," while being equal in law, "have in fact been prevented by thousands of tricks and devices from taking part in political life and from enjoying democratic rights and liberties, are now drawn unfailingly into *constant* and, moreover, *decisive* participation in the democratic administration of the state."*

That is why Soviet power is a *new form* of state organisation, different in principle from the old bourgeois-democratic and parliamentary form, a *new type* of state, adapted not to the task of exploiting and oppressing the labouring masses, but to the task of completely emancipating them from all oppression and exploitation, to the tasks facing the dictatorship of the proletariat.

Lenin is right in saying that with the appearance of Soviet power "the era of bourgeois-democratic parliamentarism has

* All italics mine.—*J. St.*

drawn to a close and a new chapter in world history—the era of proletarian dictatorship—has been opened."

Wherein lie the characteristic features of Soviet power?

In that Soviet power is the most all-embracing and most democratic state organisation of all possible state organisations while classes continue to exist; for, being the arena of the bond and collaboration between the workers and the exploited peasants in their struggle against the exploiters, and basing itself in its work on this bond and on this collaboration, Soviet power is thus the power of the majority of the population over the minority, it is the state of the majority, the expression of its dictatorship.

In that Soviet power is the most internationalist of all state organisations in class society, for, by destroying every kind of national oppression and resting on the collaboration of the labouring masses of the various nationalities, it facilitates the uniting of these masses into a single state union.

In that Soviet power, by its very structure, facilitates the task of leading the oppressed and exploited masses by the vanguard of these masses—by the proletariat, as the most united and most politically conscious core of the Soviets.

"The experience of all revolutions and of all movements of the oppressed classes, the experience of the world socialist movement teaches us," says Lenin, "that the proletariat alone is able to unite and lead the scattered and backward strata of the toiling and exploited population." The point is that the structure of Soviet power facilitates the practical application of the lessons drawn from this experience.

In that Soviet power, by combining legislative and executive power in a single state organisation and replacing territorial electoral constituencies by industrial units, factories and mills, thereby directly links the workers and the labouring masses in general with the apparatus of state administration, teaches them how to govern the country.

In that Soviet power alone is capable of releasing the army from its subordination to bourgeois command and of converting it from the instrument of oppression of the people which it is under the bourgeois order into an instrument for the liberation of the people from the yoke of the bourgeoisie, both native and foreign.

In that "the Soviet organisation of the state alone is capable of immediately and effectively smashing and finally destroying the old, i.e., the bourgeois, bureaucratic and judicial apparatus."

In that the Soviet form of state alone, by drawing the mass organisations of the toilers and exploited into constant and unrestricted participation in state administration, is capable of preparing the ground for the withering away of the state, which is one of the basic elements of the future stateless communist society.

The Republic of Soviets is thus the political form, so long sought and finally discovered, within the framework of which the economic emancipation of the proletariat, the complete victory of socialism, must be accomplished.

The Paris Commune was the embryo of this form; Soviet power is its development and culmination.

That is why Lenin says:

> "The Republic of Soviets of Workers', Soldiers', and Peasants' Deputies is not only the form of a higher type of democratic institution . . . but is the *only** form capable of ensuring the most painless transition to socialism."

V. THE PEASANT QUESTION

From this theme I take four questions:

a) the presentation of the question;

b) the peasantry during the bourgeois-democratic revolution;

c) the peasantry during the proletarian revolution;

d) the peasantry after the consolidation of Soviet power.

1) *The presentation of the question.* Some think that the fundamental thing in Leninism is the peasant question, that the point of departure of Leninism is the question of the peasantry, of its role, its relative importance. This is absolutely wrong. The fundamental question of Leninism, its point of departure, is not the peasant question, but the question of the dictatorship of the proletariat, of the conditions under which

* My italics.—*J. St.*

it can be achieved, of the conditions under which it can be consolidated. The peasant question, as the question of the ally of the proletariat in its struggle for power, is a derivative question.

This circumstance, however, does not in the least deprive the peasant question of the serious and vital importance it unquestionably has for the proletarian revolution. It is known that the serious study of the peasant question in the ranks of Russian Marxists began precisely on the eve of the first revolution (1905), when the question of overthrowing tsarism and of realising the hegemony of the proletariat confronted the Party in all its magnitude, and when the question of the ally of the proletariat in the impending bourgeois revolution became of vital importance. It is also known that the peasant question in Russia assumed a still more urgent character during the proletarian revolution, when the question of the dictatorship of the proletariat, of achieving and maintaining it, led to the question of allies for the proletariat in the impending proletarian revolution. And this was natural. Those who are marching towards and preparing to assume power cannot but be interested in the question of who are their real allies.

In this sense the peasant question is part of the general question of the dictatorship of the proletariat, and as such it is one of the most vital problems of Leninism.

The attitude of indifference and sometimes even of outright aversion displayed by the parties of the Second International towards the peasant question is to be explained not only by the specific conditions of development in the West. It is to be explained primarily by the fact that these parties do not believe in the proletarian dictatorship, that they fear revolution and have no intention of leading the proletariat to power. And those who are afraid of revolution, who do not intend to lead the proletarians to power, cannot be interested in the question of allies for the proletariat in the revolution—to them the question of allies is one of indifference, of no immediate significance. The ironical attitude of the heroes of the Second International towards the peasant question is regarded by them as a sign of good breeding, a sign of "true" Marxism. As a matter of fact, there is not a grain of Marxism in this, for indifference towards so important a question as the peasant question on the eve of the proletarian revolution is the reverse side of the repudiation of the dictatorship of the proletariat, it is an unmistakable sign of downright betrayal of Marxism.

The question is as follows: Are the revolutionary potentialities latent in the peasantry by virtue of certain conditions of its existence *already exhausted*, or not; and if not, *is there any hope, any basis*, for utilising these potentialities *for* the proletarian revolution, for transforming the peasantry, the exploited majority of it, from the reserve of the bourgeoisie which it was during the bourgeois revolutions in the West and still is even now, into a reserve of the proletariat, into its ally?

Leninism replies to this question in the affirmative, i.e., it recognises the existence of revolutionary capacities in the ranks of the majority of the peasantry, and the possibility of using these in the interests of the proletarian dictatorship.

The history of the three revolutions in Russia fully corroborates the conclusions of Leninism on this score.

Hence the practical conclusion that the toiling masses of the peasantry must be supported in their struggle against bondage and exploitation, in their struggle for deliverance from oppression and poverty. This does not mean, of course, that the proletariat must support *every* peasant movement. What we have in mind here is support for a movement or struggle of the peasantry which, directly or indirectly, facilitates the emancipation movement of the proletariat, which, in one way or another, brings grist to the mill of the proletarian revolution, and which helps to transform the peasantry into a reserve and ally of the working class.

2) *The peasantry during the bourgeois-democratic revolution.* This period extends from the first Russian revolution (1905) to the second revolution (February 1917), inclusive. The characteristic feature of this period is the emancipation of the peasantry from the influence of the liberal bourgeoisie, the peasantry's *desertion* of the Cadets, its *turn* towards the proletariat, towards the Bolshevik Party. The history of this period is the history of the struggle between the Cadets (the liberal bourgeoisie) and the Bolsheviks (the proletariat) for

the peasantry. The outcome of this struggle was decided by the Duma period, for the period of the four Dumas served as an object lesson to the peasantry, and this lesson brought home to the peasantry the fact that they would receive neither land nor liberty at the hands of the Cadets; that the tsar was wholly in favour of the landlords, and that the Cadets were supporting the tsar; that the only force they could rely on for assistance was the urban workers, the proletariat. The imperialist war merely confirmed the lessons of the Duma period and consummated the peasantry's desertion of the bourgeoisie, consummated the isolation of the liberal bourgeoisie; for the years of the war revealed the utter futility, the utter deceptiveness of all hopes of obtaining peace from the tsar and his bourgeois allies. Without the object lessons of the Duma period, the hegemony of the proletariat would have been impossible.

That is how the alliance between the workers and the peasants in the bourgeois-democratic revolution took shape. That is how the hegemony (leadership) of the proletariat in the common struggle for the overthrow of tsarism took shape—the hegemony which led to the February Revolution of 1917.

The bourgeois revolutions in the West (Britain, France, Germany, Austria) took, as is well known, a different road. There, hegemony in the revolution belonged not to the proletariat, which by reason of its weakness did not and could not represent an independent political force, but to the liberal bourgeoisie. There the peasantry obtained its emancipation from feudal regimes, not at the hands of the proletariat, which was numerically weak and unorganised, but at the hands of the bourgeoisie. There the peasantry marched against the old order side by side with the liberal bourgeoisie. There the peasantry acted as the reserve of the bourgeoisie. There the revolution, in consequence of this, led to an enormous increase in the political weight of the bourgeoisie.

In Russia, on the contrary, the bourgeois revolution produced quite opposite results. The revolution in Russia led not to the strengthening, but to the weakening of the bourgeoisie as a political force, not to an increase in its political reserves, but to the loss of its main reserve, to the loss of the peasantry. The bourgeois revolution in Russia brought to the forefront not the liberal bourgeoisie but the revolutionary proletariat, rallying around the latter the millions of the peasantry.

Incidentally, this explains why the bourgeois revolution in Russia passed into a proletarian revolution in a comparatively short space of time. The hegemony of the proletariat was the embryo of, and the transitional stage to, the dictatorship of the proletariat.

How is this peculiar phenomenon of the Russian revolution, which has no precedent in the history of the bourgeois revolutions of the West, to be explained? Whence this peculiarity?

It is to be explained by the fact that the bourgeois revolution unfolded in Russia under more advanced conditions of class struggle than in the West; that the Russian proletariat had at that time already become an independent political force, whereas the liberal bourgeoisie, frightened by the revolutionary spirit of the proletariat, lost all semblance of revolutionary spirit (especially after the lessons of 1905) and turned towards an alliance with the tsar and the landlords against the revolution, against the workers and peasants.

We should bear in mind the following circumstances, which determined the peculiar character of the Russian bourgeois revolution.

a) The unprecedented concentration of Russian industry on the eve of the revolution. It is known, for instance, that in Russia 54 per cent of all the workers were employed in enterprises employing over 500 workers each, whereas in so highly developed a country as the United States of America no more than 33 per cent of all the workers were employed in such enterprises. It scarcely needs proof that this circumstance alone, in view of the existence of a revolutionary party like the Party of the Bolsheviks, transformed the working class of Russia into an immense force in the political life of the country.

b) The hideous forms of exploitation in the factories, coupled with the intolerable police regime of the tsarist henchmen—a circumstance which transformed every important strike of the workers into an imposing political action and steeled the working class as a force that was revolutionary to the end.

c) The political flabbiness of the Russian bourgeoisie,

which after the Revolution of 1905 turned into servility to tsarism and downright counter-revolution—a fact to be explained not only by the revolutionary spirit of the Russian proletariat, which flung the Russian bourgeoisie into the embrace of tsarism, but also by the direct dependence of this bourgeoisie upon government contracts.

d) The existence in the countryside of the most hideous and most intolerable survivals of serfdom, coupled with the unlimited power of the landlords—a circumstance which threw the peasantry into the embrace of the revolution.

e) Tsarism, which stifled everything that was alive, and whose tyranny aggravated the oppression of the capitalist and the landlord—a circumstance which united the struggle of the workers and peasants into a single torrent of revolution.

f) The imperialist war, which fused all these contradictions in the political life of Russia into a profound revolutionary crisis, and which lent the revolution tremendous striking force.

To whom could the peasantry turn under these circumstances? From whom could it seek support against the unlimited power of the landlords, against the tyranny of the tsar, against the devastating war which was ruining it? From the liberal bourgeoisie? But it was an enemy, as the long years of experience of all four Dumas had proved. From the Socialist-Revolutionaries? The Socialist-Revolutionaries were "better" than the Cadets, of course, and their programme was "suitable," almost a peasant programme; but what could the Socialist-Revolutionaries offer, considering that they thought of relying only on the peasants and were weak in the towns, from which the enemy primarily drew its forces? Where was the new force which would stop at nothing either in town or country, which would boldly march in the front ranks to fight the tsar and the landlords, which would help the peasantry to extricate itself from bondage, from land hunger, from oppression, from war? Was there such a force in Russia at all? Yes, there was. It was the Russian proletariat, which had shown its strength, its ability to fight to the end, its boldness and revolutionary spirit, as far back as 1905.

At any rate, there was no other such force; nor could any other be found anywhere.

That is why the peasantry, when it turned its back on the Cadets and attached itself to the Socialist-Revolutionaries, at the same time came to realise the necessity of submitting to the leadership of such a courageous leader of the revolution as the Russian proletariat.

Such were the circumstances which determined the peculiar character of the Russian bourgeois revolution.

3) *The peasantry during the proletarian revolution.* This period extends from the February Revolution of 1917 to the October Revolution of 1917. This period is comparatively short, eight months in all; but from the point of view of the political enlightenment and revolutionary training of the masses these eight months can safely be put on a par with whole decades of ordinary constitutional development, for they were eight months of *revolution*. The characteristic feature of this period was the further revolutionisation of the peasantry, its disillusionment with the Socialist-Revolutionaries, the peasantry's *desertion* of the Socialist-Revolutionaries, its new *turn* towards a *direct rally* around the proletariat as the only consistently revolutionary force, capable of leading the country to peace. The history of this period is the history of the struggle between the Socialist-Revolutionaries (petty-bourgeois democracy) and the Bolsheviks (proletarian democracy) for the peasantry, to win over the majority of the peasantry. The outcome of this struggle was decided by the coalition period, the Kerensky period, the refusal of the Socialist-Revolutionaries and the Mensheviks to confiscate the landlords' land, the fight of the Socialist-Revolutionaries and Mensheviks to continue the war, the June offensive at the front, the introduction of capital punishment for soldiers, the Kornilov revolt.

Whereas before, in the preceding period, the basic question of the revolution had been the overthrow of the tsar and of the power of the landlords, now, in the period following the February Revolution, when there was no longer any tsar, and when the interminable war had exhausted the economy of the country and utterly ruined the peasantry, the question of liquidating the war became the main problem of the revolution. The centre of gravity had manifestly shifted from purely internal questions to the main question—the war. "End the war," "Let's get out of the war"—such was the general outcry of the war-weary nation and primarily of the peasantry.

But in order to get out of the war it was necessary to overthrow the Provisional Government, it was necessary to overthrow the power of the bourgeoisie, it was necessary to overthrow the power of the Socialist-Revolutionaries and Mensheviks, for they, and they alone, were dragging out the war to a "victorious finish." Practically, there was no way of getting out of the war except by overthrowing the bourgeoisie.

This was a new revolution, a proletarian revolution, for it ousted from power the last group of the imperialist bourgeoisie, its extreme Left wing, the Socialist-Revolutionary Party and the Mensheviks, in order to set up a new, proletarian power, the power of the Soviets, in order to put in power the party of the revolutionary proletariat, the Bolshevik Party, the party of the revolutionary struggle against the imperialist war and for a democratic peace. The majority of the peasantry supported the struggle of the workers for peace, for the power of the Soviets.

There was no other way out for the peasantry. Nor could there be any other way out.

Thus, the Kerensky period was a great object lesson for the toiling masses of the peasantry, for it showed clearly that with the Socialist-Revolutionaries and Mensheviks in power the country would not extricate itself from the war, and the peasants would never get either land or liberty; that the Mensheviks and Socialist-Revolutionaries differed from the Cadets only in their honeyed phrases and false promises, while they actually pursued the same imperialist, Cadet policy; that the only power that could lead the country on to the proper road was the power of the Soviets. The further prolongation of the war merely confirmed the truth of this lesson, spurred on the revolution, and drove millions of peasants and soldiers to *rally directly* around the proletarian revolution. The isolation of the Socialist-Revolutionaries and Mensheviks became an incontrovertible fact. Without the object lessons of the coalition period the dictatorship of the proletariat would have been impossible.

Such were the circumstances which facilitated the process

of the bourgeois revolution passing into the proletarian revolution.

That is how the dictatorship of the proletariat took shape in Russia.

4) *The peasantry after the consolidation of Soviet power.* Whereas before, in the first period of the revolution, the main objective was the overthrow of tsarism, and later, after the February Revolution, the primary objective was to get out of the imperialist war by overthrowing the bourgeoisie, now, after the liquidation of the civil war and the consolidation of Soviet power, questions of economic construction came to the forefront. Strengthen and develop the nationalised industry; for this purpose link up industry with peasant economy through state-regulated trade; replace the surplus-appropriation system by the tax in kind so as, later on, by gradually lowering the tax in kind, to reduce matters to the exchange of products of industry for the products of peasant farming; revive trade and develop the co-operatives, drawing into them the vast masses of the peasantry—this is how Lenin outlined the immediate tasks of economic construction on the way to building the foundations of socialist economy.

It is said that this task may prove beyond the strength of a peasant country like Russia. Some sceptics even say that it is simply utopian, impossible, for the peasantry is a peasantry—it consists of small producers, and therefore cannot be of use in organising the foundations of socialist production.

But the sceptics are mistaken, for they fail to take into account certain circumstances which in the present case are of decisive significance. Let us examine the most important of these:

Firstly. The peasantry in the Soviet Union must not be confused with the peasantry in the West. A peasantry that has been schooled in three revolutions, that fought against the tsar and the power of the bourgeoisie side by side with the proletariat and under the leadership of the proletariat, a peasantry that has received land and peace at the hands of the proletarian revolution and by reason of this has become the reserve of the proletariat—such a peasantry cannot but be different from a peasantry which during the bourgeois revolution fought under the leadership of the liberal bourgeoisie, which received land at the hands of that bourgeoisie, and in view of this became the reserve of the bourgeoisie. It scarcely needs proof that the Soviet peasantry, which has learnt to appreciate its political friendship and political collaboration with the proletariat and which owes its freedom to this friendship and collaboration, cannot but represent exceptionally favourable material for economic collaboration with the proletariat.

Engels said that "the conquest of political power by the Socialist Party has become a matter of the not too distant future," that "in order to conquer political power this party must first go from the towns to the country, must become a power in the countryside." (See Engels, *The Peasant Question*, 1922 ed.) He wrote this in the nineties of the last century, having in mind the Western peasantry. Does it need proof that the Russian Communists, after accomplishing an enormous amount of work in this field in the course of three revolutions, have already succeeded in gaining in the countryside an influence and backing the like of which our Western comrades dare not even dream of? How can it be denied that this circumstance must decidedly facilitate the organisation of economic collaboration between the working class and the peasantry of Russia?

The sceptics maintain that the small peasants are a factor that is incompatible with socialist construction. But listen to what Engels says about the small peasants of the West:

> "We are decidely on the side of the small peasant; we shall do everything at all permissible to make his lot more bearable, to facilitate his transition to the co-operative should he decide to do so, and even to make it possible for him to remain on his small holding for a protracted length of time to think the matter over, should he still be unable to bring himself to this decision. We do this not only because we consider the small peasant who does his own work as virtually belonging to us, but also in the direct interest of the Party. The greater the number of peasants whom we can save from being actually hurled down into the proletariat, whom we can win to our side while they are still peasants, the more quickly and easily the social transformation will be accomplished. It will serve us nought to wait with

this transformation until capitalist production has developed everywhere to its utmost consequences, until the last small handicraftsman and the last small peasant have fallen victim to capitalist large-scale production. The material sacrifices to be made for this purpose in the interest of the peasants and to be defrayed out of public funds can, from the point of view of capitalist economy, be viewed only as money thrown away, but it is nevertheless an excellent investment because it will effect a perhaps tenfold saving in the cost of the social reorganisation in general. In this sense we can, therefore, afford to deal very liberally with the peasants."

That is what Engels said, having in mind the Western peasantry. But is it not clear that what Engels said can nowhere be realised so easily and so completely as in the land of the dictatorship of the proletariat? Is it not clear that only in Soviet Russia is it possible at once and to the fullest extent for "the small peasant who does his own work" to come over to our side, for the "material sacrifices" necessary for this to be made, and for the necessary "liberality towards the peasants" to be displayed? Is it not clear that these and similar measures for the benefit of the peasantry are already being carried out in Russia? How can it be denied that this circumstance, in its turn, must facilitate and advance the work of economic construction in the land of the Soviets?

Secondly. Agriculture in Russia must not be confused with agriculture in the West. There, agriculture is developing along the ordinary lines of capitalism, under conditions of profound differentiation among the peasantry, with large landed estates and private capitalist latifundia at one extreme and pauperism, destitution and wage slavery at the other. Owing to this, disintegration and decay are quite natural there. Not so in Russia. Here agriculture cannot develop along such a path, if for no other reason than that the existence of Soviet power and the nationalisation of the principal instruments and means of production preclude such a development. In Russia the development of agriculture must proceed along a different path, along the path of organising millions of small and middle peasants in co-operatives, along the path of developing in the countryside a mass co-operative movement supported by the state by means of preferential credits. Lenin rightly pointed out in his articles on co-operation that the development of agriculture in our country must proceed along a new path, along the path of drawing the majority of the peasants into socialist construction through the co-operatives, along the path of gradually introducing into agriculture the principles of collectivism, first in the sphere of marketing and later in the sphere of production of agricultural products.

Of extreme interest in this respect are several new phenomena observed in the countryside in connection with the work of the agricultural co-operatives. It is well known that new, large organisations have sprung up within the Selskosoyuz,[5] in different branches of agriculture, such as production of flax, potatoes, butter, etc., which have a great future before them. Of these, the Flax Centre, for instance, unites a whole network of peasant flax growers' associations. The Flax Centre supplies the peasants with seeds and implements; then it buys all the flax produced by these peasants, disposes of it on the market on a large scale, guarantees the peasants a share in the profits, and in this way links peasant economy with state industry through the Selskosoyuz. What shall we call this form of organisation of production? In my opinion, it is the domestic system of large-scale state-socialist production in the sphere of agriculture. In speaking of the domestic system of state-socialist production I do so by analogy with the domestic system under capitalism, let us say, in the textile industry, where the handicraftsmen received their raw material and tools from the capitalist and turned over to him the entire product of their labour, thus being in fact semi-wage earners working in their own homes. This is one of numerous indices showing the path along which our agriculture must develop. There is no need to mention here similar indices in other branches of agriculture.

It scarcely needs proof that the vast majority of the peasantry will eagerly take this new path of development, rejecting the path of private capitalist latifundia and wage slavery, the path of destitution and ruin.

[5] Selskosoyuz: the All-Russian Union of Rural Co-operatives (1921–29).

Here is what Lenin says about the path of development of our agriculture:

> "State power over all large-scale means of production, state power in the hands of the proletariat, the alliance of this proletariat with the many millions of small and very small peasants, the assured leadership of the peasantry by the proletariat, etc.—is not this all that is necessary for building a complete socialist society from the co-operatives, from the co-operatives alone, which we formerly looked down upon as huckstering and which from a certain aspect we have the right to look down upon as such now, under the NEP? Is this not all that is necessary for building a complete socialist society? This is not yet the building of socialist society, but it is all that is necessary and sufficient for this building."

Further on, speaking of the necessity of giving financial and other assistance to the co-operatives, as a "new principal of organising the population" and a new "social system" under the dictatorship of the proletariat, Lenin continues:

> "Every social system arises only with the financial assistance of a definite class. There is no need to mention the hundreds and hundreds of millions of rubles that the birth of 'free' capitalism cost. Now we must realise, and apply in our practical work, the fact that the social system which we must now give more than usual assistance is the co-operative system. But it must be assisted in the real sense of the word, i.e., it will not be enough to interpret assistance to mean assistance for any kind of co-operative trade; by assistance we must mean assistance for co-operative trade in which *really large masses of the population really take part.*"

What do all these facts prove?

That the sceptics are wrong.

That Leninism is right in regarding the masses of labouring peasants as the reserve of the proletariat.

That the proletariat in power can and must use this reserve in order to link industry with agriculture, to advance socialist construction, and to provide for the dictatorship of the proletariat that necessary foundation without which the transition to socialist economy is impossible.

VI. THE NATIONAL QUESTION

From this theme I take two main questions:

a) the presentation of the question;

b) the liberation movement of the oppressed peoples and the proletarian revolution.

1) *The presentation of the question.* During the last two decades the national question has undergone a number of very important changes. The national question in the period of the Second International and the national question in the period of Leninism are far from being the same thing. They differ profoundly from each other, not only in their scope, but also in their intrinsic character.

Formerly, the national question was usually confined to a narrow circle of questions, concerning, primarily, "civilised" nationalities. The Irish, the Hungarians, the Poles, the Finns, the Serbs, and several other European nationalities—that was the circle of unequal peoples in whose destinies the leaders of the Second International were interested. The scores and hundreds of millions of Asiatic and African peoples who are suffering national oppression in its most savage and cruel form usually remained outside of their field of vision. They hesitated to put white and black, "civilised" and "uncivilised" on the same plane. Two or three meaningless, lukewarm resolutions, which carefully evaded the question of liberating the colonies—that was all the leaders of the Second International could boast of. Now we can say that this duplicity and half-heartedness in dealing with the national question has been brought to an end. Leninism laid bare this crying incongruity, broke down the wall between whites and blacks, between Europeans and Asiatics, between the "civilised" and "uncivilised" slaves of imperialism, and thus linked the national question with the question of the colonies. The national question was thereby transformed from a particular and internal state problem into a general and international problem, into a world problem of emancipating the oppressed peoples in the dependent countries and colonies from the yoke of imperialism.

Formerly, the principle of self-determination of nations was usually misinterpreted, and not infrequently it was narrowed down to the idea of the right of nations to autonomy. Certain leaders of the Second International even went so far as to turn the right to self-determination into the right to cultural autonomy, i.e., the right of oppressed nations to have their own cultural institutions, leaving all political power in the hands of the ruling nation. As a consequence, the idea of self-determination stood in danger of being transformed from an instrument for combating annexations into an instrument for justifying them. Now we can say that this confusion has been cleared up. Leninism broadened the conception of self-determination, interpreting it as the right of the oppressed peoples of the dependent countries and colonies to complete secession, as the right of nations to independent existence as states. This precluded the possibility of justifying annexations by interpreting the right to self-determination as the right to autonomy. Thus, the principle of self-determination itself was transformed from an instrument for deceiving the masses, which it undoubtedly was in the hands of the social-chauvinists during the imperialist war, into an instrument for exposing all imperialist aspirations and chauvinist machinations, into an instrument for the political education of the masses in the spirit of internationalism.

Formerly, the question of the oppressed nations was usually regarded as purely a juridical question. Solemn proclamations about "national equality of rights," innumerable declarations about the "equality of nations"—that was the stock-in-trade of the parties of the Second International, which glossed over the fact that "equality of nations" under imperialism, where one group of nations (a minority) lives by exploiting another group of nations, is sheer mockery of the oppressed nations. Now we can say that this bourgeois-juridical point of view on the national question has been exposed. Leninism brought the national question down from the lofty heights of high-sounding declarations to solid ground, and declared that pronouncements about the "equality of nations" not backed by the direct support of the proletarian parties for the liberation struggle of the oppressed nations are meaningless and false. In this way the question of the oppressed nations became one of supporting the oppressed nations, of rendering real and continuous assistance to them in their struggle against imperialism for real equality of nations, for their independent existence as states.

Formerly, the national question was regarded from a reformist point of view, as an independent question having no connection with the general question of the power of capital, of the overthrow of imperialism, of the proletarian revolution. It was tacitly assumed that the victory of the proletariat in Europe was possible without a direct alliance with the liberation movement in the colonies, that the national-colonial question could be solved on the quiet, "of its own accord," off the highway of the proletarian revolution, without a revolutionary struggle against imperialism. Now we can say that this anti-revolutionary point of view has been exposed. Leninism has proved, and the imperialist war and the revolution in Russia have confirmed, that the national question can be solved only in connection with and on the basis of the proletarian revolution, and that the road to victory of the revolution in the West lies through the revolutionary alliance with the liberation movement of the colonies and dependent countries against imperialism. The national question is a part of the general question of the proletarian revolution, a part of the question of the dictatorship of the proletariat.

The question is as follows: Are the revolutionary potentialities latent in the revolutionary liberation movement of the oppressed countries *already exhausted*, or not; and if not, is there any hope, any basis, for utilising these potentialities for the proletarian revolution, for transforming the dependent and colonial countries from a reserve of the imperialist bourgeoisie into a reserve of the revolutionary proletariat, into an ally of the latter?

Leninism replies to this question in the affirmative, i.e., it recognises the existence of revolutionary capacities in the national liberation movement of the oppressed countries, and the possibility of using these for overthrowing the common enemy, for overthrowing imperialism. The mechanics of the development of imperialism, the imperialist war and the revolution in Russia wholly confirm the conclusions of Leninism on this score.

Hence the necessity for the proletariat of the "dominant" nations to support—resolutely and actively to support—the national liberation movement of the oppressed and dependent peoples.

This does not mean, of course, that the proletariat must support *every* national movement, everywhere and always, in every individual concrete case. It means that support must be given to such national movements as tend to weaken, to overthrow imperialism, and not to strengthen and preserve it. Cases occur when the national movements in certain oppressed countries come into conflict with the interests of the development of the proletarian movement. In such cases support is, of course, entirely out of the question. The question of the rights of nations is not an isolated, self-sufficient question; it is a part of the general problem of the proletarian revolution, subordinate to the whole, and must be considered from the point of view of the whole. In the forties of the last century Marx supported the national movement of the Poles and Hungarians and was opposed to the national movement of the Czechs and the South Slavs. Why? Because the Czechs and the South Slavs were then "reactionary peoples," "Russian outposts" in Europe, outposts of absolutism; whereas the Poles and the Hungarians were "revolutionary peoples," fighting against absolutism. Because support of the national movement of the Czechs and the South Slavs was at that time equivalent to indirect support for tsarism, the most dangerous enemy of the revolutionary movement in Europe.

> "The various demands of democracy," writes Lenin, "including self-determination, are not an absolute, but a *small part* of the general democratic (now: general socialist) *world* movement. In individual concrete cases, the part may contradict the whole; if so, it must be rejected."

This is the position in regard to the question of particular national movements, of the possible reactionary character of these movements—if, of course, they are appraised not from the formal point of view, not from the point of view of abstract rights, but concretely, from the point of view of the interests of the revolutionary movement.

The same must be said of the revolutionary character of national movements in general. The unquestionably revolutionary character of the vast majority of national movements is as relative and peculiar as is the possible reactionary character of certain particular national movements. The revolutionary character of a national movement under the conditions of imperialist oppression does not necessarily presuppose the existence of proletarian elements in the movement, the existence of a revolutionary or a republican programme of the movement, the existence of a democratic basis of the movement. The struggle that the Emir of Afghanistan is waging for the independence of Afghanistan is objectively a *revolutionary* struggle, despite the monarchist views of the Emir and his associates, for it weakens, disintegrates and undermines imperialism; whereas the struggle waged by such "desperate" democrats and "Socialists," "revolutionaries" and republicans as, for example, Kerensky and Tsereteli, Renaudel and Scheidemann, Chernov and Dan, Henderson and Clynes, during the imperialist war was a *reactionary* struggle, for its result was the embellishment, the strengthening, the victory, of imperialism. For the same reasons, the struggle that the Egyptian merchants and bourgeois intellectuals are waging for the independence of Egypt is objectively a *revolutionary* struggle, despite the bourgeois origin and bourgeois title of the leaders of the Egyptian national movement, despite the fact that they are opposed to socialism; whereas the struggle that the British "Labour" Government is waging to preserve Egypt's dependent position is for the same reasons a *reactionary* struggle, despite the proletarian origin and the proletarian title of the members of that government, despite the fact that they are "for" socialism. There is no need to mention the national movement in other, larger, colonial and dependent countries, such as India and China, every step of which along the road to liberation, even if it runs counter to the demands of formal democracy, is a steam-hammer blow at imperialism, i.e., is undoubtedly a *revolutionary* step.

Lenin was right in saying that the national movement of the oppressed countries should be appraised not from the point of view of formal democracy, but from the point of view of the actual results, as shown by the general balance sheet of the struggle against imperialism, that is to say, "not in isolation, but on a world scale."

2) *The liberation movement of the oppressed peoples and the proletarian revolution.* In solving the national question Leninism proceeds from the following theses:

a) the world is divided into two camps: the camp of a handful of civilised nations, which possess finance capital and exploit the vast majority of the population of the globe; and the camp of the oppressed and exploited peoples in the colonies and dependent countries, which constitute that majority;

b) the colonies and the dependent countries, oppressed and exploited by finance capital, constitute a vast reserve and a very important source of strength for imperialism;

c) the revolutionary struggle of the oppressed peoples in the dependent and colonial countries against imperialism is the only road that leads to their emancipation from oppression and exploitation;

d) the most important colonial and dependent countries have already taken the path of the national liberation movement, which cannot but lead to the crisis of world capitalism;

e) the interests of the proletarian movement in the developed countries and of the national liberation movement in the colonies call for the union of these two forms of the revolutionary movement into a common front against the common enemy, against imperialism;

f) the victory of the working class in the developed countries and the liberation of the oppressed peoples from the yoke of imperialism are impossible without the formation and the consolidation of a common revolutionary front;

g) the formation of a common revolutionary front is impossible unless the proletariat of the oppressor nations renders direct and determined support to the liberation movement of the oppressed peoples against the imperialism of its "own country," for "no nation can be free if it oppresses other nations" (*Engels*);

h) this support implies the upholding, defence and implementation of the slogan of the right of nations to secession, to independent existence as states;

i) unless this slogan is implemented, the union and collaboration of nations within a single world economic system, which is the material basis for the victory of world socialism, cannot be brought about;

j) this union can only be voluntary, arising on the basis of mutual confidence and fraternal relations among peoples.

Hence the two sides, the two tendencies in the national question: the tendency towards political emancipation from the shackles of imperialism and towards the formation of an independent national state—a tendency which arose as a consequence of imperialist oppression and colonial exploitation; and the tendency towards closer economic relations among nations, which arose as a result of the formation of a world market and a world economic system.

> "Developing capitalism," says Lenin, "knows two historical tendencies in the national question. First: the awakening of national life and national movements, struggle against all national oppression, creation of national states. Second: development and acceleration of all kinds of intercourse between nations, breakdown of national barriers, creation of the international unity of capital, of economic life in general, of politics, science, etc.
>
> "Both tendencies are a world-wide law of capitalism. The first predominates at the beginning of its development, the second characterises mature capitalism that is moving towards its transformation into socialist society."

For imperialism these two tendencies represent irreconcilable contradictions; because imperialism cannot exist without exploiting colonies and forcibly retaining them within the framework of the "integral whole"; because imperialism can bring nations together only by means of annexations and colonial conquest, without which imperialism is, generally speaking, inconceivable.

For communism, on the contrary, these tendencies are but two sides of a single cause—the cause of the emancipation of the oppressed peoples from the yoke of imperialism; because communism knows that the union of peoples in a single world economic system is possible only on the basis of mutual confidence and voluntary agreement, and that the road to the formation of a voluntary union of peoples lies through the separation of the colonies from the "integral" imperialist "whole," through the transformation of the colonies into independent states.

Hence the necessity for a stubborn, continuous and determined struggle against the dominant-nation chauvinism of the "Socialists" of the ruling nations (Britain, France, America, Italy, Japan, etc.), who do not want to fight their imperialist governments, who do not want to support the struggle of the oppressed peoples in "their" colonies for emancipation from oppression, for secession.

Without such a struggle the education of the working class of the ruling nations in the spirit of true internationalism, in the spirit of closer relations with the toiling masses of the dependent countries and colonies, in the spirit of real preparation for the proletarian revolution, is inconceivable. The revolution would not have been victorious in Russia, and Kolchak and Denikin would not have been crushed, had not the Russian proletariat enjoyed the sympathy and support of the oppressed peoples of the former Russian Empire. But to win the sympathy and support of these peoples it had first of all to break the fetters of Russian imperialism and free these peoples from the yoke of national oppression.

Without this it would have been impossible to consolidate Soviet power, to implant real internationalism and to create that remarkable organisation for the collaboration of peoples which is called the Union of Soviet Socialist Republics, and which is the living prototype of the future union of peoples in a single world economic system.

Hence the necessity of fighting against the national isolationism, narrowness and aloofness of the Socialists in the oppressed countries, who do not want to rise above their national parochialism and who do not understand the connection between the liberation movement in their own countries and the proletarian movement in the ruling countries.

Without such a struggle it is inconceivable that the proletariat of the oppressed nations can maintain an independent policy and its class solidarity with the proletariat of the ruling countries in the fight for the overthrow of the common enemy, in the fight for the overthrow of imperialism.

Without such a struggle, internationalism would be impossible.

Such is the way in which the toiling masses of the dominant and of the oppressed nations must be educated in the spirit of revolutionary internationalism.

Here is what Lenin says about this twofold task of communism in educating the workers in the spirit of internationalism:

> "Can such education . . . be *concretely identical* in great, oppressing nations and in small, oppressed nations, in annexing nations and in annexed nations?
>
> "Obviously not. The way to the one goal—to complete equality, to the closest relations and the subsequent *amalgamation of all* nations—obviously proceeds here by different routes in each concrete case; in the same way, let us say, as the route to a point in the middle of a given page lies towards the left from one edge and towards the right from the opposite edge. If a Social-Democrat belonging to a great, oppressing, annexing nation, while advocating the amalgamation of nations in general, were to forget even for one moment that 'his' Nicholas II, 'his' Wilhelm, George, Poincaré, etc., *also stands for amalgamation* with small nations (by means of annexations)—Nicholas II being for 'amalgamation' with Galicia, Wilhelm II for 'amalgamation' with Belgium, etc.—such a Social-Democrat would be a ridiculous doctrinaire in theory and an abettor of imperialism in practice.
>
> "The weight of emphasis in the internationalist education of the workers in the oppressing countries must necessarily consist in their advocating and upholding freedom of secession for oppressed countries. Without this there can be *no* internationalism. It is our right and duty to treat every Social-Democrat of an oppressing nation who *fails* to conduct such propaganda as an imperialist and a scoundrel. This is an absolute demand, even if the *chance* of secession

being possible and 'feasible' before the introduction of socialism be only one in a thousand. . . .

"On the other hand, a Social-Democrat belonging to a small nation must emphasise in his agitation the *second* word of our general formula: 'voluntary *union*' of nations. He may, without violating his duties as an internationalist, be in favour of *either* the political independence of his nation *or* its inclusion in a neighbouring state X, Y, Z, etc. But in all cases he must fight *against* small-nation narrow-mindedness, isolationism and aloofness, he must fight for the recognition of the whole and the general, for the subordination of the interests of the particular to the interests of the general.

"People who have not gone thoroughly into the question think there is a 'contradiction' in Social-Democrats of oppressing nations insisting on 'freedom of *secession*,' while Social-Democrats of oppressed nations insist on 'freedom of *union*.' However, a little reflection will show that there is not, and cannot be, any *other* road leading from the *given* situation to internationalism and the amalgamation of nations, any other road to this goal."

VII. STRATEGY AND TACTICS

From this theme I take six questions:

a) strategy and tactics as the science of leadership in the class struggle of the proletariat;

b) stages of the revolution, and strategy;

c) the flow and ebb of the movement, and tactics;

d) strategic leadership;

e) tactical leadership;

f) reformism and revolutionism.

1) *Strategy and tactics as the science of leadership in the class struggle of the proletariat.* The period of the domination of the Second International was mainly a period of the formation and training of the proletarian political armies under conditions of more or less peaceful development. It was the period of parliamentarism as the predominant form of the class struggle. Questions of great class conflicts, of preparing the proletariat for revolutionary clashes, of the means

of achieving the dictatorship of the proletariat, did not seem to be on the order of the day at that time. The task was confined to utilising all means of legal development for the purpose of forming and training the proletarian armies, to utilising parliamentarism in conformity with the conditions under which the status of the proletariat remained, and, as it seemed, had to remain, that of an opposition. It scarcely needs proof that in such a period and with such a conception of the tasks of the proletariat there could be neither an integral strategy nor any elaborated tactics. There were fragmentary and detached ideas about tactics and strategy, but no tactics or strategy as such.

The mortal sin of the Second International was not that it pursued at that time the tactics of utilising parliamentary forms of struggle, but that it overestimated the importance of these forms, that it considered them virtually the only forms; and that when the period of open revolutionary battles set in and the question of extra-parliamentary forms of struggle came to the fore, the parties of the Second International turned their backs on these new tasks, refused to shoulder them.

Only in the subsequent period, the period of direct action by the proletariat, the period of proletarian revolution, when the question of overthrowing the bourgeoisie became a question of immediate practical action; when the question of the reserves of the proletariat (strategy) became one of the most burning questions; when all forms of struggle and of organisation, parliamentary and extra-parliamentary (tactics), had quite clearly manifested themselves—only in this period could an integral strategy and elaborated tactics for the struggle of the proletariat be worked out. It was precisely in this period that Lenin brought out into the light of day the brilliant ideas of Marx and Engels on tactics and strategy that had been suppressed by the opportunists of the Second International. But Lenin did not confine himself to restoring particular tactical propositions of Marx and Engels. He developed them further and supplemented them with new ideas and propositions, combining them all into a system of rules and guiding principles for the leadership of the class struggle of the proletariat. Lenin's pamphlets, such as *What Is To*

Be Done?, *Two Tactics*, *Imperialism*, *The State and Revolution*, *The Proletarian Revolution and the Renegade Kautsky*, *"Left-Wing" Communism*, undoubtedly constitute priceless contributions to the general treasury of Marxism, to its revolutionary arsenal. The strategy and tactics of Leninism constitute the science of leadership in the revolutionary struggle of the proletariat.

2) *Stages of the revolution, and strategy.* Strategy is the determination of the direction of the main blow of the proletariat at a given stage of the revolution, the elaboration of a corresponding plan for the disposition of the revolutionary forces (main and secondary reserves), the fight to carry out this plan throughout the given stage of the revolution.

Our revolution had already passed through two stages, and after the October Revolution it entered a third one. Our strategy changed accordingly.

First stage. 1903 to February 1917. Objective: to overthrow tsarism and completely wipe out the survivals of medievalism. The main force of the revolution: the proletariat. Immediate reserves: the peasantry. Direction of the main blow: the isolation of the liberal-monarchist bourgeoisie, which was striving to win over the peasantry and liquidate the revolution by a *compromise* with tsarism. Plan for the disposition of forces: alliance of the working class with the peasantry. "The proletariat must carry to completion the democratic revolution, by allying to itself the mass of the peasantry in order to crush by force the resistance of the autocracy and to paralyse the instability of the bourgeoisie."

Second stage. March 1917 to October 1917. Objective: to overthrow imperialism in Russia and to withdraw from the imperialist war. The main force of the revolution: the proletariat. Immediate reserves: the poor peasantry. The proletariat of neighbouring countries as probable reserves. The protracted war and the crisis of imperialism as a favourable factor. Direction of the main blow: isolation of the petty-bourgeois democrats (Mensheviks and Socialist-Revolutionaries), who were striving to win over the toiling masses of the peasantry and to put an end to the revolution by a *compromise* with imperialism. Plan for the disposition of forces: alliance of the proletariat with the poor peasantry. "The proletariat must accomplish the socialist revolution, by allying to itself the mass of the semi-proletarian elements of the population in order to crush by force the resistance of the bourgeoisie and to paralyse the instability of the peasantry and the petty bourgeoisie."

Third stage. Began after the October Revolution. Objective: to consolidate the dictatorship of the proletariat in one country, using it as a base for the defeat of imperialism in all countries. The revolution spreads beyond the confines of one country; the epoch of world revolution has begun. The main forces of the revolution: the dictatorship of the proletariat in one country, the revolutionary movement of the proletariat in all countries. Main reserves: the semi-proletarian and small-peasant masses in the developed countries, the liberation movement in the colonies and dependent countries. Direction of the main blow: isolation of the petty-bourgeois democrats, isolation of the parties of the Second International, which constitute the main support of the policy of *compromise* with imperialism. Plan for the disposition of forces: alliance of the proletarian revolution with the liberation movement in the colonies and the dependent countries.

Strategy deals with the main forces of the revolution and their reserves. It changes with the passing of the revolution from one stage to another, but remains basically unchanged throughout a given stage.

3) *The flow and ebb of the movement, and tactics.* Tactics are the determination of the line of conduct of the proletariat in the comparatively short period of the flow or ebb of the movement, of the rise or decline of the revolution, the fight to carry out this line by means of replacing old forms of struggle and organisation by new ones, old slogans by new ones, by combining these forms, etc. While the object of strategy is to win the war against tsarism, let us say, or against the bourgeoisie, to carry through the struggle against tsarism or against the bourgeoisie to its end, tactics pursue less important objects, for their aim is not the winning of the war as a whole, but the winning of some particular engagements or some particular battles, the carrying through successfully of some particular campaigns or actions corresponding to the concrete circumstances in the given period

of rise or decline of the revolution. Tactics are a part of strategy, subordinate to it and serving it.

Tactics change according to flow and ebb. While the strategic plan remained unchanged during the first stage of the revolution (1903 to February 1917), tactics changed several times during that period. In the period from 1903 to 1905 the Party pursued offensive tactics, for the tide of the revolution was rising, the movement was on the upgrade, and tactics had to proceed from this fact. Accordingly, the forms of struggle were revolutionary, corresponding to the requirements of the rising tide of the revolution. Local political strikes, political demonstrations, the general political strike, boycott of the Duma, uprising, revolutionary fighting slogans—such were the successive forms of struggle during that period. These changes in the forms of struggle were accompanied by corresponding changes in the forms of organisation. Factory committees, revolutionary peasant committees, strike committees, Soviets of workers' deputies, a workers' party operating more or less openly—such were the forms of organisation during that period.

In the period from 1907 to 1912 the Party was compelled to resort to tactics of retreat; for we then experienced a decline in the revolutionary movement, the ebb of the revolution, and tactics necessarily had to take this fact into consideration. The forms of struggle, as well as the forms of organisation, changed accordingly: instead of the boycott of the Duma—participation in the Duma; instead of open revolutionary actions outside the Duma—actions and work in the Duma; instead of general political strikes—partial economic strikes, or simply a lull in activities. Of course, the Party had to go underground during that period, while the revolutionary mass organisations were replaced by cultural, educational, co-operative, insurance and other legal organisations.

The same must be said of the second and third stages of the revolution, during which tactics changed dozens of times, whereas the strategic plans remained unchanged.

Tactics deal with the forms of struggle and the forms of organisation of the proletariat, with their changes and combinations. During a given stage of the revolution tactics may change several times, depending on the flow or ebb, the rise or decline, of the revolution.

4) *Strategic leadership.* The reserves of the revolution can be:

direct: a) the peasantry and in general the intermediate strata of the population within the country; b) the proletariat of neighbouring countries; c) the revolutionary movement in the colonies and dependent countries; d) the conquests and gains of the dictatorship of the proletariat—part of which the proletariat may give up temporarily, while retaining superiority of forces, in order to buy off a powerful enemy and gain a respite; and

indirect: a) the contradictions and conflicts among the non-proletarian classes within the country, which can be utilised by the proletariat to weaken the enemy and to strengthen its own reserves; b) contradictions, conflicts and wars (the imperialist war, for instance) among the bourgeois states hostile to the proletarian state, which can be utilised by the proletariat in its offensive or in manoeuvring in the event of a forced retreat.

There is no need to speak at length about the reserves of the first category, as their significance is clear to everyone. As for the reserves of the second category, whose significance is not always clear, it must be said that sometimes they are of prime importance for the progress of the revolution. One can hardly deny the enormous importance, for example, of the conflict between the petty-bourgeois democrats (Socialist-Revolutionaries) and the liberal-monarchist bourgeoisie (the Cadets) during and after the first revolution, which undoubtedly played its part in freeing the peasantry from the influence of the bourgeoisie. Still less reason is there for denying the colossal importance of the fact that the principal groups of imperialists were engaged in a deadly war during the period of the October Revolution, when the imperialists, engrossed in war among themselves, were unable to concentrate their forces against the young Soviet power, and the proletariat, for this very reason, was able to get down to the work of organising its forces and consolidating its power, and to prepare the rout of Kolchak and Denikin. It must be presumed that now, when the contradictions among the imperialist groups are becoming more and more profound, and when a new war among them is becoming inevitable, reserves of this description will assume ever greater importance for the proletariat.

The task of strategic leadership is to make proper use of all these reserves for the achievement of the main object of the revolution at the given stage of its development.

What does making proper use of reserves mean?

It means fulfilling certain necessary conditions, of which the following must be regarded as the principal ones:

Firstly. The concentration of the main forces of the revolution at the enemy's most vulnerable spot at the decisive moment, when the revolution has already become ripe, when the offensive is going full-steam ahead, when insurrection is knocking at the door, and when bringing the reserves up to the vanguard is the decisive condition of success. The Party's strategy during the period from April to October 1917 can be taken as an example of this manner of utilising reserves. Undoubtedly, the enemy's most vulnerable spot at that time was the war. Undoubtedly, it was on this question, as the fundamental one, that the Party rallied the broadest masses of the population around the proletarian vanguard. The Party's strategy during that period was, while training the vanguard for street action by means of manifestations and demonstrations, to bring the reserves up to the vanguard through the medium of the Soviets in the rear and the soldiers' committees at the front. The outcome of the revolution has shown that the reserves were properly utilised.

Here is what Lenin, paraphrasing the well-known theses of Marx and Engels on insurrection, says about this condition of the strategic utilisation of the forces of the revolution:

> "1) Never *play* with insurrection, but when beginning it firmly realise that you must *go to the end.*
>
> "2) Concentrate a great *superiority of forces* at the decisive point, at the decisive moment, otherwise the enemy, who has the advantage of better preparation and organisation, will destroy the insurgents.
>
> "3) Once the insurrection has begun, you must act with the greatest *determination,* and by all means, without

fail, take the *offensive*. 'The defensive is the death of every armed rising.'

"4) You must try to take the enemy by surprise and seize the moment when his forces are scattered.

"5) You must strive for *daily* successes, even if small (one might say hourly, if it is the case of one town), and at all costs retain the '*moral ascendancy*'."

Secondly. The selection of the moment for the decisive blow, of the moment for starting the insurrection, so timed as to coincide with the moment when the crisis has reached its climax, when it is already the case that the vanguard is prepared to fight to the end, the reserves are prepared to support the vanguard, and maximum consternation reigns in the ranks of the enemy.

The decisive battle, says Lenin, may be deemed to have fully matured *if* "(1) all the class forces hostile to us have become sufficiently entangled, are sufficiently at loggerheads, have sufficiently weakened themselves in a struggle which is beyond their strength"; *if* "(2) all the vacillating, wavering, unstable, intermediate elements—the petty bourgeoisie, the petty-bourgeois democrats as distinct from the bourgeoisie—have sufficiently exposed themselves in the eyes of the people, have sufficiently disgraced themselves through their practical bankruptcy"; *if* "(3) among the proletariat a mass sentiment in favour of supporting the most determined, supremely bold, revolutionary action against the bourgeoisie has arisen and begun vigorously to grow. Then revolution is indeed ripe; then, indeed, if we have correctly gauged all the conditions indicated above . . . and if we have chosen the moment rightly, our victory is assured."

The manner in which the October uprising was carried out may be taken as a model of such strategy.

Failure to observe this condition leads to a dangerous error called "loss of tempo," when the Party lags behind the movement or runs far ahead of it, courting the danger of failure. An example of such "loss of tempo," of how the moment for an uprising should not be chosen, may be seen in the attempt made by a section of our comrades to begin the uprising by arresting the Democratic Conference in September 1917, when wavering was still apparent in the Soviets, when the armies at the front were still at the crossroads, when the reserves had not yet been brought up to the vanguard.

Thirdly. Undeviating pursuit of the course adopted, no matter what difficulties and complications are encountered on the road towards the goal; this is necessary in order that the vanguard may not lose sight of the main goal of the struggle and that the masses may not stray from the road while marching towards that goal and striving to rally around the vanguard. Failure to observe this condition leads to a grave error, well known to sailors as "losing one's bearings." As an example of this "losing one's bearings" we may take the erroneous conduct of our Party when, immediately after the Democratic Conference, it adopted a resolution to participate in the Pre-parliament. For the moment the Party, as it were, forgot that the Pre-parliament was an attempt of the bourgeoisie to switch the country from the path of the Soviets to the path of bourgeois parliamentarism, that the Party's participation in such a body might result in mixing everything up and confusing the workers and peasants, who were waging a revolutionary struggle under the slogan: "All Power to the Soviets." This mistake was rectified by the withdrawal of the Bolsheviks from the Pre-parliament.

Fourthly. Manoeuvring the reserves with a view to effecting a proper retreat when the enemy is strong, when retreat is inevitable, when to accept battle forced upon us by the enemy is obviously disadvantageous, when, with the given relation of forces, retreat becomes the only way to escape a blow against the vanguard and to retain the reserves for the latter.

> "The revolutionary parties," says Lenin, "must complete their education. They have learned to attack. Now they have to realise that this knowledge must be supplemented with the knowledge how to retreat properly. They have to realise—and the revolutionary class is taught to realise it by its own bitter experience—that victory is impossible unless

> they have learned both how to attack and how to retreat properly."

The object of this strategy is to gain time, to disrupt the enemy, and to accumulate forces in order later to assume the offensive.

The signing of the Brest Peace may be taken as a model of this strategy, for it enabled the Party to gain time, to take advantage of the conflicts in the camp of the imperialists, to disrupt the forces of the enemy, to retain the support of the peasantry, and to accumulate forces in preparation for the offensive against Kolchak and Denikin.

> "In concluding a separate peace," said Lenin at that time, "we free ourselves as much *as is possible at the present moment* from both warring imperialist groups, we take advantage of their mutual enmity and warfare, which hinder them from making a deal against us, and for a certain period have our hands free to advance and to consolidate the socialist revolution." (See Vol. XXII, p. 198.)
>
> "Now even the biggest fool," said Lenin three years after the Brest Peace, can see "that the 'Brest Peace' was a concession that strengthened us and broke up the forces of international imperialism."

Such are the principal conditions which ensure correct strategic leadership.

5) *Tactical leadership.* Tactical leadership is a part of strategic leadership, subordinated to the tasks and the requirements of the latter. The task of tactical leadership is to master all forms of struggle and organisation of the proletariat and to ensure that they are used properly so as to achieve, with the given relation of forces, the maximum results necessary to prepare for strategic success.

What is meant by making proper use of the forms of struggle and organisation of the proletariat?

It means fulfilling certain necessary conditions, of which the following must be regarded as the principal ones:

Firstly. To put in the forefront precisely those forms of struggle and organisation which are best suited to the conditions prevailing during the flow or ebb of the movement at a given moment, and which therefore can facilitate and ensure the bringing of the masses to the revolutionary positions, the bringing of the millions to the revolutionary front, and their disposition at the revolutionary front.

The point here is not that the vanguard should realise the impossibility of preserving the old regime and the inevitability of its overthrow. The point is that the masses, the millions, should understand this inevitability and display their readiness to support the vanguard. But the masses can understand this only from their own experience. The task is to enable the vast masses to realise from their own experience the inevitability of the overthrow of the old regime, to promote such methods of struggle and forms of organisation as will make it easier for the masses to realise from experience the correctness of the revolutionary slogans.

The vanguard would have become detached from the working class, and the working class would have lost contact with the masses, if the Party had not decided at the time to participate in the Duma, if it had not decided to concentrate its forces on work in the Duma and to develop a struggle on the basis of this work, in order to make it easier for the masses to realise from their own experience the futility of the Duma, the falsity of the promises of the Cadets, the impossibility of compromise with tsarism, and the inevitability of an alliance between the peasantry and the working class. Had the masses not gained their experience during the period of the Duma, the exposure of the Cadets and the hegemony of the proletariat would have been impossible.

The danger of the "Otzovist" tactics was that they threatened to detach the vanguard from the millions of its reserves.

The Party would have become detached from the working class, and the working class would have lost its influence among the broad masses of the peasants and soldiers, if the proletariat had followed the "Left" Communists, who called for an uprising in April 1917, when the Mensheviks and Socialist-Revolutionaries had not yet exposed themselves as advocates of war and imperialism, when the masses had not yet realised from their own experience the falsity of the speeches of the Mensheviks and Socialist-Revolutionaries about peace, land and freedom. Had the masses not gained this experience during the Kerensky period, the Mensheviks and Socialist-Revolutionaries would not have been isolated and the dictatorship of the proletariat would have been impossible. Therefore, the tactics of "patiently explaining" the mistakes of the petty-bourgeois parties and of open struggle in the Soviets were the only correct tactics.

The danger of the tactics of the "Left" Communists was that they threatened to transform the Party from the leader of the proletarian revolution into a handful of futile conspirators with no ground to stand on.

> "Victory cannot be won with the vanguard alone," says Lenin. "To throw the vanguard alone into the decisive battle, before the whole class, before the broad masses have taken up a position either of direct support of the vanguard, or at least of benevolent neutrality towards it . . . would be not merely folly but a crime. And in order that actually the whole class, that actually the broad masses of the working people and those oppressed by capital may take up such a position, propaganda and agitation alone are not enough. For this the masses must have their own political experience. Such is the fundamental law of all great revolutions, now confirmed with astonishing force and vividness not only in Russia but also in Germany. Not only the uncultured, often illiterate masses of Russia, but the highly cultured, entirely literate masses of Germany had to realise through their own painful experience the absolute impotence and spinelessness, the absolute helplessness and servility to the bourgeoisie, the utter vileness, of the government of the knights of the Second International, the absolute inevitability of a dictatorship of the extreme reactionaries (Kornilov in Russia, Kapp and Co. in Germany) as the only alternative to a dictatorship of the proletariat, in order to turn resolutely towards communism."

Secondly. To locate at any given moment the particular link in the chain of processes which, if grasped, will enable us to keep hold of the whole chain and to prepare the conditions for achieving strategic success.

The point here is to single out from all the tasks confronting the Party the particular immediate task, the fulfilment of which constitutes the central point, and the accomplishment of which ensures the successful fulfilment of the other immediate tasks.

The importance of this thesis may be illustrated by two examples, one of which could be taken from the remote past (the period of the formation of the Party) and the other from the immediate present (the period of the NEP).

In the period of the formation of the Party, when the innumerable circles and organisations had not yet been linked together, when amateurishness and the parochial outlook of the circles were corroding the Party from top to bottom, when ideological confusion was the characteristic feature of the internal life of the Party, the main link and the main task in the chain of links and in the chain of tasks then confronting the Party proved to be the establishment of an all-Russian illegal newspaper (*Iskra*). Why? Because, under the conditions then prevailing, only by means of an all-Russian illegal newspaper was it possible to create a solid core of the Party capable of uniting the innumerable circles and organisations into one whole, to prepare the conditions for ideological and tactical unity, and thus to build the foundations for the formation of a real party.

During the period of transition from war to economic construction, when industry was vegetating in the grip of disruption and agriculture was suffering from a shortage of urban manufactured goods, when the establishment of a bond between state industry and peasant economy became the fundamental condition for successful socialist construction—in that period it turned out that the main link in the chain of processes, the main task among a number of tasks, was to develop trade. Why? Because under the conditions of the NEP the bond between industry and peasant economy cannot be established except through trade; because under the conditions of the NEP production without sale is fatal for industry; because industry can be expanded only by the expansion of sales as a result of developing trade; because only after we have consolidated our position in the sphere of trade, only after we have secured control of trade, only after we have secured this link can there be any hope of linking industry with the peasant market and successfully fulfilling the other immediate tasks in order to create the conditions for building the foundations of socialist economy.

> "It is not enough to be a revolutionary and an adherent of socialism or a Communist in general," says Lenin. "One must be able at each particular moment to find the particular link in the chain which one must grasp with all one's might in order to keep hold of the whole chain and to prepare firmly for the transition to the next link." . . .
>
> "At the present time . . . this link is the revival of internal *trade* under proper state regulation (direction). Trade—that is the 'link' in the historical chain of events, in the transitional forms of our socialist construction in 1921–22, *'which we must grasp with all our might'*. . . ."

Such are the principal conditions which ensure correct tactical leadership.

6) *Reformism and revolutionism.* What is the difference between revolutionary tactics and reformist tactics?

Some think that Leninism is opposed to reforms, opposed to compromises and to agreements in general. This is absolutely wrong. Bolsheviks know as well as anybody else that in a certain sense "every little helps," that under certain conditions reforms in general, and compromises and agreements in particular, are necessary and useful.

> "To carry on a war for the overthrow of the international bourgeoisie," says Lenin, "a war which is a hundred times more difficult, protracted and complicated than the most stubborn of ordinary wars between states, and to refuse beforehand to manoeuvre, to utilise the conflict of interests (even though temporary) among one's enemies, to reject agreements and compromises with possible (even though temporary, unstable, vacillating and conditional) allies—is not this ridiculous in the extreme? Is it not as though, when making a difficult ascent of an unexplored and hitherto inaccessible mountain, we were to refuse before-

hand ever to move in zigzags, ever to retrace our steps, ever to abandon the course once selected and to try others?"

Obviously, therefore, it is not a matter of reforms or of compromises and agreements, but of the use people make of reforms and agreements.

To a reformist, reforms are everything, while revolutionary work is something incidental, something just to talk about, mere eyewash. That is why, with reformist tactics under the conditions of bourgeois rule, reforms are inevitably transformed into an instrument for strengthening that rule, an instrument for disintegrating the revolution.

To a revolutionary, on the contrary, the main thing is revolutionary work and not reforms; to him reforms are a by-product of the revolution. That is why, with revolutionary tactics under the conditions of bourgeois rule, reforms are naturally transformed into an instrument for disintegrating that rule, into an instrument for strengthening the revolution, into a strongpoint for the further development of the revolutionary movement.

The revolutionary will accept a reform in order to use it as an aid in combining legal work with illegal work and to intensify, under its cover, the illegal work for the revolutionary preparation of the masses for the overthrow of the bourgeoisie.

That is the essence of making revolutionary use of reforms and agreements under the conditions of imperialism.

The reformist, on the contrary, will accept reforms in order to renounce all illegal work, to thwart the preparation of the masses for the revolution and to rest in the shade of "bestowed" reforms.

That is the essence of reformist tactics.

Such is the position in regard to reforms and agreements under the conditions of imperialism.

The situation changes somewhat, however, after the overthrow of imperialism, under the dictatorship of the proletariat. Under certain conditions, in a certain situation, the proletarian power may find itself compelled temporarily to leave the path of the revolutionary reconstruction of the existing order of things and to take the path of its gradual transformation, the "reformist path," as Lenin says in his well-known article "The Importance of Gold," the path of flanking movements, of reforms and concessions to the non-proletarian classes—in order to disintegrate these classes, to give the revolution a respite, to recuperate one's forces and prepare the conditions for a new offensive. It cannot be denied that in a sense this is a "reformist" path. But it must be borne in mind that there is a fundamental distinction here, which consists in the fact that in this case the reform emanates from the proletarian power, it strengthens the proletarian power, it procures for it a necessary respite, its purpose is to disintegrate, not the revolution, but the non-proletarian classes.

Under such conditions a reform is thus transformed into its opposite.

The proletarian power is able to adopt such a policy because, and only because, the sweep of the revolution in the preceding period was great enough and therefore provided a sufficiently wide expanse within which to retreat, substituting for offensive tactics the tactics of temporary retreat, the tactics of flanking movements.

Thus, while formerly, under bourgeois rule, reforms were a by-product of revolution, now, under the dictatorship of the proletariat, the source of reforms is the revolutionary gains of the proletariat, the reserves accumulated in the hands of the proletariat and consisting of these gains.

> "Only Marxism," says Lenin, "has precisely and correctly defined the relation of reforms to revolution. However, Marx was able to see this relation only from one aspect, namely, under the conditions preceding the first to any extent permanent and lasting victory of the proletariat, if only in a single country. Under those conditions, the basis of the proper relation was: reforms are a by-product of the revolutionary class struggle of the proletariat. . . . After the victory of the proletariat, if only in a single country, something new enters into the relation between reforms and revolution. In principle, it is the same as before, but a change in form takes place, which Marx himself could not foresee, but which can be appreciated only on the basis of the philosophy and politics of Marxism. . . . After the

victory (while still remaining a 'by-product' on an international scale) they (i.e., reforms—*J. St.*) are, in addition, for the country in which victory has been achieved, a necessary and legitimate respite in those cases when, after the utmost exertion of effort, it becomes obvious that sufficient strength is lacking for the revolutionary accomplishment of this or that transition. Victory creates such a 'reserve of strength' that it is possible to hold out even in a forced retreat, to hold out both materially and morally."

VIII. THE PARTY

In the pre-revolutionary period, the period of more or less peaceful development, when the parties of the Second International were the predominant force in the working-class movement and parliamentary forms of struggle were regarded as the principal forms—under these conditions the Party neither had nor could have had that great and decisive importance which it acquired afterwards, under conditions of open revolutionary clashes. Defending the Second International against attacks made upon it, Kautsky says that the parties of the Second International are an instrument of peace and not of war, and that for this very reason they were powerless to take any important steps during the war, during the period of revolutionary action by the proletariat. That is quite true. But what does it mean? It means that the parties of the Second International are unfit for the revolutionary struggle of the proletariat, that they are not militant parties of the proletariat, leading the workers to power, but election machines adapted for parliamentary elections and parliamentary struggle. This, in fact, explains why, in the days when the opportunists of the Second International were in the ascendancy, it was not the party but its parliamentary group that was the chief political organisation of the proletariat. It is well known that the party at that time was really an appendage and subsidiary of the parliamentary group. It scarcely needs proof that under such circumstances and with such a party at the helm there could be no question of preparing the proletariat for revolution.

But matters have changed radically with the dawn of the

new period. The new period is one of open class collisions, of revolutionary action by the proletariat, of proletarian revolution, a period when forces are being directly mustered for the overthrow of imperialism and the seizure of power by the proletariat. In this period the proletariat is confronted with new tasks, the tasks of reorganising all party work on new, revolutionary lines; of educating the workers in the spirit of revolutionary struggle for power; of preparing and moving up reserves; of establishing an alliance with the proletarians of neighbouring countries; of establishing firm ties with the liberation movement in the colonies and dependent countries, etc., etc. To think that these new tasks can be performed by the old Social-Democratic parties, brought up as they were in the peaceful conditions of parliamentarism, is to doom oneself to hopeless despair, to inevitable defeat. If, with such tasks to shoulder, the proletariat remained under the leadership of the old parties, it would be completely unarmed. It scarcely needs proof that the proletariat could not consent to such a state of affairs.

Hence the necessity for a new party, a militant party, a revolutionary party, one bold enough to lead the proletarians in the struggle for power, sufficiently experienced to find its bearings amidst the complex conditions of a revolutionary situation, and sufficiently flexible to steer clear of all submerged rocks in the path to its goal.

Without such a party it is useless even to think of overthrowing imperialism, of achieving the dictatorship of the proletariat.

This new party is the party of Leninism.

What are the specific features of this new party?

1) *The Party as the advanced detachment of the working class.* The Party must be, first of all, the *advanced* detachment of the working class. The Party must absorb all the best elements of the working class, their experience, their revolutionary spirit, their selfless devotion to the cause of the proletariat. But in order that it may really be the advanced detachment, the Party must be armed with revolutionary theory, with a knowledge of the laws of the movement, with a knowledge of the laws of revolution. Without this it will be incapable of directing the struggle of the proletariat, of

leading the proletariat. The Party cannot be a real party if it limits itself to registering what the masses of the working class feel and think, if it drags at the tail of the spontaneous movement, if it is unable to overcome the inertia and the political indifference of the spontaneous movement, if it is unable to rise above the momentary interests of the proletariat, if it is unable to raise the masses to the level of understanding the class interests of the proletariat. The Party must stand at the head of the working class; it must see farther than the working class; it must lead the proletariat, and not drag at the tail of the spontaneous movement. The parties of the Second International, which preach "khvostism," are vehicles of bourgeois policy, which condemns the proletariat to the role of a tool in the hands of the bourgeoisie. Only a party which adopts the standpoint of advanced detachment of the proletariat and is able to raise the masses to the level of understanding the class interests of the proletariat—only such a party can divert the working class from the path of trade unionism and convert it into an independent political force.

The Party is the political leader of the working class.

I have already spoken of the difficulties of the struggle of the working class, of the complicated conditions of the struggle, of strategy and tactics, of reserves and manoeuvring, of attack and retreat. These conditions are no less complicated, if not more so, than the conditions of war. Who can see clearly in these conditions, who can give correct guidance to the proletarian millions? No army at war can dispense with an experienced General Staff if it does not want to be doomed to defeat. Is it not clear that the proletariat can still less dispense with such a General Staff if it does not want to allow itself to be devoured by its mortal enemies? But where is this General Staff? Only the revolutionary party of the proletariat can serve as this General Staff. The working class without a revolutionary party is an army without a General Staff.

The Party is the General Staff of the proletariat.

But the Party cannot be only an *advanced* detachment. It must at the same time be a detachment of the *class*, part of the class, closely bound up with it by all the fibres of its being. The distinction between the advanced detachment and the rest of the working class, between Party members and non-Party people, cannot disappear until classes disappear; it will exist as long as the ranks of the proletariat continue to be replenished with former members of other classes, as long as the working class as a whole is not in a position to rise to the level of the advanced detachment. But the Party would cease to be a party if this distinction developed into a gap, if the Party turned in on itself and became divorced from the non-Party masses. The Party cannot lead the class if it is not connected with the non-Party masses, if there is no bond between the Party and the non-Party masses, if these masses do not accept its leadership, if the Party enjoys no moral and political credit among the masses.

Recently two hundred thousand new members from the ranks of the workers were admitted into our Party. The remarkable thing about this is the fact that these people did not merely join the Party themselves, but were rather sent there by all the rest of the non-Party workers, who took an active part in the admission of the new members, and without whose approval no new member was accepted. This fact shows that the broad masses of non-Party workers regard our Party as *their* Party, as a Party *near* and *dear* to them, in whose expansion and consolidation they are vitally interested and to whose leadership they voluntarily entrust their destiny. It scarcely needs proof that without these intangible moral threads which connect the Party with the non-Party masses, the Party could not have become the decisive force of its class.

The Party is an inseparable part of the working class.

> "We," says Lenin, "are the Party of a class, and therefore *almost the whole class* (and in times of war, in the period of civil war, the whole class) should act under the leadership of our Party, should adhere to our Party as closely as possible. But it would be Manilovism and 'khvostism' to think that at any time under capitalism almost the whole class, or the whole class, would be able to rise to the level of consciousness and activity of its advanced detachment, of its Social-Democratic Party. No sensible Social-Democrat has ever yet doubted that under

capitalism even the trade union organisations (which are more primitive and more comprehensible to the undeveloped strata) are unable to embrace almost the whole, or the whole, working class. To forget the distinction between the advanced detachment and the whole of the masses which gravitate towards it, to forget the constant duty of the advanced detachment to *raise* ever wider strata to this most advanced level, means merely to deceive oneself, to shut one's eyes to the immensity of our tasks, and to narrow down these tasks."

2) *The Party as the organised detachment of the working class.* The Party is not only the *advanced* detachment of the working class. If it desires really to direct the struggle of the class it must at the same time be the *organised* detachment of its class. The Party's tasks under the conditions of capitalism are immense and extremely varied. The Party must direct the struggle of the proletariat under the exceptionally difficult conditions of internal and external development; it must lead the proletariat in the offensive when the situation calls for an offensive; it must lead the proletariat so as to escape the blow of a powerful enemy when the situation calls for retreat; it must imbue the millions of unorganised non-Party workers with the spirit of discipline and system in the struggle, with the spirit of organisation and endurance. But the Party can fulfil these tasks only if it is itself the embodiment of discipline and organisation, if it is itself the *organised* detachment of the proletariat. Without these conditions there can be no question of the Party really leading the vast masses of the proletariat.

The Party is the organised detachment of the working class.

The conception of the Party as an organized whole is embodied in Lenin's well-known formulation of the first paragraph of our Party Rules, in which the Party is regarded as the *sum total* of its organisations, and the Party member as a member of one of the organisations of the Party. The Mensheviks, who objected to this formulation as early as 1903, proposed to substitute for it a "system" of self-enrolment in the Party, a "system" of conferring the "title" of Party member upon every "professor" and "high-school student," upon every "sympathiser" and "striker" who supported the Party in one way or another, but who did not join and did not want to join any one of the Party organisations. It scarcely needs proof that had this singular "system" become entrenched in our Party it would inevitably have led to our Party becoming inundated with professors and high-school students and to its degeneration into a loose, amorphous, disorganised "formation," lost in a sea of "sympathisers," that would have obliterated the dividing line between the Party and the class and would have upset the Party's task of raising the unorganised masses to the level of the advanced detachment. Needless to say, under such an opportunist "system" our Party would have been unable to fulfil the role of the organising core of the working class in the course of our revolution.

> "From the point of view of Comrade Martov," says Lenin, "the border-line of the Party remains quite indefinite, for 'every striker' may 'proclaim himself a Party member.' What is the use of this vagueness? A wide extension of the 'title.' Its harm is that it introduces a *disorganising* idea, the confusing of class and Party."

But the Party is not merely the *sum total* of Party organisations. The Party is at the same time a single *system* of these organisations, their formal union into a single whole, with higher and lower leading bodies, with subordination of the minority to the majority, with practical decisions binding on all members of the Party. Without these conditions the Party cannot be a single organised whole capable of exercising systematic and organised leadership in the struggle of the working class.

> "*Formerly*," says Lenin, "our Party was not a formally organised whole, but only the sum of separate groups, and therefore no other relations except those of ideological influence were possible between these groups. *Now* we have become an organised Party, and this implies the establishment of authority, the transformation of the power of ideas

into the power of authority, the subordination of lower Party bodies to higher Party bodies."

The principle of the minority submitting to the majority, the principle of directing Party work from a centre, not infrequently gives rise to attacks on the part of wavering elements, to accusations of "bureaucracy," "formalism," etc. It scarcely needs proof that systematic work by the Party as one whole, and the directing of the struggle of the working class, would be impossible without putting these principles into effect. Leninism in questions of organisation is the unswerving application of these principles. Lenin terms the fight against these principles "Russian nihilism" and "aristocratic anarchism," which deserves to be ridiculed and swept aside.

Here is what Lenin says about these wavering elements in his book *One Step Forward:*

> "This aristocratic anarchism is particularly characteristic of the Russian nihilist. He thinks of the Party organisation as a monstrous 'factory'; he regards the subordination of the part to the whole and of the minority to the majority as 'serfdom'. . . , division of labour under the direction of a centre evokes from him a tragi-comical outcry against people being transformed into 'wheels and cogs'. . . , mention of the organisational rules of the Party calls forth a contemptuous grimace and the disdainful . . . remark that one could very well dispense with rules altogether."
>
> "It is clear, I think, that the cries about this celebrated bureaucracy are just a screen for dissatisfaction with the personal composition of the central bodies, a fig leaf. . . . You are a bureaucrat because you were appointed by the congress not by my will, but against it; you are a formalist because you rely on the formal decisions of the congress, and not on my consent; you are acting in a grossly mechanical way because you plead the 'mechanical' majority at the Party Congress and pay no heed to my wish to be co-opted; you are an autocrat because you refuse to hand over the power to the old gang."*

* The "gang" here referred to is that of Axelrod, Martov, Potresov

3) *The Party as the highest form of class organisation of the proletariat.* The Party is the organised detachment of the working class. But the Party is not the only organisation of the working class. The proletariat has also a number of other organisations, without which it cannot wage a successful struggle against capital: trade unions, co-operatives, factory organisations, parliamentary groups, non-Party women's associations, the press, cultural and educational organisations, youth leagues, revolutionary fighting organisations (in times of open revolutionary action), Soviets of deputies as the form of state organisation (if the proletariat is in power), etc. The overwhelming majority of these organisations are non-Party, and only some of them adhere directly to the Party, or constitute offshoots from it. All these organisations, under certain conditions, are absolutely necessary for the working class, for without them it would be impossible to consolidate the class positions of the proletariat in the diverse spheres of struggle; for without them it would be impossible to steel the proletariat as the force whose mission it is to replace the bourgeois order by the socialist order. But how can single leadership be exercised with such an abundance of organisations? What guarantee is there that this multiplicity of organisations will not lead to divergency in leadership? It may be said that each of these organisations carries on its work in its own special field, and that therefore these organisations cannot hinder one another. That, of course, is true. But it is also true that all these organisations should work in one direction for they serve *one* class, the class of the proletarians. The question then arises: who is to determine the line, the general direction, along which the work of all these organisations is to be conducted? Where is the central organisation which is not only able, because it has the necessary experience, to work out such a general line, but, in addition, is in a position, because it has sufficient prestige, to induce all these organisations to carry out this line, so as to attain unity of leadership and to make hitches impossible?

That organisation is the Party of the proletariat.

---

and others, who would not submit to the decisions of the Second Congress and who accused Lenin of being a "bureaucrat."—*J. St.*

The Party possesses all the necessary qualifications for this because, in the first place, it is the rallying centre of the finest elements in the working class, who have direct connections with the non-Party organisations of the proletariat and very frequently lead them; because, secondly, the Party, as the rallying centre of the finest members of the working class, is the best school for training leaders of the working class, capable of directing every form of organisation of their class; because, thirdly, the Party, as the best school for training leaders of the working class, is, by reason of its experience and prestige, the only organisation capable of centralising the leadership of the struggle of the proletariat, thus transforming each and every non-Party organisation of the working class into an auxiliary body and transmission belt linking the Party with the class.

The Party is the highest form of class organisation of the proletariat.

This does not mean, of course, that non-Party organisations, trade unions, co-operatives, etc., should be officially subordinated to the Party leadership. It only means that the members of the Party who belong to these organisations and are doubtlessly influential in them should do all they can to persuade these non-Party organisations to draw nearer to the Party of the proletariat in their work and voluntarily accept its political leadership.

That is why Lenin says that the Party is "the *highest* form of proletarian class association," whose political leadership must extend to every other form of organisation of the proletariat.

That is why the opportunist theory of the "independence" and "neutrality" of the non-Party organisations, which breeds *independent* members of parliament and journalists *isolated* from the Party, *narrow-minded* trade union leaders and *philistine* co-operative officials, is wholly incompatible with the theory and practice of Leninism.

4) *The Party as an instrument of the dictatorship of the proletariat.* The Party is the highest form of organisation of the proletariat. The Party is the principal guiding force within the class of the proletarians and among the organisations of that class. But it does not by any means follow from

this that the Party can be regarded as an end in itself, as a self-sufficient force. The Party is not only the highest form of class association of the proletarians; it is at the same time an *instrument* in the hands of the proletariat *for* achieving the dictatorship when that has not yet been achieved and *for* consolidating and expanding the dictatorship when it has already been achieved. The Party could not have risen so high in importance and could not have exerted its influence over all other forms of organisation of the proletariat, if the latter had not been confronted with the question of power, if the conditions of imperialism, the inevitability of wars, and the existence of a crisis had not demanded the concentration of all the forces of the proletariat at one point, the gathering of all the threads of the revolutionary movement in one spot in order to overthrow the bourgeoisie and to achieve the dictatorship of the proletariat. The proletariat needs the Party first of all as its General Staff, which it must have for the successful seizure of power. It scarcely needs proof that without a party capable of rallying around itself the mass organisations of the proletariat, and of centralising the leadership of the entire movement during the progress of the struggle, the proletariat in Russia could not have established its revolutionary dictatorship.

But the proletariat needs the Party not only to achieve the dictatorship; it needs it still more to maintain the dictatorship, to consolidate and expand it in order to achieve the complete victory of socialism.

> "Certainly, almost everyone now realises," says Lenin, "that the Bolsheviks could not have maintained themselves in power for two-and-a-half months, let alone two-and-a-half years, without the strictest, truly iron discipline in our Party, and without the fullest and unreserved support of the latter by the whole mass of the working class, that is, by all its thinking, honest, self-sacrificing and influential elements, capable of leading or of carrying with them the backward strata."

Now, what does to "maintain" and "expand" the dictatorship mean? It means imbuing the millions of proletarians with the spirit of discipline and organisation; it means creating among the proletarian masses a cementing force and a bulwark against the corrosive influences of the petty-bourgeois elemental forces and petty-bourgeois habits; it means enhancing the organising work of the proletarians in re-educating and remoulding the petty-bourgeois strata; it means helping the masses of the proletarians to educate themselves as a force capable of abolishing classes and of preparing the conditions for the organisation of socialist production. But it is impossible to accomplish all this without a party which is strong by reason of its solidarity and discipline.

> "The dictatorship of the proletariat," says Lenin, "is a stubborn struggle—bloody and bloodless, violent and peaceful, military and economic, educational and administrative —against the forces and traditions of the old society. The force of habit of millions and tens of millions is a most terrible force. Without an iron party tempered in the struggle, without a party enjoying the confidence of all that is honest in the given class, without a party capable of watching and influencing the mood of the masses, it is impossible to conduct such a struggle successfully."

The proletariat needs the Party *for* the purpose of achieving and maintaining the dictatorship. The Party is an instrument of the dictatorship of the proletariat.

But from this it follows that when classes disappear and the dictatorship of the proletariat withers away, the Party also will wither away.

5) *The Party as the embodiment of unity of will, unity incompatible with the existence of factions.* The achievement and maintenance of the dictatorship of the proletariat is impossible without a party which is strong by reason of its solidarity and iron discipline. But iron discipline in the Party is inconceivable without unity of will, without complete and absolute unity of action on the part of all members of the Party. This does not mean, of course, that the possibility of conflicts of opinion within the Party is thereby precluded. On the contrary, iron discipline does not preclude but presupposes criticism and conflict of opinion within the Party.

Least of all does it mean that discipline must be "blind." On the contrary, iron discipline does not preclude but presupposes conscious and voluntary submission, for only conscious discipline can be truly iron discipline. But after a conflict of opinion has been closed, after criticism has been exhausted and a decision has been arrived at, unity of will and unity of action of all Party members are the necessary conditions without which neither Party unity nor iron discipline in the Party is conceivable.

> "In the present epoch of acute civil war," says Lenin, "the Communist Party will be able to perform its duty only if it is organised in the most centralised manner, if iron discipline bordering on military discipline prevails in it, and if its Party centre is a powerful and authoritative organ, wielding wide powers and enjoying the universal confidence of the members of the Party."

This is the position in regard to discipline in the Party in the period of struggle preceding the achievement of the dictatorship.

The same, but to an even greater degree, must be said about discipline in the Party after the dictatorship has been achieved.

> "Whoever," says Lenin, "weakens in the least the iron discipline of the Party of the proletariat (especially during the time of its dictatorship), actually aids the bourgeoisie against the proletariat."

But from this it follows that the existence of factions is compatible neither with the Party's unity nor with its iron discipline. It scarcely needs proof that the existence of factions leads to the existence of a number of centres, and the existence of a number of centres means the absence of one common centre in the Party, the breaking up of unity of will, the weakening and disintegration of discipline, the weakening and disintegration of the dictatorship. Of course, the parties of the Second International, which are fighting against the dictatorship of the proletariat and have no desire to lead the proletarians to power, can afford such liberalism as freedom of factions, for they have no need at all for iron discipline. But the parties of the Communist International, whose activities are conditioned by the task of achieving and consolidating the dictatorship of the proletariat, cannot afford to be "liberal" or to permit freedom of factions.

The Party represents unity of will, which precludes all factionalism and division of authority in the Party.

Hence Lenin's warning about the "danger of factionalism from the point of view of Party unity and of effecting the unity of will of the vanguard of the proletariat as the fundamental condition for the success of the dictatorship of the proletariat," which is embodied in the special resolution of the Tenth Congress of our Party "On Party Unity."

Hence Lenin's demand for the "complete elimination of all factionalism" and the "immediate dissolution of all groups, without exception, that have been formed on the basis of various platforms," on pain of "unconditional and immediate expulsion from the Party." (See the resolution "On Party Unity.")

6) *The Party becomes strong by purging itself of opportunist elements.* The source of factionalism in the Party is its opportunist elements. The proletariat is not an isolated class. It is constantly replenished by the influx of peasants, petty bourgeois and intellectuals proletarianised by the development of capitalism. At the same time the upper stratum of the proletariat, principally trade union leaders and members of parliament who are fed by the bourgeoisie out of the super-profits extracted from the colonies, is undergoing a process of decay. "This stratum of bourgeoisified workers, or the 'labour aristocracy,'" says Lenin, "who are quite philistine in their mode of life, in the size of their earnings and in their entire outlook, is the principal prop of the Second International, and, in our days, the principal *social* (not military) *prop of the bourgeoisie*. For they are real *agents of the bourgeoisie in the working-class* movement, the labour lieutenants of the capitalist class . . . , real channels of reformism and chauvinism."

In one way or another, all these petty-bourgeois groups penetrate into the Party and introduce into it the spirit of hesitancy and opportunism, the spirit of demoralisation and uncertainty. It is they, principally, that constitute the source of factionalism and disintegration, the source of disorganisation and disruption of the Party from within. To fight imperialism with such "allies" in one's rear means to put oneself in the position of being caught between two fires, from the front and from the rear. Therefore, ruthless struggle against such elements, their expulsion from the Party, is a prerequisite for the successful struggle against imperialism.

The theory of "defeating" opportunist elements by ideological struggle within the Party, the theory of "overcoming" these elements within the confines of a single party, is a rotten and dangerous theory, which threatens to condemn the Party to paralysis and chronic infirmity, threatens to make the Party a prey to opportunism, threatens to leave the proletariat without a revolutionary party, threatens to deprive the proletariat of its main weapon in the fight against imperialism. Our Party could not have emerged on to the broad highway, it could not have seized power and organised the dictatorship of the proletariat, it could not have emerged victorious from the civil war, if it had had within its ranks people like Martov and Dan, Potresov and Axelrod. Our Party succeeded in achieving internal unity and unexampled cohesion of its ranks primarily because it was able in good time to purge itself of the opportunist pollution, because it was able to rid its ranks of the Liquidators and Mensheviks. Proletarian parties develop and become strong by purging themselves of opportunists and reformists, social-imperialists and social-chauvinists, social-patriots and social-pacifists.

The Party becomes strong by purging itself of opportunist elements.

> "With reformists, Mensheviks, in our ranks," says Lenin, "it is *impossible* to be victorious in the proletarian revolution, it is *impossible* to defend it. That is obvious in principle, and it has been strikingly confirmed by the experience of both Russia and Hungary. . . . In Russia, difficult situations have arisen *many times*, when the Soviet regime would *most certainly* have been overthrown had Mensheviks, reformists and petty-bourgeois democrats re-

mained in our Party. . . . In Italy, where, as is generally admitted, decisive battles between the proletariat and the bourgeoisie for the possession of state power are imminent. At such a moment it is not only absolutely necessary to remove the Mensheviks, reformists, the Turatists from the Party, but it may even be useful to remove excellent Communists who are liable to waver, and who reveal a tendency to waver towards 'unity' with the reformists, to remove them from all responsible posts. . . . On the eve of a revolution, and at a moment when a most fierce struggle is being waged for its victory, the slightest wavering in the ranks of the Party may *wreck everything*, frustrate the revolution, wrest the power from the hands of the proletariat; for this power is not yet consolidated, the attack upon it is still very strong. The desertion of wavering leaders at such a time does not weaken but strengthens the Party, the working-class movement and the revolution."

IX. STYLE IN WORK

I am not referring to literary style. What I have in mind is style in work, that specific and peculiar feature in the practice of Leninism which creates the special type of Leninist worker. Leninism is a school of theory and practice which trains a special type of Party and state worker, creates a special Leninist style in work.

What are the characteristic features of this style? What are its peculiarities?

It has two specific features:

a) Russian revolutionary sweep and

b) American efficiency.

The style of Leninism consists in combining these two specific features in Party and state work.

Russian revolutionary sweep is an antidote to inertia, routine, conservatism, mental stagnation and slavish submission to ancient traditions. Russian revolutionary sweep is the life-giving force which stimulates thought, impels things forward, breaks the past and opens up perspectives. Without it no progress is possible.

But Russian revolutionary sweep has every chance of degenerating in practice into empty "revolutionary" Manilovism if it is not combined with American efficiency in work. Examples of this degeneration are only too numerous. Who does not know the disease of "revolutionary" scheme concocting and "revolutionary" plan drafting, which springs from the belief in the power of decrees to arrange everything and re-make everything? A Russian writer, I. Ehrenburg, in his story *The Percomman* (*The Perfect Communist Man*), has portrayed the type of a "Bolshevik" afflicted with this disease, who set himself the task of finding a formula for the ideally perfect man and . . . became "submerged" in this "work." The story contains a great exaggeration, but it certainly gives a correct likeness of the disease. But no one, I think, has so ruthlessly and bitterly ridiculed those afflicted with this disease as Lenin. Lenin stigmatised this morbid belief in concocting schemes and in turning out decrees as "communist vainglory."

> "Communist vainglory," says Lenin, "means that a man, who is a member of the Communist Party, and has not yet been purged from it, imagines that he can solve all his problems by issuing communist decrees."

Lenin usually contrasted hollow "revolutionary" phrasemongering with plain everyday work, thus emphasising that "revolutionary" scheme concocting is repugnant to the spirit and the letter of true Leninism.

> "Fewer pompous phrases, more plain, *everyday* work . . ." says Lenin.
>
> "Less political fireworks and more attention to the simplest but vital . . . facts of communist construction. . . ."

American efficiency, on the other hand, is an antidote to "revolutionary" Manilovism and fantastic scheme concocting. American efficiency is that indomitable force which neither knows nor recognises obstacles; which with its business-like perseverance brushes aside all obstacles; which continues at a task once started until it is finished, even if it is a minor task; and without which serious constructive work is inconceivable.

But American efficiency has every chance of degenerating into narrow and unprincipled practicalism if it is not combined with Russian revolutionary sweep. Who has not heard of that disease of narrow empiricism and unprincipled practicalism which has not infrequently caused certain "Bolsheviks" to degenerate and to abandon the cause of the revolution? We find a reflection of this peculiar disease in a story by B. Pilnyak, entitled *The Barren Year*, which depicts types of Russian "Bolsheviks" of strong will and practical determination who "function" very "energetically," but without vision, without knowing "what it is all about," and who, therefore, stray from the path of revolutionary work. No one has ridiculed this disease of practicalism so incisively as Lenin. He branded it as "narrow-minded empiricism" and "brainless practicalism." He usually contrasted it with vital revolutionary work and the necessity of having a revolutionary perspective in all our daily activities, thus emphasising that this unprincipled practicalism is as repugnant to true Leninism as "revolutionary" scheme concocting.

The combination of Russian revolutionary sweep with American efficiency is the essence of Leninism in Party and state work.

This combination alone produces the finished type of Leninist worker, the style of Leninism in work.

1924

CONCERNING THE QUESTION OF THE PROLETARIAT AND THE PEASANTRY[1]

Comrades, I should like to say a few words about the principles underlying the policy which the Party has now adopted towards the peasantry. That the question of the peasantry is particularly important at the present time there can be no doubt. Many comrades have gone to extremes and even say that a new era has begun—the peasant era. Others have begun to interpret the slogan "face to the countryside" as meaning that we must turn our backs on the towns. Some have even gone to the length of talking about a political NEP. That is nonsense, of course. All that means going to extremes, of course. If, however, we put those extremes aside, one thing

[1] Speech delivered by Stalin to a Moscow Party conference, January 27, 1925.

In the early 1920s, with much of the economy ruined by the Civil War, massive famines swept through the Soviet Union. Serious peasant rebellions broke out, particularly in Stalin's native land of Georgia. Stalin's policy toward the peasantry was to be the basis for the gradual collectivization and mechanization of agriculture.

Here Stalin speaks to the main difference with Trotsky on internal policy. Trotsky believed the proletariat to be the only revolutionary class. Hence he saw the industrial proletariat of Western Europe as the only ally that could immediately come to the aid of the Soviet workers. Stalin, on the other hand, saw that the industrial proletariat of Western Europe was not yet ready to make a revolution and that the Soviet workers would have to look to the Soviet peasants as their main immediate ally.

Stalin also avoids the opposite extreme: seeing the Russian revolution as peasant rather than proletarian. This idea had been very powerful during the late-nineteenth century, when many revolutionary intellectuals looked with romantic eyes to the countryside as a base for a kind of utopian communism. The difficulties of building heavy industry in Russia helped revive this notion.

remains, namely, that at the present time, particularly just now, the question of the peasantry acquires exceptional importance.

Why? What is the reason?

There are two reasons for it. I am speaking of fundamental reasons.

The first reason why the peasant question has assumed exceptional importance for us at the present moment is that, of the allies of the Soviet power, of all the proletariat's principal allies—of whom there are four, in my opinion—the peasantry is the only ally that can be of direct assistance to our revolution *at this very moment*. It is a question of direct assistance just now, at the present moment. All the other allies, while they will be of great importance in the future and while they constitute an immense reserve for our revolution, nevertheless, unfortunately, cannot render our regime, our state, direct assistance now.

What are these allies?

The first ally, our principal ally, is the proletariat in the developed countries. The advanced proletariat, the proletariat in the West, is an immense force, and it is the most faithful and most important ally of our revolution and our regime. But, unfortunately, the situation, the state of the revolutionary movement in the developed capitalist countries, is such that the proletariat in the West is unable to render us direct and decisive assistance at the present moment. We have its indirect, moral support, and this is so important that its value cannot even be measured, it is inestimable. Nevertheless, it does not constitute that direct and immediate assistance that we need now.

The second ally is the colonies, the oppressed peoples in the under-developed countries, which are oppressed by the more developed countries. Comrades, they constitute an immense reserve for our revolution. But they are very slow in getting into their stride. They are coming directly to our help, but it is evident that they will not arrive quickly. For that very reason they are unable to render us direct and immediate assistance in our work of socialist construction, of strengthening the Soviet regime, of building our socialist economy.

We have a third ally, intangible, impersonal, but for all

that an extremely important one, namely, the conflicts and contradictions between the capitalist countries; they cannot be personified, but they certainly render our regime and our revolution very great support. That may seem strange, comrades, but it is a fact. Had the two chief coalitions of capitalist countries not been engaged in mortal combat during the imperialist war in 1917, had they not been clutching at each other's throats, had they not been busy with their own affairs and unable to spare time to wage a struggle against the Soviet power, it is doubtful whether the Soviet power would have survived. The struggle, conflicts and wars between our enemies, I repeat, constitute an extremely important ally for us. But what is the situation with regard to this ally? The situation is that world capital after the war, after passing through several crises, has begun to recover. That must be admitted. The chief victor countries—Britain and America—have now acquired such strength that they have the material possibility not only of putting capital's affairs in more or less tolerable order at home, but also of infusing new blood into France, Germany and other capitalist countries. That is one aspect of the matter. And as a result of that aspect of the matter, the contradictions between the capitalist countries are, for the time being, not developing with the same intensity as was the case immediately after the war. That is a gain for capital, and a loss for us. But this process has also another aspect, a reverse side. The reverse side is that, notwithstanding the relative stability which capital has been able to create for the time being, the contradictions at the other end of the interrelations, the contradictions between the exploiting advanced countries and the exploited backward countries, the colonies and dependent countries, are becoming sharper and deeper and are threatening to disrupt capital's "work" from a new and "unexpected" end. The crisis in Egypt and in the Sudan —you have probably read about it in the newspapers—also a number of key points of contradiction in China, which may set the present "allies" at loggerheads and wreck the strength of capital, a new series of key points of contradiction in North Africa, where Spain is losing Morocco, towards which France is stretching out her hands, but which she will be unable to take because Britain will not permit France to gain control over Gibraltar—all these are facts which are in many ways reminiscent of the pre-war period and which are bound to imperil the "constructive work" of international capital.

Such are the gains and losses in the total balance-sheet of the development of contradictions. But as, for the time being, capital's gains in this sphere are bigger than its losses, and as there are no grounds for expecting that armed conflicts between the capitalists will break out in the immediate future, it is evident that the situation as regards our third ally is still not what we would like it to be.

There remains the fourth ally—the peasantry. It is by our side, we are living together, together we are building the new life; well or ill, we are building together. As you yourselves are aware, this ally is not a very staunch one; the peasantry is not as reliable an ally as the proletariat in the developed capitalist countries. But, for all that, it is an ally, and of all our existing allies it is the only one that can render us, and is rendering us, direct assistance at this very moment, receiving our assistance in exchange.

That is why, particularly at the present moment, when the course of development of revolutionary and all other crises has slowed down somewhat, the question of the peasantry acquires exceptional importance.

Such is the first reason for the exceptional importance of the peasant question.

The second reason for our making the question of the peasantry the corner-stone of our policy at the present moment is that our industry, which is the basis of socialism and the basis of our regime, rests on the home market, the peasant market. I do not know what the situation will be when our industry develops to the full, when we are able to cope with the home market, and when we are faced with the question of winning foreign markets. We shall be faced with that question in the future, you can have no doubt about that. It is doubtful whether we shall be able in the future to count on capturing foreign markets in the West from capital, which is more experienced than we are. But as regards markets in the East, our relations with which cannot be considered bad—and they will improve still further—here we shall find more favourable conditions. There can be no doubt that textile goods, means of defence, machinery, and so forth, will be the principal commodities with which we shall supply the East in competition with the capitalists. But that concerns the future of our industry. As for the present, when we have not yet fully utilised even a third of our peasant market, at the present moment, the chief question that faces us is that of the home market, and above all the peasant market. The fact that the peasant market is at the present moment the chief basis of our industry is precisely the reason why we, as the government, and we, as the proletariat, are interested in improving to the utmost the condition of peasant economy, in improving the material conditions of the peasantry, in raising the purchasing power of the peasantry, in improving the relations between the proletariat and the peasantry, in establishing that bond which Lenin spoke about, but which we have not yet established properly.

That is the second reason why we, as the Party, must put the question of the peasantry in the forefront at the present moment, why we must devote special attention and special care to the peasantry.

Such are the premises of our Party's policy in regard to the peasantry.

The whole trouble, comrades, is that many of our comrades do not understand, or do not want to understand, how extremely important this question is.

It is often said: our leaders in Moscow have made it the fashion to talk about the peasantry; probably, they don't mean it seriously, it is diplomacy. Moscow needs these speeches to be made for the outside world, but we can continue the old policy. That is what some say. Others say that the talk about the peasantry is just talk. If the Moscow people did not stick in their offices, but were to visit the countryside, they would see what the peasants are, and how the taxes are collected. That is the sort of talk one hears. I think, comrades, that of all the dangers that face us, this failure of our local responsible workers to understand the tasks before us is the most serious danger.

One thing or the other:

Either our local comrades will realise how very serious the question of the peasantry is, in which case they will really set about drawing the peasantry into our constructive work, improving peasant economy and strengthening the bond; or the comrades will fail to realise it, in which case things may end in the collapse of the Soviet power.

Let not the comrades think that I am trying to frighten somebody. No, comrades, there would be no sense in trying to frighten anybody. The question is too serious, and it must be dealt with in a way that befits serious people.

On arriving in Moscow, comrades often try to show the "right side of the cloth," saying that all is well in the countryside where they are. This official optimism is sometimes sickening, for it is obvious that all is not well, nor can it be. Obviously, there are defects, which must be exposed without fear of criticism, and then eliminated. The issue is as follows: either we, the entire Party, allow the non-Party peasants and workers to criticise us, or we shall be criticised by means of revolts. The revolt in Georgia was criticism. The revolt in Tambov was also criticism. The revolt in Kronstadt—was not that criticism? One thing or the other: either we abandon this official optimism and official approach to the matter, do not fear criticism and allow ourselves to be criticised by the non-Party workers and peasants, who, after all, are the ones to feel the effects of our mistakes, or we do not do this, and discontent will accumulate and grow, and we shall have criticism in the form of revolts.

The greatest danger now is that many of our comrades fail to understand this specific feature of the present situation.

Has this question—the question of the peasantry—any connection with the question of Trotskyism, which you have discussed here? Undoubtedly it has.

What is Trotskyism?

Trotskyism is disbelief in the forces of our revolution, disbelief in the alliance between the workers and peasants, disbelief in the bond. What is our principal task at the present time? In the words of Ilyich, it is to convert NEP Russia into socialist Russia. Can this task be carried out if the bond is not established? No, it cannot. Can the bond, the alliance between the workers and peasants, be established if the theory which involves disbelief in that alliance, i.e., the theory of Trotskyism, is not smashed? No, it cannot. The conclusion is obvious: whoever wants to emerge from NEP as the victor must bury Trotskyism as an ideological trend.

Before the revolution in October, Ilyich would often say that of all our ideological opponents the most dangerous were the Mensheviks, for they were trying to instil disbelief in the victory of the October Revolution. Therefore, he said, the victory of October could not be achieved unless Menshevism was smashed. I think that there is some analogy between Menshevism at that time, in the period of October, and Trotskyism at the present time, in the period of NEP. I think that of all the ideological trends in communism today, after the victory of October, under the present conditions of NEP, Trotskyism must be regarded as the most dangerous, for it tries to instil disbelief in the forces of our revolution, disbelief in the alliance of the workers and peasants, disbelief in the work of converting NEP Russia into socialist Russia. Therefore, unless Trotskyism is smashed, it will be impossible to achieve victory under the conditions of NEP, it will be impossible to achieve the conversion of present-day Russia into socialist Russia.

Such is the connection between the Party's policy towards the peasantry and Trotskyism.

1925

NOTES ON CONTEMPORARY THEMES: CHINA[1]

Now that the revolution in China has entered a new phase of development, we can to some extent sum up the path already travelled and proceed to verify the line of the Comintern in China.

There are certain tactical principles of Leninism, without due regard for which there can be neither correct leadership of the revolution, nor verification of the Comintern's line in China. These principles have been forgotten by our opponents long ago. But just because the opposition suffers from forgetfulness, it has to be reminded of them again and again.

I have in mind such tactical principles of Leninism as:

a) the principle that the nationally peculiar and nationally specific features in each separate country must unfailingly be taken into account by the Comintern when drawing up guiding directives for the working-class movement of the country concerned;

b) the principle that the Communist Party of each

[1] Article in *Pravda*, July 28, 1927.

This article appeared at a crucial moment in the Chinese revolution. Chiang Kai-shek's forces had just broken the alliance with the Communists and begun the massacre of Communists and other workers in Canton and Shanghai. To many, it seemed that the revolution had been decisively defeated. But just as Stalin here argues, it was precisely this betrayal that could make it possible for the Communists themselves to lead the workers and peasants and establish the first revolutionary bases. A month after this article appeared, Mao Tse-tung led the Autumn Harvest Uprising and created the first units of the Red Army.

Stalin here outlines the basic theory for the Chinese revolution: a united front led by the workers, relying on the peasant masses, and rallying all who would oppose the three major forms of oppression—foreign imperialism, feudalism, and bureaucrat-capitalism. This was the theory adopted by Mao, who acknowledged Stalin as his teacher.

country must unfailingly avail itself of even the smallest opportunity of gaining a mass ally for the proletariat, even if a temporary, vacillating, unstable and unreliable ally;

c) the principle that unfailing regard must be paid to the truth that propaganda and agitation alone are not enough for the political education of the vast masses, that what is required for that is the political experience of the masses themselves.

I think that due regard for these tactical principles of Leninism is an essential condition, without which a Marxist verification of the Comintern's line in the Chinese revolution is impossible.

Let us examine the questions of the Chinese revolution in the light of these tactical principles.

Notwithstanding the ideological progress of our Party, there are still, unfortunately, "leaders" of a sort in it who sincerely believe that the revolution in China can be directed, so to speak, by telegraph, on the basis of the universally recognised general principles of the Comintern, *disregarding* the national peculiarities of China's economy, political system, culture, manners and customs, and traditions. What, in fact, distinguishes these "leaders" from real leaders is that they always have in their pockets two or three ready-made formulas, "suitable" for all countries and "obligatory" under all conditions. The necessity of taking into account the nationally peculiar and nationally specific features of each country does not exist for them. Nor does the necessity exist for them of co-ordinating the general principles of the Comintern with the national peculiarities of the revolutionary movement in each country, the necessity of adapting these general principles to the national peculiarities of the state in each country.

They do not understand that the chief task of leadership, now that the Communist Parties have grown and become mass parties, is to discover, to grasp, the nationally peculiar features of the movement in each country and skilfully co-ordinate them with the Comintern's general principles, in order to facilitate and make feasible the basic aims of the Communist movement.

Hence the attempts to stereotype the leadership for all countries. Hence the attempts mechanically to implant certain general formulas, regardless of the concrete conditions of the movement in different countries. Hence the endless conflicts between the formulas and the revolutionary movement in the different countries, as the main outcome of the leadership of these pseudo-leaders.

It is precisely to this category of pseudo-leaders that our oppositionists belong.

The opposition has heard that a bourgeois revolution is taking place in *China.* It knows, furthermore, that the bourgeois revolution in *Russia* took place in opposition to the bourgeoisie. Hence the ready-made formula for *China:* down with all joint action with the bourgeoisie, long live the immediate withdrawal of the Communists from the Kuomintang (April 1926).

But the opposition has forgotten that, unlike the Russia of 1905, China is a semi-colonial country oppressed by imperialism; that, in consequence of this, the revolution in China is not simply a bourgeois revolution, but a bourgeois revolution of an anti-imperialist type; that, in China, imperialism controls the principal threads of industry, trade and transport; that imperialist oppression affects not only the Chinese labouring masses, but also certain sections of the Chinese bourgeoisie; and that, in consequence, the Chinese bourgeoisie may, under certain conditions and for a certain period, support the Chinese revolution.

And that, as we know, is in fact what occurred. If we take the Canton period of the Chinese revolution, the period when the national armies had reached the Yangtse, the period prior to the split in the Kuomintang, it has to be admitted that the Chinese bourgeoisie supported the revolution in China, that the Comintern's line that joint action with this bourgeoisie is permissible for a certain period and under certain conditions proved to be absolutely correct.

The result is the retreat of the opposition from its old formula and its proclamation of a "new" formula, namely, joint action with the Chinese bourgeoisie is essential, the Communists must not withdraw from the Kuomintang (April 1927).

That was the first punishment that befell the opposition for refusing to take into account the national peculiarities of the Chinese revolution.

The opposition has heard that the Peking government is squabbling with the representatives of the imperialist states over the question of customs autonomy for China. The opposition knows that it is primarily the Chinese capitalists that need customs autonomy. Hence the ready-made formula: the Chinese revolution is a national, anti-imperialist revolution, because its chief aim is to win customs autonomy for China.

But the opposition has forgotten that the strength of imperialism in China does not lie mainly in the customs restrictions in China, but in the fact that it owns mills, factories, mines, railways, steamships, banks and trading firms in that country, which suck the blood of the millions of Chinese workers and peasants.

The opposition has forgotten that the revolutionary struggle of the Chinese people against imperialism is due first and foremost to the fact that imperialism in China is the force that supports and inspires the immediate exploiters of the Chinese people—the feudal lords, militarists, capitalists, bureaucrats, etc.—and that the Chinese workers and peasants cannot defeat their exploiters without at the same time waging a revolutionary struggle against imperialism.

The opposition forgets that it is precisely this circumstance that is one of the major factors making possible the growing over of the bourgeois revolution in China into a socialist revolution.

The opposition forgets that anyone who declares that the Chinese anti-imperialist revolution is a revolution for customs autonomy denies the possibility of the growing over of the bourgeois revolution in China into a socialist revolution, for he places the revolution under the leadership of the Chinese bourgeoisie.

And, indeed, the facts have since shown that customs autonomy is in essence the platform of the Chinese bourgeoisie, because even such inveterate reactionaries as Chang Tso-lin and Chiang Kai-shek now declare in favour of the abolition of the unequal treaties and the establishment of customs autonomy in China.

Hence the opposition's divided stand, its attempts to wriggle out of its own formula about customs autonomy, its surreptitious attempts to renounce this formula and to hitch on to the

Comintern's stand that the growing over of the bourgeois revolution in China into a socialist revolution is possible.

That was the second punishment that befell the opposition for refusing to make a serious study of the national peculiarities of the Chinese revolution.

The opposition has heard that the merchant bourgeoisie has penetrated the Chinese countryside, leasing land to poor peasants. The opposition knows that the merchant is not a feudal lord. Hence the ready-made formula: feudal survivals, hence also the struggle of the peasantry against feudal survivals, are of no serious importance in the Chinese revolution, and that the chief thing in China today is not the agrarian revolution, but the question of China's state-customs dependence on the imperialist countries.

The opposition, however, fails to see that the specific feature of China's economy is not the penetration of merchant capital into the countryside, but a combination of the *domination* of feudal survivals with the existence of merchant capital in the Chinese countryside, *along with the preservation* of medieval feudal methods of exploiting and oppressing the peasantry.

The opposition fails to understand that the entire military-bureaucratic machine which today so inhumanly robs and oppresses the Chinese peasantry is essentially a political superstructure on this combination of the *domination* of feudal survivals and feudal methods of exploitation with the existence of merchant capital in the countryside.

And, indeed, the facts have since shown that a gigantic agrarian revolution has developed in China, directed first and foremost against the Chinese feudal lords, big and small.

The facts have shown that this revolution embraces tens of millions of peasants and is tending to spread over the whole of China.

The facts have shown that feudal lords—real feudal lords of flesh and blood—not only exist in China, but wield power in a number of provinces, dictate their will to the military commanders, subordinate the Kuomintang leadership to their influence, and strike blow after blow at the Chinese revolution.

To deny, after this, the existence of feudal survivals and a feudal system of exploitation as the main form of oppression in the Chinese countryside, to refuse to recognise that the agrarian revolution is the main factor in the Chinese revolutionary movement at the present time, would be flying in the face of obvious facts.

Hence the opposition's retreat from its old formula regarding feudal survivals and the agrarian revolution. Hence the opposition's attempt to slink away from its old formula and tacitly to recognise the correctness of the Comintern's position.

That is the third punishment which has befallen the opposition for its unwillingness to take into account the national peculiarities of China's economy.

And so on and so forth.

Disharmony between formulas and reality—such is the lot of the oppositionist pseudo-leaders.

And this disharmony is a direct result of the opposition's repudiation of the well-known tactical principle of Leninism that the nationally peculiar and nationally specific features in the revolutionary movement of each separate country must unfailingly be taken into account.

Here is how Lenin formulates this principle:

> "The whole point now is that the Communists of every country should quite consciously take into account both the main fundamental tasks of the struggle against opportunism and 'Left' doctrinairism and the *specific features* which this struggle assumes and inevitably must assume in each separate country in conformity with the peculiar features of its economics, politics, culture, national composition (Ireland, etc.), its colonies, religious divisions, and so on and so forth. Everywhere it is felt that dissatisfaction with the Second International is spreading and growing, both because of its opportunism and because of its inability, or incapacity, to create a really centralised, really leading, centre capable of directing the international tactics of the revolutionary proletariat in its struggle for a world Soviet republic. We must clearly realise that *such a leading centre cannot under any circumstances be built up on stereotyped, mechanically equalised and identical tactical rules of strug-*

> *gle.** As long as national and state differences exist among peoples and countries—and these differences will continue to exist for a very long time even after the dictatorship of the proletariat has been established on a world scale—the unity of international tactics of the communist working-class movement of all countries demands, not the elimination of variety, not the abolition of national differences (that is a foolish dream at the present moment), but such an application of the fundamental principles of communism (Soviet power and the dictatorship of the proletariat) as would *correctly modify* these principles in certain *particulars,* correctly adapt and apply them to national and national-state differences. *Investigate, study, seek, divine, grasp that which is nationally peculiar, nationally specific in the concrete manner in which each country approaches the fulfilment of the single international task, in which it approaches the victory over opportunism and Left doctrinairism within the working-class movement, the overthrow of the bourgeoisie, and the establishment of a Soviet republic and a proletarian dictatorship**—such is the main task of the historical period through which all the advanced countries (and not only the advanced countries) are now passing" (see *"Left-Wing" Communism, an Infantile Disorder*).

The line of the Comintern is the line of unfailingly taking this tactical principle of Leninism into account.

The line of the opposition, on the contrary, is the line of repudiating this tactical principle.

In that repudiation lies the root of the opposition's misadventures in the questions of the character and prospects of the Chinese revolution.

* * *

Let us pass to the second tactical principle of Leninism.

Out of the character and prospects of the Chinese revolution there arises the question of the allies of the proletariat in its struggle for the victory of the revolution.

* My italics.—*J. St.*

The question of the allies of the proletariat is one of the main questions of the Chinese revolution. The Chinese proletariat is confronted by powerful enemies: the big and small feudal lords, the military-bureaucratic machine of the old and the new militarists, the counter-revolutionary national bourgeoisie, and the Eastern and Western imperialists, who have seized control of the principal threads of China's economic life and who reinforce their right to exploit the Chinese people by their troops and fleets.

To smash these powerful enemies requires, apart from everything else, a flexible and well-considered policy on the part of the proletariat, the ability to take advantage of every rift in the camp of its enemies, and the ability to find allies, even if they are vacillating and unstable allies, provided that they are *mass* allies, that they *do not restrict* the revolutionary propaganda and agitation of the party of the proletariat, and *do not restrict* the party's work of organising the working class and the labouring masses.

This policy is a fundamental requirement of the second tactical principle of Leninism. Without such a policy, the victory of the proletariat is impossible.

The opposition regards such a policy as incorrect, un-Leninist. But that only indicates that it has shed the last remnants of Leninism, that it is as far from Leninism as heaven is from earth.

Did the Chinese proletariat have such allies in the recent past?

Yes, it did.

In the period of the first stage of the revolution, when it was a revolution of an all-national *united* front (the Canton period), the proletariat's allies were the peasantry, the urban poor, the petty-bourgeois intelligentsia, and the national bourgeoisie.

One of the specific features of the Chinese revolutionary movement is that the representatives of those classes worked jointly with the Communists within a single, bourgeois-revolutionary organisation, called the Kuomintang.

Those allies were not, and could not be, all equally reliable. Some of them were more or less reliable allies (the peasantry, the urban poor), others were less reliable and vacillating (the petty-bourgeois intelligentsia), others again were entirely unreliable (the national bourgeoisie).

At that time the Kuomintang was unquestionably more or less a mass organisation. The policy of the Communists within the Kuomintang consisted in isolating the representatives of the national bourgeoisie (the Rights) and utilising them in the interests of the revolution, in impelling the petty-bourgeois intelligentsia (the Lefts) leftwards, and in rallying the peasantry and the urban poor around the proletariat.

Was Canton at that time the centre of the Chinese revolutionary movement? It certainly was. Only lunatics can deny that now.

What were the achievements of the Communists during that period? Extension of the territory of the revolution, inasmuch as the Canton armies reached the Yangtse; the possibility of openly organising the proletariat (trade unions, strike committees); the formation of the communist organisations into a party; the creation of the first nuclei of peasant organisations (the peasant associations); communist penetration into the army.

It follows that the Comintern's leadership during that period was quite correct.

In the period of the second stage of the revolution, when Chiang Kai-skek and the national bourgeoisie deserted to the camp of counter-revolution, and the centre of the revolutionary movement shifted from Canton to Wuhan, the proletariat's allies were the peasantry, the urban poor, and the petty-bourgeois intelligentsia.

How is the desertion of the national bourgeoisie to the camp of counter-revolution to be explained? By fear of the scope assumed by the revolutionary movement of the workers, in the first place, and, secondly, by the pressure exerted on the national bourgeoisie by the imperialists in Shanghai.

Thus the revolution lost the national bourgeoisie. That was a partial loss for the revolution. But, on the other hand, it entered a higher phase of its development, the phase of agrarian revolution, by bringing the broad masses of the peasantry closer to itself. That was a gain for the revolution.

Was the Kuomintang at that time, in the period of the second stage of the revolution, a mass organisation? It certainly was. It was unquestionably more of a mass organisation than was the Kuomintang of the Canton period.

Was Wuhan at that time the centre of the revolutionary movement? It certainly was. Surely only the blind could deny that now. Otherwise Wuhan's territory (Hupeh, Hunan) would not have been the base for the maximum development of the agrarian revolution, which was led by the Communist Party.

The policy of the Communists towards the Kuomintang at that time was to impel it leftwards and to transform it into the core of a revolutionary-democratic dictatorship of the proletariat and peasantry.

Was such a transformation possible at that time? It was. At any rate, there was no reason to believe such a possibility out of the question. We plainly said at the time that to transform the Wuhan Kuomintang into the core of a revolutionary-democratic dictatorship of the proletariat and peasantry at least two conditions were required: a radical democratisation of the Kuomintang, and direct assistance by the Kuomintang to the agrarian revolution. It would have been foolish for the Communists to have refrained from attempting such a transformation.

What were the achievements of the Communists during that period?

The Communist Party during that period grew from a small party of 5–6 thousand members into a large mass party of 50–60 thousand members.

The workers' trade unions grew into a huge national federation with about three million members.

The primary peasant organisations expanded into huge associations embracing several tens of millions of members. The agrarian movement of the peasantry grew to gigantic proportions and came to occupy the central place in the Chinese revolutionary movement. The Communist Party gained the possibility of openly organising the revolution. The Communist Party became the leader of the agrarian revolution. The hegemony of the proletariat began to change from a wish into a reality.

It is true that the Chinese Communist Party failed to exploit all the possibilities of that period. It is true that during that period the Central Committee of the Chinese Communist Party committed a number of grave errors. But it would be ridiculous to think that the Chinese Communist Party can become a real Bolshevik party at one stroke, so to speak, on the basis of the Comintern's directives. One has only to recall the history of our Party, which passed through a series of splits, secessions, betrayals, treacheries and so forth, to realise that real Bolshevik parties do not come into being at one stroke.

It follows, then, that the Comintern's leadership during that period, too, was quite correct.

Does the Chinese proletariat have allies today?

It does.

These allies are the peasantry and the urban poor.

The present period is marked by the desertion of the Wuhan leadership of the Kuomintang to the camp of counter-revolution, by the desertion of the petty-bourgeois intelligentsia from the revolution.

This desertion is due, firstly, to the fear of the petty-bourgeois intelligentsia in face of the spread of the agrarian revolution and to the pressure of the feudal lords on the Wuhan leadership, and, secondly, to the pressure of the imperialists in the Tientsin area, who are demanding that the Kuomintang break with the Communists as the price for permitting its passage northward.

The opposition has doubts about the existence of feudal survivals in China. But it is now clear to all that not only do feudal survivals exist in China, but that they have proved to be even stronger than the onslaught of the revolution at the present time. And it is because the imperialists and the feudal lords in China have for the time being proved to be stronger that the revolution has sustained a temporary defeat.

On this occasion the revolution has lost the petty-bourgeois intelligentsia.

That indeed is a sign that the revolution has sustained a temporary defeat.

But, on the other hand, it has rallied the broad masses of the peasantry and urban poor more closely around the proletariat, and has thereby created the basis for the hegemony of the proletariat.

That is a gain for the revolution.

The opposition ascribes the temporary defeat of the revolution to the Comintern's policy. But only people who have broken with Marxism can say that. Only people who have broken with Marxism can demand that a correct policy should always and necessarily lead to *immediate* victory over the enemy.

Was the policy of the Bolsheviks in the 1905 Revolution a correct one? Yes, it was. Why, then, did the 1905 Revolution suffer defeat, despite the existence of Soviets, despite the correct policy of the Bolsheviks? Because the feudal survivals and the autocracy proved at that time to be stronger than the revolutionary movement of the workers.

Was the policy of the Bolsheviks in July 1917 a correct one? Yes, it was. Why, then, did the Bolsheviks sustain defeat, again despite the existence of Soviets, which at that time betrayed the Bolsheviks, and despite the correct policy of the Bolsheviks? Because Russian imperialism proved at that time to be stronger than the revolutionary movement of the workers.

A correct policy is by no means bound to lead always and without fail to direct victory over the enemy. Direct victory over the enemy is not determined by correct policy alone; it is determined first and foremost by the correlation of class forces, by a marked preponderance of strength on the side of the revolution, by disintegration in the enemy's camp, by a favourable international situation.

Only given those conditions can a correct policy of the proletariat lead to direct victory.

But there is one obligatory requirement which a correct policy must satisfy always and under all conditions. That requirement is that the party's policy must enhance the fighting capacity of the proletariat, multiply its ties with the labouring masses, increase its prestige among these masses, and convert the proletariat into the hegemon of the revolution.

Can it be affirmed that this past period has presented the maximum favourable conditions for the direct victory of the revolution in China? Clearly, it cannot.

Can it be affirmed that communist policy in China has not enhanced the fighting capacity of the proletariat, has not multiplied its ties with the broad masses, and has not increased its prestige among these masses? Clearly, it cannot.

Only the blind could fail to see that the Chinese proletariat has succeeded in this period in severing the broad mass of the peasantry both from the national bourgeoisie and from the petty-bourgeois intelligentsia, so as to rally them around its own standard.

The Communist Party went through a bloc with the national bourgeoisie in Canton at the first stage of the revolution in order to extend the area of the revolution, to form itself into a mass party, to secure the possibility of openly organising the proletariat, and to open up a road for itself to the peasantry.

The Communist Party went through a bloc with the Kuomintang petty-bourgeois intelligentsia in Wuhan at the second stage of the revolution in order to multiply its forces, to extend the organisation of the proletariat, to sever the broad masses of the peasantry from the Kuomintang leadership, and to create the conditions for the hegemony of the proletariat.

The national bourgeoisie has gone over to the camp of counter-revolution, having lost contact with the broad masses of the people.

The Kuomintang petty-bourgeois intelligentsia in Wuhan has trailed in the wake of the national bourgeoisie, having taken fright at the agrarian revolution and having utterly discredited itself in the eyes of the peasant millions.

On the other hand, however, the vast masses of the peasantry have rallied more closely around the proletariat, seeing in it their only reliable leader and guide.

Is it not clear that only a correct policy could have led to such results?

Is it not clear that only such a policy could have enhanced the fighting capacity of the proletariat?

Who but the pseudo-leaders belonging to our opposition can deny the correctness and revolutionary character of such a policy?

The opposition asserts that the swing of the Wuhan Kuomintang leadership to the side of the counter-revolution indicates that the policy of a bloc with the Wuhan Kuomintang at the second stage of the revolution was incorrect.

But only people who have forgotten the history of Bolshevism and who have shed the last remnants of Leninism can say that.

Was the Bolshevik policy of a revolutionary bloc with the Left Socialist-Revolutionaries in October and after October, down to the spring of 1918, a correct one? I believe that nobody has yet ventured to deny that this bloc was correct. How did this bloc end? With a revolt of the Left Socialist-Revolutionaries against the Soviet government. Can it be affirmed *on these grounds* that the policy of a bloc with the Socialist-Revolutionaries was incorrect? Obviously, it cannot.

Was the policy of a revolutionary bloc with the Wuhan Kuomintang at the second stage of the Chinese revolution a correct one? I believe that nobody has yet ventured to deny that this bloc was correct during the second stage of the revolution. The opposition itself declared at that time (April 1927) that such a bloc was correct. How, then, can it be asserted now, after the Wuhan Kuomintang leadership has deserted the revolution, and because of this desertion, that the revolutionary bloc with the Wuhan Kuomintang was incorrect?

Is it not clear that only spineless people can employ such "arguments"?

Did anyone assert that the bloc with the Wuhan Kuomintang would be eternal and unending? Do such things as eternal and unending blocs exist at all? Is it not clear that the opposition has no understanding, no understanding whatever, of the second tactical principle of Leninism, concerning a revolutionary bloc of the proletariat with non-proletarian classes and groups.

Here is how Lenin formulates this tactical principle:

> "The more powerful enemy can be vanquished only by exerting the utmost effort, and by making, *without fail*, the most thorough, careful, attentive and skilful use both of every, even the smallest, 'rift' among the enemies, every antagonism of interests among the bourgeoisie of the various countries and among the various groups or types of bourgeoisie within individual countries, *as well as of every, even the smallest, opportunity of gaining a mass ally,*

*even though a temporary, vacillating, unstable, unreliable and conditional ally. He who has not understood this, has not understood even a particle of Marxism, or of scientific, modern socialism in general.** He who has not proved by *deeds* over a fairly considerable period of time, and in fairly varied political situations, his ability to apply this truth in practice has not yet learned to assist the revolutionary class in its struggle to emancipate all toiling humanity from the exploiters. And this applies equally to the period before and after the proletariat has conquered political power" (see *"Left-Wing" Communism, an Infantile Disorder*).

Is it not clear that the line of the opposition is the line of repudiating this tactical principle of Leninism?

Is it not clear that the line of the Comintern, on the contrary, is the line of unfailingly taking this tactical principle into account?

* * *

Let us pass to the third tactical principle of Leninism.

This tactical principle concerns the question of change of slogans, the order and methods of such change. It concerns the question how to convert a slogan for the party into a slogan for the masses, how and in what way to bring the masses to the revolutionary positions, so that they may convince themselves by their own political experience of the correctness of the party's slogans.

And the masses cannot be convinced by propaganda and agitation alone. What is required for that is the political experience of the masses themselves. What is required for that is that the broad masses shall come to feel, from painful experience, the inevitability, say, of overthrowing a given system, the inevitability of establishing a new political and social order.

It was a good thing that the advanced group, the Party, had already convinced itself of the inevitability of the overthrow, say, of the Milyukov-Kerensky Provisional Government in April 1917. But that was not yet enough for coming forward

* My italics.—*J. St.*

and advocating the overthrow of that government, for putting forward the slogan of the overthrow of the Provisional Government and the establishment of Soviet power as a *slogan of the day*. In order to convert the formula "All power to the Soviets" from a *perspective* for the immediate future into a *slogan of the day*, into a slogan of immediate action, one other decisive factor was required, namely, that the masses themselves should become convinced of the correctness of this slogan, and should help the Party in one way or another to put it into effect.

A strict distinction must be drawn between a formula as a *perspective* for the immediate future and a formula as a *slogan of the day*. It was precisely on this point that the group of Petrograd Bolsheviks headed by Bagdatyev came to grief in April 1917, when they *prematurely* put forward the slogan "Down with the Provisional Government, all power to the Soviets." Lenin at the time qualified that attempt of the Bagdatyev group as dangerous adventurism and publicly denounced it.

Why?

Because the broad masses of the working people in the rear and at the front were not yet ready to accept that slogan. Because that group confused the formula "All power to the Soviets," as a perspective, with the slogan "All power to the Soviets," as a slogan of the day. Because that group was *running too far ahead*, exposing the Party to the threat of being completely isolated from the broad masses, from the Soviets, which at that time still believed that the Provisional Government was revolutionary.

Should the Chinese Communists have put forward the slogan "Down with the Kuomintang leadership in Wuhan" six months ago, say? No, they should not.

They should not, because that would have been dangerously *running too far ahead*, it would have made it difficult for the Communists to gain access to the broad masses of the working people, who still believed in the Kuomintang leadership; it would have isolated the Communist Party from the broad masses of the peasantry.

They should not, because the Wuhan Kuomintang leadership, the Wuhan Central Committee of the Kuomintang had not yet exhausted its potentialities as a bourgeois-revolutionary government, had not yet disgraced and discredited itself in the eyes of the broad masses of the working people by its fight against the agrarian revolution, by its fight against the working class, and by its swing over to the counter-revolution.

We always said that it would be wrong to adopt the course of discrediting and replacing the Wuhan Kuomintang leadership so long as it had not yet exhausted its potentialities as a bourgeois-revolutionary government; that it should first be allowed to do so before raising in practice the question of replacing it.

Should the Chinese Communists now put forward the slogan "Down with the Kuomintang leadership in Wuhan"? Yes, they certainly should.

Now that the Kuomintang leadership has disgraced itself by its struggle against the revolution and has taken up an attitude of hostility towards the broad masses of the workers and peasants, this slogan will meet with a powerful response among the masses of the people.

Every worker and every peasant will now understand that the Communists acted rightly in withdrawing from the Wuhan government and the Wuhan Central Committee of the Kuomintang, and in putting forward the slogan "Down with the Kuomintang leadership in Wuhan."

For the masses of the peasants and workers are now faced with the choice: *either* the present Kuomintang leadership—which means refusing to satisfy the vital needs of these masses, repudiating the agrarian revolution; *or* agrarian revolution and a radical improvement of the position of the working class—which means that replacing the Kuomintang leadership in Wuhan becomes a slogan of the day for the masses.

Such are the demands of the third tactical principle of Leninism, concerning the question of change of slogans, the question of the ways and means of bringing the broad masses to the new revolutionary positions, the question how, by the policy and actions of the Party and the *timely* replacement of one slogan by another, to help the broad masses of the working people to recognise the correctness of the Party's line on the basis of their own experience.

Here is how Lenin formulates this tactical principle:

"Victory cannot be won with the vanguard alone. To throw the vanguard alone into the decisive battle, before the whole class, before the broad masses have taken up a position either of direct support of the vanguard, or at least of benevolent neutrality towards it, and one in which they cannot possibly support the enemy, would be not merely folly but a crime. *And in order that actually the whole class, that actually the broad masses of the working people and those oppressed by capital may take up such a position, propaganda and agitation alone are not enough. For this the masses must have their own political experience.** Such is the fundamental law of all great revolutions, now confirmed with astonishing force and vividness not only in Russia but also in Germany. Not only the uncultured, often illiterate, masses of Russia, but the highly cultured, entirely literate masses of Germany had to realise through their own painful experience the absolute impotence and spinelessness, the absolute helplessness and servility to the bourgeoisie, the utter vileness, of the government of the knights of the Second International, the absolute inevitability of a dictatorship of the extreme reactionaries (Kornilov in Russia, Kapp and Co. in Germany) as the only alternative to a dictatorship of the proletariat, in order to turn resolutely towards communism. The immediate task that confronts the class-conscious vanguard of the international labour movement, i.e. the Communist Parties, groups and trends, is to be able *to lead* the broad masses (as yet, for the most part, slumbering, apathetic, bound by routine, inert and dormant) to their new position, or, rather, to be able to lead *not only* their own party, but also these masses, in their approach, their transition to the new position" (see *"Left-Wing" Communism, an Infantile Disorder*).

* My italics.—*J. St.*

The basic error of the opposition is that it does not understand the meaning and importance of this tactical principle of Leninism, that it does not recognise it and systematically violates it.

It (Trotskyists) violated this tactical principle at the beginning of 1917, when it attempted to "skip over" the agrarian movement which had not yet been completed (see Lenin).

It (Trotsky-Zinoviev) violated this principle when it attempted to "skip over" the reactionary character of the trade unions, failing to recognise the expediency of Communists working in reactionary trade unions, and denying the necessity for temporary blocs with them.

It (Trotsky-Zinoviev-Radek) violated this principle when it attempted to "skip over" the national peculiarities of the Chinese revolutionary movement (the Kuomintang), the backwardness of the masses of the Chinese people, by demanding, in April 1926, the immediate withdrawal of the Communists from the Kuomintang, and, in April 1927, by putting forward the slogan of immediate organisation of Soviets, at a time when the Kuomintang phase of development had not yet been completed and had not yet outlived its day.

The opposition thinks that if it has understood, has recognised, the half-heartedness, vacillation and unreliability of the Kuomintang leadership, if it has recognised the temporary and conditional character of the bloc with the Kuomintang (and that is not difficult for any competent political worker to recognise), that is quite sufficient to warrant starting "determined action" against the Kuomintang, against the Kuomintang government, quite sufficient to induce the masses, the broad masses of the workers and peasants "at once" to support "us" and "our" "determined action."

The opposition forgets that "our" understanding all this is still very far from enough to enable the Chinese Communists to get the masses to follow them. The opposition forgets that what this also requires is that the masses themselves should recognise from their own experience the unreliable, reactionary and counter-revolutionary character of the Kuomintang leadership.

The opposition forgets that it is not only the advanced

group, not only the party, not only individual, even if "exalted," "personalities," but first and foremost the vast masses of the people, that "make" a revolution.

It is strange that the opposition should forget about the state of the vast masses of the people, about their level of understanding, about their readiness for determined action.

Did we, the Party, Lenin, know in April 1917 that the Milyukov-Kerensky Provisional Government would have to be overthrown, that the existence of the Provisional Government was incompatible with the activity of the Soviets, and that the power would have to pass into the hands of the Soviets? Yes, we did.

Why, then, did Lenin brand as adventurers the group of Petrograd Bolsheviks headed by Bagdatyev in April 1917, when that group put forward the slogan "Down with the Provisional Government, all power to the Soviets," and attempted to overthrow the Provisional Government?

Because the broad masses of the working people, a certain section of the workers, millions of the peasantry, the broad mass of the army and, lastly, the Soviets themselves, were not yet prepared to accept that slogan as a slogan of the day.

Because the Provisional Government and the Socialist-Revolutionary and Menshevik petty-bourgeois parties had not yet exhausted their potentialities, had not yet sufficiently discredited themselves in the eyes of the vast masses of the working people.

Because Lenin knew that the understanding, the political consciousness, of the advanced group of the proletariat, the Party of the proletariat, was not enough by itself for the overthrow of the Provisional Government and the establishment of Soviet power—that this required also that the masses themselves should become convinced of the correctness of this line through their own experience.

Because it was necessary to go through the whole coalition orgy, through the betrayals and treacheries of the petty-bourgeois parties in June, July and August 1917; it was necessary to go through the shameful offensive at the front in June 1917, through the "honest" coalition of the petty-bourgeois parties with the Kornilovs and Milyukovs, through the Kornilov revolt and so on, in order that the vast masses of the working people should become convinced that the overthrow of the Provisional Government and the establishment of Soviet power were unavoidable.

Because only under those circumstances could the slogan of Soviet power be transformed from a slogan that was a *perspective* into a *slogan of the day*.

The trouble with the opposition is that it continually commits the same error as the Bagdatyev group committed in their day, that it abandons Lenin's road and prefers to "march" along the road of Bagdatyev.

Did we, the Party, Lenin, know that the Constituent Assembly was incompatible with the system of Soviet power when we took part in the elections to the Constituent Assembly and when we convened it in Petrograd? Yes, we did.

Why, then, did we convene it? How could it happen that the Bolsheviks, who were enemies of bourgeois parliamentarism and who established Soviet power, not only took part in the elections but even themselves convened the Constituent Assembly? Was this not "khvostism," lagging behind events, "holding the masses in check," violating "long-range" tactics? Of course not.

The Bolsheviks took this step in order to make it easier for the backward masses of the people to convince themselves with their own eyes that the Constituent Assembly was unsuitable, reactionary and counter-revolutionary. Only in that way was it possible to draw to our side the vast masses of the peasantry and make it easier for us to disperse the Constituent Assembly.

Here is what Lenin writes about it:

> "We took part in the elections to the Russian bourgeois parliament, the Constituent Assembly, in September-November 1917. Were our tactics correct or not? . . . Did not we, the Russian Bolsheviks, have more right in September-November 1917 than any Western Communists to consider that parliamentarism was politically obsolete in Russia? Of course we did, for the point is not whether bourgeois parliaments have existed for a long time or a short time, but how far the broad masses of the working

people are *prepared* (ideologically, politically and practically) to accept the Soviet system and to disperse the bourgeois-democratic parliament (or allow it to be dispersed). That in Russia in September-November 1917, owing to a number of special conditions, the urban working class and the soldiers and peasants were exceptionally well prepared to accept the Soviet system and to disperse the most democratic of bourgeois parliaments, is an absolutely incontestable and fully established historical fact. Nevertheless, the Bolsheviks did *not* boycott the Constituent Assembly, but took part in the elections both before the proletariat conquered political power and *after*. . . .

"The conclusion which follows from this is absolutely incontrovertible: it has been proved that participation in a bourgeois-democratic parliament even a few weeks before the victory of a Soviet Republic, and even *after* such a victory, not only does not harm the revolutionary proletariat, but actually helps it to *prove* to the backward masses why such parliaments deserve to be dispersed; it *helps* their successful dispersal, and *helps* to make bourgeois parliamentarism 'politically obsolete'" (see *"Left-Wing" Communism, an Infantile Disorder*).

That is how the Bolsheviks applied the third tactical principle of Leninism in practice.

That is how Bolshevik tactics must be applied in China, whether in relation to the agrarian revolution, or to the Kuomintang, or to the slogan of Soviets.

The opposition is apparently inclined to think that the revolution in China has suffered a complete fiasco. That, of course, is wrong. That the revolution in China has sustained a temporary defeat, of that there can be no doubt. But what sort of defeat, and how profound it is—that is the question now.

It is possible that it will be approximately as prolonged a defeat as was the case in Russia in 1905, when the revolution was interrupted for a full twelve years, only to break out later, in February 1917, with fresh force, sweep away the autocracy, and clear the way for a new, Soviet revolution.

That prospect cannot be considered excluded. It is still

not a complete defeat of the revolution, just as the defeat of 1905 could not be considered a final defeat. It is not a complete defeat, since the basic tasks of the Chinese revolution at the present stage of its development—agrarian revolution, revolutionary unification of China, emancipation from the imperialist yoke—still await their accomplishment. And if this prospect should become a reality, then, of course, there can be no question of the immediate formation of Soviets of workers' and peasants' deputies in China, because Soviets are formed and flourish only in circumstances of revolutionary upsurge.

But that prospect can scarcely be considered a likely one. At all events, there are no grounds so far for considering it likely. There are none, because the counter-revolution is not yet united, and will not be soon, if indeed it is ever destined to be united.

For the war of the old and the new militarists among themselves is flaring up with fresh force and cannot but weaken the counter-revolution, at the same time as it ruins and infuriates the peasantry.

For there is still no group or government in China capable of undertaking something in the nature of a Stolypin reform which might serve the ruling groups as a lightning conductor.

For the millions of the peasantry, who have already begun to lay hands on the landlords' land, cannot be so easily curbed and crushed to the ground.

For the prestige of the proletariat in the eyes of the labouring masses is growing from day to day, and its forces are still very far from having been demolished.

It is possible that the defeat of the Chinese revolution is analogous in degree to that suffered by the Bolsheviks in July 1917, when the Menshevik and Socialist-Revolutionary Soviets betrayed them, when they were forced to go underground, and when, a few months later, the revolution again came out into the streets in order to sweep away the imperialist government of Russia.

The analogy, of course, is a qualified one. I make it with all the necessary reservations, bearing in mind the difference between the situation of China in our day and that of Russia in 1917. I resort to such an analogy only in order to indicate the approximate degree of defeat of the Chinese revolution.

I think that this prospect is the more likely one. And if it should become a reality, if in the near future—not necessarily in a couple of months, but in six months or a year from now—*a new upsurge of the revolution should become a fact*, the question of forming Soviets of workers' and peasants' deputies may become a live issue, as a slogan of the day, and as a counterpoise to the bourgeois government.

Why?

Because, if there is a *new upsurge of the revolution* in its present phase of development, the formation of Soviets will be an issue that has become fully mature.

Recently, a few months ago, it would have been wrong for the Chinese Communists to issue the slogan of forming Soviets, for that would have been adventurism, which is characteristic of our opposition, for the Kuomintang leadership had not yet discredited itself as an enemy of the revolution.

Now, on the contrary, the slogan of forming Soviets may become a really revolutionary slogan, *if* (if!) a new and powerful revolutionary upsurge takes place in the near future.

Consequently, alongside the fight to replace the present Kuomintang leadership by a revolutionary leadership, it is necessary at once, even before the upsurge begins, to conduct the widest propaganda for the idea of Soviets among the broad masses of the working people, without running too far ahead and forming Soviets immediately, remembering that Soviets can flourish only at a time of powerful revolutionary upsurge.

The opposition may say that it said this "first," that this is precisely what it calls "long-range" tactics.

You are wrong, my dear sirs, absolutely wrong! That is not "long-range" tactics; it is haphazard tactics, the tactics of perpetually overshooting and undershooting the mark.

When, in April 1926, the opposition demanded that the Communists should immediately withdraw from the Kuomintang, that was *overshooting* tactics, because the opposition itself was subsequently compelled to admit that the Communists ought to remain in the Kuomintang.

When the opposition declared that the Chinese revolution was a revolution for customs autonomy, that was *undershooting* tactics, because the opposition itself was subsequently compelled to slink away from its own formula.

When, in April 1927, the opposition declared that to talk of feudal survivals in China was an exaggeration, forgetting the existence of the mass agrarian movement, that was *undershooting* tactics, because the opposition itself was subsequently compelled tacitly to admit its error.

When, in April 1927, the opposition issued the slogan of immediate formation of Soviets, that was *overshooting* tactics, because the oppositionists themselves were compelled at the time to admit the contradictions in their own camp, one of them (Trotsky) demanding adoption of the course of overthrowing the Wuhan government, and another (Zinoviev), on the contrary, demanding the "utmost assistance" for this same Wuhan government.

But since when have haphazard tactics, the tactics of perpetually overshooting and undershooting the mark, been called "long-range" tactics?

As to Soviets, it should be said that, long before the opposition, the Comintern in its documents spoke of Soviets in China as a *perspective*. As to Soviets as a *slogan of the day*—put forward by the opposition in the spring of this year as a counterblast to the revolutionary Kuomintang (the Kuomintang was then revolutionary, otherwise there was no point in Zinoviev clamouring for the "utmost assistance" for the Kuomintang)—that was adventurism, vociferous running too far ahead, the same adventurism and the same running too far ahead that Bagdatyev was guilty of in April 1917.

From the fact that the slogan of Soviets may become a slogan of the day in China *in the near future*, it does not by any means follow that it was not dangerous and harmful adventurism on the part of the opposition to put forward the slogan of Soviets in *the spring of this year*.

Just as it by no means follows from the fact that Lenin recognised the slogan "All power to the Soviets" to be necessary and timely in *September* 1917 (the Central Committee's decision on the uprising), that it was not harmful and dangerous adventurism on the part of Bagdatyev to put forward this slogan in *April* 1917.

Bagdatyev, in September 1917, might also have said that he had been the "first" to call for Soviet power, having done so in April 1917. Does this mean that Bagdatyev was right, and that Lenin was wrong in qualifying his action in April 1917 as adventurism?

Apparently, our opposition is envious of Bagdatyev's "laurels."

The opposition does not understand that the point is not at all to be "first" in saying a thing, running too far ahead and disorganising the cause of the revolution, but to say it *at the right time*, and to say it in such a way that it will be taken up by the masses and *put into practice.*

Such are the facts.

The opposition has departed from Leninist tactics, its policy is one of "ultra-Left" adventurism—such is the conclusion.

1927

ORGANISE MASS CRITICISM FROM BELOW[1]

Bureaucracy is one of the worst enemies of our progress. It exists in all our organisations—Party, Y.C.L., trade-union and economic. When people talk of bureaucrats, they usually point to the old non-Party officials, who as a rule are depicted in our cartoons as men wearing spectacles. (*Laughter.*) That is not quite true, comrades. If it were only a question of the old bureaucrats, the fight against bureaucracy would be very easy. The trouble is that it is not a matter of the old bureaucrats. It is a matter of the new bureaucrats, bureaucrats who sympathise with the Soviet Government, and finally, communist bureaucrats. The communist bureaucrat is the most dangerous type of bureaucrat. Why? Because he masks his bureaucracy with the title of Party member. And, unfortunately, we have quite a number of such communist bureaucrats.

Take our Party organisations. You have no doubt read about the Smolensk affair, the Artyomovsk affair and so on. What do you think, were they matters of chance? What is the explanation of these shameful instances of corruption and moral deterioration in certain of our Party organisations? The fact that Party monopoly was carried to absurd lengths, that the voice of the rank and file was stifled, that inner-Party democracy was abolished and bureaucracy became rife. How is this evil to be combated? I think that there is not and cannot be any other way of combating this evil than by organising control from below by the Party masses, by implanting inner-Party democracy. What objection can there be to rousing the fury of the mass of the Party membership

[1] From a speech delivered to the Eighth Congress of the Young Communist League, May 16, 1928.

against these corrupt elements and giving it the opportunity to send such elements packing? There can hardly be any objection to that.

Or take the Young Communist League, for instance. You will not deny, of course, that here and there in the Young Communist League there are utterly corrupt elements against whom it is absolutely essential to wage a ruthless struggle. But let us leave aside the corrupt elements. Let us take the latest fact of an unprincipled struggle waged by groups within the Young Communist League around personalities, a struggle which is poisoning the atmosphere in the Young Communist League. Why is it that you can find as many "Kosarevites" and "Sobolevites" as you like in the Young Communist League, while Marxists have to be looked for with a candle? (*Applause.*) What does this indicate, if not that a process of bureaucratic petrification is taking place in certain sections of the Y.C.L. top leadership?

And the trade unions? Who will deny that in the trade unions there is bureaucracy in plenty? We have production conferences in the factories. We have temporary control commissions in the trade unions. It is the task of these organisations to rouse the masses, to bring our shortcomings to light and to indicate ways and means of improving our constructive work. Why are these organisations not developing? Why are they not seething with activity? Is it not obvious that it is bureaucracy in the trade unions, coupled with bureaucracy in the Party organisations, that is preventing these highly important organisations of the working class from developing?

Lastly, our economic organisations. Who will deny that our economic bodies suffer from bureaucracy? Take the Shakhty affair as an illustration. Does not the Shakhty affair indicate that our economic bodies are not speeding ahead, but crawling, dragging their feet?

How are we to put an end to bureaucracy in all these organisations?

There is only one sole way of doing this, and that is to organise control from below, to organise criticism of the bureaucracy in our institutions, of their shortcomings and their mistakes, by the vast masses of the working class.

I know that by rousing the fury of the masses of the working people against the bureaucratic distortions in our organisations, we sometimes have to tread on the toes of some of our comrades who have past services to their credit, but who are now suffering from the disease of bureaucracy. But ought this to stop our work of organising control from below? I think that it ought not and must not. For their past services we should take off our hats to them, but for their present blunders and bureaucracy it would be quite in order to give them a good drubbing. (*Laughter and applause.*) How else? Why not do this if the interests of the work demand it?

There is talk of criticism from above, criticism by the Workers' and Peasants' Inspection, by the Central Committee of our Party and so on. That, of course, is all very good. But it is still far from enough. More, it is by no means the chief thing now. The chief thing now is to start a broad tide of criticism from below against bureaucracy in general, against shortcomings in our work in particular. Only by organising twofold pressure—from above and from below—and only by shifting the principal stress to criticism from below, can we count on waging a successful struggle against bureaucracy and on rooting it out.

It would be a mistake to think that only the leaders possess experience in constructive work. That is not true, comrades. The vast masses of the workers who are engaged in building our industry are day by day accumulating vast experience in construction, experience which is not a whit less valuable to us than the experience of the leaders. Mass criticism from below, control from below, is needed by us in order that, among other things, this experience of the vast masses should not be wasted, but be reckoned with and translated into practice.

From this follows the immediate task of the Party: *to wage a ruthless struggle against bureaucracy, to organise mass criticism from below, and to take this criticism into account when adopting practical decisions for eliminating our shortcomings.*

It cannot be said that the Young Communist League, and especially *Komsomolskaya Pravda,* have not appreciated the importance of this task. The shortcoming here is that often the fulfilment of this task is not carried out completely. And in order to carry it out completely, it is necessary to give heed not only to criticism, but also to the results of criticism, to the improvements that are introduced as a result of criticism.

1928

REPORT TO THE SEVENTEENTH CONGRESS OF THE COMMUNIST PARTY OF THE SOVIET UNION (BOLSHEVIK)[1] ON THE WORK OF THE CENTRAL COMMITTEE

January 26, 1934

I. THE CONTINUING CRISIS OF WORLD CAPITALISM AND THE EXTERNAL SITUATION OF THE SOVIET UNION

Comrades, more than three years have passed since the Sixteenth Congress. That is not a very long period. But it has been fuller in content than any other period. I do not think that any period in the last decade has been so rich in events as this one.

In the *economic* sphere these years have been years of continuing world economic crisis. The crisis has affected not only industry, but also agriculture as a whole. The crisis has raged not only in the sphere of production and trade; it has also extended to the sphere of credit and money circulation, and has completely upset the established credit and currency relations among countries. While formerly people here and there still disputed whether there was a world economic

[1] The Seventeenth Party Congress, held in Moscow, January 26 to February 10, 1934, represented the consolidation of Stalin's line on all major policies. Stalin's opening report to the Congress is obviously a document of enormous historical significance.

crisis or not, now they no longer do so, for the existence of the crisis and its devastating effects are only too obvious. Now the controversy centres around another question: Is there a way out of the crisis or not; and if there is, then what is to be done?

In the *political* sphere these years have been years of further tension both in the relations between the capitalist countries and in the relations within them. Japan's war against China and the occupation of Manchuria, which have strained relations in the Far East; the victory of fascism in Germany and the triumph of the idea of revenge, which have strained relations in Europe; the withdrawal of Japan and Germany from the League of Nations, which has given a new impetus to the growth of armaments and to the preparations for an imperialist war; the defeat of fascism in Spain,[2] which is one more indication that a revolutionary crisis is maturing and that fascism is far from being long-lived—such are the most important events of the period under review. It is not surprising that bourgeois pacifism is breathing its last and that the trend towards disarmament is openly and definitely giving way to a trend towards armament and rearmament.

Amid the surging waves of economic perturbations and military-political catastrophes, the U.S.S.R. stands out like a rock, continuing its work of socialist construction and its fight to preserve peace. Whereas in the capitalist countries the economic crisis is still raging, in the U.S.S.R. the advance continues both in industry and in agriculture. Whereas in the capitalist countries feverish preparations are in progress for a new war for a new redivision of the world and of spheres of influence, the U.S.S.R. is continuing its systematic and persistent struggle against the menace of war and for peace; and it cannot be said that the efforts of the U.S.S.R. in this direction have had no success.

Such is the general picture of the international situation at the present moment.

[2] In 1931, the military-fascist Spanish dictatorship of General Primo de Rivera was overthrown. The resulting election abolished the monarchy and created a democratic republic, with strong representation from the workers and peasants. Franco's fascist rebellion began in 1936.

Let us pass to an examination of the principal data on the economic and political situation in the capitalist countries.

1. THE COURSE OF THE ECONOMIC CRISIS IN THE CAPITALIST COUNTRIES

The present economic crisis in the capitalist countries differs from all analogous crises, among other things, in that it is the longest and most protracted crisis. Formerly crises would come to an end in a year or two; the present crisis, however, is now in its fifth year, devastating the economy of the capitalist countries year after year and draining it of the fat accumulated in previous years. It is not surprising that this is the most severe of all the crises that have taken place.

How is this unprecedentedly protracted character of the present industrial crisis to be explained?

It is to be explained, first of all, by the fact that the industrial crisis has affected every capitalist country without exception, which has made it difficult for some countries to manoeuvre at the expense of others.

Secondly, it is to be explained by the fact that the industrial crisis has become interwoven with the agrarian crisis which has affected all the agrarian and semi-agrarian countries without exception, which could not but make the industrial crisis more complicated and more profound.

Thirdly, it is to be explained by the fact that the agrarian crisis has grown more acute in this period, and has affected all branches of agriculture, including livestock farming; that it has brought about a retrogression of agriculture, a reversion from machines to hand labour, a substitution of horses for tractors, a sharp reduction in the use of artificial fertilisers, and in some cases a complete abandonment of them—all of which has caused the industrial crisis to become still more protracted.

Fourthly, it is to be explained by the fact that the monopolist cartels which dominate industry strive to maintain high commodity prices, a circumstance which makes the crisis particularly painful and hinders the absorption of commodity stocks.

Lastly—and this is the chief thing—it is to be explained by the fact that the industrial crisis broke out in the conditions of the *general* crisis of capitalism, when capitalism no longer has, nor can have, either in the major countries or in the colonial and dependent countries, the strength and stability it had before the war and the October Revolution; when industry in the capitalist countries has acquired, as a heritage from the imperialist war, chronic under-capacity operation of plants, and armies of millions of unemployed of which it is no longer able to rid itself.

Such are the circumstances that have given rise to the extremely protracted character of the present industrial crisis.

It is these circumstances also that explain the fact that the crisis has not been confined to the sphere of production and trade, but has also affected the credit system, foreign exchange, the debt settlements, etc., and has broken down the traditionally established relations both between countries and between social groups in the various countries.

An important part was played by the fall in commodity prices. In spite of the resistance of the monopolist cartels, the fall in prices increased with elemental force, affecting primarily and mainly the commodities of the unorganised commodity owners—peasants, artisans, small capitalists—and only gradually and to a smaller degree those of the organised commodity owners—the capitalists united in cartels. The fall in prices made the position of debtors (manufacturers, artisans, peasants, etc.) intolerable, while, on the other hand, it placed creditors in an unprecedentedly privileged position. Such a situation was bound to lead, and actually did lead, to the mass bankruptcy of firms and of individual capitalists. As a result, tens of thousands of joint-stock companies have failed in the United States, Germany, Britain and France during the past three years. The bankruptcy of joint-stock companies was followed by a depreciation of currency, which slightly alleviated the position of debtors. The depreciation of currency was followed by the non-payment of debts, both foreign and internal, legalised by the state. The collapse of such banks as the Darmstadt and Dresden banks in Germany and the Kreditanstalt in Austria, and of concerns like

Kreuger's in Sweden, the Insull corporation in the United States, etc., is well known to all.

Naturally, these phenomena, which shook the foundations of the credit system, were bound to be followed, and actually were followed, by the cessation of payments on credits and foreign loans, the cessation of payments on inter-Allied debts, the cessation of export of capital, a further decline in foreign trade, a further decline in the export of commodities, an intensification of the struggle for foreign markets, trade war between countries, and—dumping. Yes, comrades, dumping. I am not referring to the alleged Soviet dumping, about which only very recently certain honourable members of honourable parliaments in Europe and America were shouting themselves hoarse. I am referring to the real dumping that is now being practised by almost all "civilised" states, and about which these gallant and honourable members of parliaments maintain a prudent silence.

Naturally, also, these destructive phenomena accompanying the industrial crisis, which took place outside the sphere of production, could not but in their turn influence the course of the industrial crisis, aggravating it and complicating the situation still further.

Such is the general picture of the course of the industrial crisis.

Here are a few figures, taken from official data, that illustrate the course of the industrial crisis during the period under review.

Volume of Industrial Output
(Per cent of 1929)

	1929	1930	1931	1932	1933
U.S.S.R.	100	129.7	161.9	184.7	201.6
U.S.A.	100	80.7	68.1	53.8	64.9
Britain	100	92.4	83.8	83.8	86.1
Germany	100	88.3	71.7	59.8	66.8
France	100	100.7	89.2	69.1	77.4

As you see, this table speaks for itself.

While industry in the principal capitalist countries declined from year to year, compared with 1929, and began to recover somewhat only in 1933—although still far from reaching the level of 1929—industry in the U.S.S.R. grew from year to year, experiencing an uninterrupted rise.

While industry in the principal capitalist countries at the end of 1933 shows on the average a *reduction* of 25 per cent and more in volume of output compared with 1929, industrial output in the U.S.S.R. has more than doubled during this period, i.e., it has *increased* more than 100 per cent. (*Applause.*)

Judging by this table, it may seem that of these four capitalist countries Britain is in the most favourable position. But that is not quite true. If we compare industry in these countries with its pre-war level we get a somewhat different picture.

Here is the corresponding table:

Volume of Industrial Output
(*Per cent of pre-war level*)

	1913	1929	1930	1931	1932	1933
U.S.S.R.	100	194.3	252.1	314.7	359.0	391.9
U.S.A.	100	170.2	137.3	115.9	91.4	110.2
Britain	100	99.1	91.5	83.0	82.5	85.2
Germany	100	113.0	99.8	81.0	67.6	75.4
France	100	139.0	140.0	124.0	96.1	107.6

As you see, industry in Britain and Germany has not yet reached the pre-war level, while the United States and France have exceeded it by several per cent, and the U.S.S.R. has raised, increased its industrial output during this period by more than 290 per cent over the pre-war level. (*Applause.*)

But there is still another conclusion to be drawn from these tables.

While industry in the principal capitalist countries declined steadily after 1930, and particularly after 1931, and reached its lowest point in 1932, in 1933 it began to recover and pick up somewhat. If we take the monthly returns for 1932 and 1933 we find still further confirmation of this conclusion; for they show that, despite fluctuations of output in the course of 1933, industry in these countries revealed no tendency to fall to the lowest point reached in the summer of 1932.

What does this mean?

It means that, apparently, industry in the principal capitalist countries had already reached the lowest point of decline and did not return to it in the course of 1933.

Some people are inclined to ascribe this phenomenon exclusively to the influence of artificial factors, such as the war-inflation boom. There can be no doubt that the war-inflation boom plays no small part in it. This is particularly true in regard to Japan, where this artificial factor is the principal and decisive force stimulating a certain revival in some industries, mainly war industries. But it would be a gross mistake to explain everything by the war-inflation boom. Such an explanation would be incorrect, if only for the reason that the changes in industry which I have described are observed, not in separate and chance areas, but in all, or nearly all, the industrial countries, including the countries with a stable currency. Apparently, in addition to the war-inflation boom, the internal economic forces of capitalism are also operating here.

Capitalism has succeeded in somewhat alleviating the position of industry *at the expense of the workers*, by heightening their exploitation through increased intensity of labour; *at the expense of the farmers*, by pursuing a policy of paying the lowest prices for the products of their labour, for foodstuffs and, partly, raw materials; and *at the expense of the peasants in the colonies and economically weak countries*, by still further forcing down prices for the products of their labour, principally for raw materials, and also foodstuffs.

Does this mean that we are witnessing a transition from a crisis to an ordinary depression, to be followed by a new upswing and flourishing of industry? No, it does not. At any rate, at the present time there is no evidence, direct or indirect, to indicate the approach of an upswing of industry in the capitalist countries. More than that, judging by all things, there can be no such evidence, at least in the near future. There can be no such evidence, because all the unfavourable conditions which prevent industry in the capitalist countries from making any considerable advance continue to operate. I have in mind the continuing *general* crisis of capitalism, in the circumstances of which the *economic* crisis is proceeding; the chronic under-capacity operation of the enterprises; chronic mass unemployment; the interweaving of the industrial crisis with an agricultural crisis; the absence of tendencies towards a more or less serious renewal of fixed capital, which usually heralds the approach of a boom, etc., etc.

Evidently, what we are witnessing is a transition from the lowest point of decline of industry, from the lowest point of the industrial crisis, to a depression—not an ordinary depression, but a depression of a special kind, which does not lead to a new upswing and flourishing of industry, but which, on the other hand, does not force industry back to the lowest point of decline.

2. THE GROWING TENSION IN THE POLITICAL SITUATION IN THE CAPITALIST COUNTRIES

A result of the protracted economic crisis has been an unprecedented increase in the tension of the political situation in the capitalist countries, both within those countries and in their mutual relations.

The intensified struggle for foreign markets, the abolition of the last vestiges of free trade, the prohibitive tariffs, the trade war, the foreign currency war, dumping, and many other analogous measures which demonstrate extreme *nationalism* in economic policy have strained to the utmost the relations among the various countries, have created the basis for military conflicts, and have put war on the order of the day as a means for a new redivision of the world and of spheres of influence in favour of the stronger states.

Japan's war against China, the occupation of Manchuria, Japan's withdrawal from the League of Nations, and her advance in North China, have made the situation still more tense. The intensified struggle for the Pacific and the growth of naval armaments in Japan, the United States, Britain and France are results of this increased tension.

Germany's withdrawal from the League of Nations and the spectre of revanchism have further added to the tension and have given a fresh impetus to the growth of armaments in Europe.

It is not surprising that bourgeois pacifism is now dragging out a miserable existence, and that idle talk of disarmament is giving way to "business-like" talk about armament and rearmament.

Once again, as in 1914, the parties of bellicose imperialism, the parties of war and revanchism are coming into the foreground.

Quite clearly things are heading for a new war.

The internal situation of the capitalist countries, in view of the operation of these same factors, is becoming still more tense. Four years of industrial crisis have exhausted the working class and reduced it to despair. Four years of agricultural crisis have utterly ruined the poorer strata of the peasantry, not only in the principal capitalist countries, but also—and particularly—in the dependent and colonial countries. It is a fact that, notwithstanding all kinds of statistical trickery designed to minimise unemployment, the number of unemployed, according to the official figures of bourgeois institutions, reaches 3,000,000 in Britain, 5,000,000 in Germany and 10,000,000 in the United States, not to mention the other European countries. Add to this the more than ten million partially unemployed; add the vast masses of ruined peasants—and you will get an approximate picture of the poverty and despair of the labouring masses. The masses of the people have not yet reached the stage when they are ready to storm capitalism; but the idea of storming it is maturing in the minds of the masses—of that there can hardly be any doubt. This is eloquently testified to by such facts as, say, the Spanish revolution which overthrew the fascist regime, and the expansion of the Soviet districts in China, which the united counter-revolution of the Chinese and foreign bourgeoisie is unable to stop.

This, indeed, explains why the ruling classes in the capitalist countries are so zealously destroying or nullifying the last vestiges of parliamentarism and bourgeois democracy which might be used by the working class in its struggle against the oppressors, why they are driving the Communist Parties underground and resorting to openly terrorist methods of maintaining their dictatorship.

Chauvinism and preparation of war as the main elements

of foreign policy; repression of the working class and terrorism in the sphere of home policy as a necessary means for strengthening the rear of future war fronts—that is what is now particularly engaging the minds of contemporary imperialist politicians.

It is not surprising that fascism has now become the most fashionable commodity among war-mongering bourgeois politicians. I am referring not only to fascism in general, but, primarily, to fascism of the German type, which is wrongly called national-socialism—wrongly because the most searching examination will fail to reveal even an atom of socialism in it.

In this connection the victory of fascism in Germany must be regarded not only as a symptom of the weakness of the working class and a result of the betrayals of the working class by Social-Democracy, which paved the way for fascism; it must also be regarded as a sign of the weakness of the bourgeoisie, a sign that the bourgeoisie is no longer able to rule by the old methods of parliamentarism and bourgeois democracy, and, as a consequence, is compelled in its home policy to resort to terrorist methods of rule—as a sign that it is no longer able to find a way out of the present situation on the basis of a peaceful foreign policy, and, as a consequence, is compelled to resort to a policy of war.

Such is the situation.

As you see, things are heading towards a new imperialist war as a way out of the present situation.

Of course, there are no grounds for assuming that war can provide a real way out. On the contrary, it is bound to confuse the situation still more. More than that, it is sure to unleash revolution and jeopardise the very existence of capitalism in a number of countries, as happened in the course of the first imperialist war. And if, in spite of the experience of the first imperialist war, the bourgeois politicians clutch at war as a drowning man clutches at a straw, that shows that they have got into a hopeless muddle, have landed in an impasse, and are ready to rush headlong into the abyss.

It is worth while, therefore, briefly to examine the plans for the organisation of war which are now being hatched in the circles of bourgeois politicians.

Some think that war should be organised against one of the

great powers. They think of inflicting a crushing defeat upon that power and of improving their affairs at its expense. Let us assume that they organise such a war. What may be the result of that?

As is well known, during the first imperialist war it was also intended to destroy one of the great powers, viz., Germany, and to profit at her expense. But what was the upshot of this? They did not destroy Germany; but they sowed in Germany such a hatred of the victors, and created such a rich soil for revenge, that even to this day they have not been able to clear up the revolting mess they made, and will not, perhaps, be able to do so for some time. On the other hand, the result they obtained was the smashing of capitalism in Russia, the victory of the proletarian revolution in Russia, and—of course—the Soviet Union. What guarantee is there that a second imperialist war will produce "better" results for them than the first? Would it not be more correct to assume that the opposite will be the case?

Others think that war should be organised against a country that is weak in the military sense, but represents an extensive market—for example, against China, which, it is claimed, cannot even be described as a state in the strict sense of the word, but is merely "unorganised territory" which needs to be seized by strong states. They evidently want to divide her up completely and improve their affairs at her expense. Let us assume that they organise such a war. What may be the result of that?

It is well known that at the beginning of the nineteenth century Italy and Germany were regarded in the same light as China is today, i.e., they were considered "unorganised territories" and not states, and they were subjugated. But what was the result of that? As is well known, it resulted in wars for independence waged by Germany and Italy, and the union of these countries into independent states. It resulted in increased hatred for the oppressors in the hearts of the peoples of these countries, the effects of which have not been removed to this day and will not, perhaps, be removed for some time. The question arises: What guarantee is there that the same thing will not result from a war of the imperialists against China?

Still others think that war should be organised by a "superior race," say, the German "race," against an "inferior race," primarily against the Slavs; that only such a war can provide a way out of the situation, for it is the mission of the "superior race" to render the "inferior race" fruitful and to rule over it. Let us assume that this queer theory, which is as far removed from science as the sky from the earth, let us assume that this queer theory is put into practice. What may be the result of that?

It is well known that ancient Rome looked upon the ancestors of the present-day Germans and French in the same way as the representatives of the "superior race" now look upon the Slav races. It is well known that ancient Rome treated them as an "inferior race," as "barbarians," destined to live in eternal subordination to the "superior race," to "great Rome"; and, between ourselves be it said, ancient Rome had some grounds for this, which cannot be said of the representatives of the "superior race" of today. (*Thunderous applause.*) But what was the upshot of this? The upshot was that the non-Romans, i.e., all the "barbarians," united against the common enemy and brought Rome down with a crash. The question arises: What guarantee is there that the claims of the representatives of the "superior race" of today will not lead to the same lamentable results? What guarantee is there that the fascist literary politicians in Berlin will be more fortunate than the old and experienced conquerors in Rome? Would it not be more correct to assume that the opposite will be the case?

Finally, there are others who think that war should be organised against the U.S.S.R. Their plan is to defeat the U.S.S.R., divide up its territory, and profit at its expense. It would be a mistake to believe that it is only certain military circles in Japan who think in this way. We know that similar plans are being hatched in the circles of the political leaders of certain states in Europe. Let us assume that these gentlemen pass from words to deeds. What may be the result of that?

There can hardly be any doubt that such a war would be the most dangerous war for the bourgeoisie. It would be the most dangerous war, not only because the peoples of the U.S.S.R. would fight to the death to preserve the gains of the revolution; it would be the most dangerous war for the bourgeoisie for the added reason that it would be waged not only at the fronts, but also in the enemy's rear. The bourgeoisie need have no doubt that the numerous friends of the working class of the U.S.S.R. in Europe and Asia will endeavour to strike a blow in the rear at their oppressors who have launched a criminal war against the fatherland of the working class of all countries. And let not Messieurs the bourgeoisie blame us if some of the governments near and dear to them, which today rule happily "by the grace of God," are missing on the morrow after such a war. (*Thunderous applause.*)

There has already been one such war against the U.S.S.R., if you remember, fifteen years ago. As is well known, the universally esteemed Churchill clothed that war in a poetic formula—"the campaign of fourteen states." You remember, of course, that that war rallied all the working people of our country into one united camp of self-sacrificing warriors, who with their lives defended their workers' and peasants' motherland against the foreign foe. You know how it ended. It ended in the ejection of the invaders from our country and the formation of revolutionary Councils of Action[3] in Europe. It can hardly be doubted that a second war against the U.S.S.R. will lead to the complete defeat of the aggressors, to revolution in a number of countries in Europe and in Asia, and to the destruction of the bourgeois-landlord governments in those countries.

Such are the war plans of the perplexed bourgeois politicians.

As you see, they are not distinguished either for their brains or for their valour. (*Applause.*)

But while the bourgeoisie chooses the path of war, the working class in the capitalist countries, brought to despair by four years of crisis and unemployment, is beginning to take the path of revolution. This means that a revolutionary crisis is maturing and will continue to mature. And the more the bour-

[3] Inside the various capitalist countries that intervened militarily against the Soviet government in 1918–20 arose the Councils of Action, revolutionary organizations of workers. Under the slogan "Hands off Soviet Russia," they organized strikes and demonstrations and refused to load war equipment.

geoisie becomes entangled in its war schemes, the more frequently it resorts to terrorist methods of fighting against the working class and the labouring peasantry, the more rapidly will the revolutionary crisis develop.

Some comrades think that, once there is a revolutionary crisis, the bourgeoisie is bound to get into a hopeless position, that its end is therefore a foregone conclusion, that the victory of the revolution is thus assured, and that all they have to do is to wait for the fall of the bourgeoisie and to draw up victorious resolutions. That is a profound mistake. The victory of the revolution never comes of itself. It must be prepared for and won. And only a strong proletarian revolutionary party can prepare for and win victory. Moments occur when the situation is revolutionary, when the rule of the bourgeoisie is shaken to its very foundations, and yet the victory of the revolution does not come, because there is no revolutionary party of the proletariat with sufficient strength and prestige to lead the masses and to take power. It would be unwise to believe that such "cases" cannot occur.

It is worth while in this connection to recall Lenin's prophetic words on revolutionary crises, uttered at the Second Congress of the Communist International:

> "We have now come to the question of the revolutionary crisis as the basis of our revolutionary action. And here we must first of all note two widespread errors. On the one hand, the bourgeois economists depict this crisis as mere 'unrest,' as the English so elegantly express it. On the other hand, revolutionaries sometimes try to prove that the crisis is absolutely hopeless. That is a mistake. There is no such thing as an absolutely hopeless situation. The bourgeoisie behaves like an arrogant brigand who has lost his head; it commits blunder after blunder, making the situation more acute and hastening its own doom. All this is true. But it cannot be 'proved' that there is absolutely no chance of its gulling some minority of the exploited with some kind of minor concessions, or of suppressing some movement or uprising of some section or another of the oppressed and exploited. To try to 'prove' beforehand that a situation is 'absolutely' hopeless would be sheer pedantry, or juggling

with concepts and catchwords. In this and similar questions the only real 'proof' is practice. The bourgeois system all over the world is experiencing a most profound revolutionary crisis. The revolutionary parties must now 'prove' by their practical actions that they are sufficiently intelligent and organised, are sufficiently in contact with the exploited masses, are sufficiently determined and skilful, to utilise this crisis for a successful and victorious revolution."

3. THE RELATIONS BETWEEN THE U.S.S.R. AND THE CAPITALIST STATES

It is easy to understand how difficult it has been for the U.S.S.R. to pursue its peace policy in this atmosphere poisoned with the miasma of war schemes.

In the midst of this eve-of-war frenzy which has affected a number of countries, the U.S.S.R. during these years has stood firmly and unshakably by its position of peace: fighting against the menace of war; fighting to preserve peace; meeting halfway those countries which in one way or another stand for the preservation of peace; exposing and tearing the masks from those who are preparing for and provoking war.

What did the U.S.S.R. rely on in this difficult and complicated struggle for peace?

a) On its growing economic and political might.

b) On the moral support of the vast masses of the working class of all countries, who are vitally interested in the preservation of peace.

c) On the prudence of those countries which for one motive or another are not interested in disturbing the peace, and which want to develop trade relations with such a punctual client as the U.S.S.R.

d) Finally—on our glorious army, which stands ready to defend our country against assaults from without.

It was on this basis that we began our campaign for the conclusion with neighbouring states of pacts of non-aggression and of pacts defining aggression. You know that this campaign has been successful. As you know, pacts of non-aggression have been concluded not only with the majority of our neighbours in the West and in the South, including Finland and

Poland, but also with such countries as France and Italy; and pacts defining aggression have been concluded with those same neighbouring states, including the Little Entente.[4]

On the same basis the friendship between the U.S.S.R and Turkey has been consolidated; relations between the U.S.S.R. and Italy have improved and have indisputably become satisfactory; relations with France, Poland and other Baltic states have improved; relations have been restored with the U.S.A., China, etc.

Of the many facts reflecting the successes of the peace policy of the U.S.S.R. two facts of indisputably material significance should be noted and singled out.

1) I have in mind, firstly, the change for the better that has taken place recently in the relations between the U.S.S.R. and Poland and between the U.S.S.R. and France. In the past, as you know, our relations with Poland were not at all good. Representatives of our state were assassinated in Poland. Poland regarded herself as the barrier of the Western states against the U.S.S.R. All the various imperialists counted on Poland as their advanced detachment in the event of a military attack on the U.S.S.R. The relations between the U.S.S.R. and France were no better. We need only recall the facts relating to the trial of the Ramzin group of wreckers in Moscow to bring to mind a picture of the relations between the U.S.S.R. and France. But now those undesirable relations are gradually beginning to disappear. They are giving way to other relations, which can only be called relations of rapprochement.

The point is not merely that we have concluded pacts of non-aggression with these countries, although the pacts in themselves are of very great importance. The point is, primarily, that the atmosphere of mutual distrust is beginning to be dissipated. This does not mean, of course, that the incipient process of rapprochement can be regarded as sufficiently stable and as guaranteeing ultimate success. Surprises

[4] The Little Entente was a political alliance of Czechoslovakia, Romania, and Yugoslavia from 1920 to 1938. Originally designed to check the spread of revolution in Eastern and Central Europe, it later moved, under the threat of Nazi expansion, toward a rapprochement with the Soviet Union.

and zigzags in policy, for example in Poland, where anti-Soviet sentiments are still strong, can as yet by no means be regarded as out of the question. But the change for the better in our relations, irrespective of its results in the future, is a fact worthy of being noted and emphasised as a factor in the advancement of the cause of peace.

What is the cause of this change? What stimulates it?

Primarily, the growth of the strength and might of the U.S.S.R.

In our times it is not the custom to take any account of the weak—only the strong are taken into account. Furthermore, there have been some changes in the policy of Germany which reflect the growth of revanchist and imperialist sentiments in Germany.

In this connection some German politicians say that the U.S.S.R. has now taken an orientation towards France and Poland; that from an opponent of the Versailles Treaty it has become a supporter of it, and that this change is to be explained by the establishment of the fascist regime in Germany. That is not true. Of course, we are far from being enthusiastic about the fascist regime in Germany. But it is not a question of fascism here, if only for the reason that fascism in Italy, for example, has not prevented the U.S.S.R. from establishing the best relations with that country. Nor is it a question of any alleged change in our attitude towards the Versailles Treaty. It is not for us, who have experienced the shame of the Brest Peace, to sing the praises of the Versailles Treaty. We merely do not agree to the world being flung into the abyss of a new war on account of that treaty. The same must be said of the alleged new orientation taken by the U.S.S.R. We never had any orientation towards Germany, nor have we any orientation towards Poland and France. Our orientation in the past and our orientation at the present time is towards the U.S.S.R., and towards the U.S.S.R. alone. (*Stormy applause.*) And if the interests of the U.S.S.R. demand rapprochement with one country or another which is not interested in disturbing peace, we adopt this course without hesitation.

No, that is not the point. The point is that Germany's policy has changed. The point is that even before the present German politicians came to power, and particularly after they came to power, a contest began in Germany between two political lines: between the old policy, which was reflected in the treaties between the U.S.S.R. and Germany, and the "new" policy, which, in the main, recalls the policy of the former German Kaiser, who at one time occupied the Ukraine and marched against Leningrad, after converting the Baltic countries into a place d'armes for this march; and this "new" policy is obviously gaining the upper hand over the old policy. The fact that the advocates of the "new" policy are gaining supremacy in all things, while the supporters of the old policy are in disfavour, cannot be regarded as an accident. Nor can the well-known statement made by Hugenberg in London, and the equally well-known declarations of Rosenberg, who directs the foreign policy of the ruling party in Germany, be regarded as accidents. That is the point, comrades.

2) I have in mind, secondly, the restoration of normal relations between the U.S.S.R. and the United States of America. There cannot be any doubt that this act is of very great significance for the whole system of international relations. The point is not only that it improves the chances of preserving peace, improves the relations between the two countries, strengthens trade connections between them and creates a basis for mutual collaboration. The point is that it forms a landmark between the old position, when in various countries the U.S.A. was regarded as the bulwark for all sorts of anti-Soviet trends, and the new position, when that bulwark has been voluntarily removed, to the mutual advantage of both countries.

Such are the two main facts which reflect the successes of the Soviet policy of peace.

It would be wrong, however, to think that everything went smoothly in the period under review. No, not everything went smoothly, by a long way.

Recall, say, the pressure that was brought to bear upon us by Britain; the embargo on our exports, the attempt to interfere in our internal affairs and to use this as a probe—to test our power of resistance. True, nothing came of this attempt, and later the embargo was lifted; but the unpleasant after-effect of these sallies still makes itself felt in everything connected with the relations between Britain and the U.S.S.R., including the negotiations for a commercial treaty. And these sallies against the U.S.S.R. must not be regarded as accidental. It is well known that a certain section of the British Conservatives cannot live without such sallies. And precisely because they are not accidental we must reckon that in the future, too, sallies will be made against the U.S.S.R., all sorts of menaces will be created, attempts will be undertaken to damage the U.S.S.R., etc.

Nor must we lose sight of the relations between the U.S.S.R. and Japan, which stand in need of considerable improvement. Japan's refusal to conclude a pact of non-aggression, of which Japan stands in no less need than the U.S.S.R., once again emphasises the fact that all is not well in the sphere of our relations. The same must be said of the rupture of negotiations concerning the Chinese-Eastern Railway, due to no fault of the U.S.S.R.; and also of the outrageous actions of the Japanese agents on the Chinese-Eastern Railway, the illegal arrests of Soviet employees on the Chinese-Eastern Railway, etc. That is apart from the fact that one section of the military in Japan, with the obvious approval of another section of the military, is openly advocating in the press the necessity for a war against the U.S.S.R. and the seizure of the Maritime Province; while the Japanese Government, instead of calling these instigators of war to order, pretends that the matter is no concern of its. It is not difficult to understand that such circumstances cannot but create an atmosphere of uneasiness and uncertainty. Of course, we shall persistently continue to pursue a policy of peace and strive for an improvement in our relations with Japan, because we want to improve these relations. But it does not depend entirely upon us. That is why we must at the same time take all measures to guard our country against surprises, and be prepared to defend it against attack. (*Stormy applause.*)

As you see, alongside the successes in our peace policy there are also a number of unfavourable features.

Such is the external situation of the U.S.S.R.

Our foreign policy is clear. It is a policy of preserving peace and strengthening trade relations with all countries. The

U.S.S.R. does not think of threatening anybody—let alone of attacking anybody. We stand for peace and uphold the cause of peace. But we are not afraid of threats and are prepared to answer the instigators of war blow for blow. (*Stormy applause.*) Those who want peace and seek business relations with us will always have our support. But those who try to attack our country will receive a crushing repulse to teach them in future not to poke their pig snouts into our Soviet garden. (*Thunderous applause.*)

Such is our foreign policy. (*Thunderous applause.*)

The task is to continue to implement this policy with unflagging perseverance and consistency.

II. THE CONTINUING PROGRESS OF THE NATIONAL ECONOMY AND THE INTERNAL SITUATION IN THE U.S.S.R.

I pass to the question of the internal situation in the U.S.S.R.

From the point of view of the internal situation in the U.S.S.R. the period under review presents a picture of ever-increasing progress, both in the sphere of the national economy and in the sphere of culture.

This progress has not been merely a simple quantitative accumulation of strength. This progress is remarkable in that it has introduced fundamental changes into the structure of the U.S.S.R., and has radically changed the face of the country.

During this period, the U.S.S.R. has become radically transformed and has cast off the aspect of backwardness and medievalism. From an agrarian country it has become an industrial country. From a country of small individual agriculture it has become a country of collective, large-scale mechanised agriculture. From an ignorant, illiterate and uncultured country it has become—or rather it is becoming—a literate and cultured country covered by a vast network of higher, secondary and elementary schools functioning in the languages of the nationalities of the U.S.S.R.

New industries have been created: the production of machine tools, automobiles, tractors, chemicals, motors, aircraft, harvester combines, powerful turbines and generators, high-grade steel, ferro-alloys, synthetic rubber, nitrates, artificial fibre, etc., etc. (*Prolonged applause.*)

During this period thousands of new, fully up-to-date industrial plants have been built and put into operation. Giants like the Dnieprostroi, Magnitostroi, Kuznetskstroi, Chelyabstroi, Bobriki, Uralmashstroi and Krammashstroi have been built. Thousands of old plants have been reconstructed and provided with modern technical equipment. New plants have been built, and industrial centres created, in the national republics and in the border regions of the U.S.S.R.: in Byelorussia, in the Ukraine, in the North Caucasus, in Transcaucasia, in Central Asia, in Kazakhstan, in Buryat-Mongolia, in Tataria, in Bashkiria, in the Urals, in Eastern and Western Siberia, in the Far East, etc.

More than 200,000 collective farms and 5,000 state farms have been organised, with new district centres and industrial centres serving them.

New large towns, with large populations, have sprung up in what were almost uninhabited places. The old towns and industrial centres have grown enormously.

The foundations have been laid for the Urals-Kuznetsk Combine, which unites the coking coal of Kuznetsk with the iron ore of the Urals. Thus, we may consider that the dream of a new metallurgical base in the East has become a reality.

The foundations for a powerful new oil base have been laid in areas of the western and southern slopes of the Urals range—in the Urals region, Bashkiria and Kazakhstan.

It is obvious that the huge capital investments of the state in all branches of the national economy, amounting in the period under review to over 60,000 million rubles, have not been spent in vain, and are already beginning to bear fruit.

As a result of these achievements the national income of the U.S.S.R. has increased from 29,000 million rubles in 1929 to 50,000 million in 1933; whereas during the same period there has been an enormous decline in the national income of all the capitalist countries without exception.

Naturally, all these achievements and all this progress were bound to lead—and actually have led—to the further consolidation of the internal situation in the U.S.S.R.

How was it possible for these colossal changes to take place in a matter of three or four years on the territory of a vast state with a backward technique and a backward culture? Was it not a miracle? It would have been a miracle if this development had taken place on the basis of capitalism and individual small farming. But it cannot be described as a miracle if we bear in mind that this development took place on the basis of expanding socialist construction.

Naturally, this enormous progress could take place only on the basis of the successful building of socialism; on the basis of the socially organised work of scores of millions of peoples; on the basis of the advantages which the socialist system of economy has over the capitalist and individual peasant system.

It is not surprising, therefore, that the colossal progress in the economy and culture of the U.S.S.R. during the period under review has at the same time meant the elimination of the capitalist elements and the relegation of individual peasant economy to the background. It is a fact that the socialist system of economy in the sphere of industry now constitutes 99 per cent of the total; and in agriculture, according to the area sown to grain crops, it constitutes 84.5 per cent of the total, whereas individual peasant economy accounts for only 15.5 per cent.

It follows, then, that capitalist economy in the U.S.S.R. has already been eliminated and that the individual peasant sector in the countryside has been relegated to a secondary position.

At the time when the New Economic Policy was being introduced, Lenin said that there were elements of five forms of social and economic structure in our country: 1) patriarchal economy (largely natural economy); 2) small-commodity production (the majority of the peasants who sell grain); 3) private capitalism; 4) state capitalism; 5) socialism. Lenin considered that, of all these forms, the socialist form must in the end gain the upper hand. We can now say that the first, the third and the fourth forms of social and economic structure no longer exist; the second form has been forced into a secondary position, while the fifth form—the socialist form of social and economic structure—now holds undivided sway and is the sole commanding force in the whole national economy. (*Stormy and prolonged applause.*)

Such is the result.

In this result is contained the basis of the stability of the internal situation in the U.S.S.R., the basis of the firmness of its front and rear positions in the circumstances of the capitalist encirclement.

Let us pass to an examination of the concrete material relating to various questions of the economic and political situation in the Soviet Union.

1. THE PROGRESS OF INDUSTRY

Of all branches of our national economy, the one that has grown most rapidly is industry. During the period under review, i.e., beginning with 1930, our industry has more than doubled—namely, it has increased by 101.6 per cent; and compared with the pre-war level it has grown almost four-fold—namely, by 291.9 per cent.

This means that our industrialisation has been going ahead at full speed.

As a result of the rapid growth of industrialisation the output of industry has advanced to first place in the gross output of the whole national economy.

Here is the corresponding table:

Relative Importance of Industry in the Gross Output of the National Economy
(Per cent of total, in prices of 1926–27)

	1913	1929	1930	1931	1932	1933
1. Industry (without small industry)	42.1	54.5	61.6	66.7	70.7	70.4
2. Agriculture	57.9	45.5	38.4	33.3	29.3	29.6
Total	100.0	100.0	100.0	100.0	100.0	100.0

This means that our country has definitely and finally become an industrial country.

Of decisive significance for the industrialisation of the country is the growth of the output of instruments and means of production in the total development of industry. The figures for the period under review show that this item has become predominant in the gross output of industry.

Here is the corresponding table:

Relative Importance of the Output of the Two Main Branches of Large-Scale Industry
(In prices of 1926–27)

	Gross output (in thousand million rubles)				
	1929	1930	1931	1932	1933
Total large-scale industry	21.0	27.5	33.9	38.5	41.9
Of which:					
Group "A": instruments and means of production	10.2	14.5	18.8	22.0	24.3
Group "B": consumer goods	10.8	13.0	15.1	16.5	17.6
Relative importance	(per cent of total)				
Group "A": instruments and means of production	48.5	52.6	55.4	57.0	58.0
Group "B": consumer goods	51.5	47.4	44.6	43.0	42.0
Total	100.0	100.0	100.0	100.0	100.0

As you see, this table requires no explanation.

In our country, which is still young as regards technical development, industry has a special task to fulfil. It must reconstruct on a new technical basis not only itself, not only all branches of industry, including light industry, the food industry, and the timber industry; it must also reconstruct all forms of transport and all branches of agriculture. It can fulfil this task, however, only if the machine-building industry—which is the main lever for the reconstruction of the national economy—occupies a predominant place in it. The figures for the period under review show that our machine-building industry has advanced to the leading place in the total volume of industrial output.

Here is the corresponding table:

Relative Importance of Various Branches of Industry
(Per cent of total gross output)

	U.S.S.R.			
	1913	1929	1932	1933
Coal	2.9	2.1	1.7	2.0
Coke	0.8	0.4	0.5	0.6
Oil (extraction)	1.9	1.8	1.5	1.4
Oil (refining)	2.3	2.5	2.9	2.6
Iron and steel	No data	4.5	3.7	4.0
Non-ferrous metals	" "	1.5	1.3	1.2
Machine building	11.0	14.8	25.0	26.1
Basic chemicals	0.8	0.6	0.8	0.9
Cotton textiles	18.3	15.2	7.6	7.3
Woollen textiles	3.1	3.1	1.9	1.8

This means that our industry is developing on a sound foundation, and that the key to reconstruction—the machine-building industry—is entirely in our hands. All that is required is that we use it skilfully and rationally.

The development of industry according to social sectors during the period under review present an interesting picture.

Here is the corresponding table:

Gross Output of Large-Scale Industry
According to Social Sectors
(In prices of 1926–27)

	(In million rubles)				
	1929	1930	1931	1932	1933
Total output	21,025	27,477	33,903	38,464	41,968
Of which:					
I. Socialised industry	20,891	27,402	No data	38,436	41,940
Of which:					
a) State industry	19,143	24,989	" "	35,587	38,932
b) Co-operative industry	1,748	2,413	" "	2,849	3,008
II. Private industry	134	75	" "	28	28

	(Per cent of total)				
Total output	100	100	100	100	100
Of which:					
I. Socialised industry	99.4	99.7	No data	99.93	99.93
Of which:					
a) State industry	91.1	90.9	” ”	92.52	92.76
b) Co-operative industry	8.3	8.8	” ”	7.41	7.17
II. Private industry	0.6	0.3	” ”	0.07	0.07

From this table it is evident that the capitalist elements in industry have already come to an end and that the socialist system of economy is now the sole system, holding a position of monopoly, in our industry. (*Applause.*)

However, of all the achievements of industry in the period under review the most important is the fact that it has succeeded in this period in training and moulding thousands of new men and women, of new leaders of industry, whole strata of new engineers and technicians, hundreds of thousands of young skilled workers who have mastered the new technique and who have advanced our socialist industry. There can be no doubt that without these men and women industry could not have achieved the successes it has achieved, and of which it has a right to be proud. The figures show that in the period under review about 800,000 more or less skilled workers have graduated into industry from factory training schools, and over 180,000 engineers and technicians from higher technical educational institutions, other higher educational institutions and technical schools. If it is true that the problem of cadres is a most important problem of our development, then it must be admitted that our industry is beginning really to cope with this problem.

Such are the principal achievements of our industry.

It would be wrong, however, to think that industry has only successes to record. No, it also has its defects. The chief of these are:

a) The continuing lag of the *iron and steel industry;*

b) The lack of order in the *non-ferrous metals industry;*

c) The underestimation of the great importance of developing the mining of *local coal* for the general fuel supply of the country (Moscow Region, the Caucasus, the Urals,

Karaganda, the Central Asia, Siberia, the Far East, the Northern Territory, etc.);

d) The absence of proper attention to the question of organising a new *oil centre* in areas of the Urals, Bashkiria, and the Emba;

e) The absence of serious concern for expanding the production of *goods for mass consumption* both in the light and food industries and in the timber industry;

f) The absence of proper attention to the question of developing *local industry;*

g) An absolutely impermissible attitude towards the question of improving the *quality of output;*

h) The continuing lag as regards increasing the *productivity of labour,* reducing the *cost of production,* and adopting *business accounting;*

i) The fact that bad organisation of work and wages, lack of personal responsibility in work, and wage equalisation have not yet been eliminated;

j) The fact that *red-tape and bureaucratic* methods of management in the economic People's Commissariats and their bodies, including the People's Commissariats of the light and food industries, are still far from having been eliminated.

The absolute necessity for the speedy elimination of these defects scarcely needs any further explanation. As you know, the iron and steel and non-ferrous metals industries failed to fulfil their plan throughout the first five-year plan period; nor have they fulfilled the plan for the first year of the second five-year plan period. If they continue to lag behind they may become a brake on industry and the cause of failures in its work. As to the creation of new centres of the coal and oil industries, it is not difficult to understand that unless this urgent task is fulfilled both industry and transport may run aground. The question of goods for mass consumption and of developing local industry, as well as the questions of improving the quality of output, of increasing the productivity of labour, of reducing production costs, and of adopting business accounting also need no further explanation. As for the bad organisation of work and wages, and red-tape and bureaucratic methods of management, the case of the Donbas and of the enterprises of the light and food industries has shown that this dangerous disease is to be found in all branches of industry and hinders their development. If it is not eliminated, industry will be in a bad way.

Our immediate tasks are:

1) To maintain the present leading role of machine building in the system of industry.

2) To eliminate the lag of the iron and steel industry.

3) To put the non-ferrous metals industries in order.

4) To develop to the utmost the mining of local coal in all the areas already known; to develop new coal-fields (for example, in the Bureya district in the Far East), and to convert the Kuzbas into a second Donbas. (*Prolonged applause.*)

5) Seriously to set about organising a centre of the oil industry in the areas of the western and southern slopes of the Urals range.

6) To expand the production of goods for mass consumption by all the economic People's Commissariats.

7) To develop local Soviet industry; to give it the opportunity of displaying initiative in the production of goods for mass consumption and to give it all possible assistance in the way of raw materials and funds.

8) To improve the quality of the goods produced; to stop turning out incomplete sets of goods, and to punish all those comrades, irrespective of their post, who violate or evade Soviet laws concerning the quality and completeness of sets of goods.

9) To secure a systematic increase in the productivity of labour, a reduction in production costs, and the adoption of business accounting.

10) To put an end to lack of personal responsibility in work and to wage equalisation.

11) To eliminate red-tape and bureaucratic methods of management in all the departments of the economic Commissariats, and to check systematically the fulfilment of the decisions and instructions of the directing centres by the subordinate bodies.

2. THE PROGRESS OF AGRICULTURE

Development in the sphere of agriculture has proceeded somewhat differently. In the period under review progress in the main branches of agriculture proceeded many times more slowly than in industry, but nevertheless more rapidly than in the period when individual farming predominated. In livestock farming, however, there was even a reverse process —a decline in the number of livestock, and it was only in 1933, and then only in pig breeding, that signs of progress were observed.

Evidently, the enormous difficulties of uniting the scattered small peasant farms into collective farms, the difficult task of creating a large number of big grain and livestock farms, starting almost from nothing, and, in general, the period of *reorganisation*, when individual agriculture was being remodelled and transferred to the new, collective-farm basis, which required much time and considerable outlay—all these factors inevitably predetermined both the slow rate of progress of agriculture, and the relatively long period of decline in the number of livestock.

In point of fact, in agriculture the period under review was not so much one of rapid progress and powerful upswing as one during which the conditions were created for such a progress and upswing in the near future.

If we take the figures for the increase in the area under all

Area under All Crops in the U.S.S.R.

	(In million hectares)					
	1913	1929	1930	1931	1932	1933
Total crop area	105.0	118.0	127.2	136.3	134.4	129.7
Of which:						
a) Grain crops	94.4	96.0	101.8	104.4	99.7	101.5
b) Industrial crops	4.5	8.8	10.5	14.0	14.9	12.0
c) Vegetables and melons	3.8	7.6	8.0	9.1	9.2	8.6
d) Fodder crops	2.1	5.0	6.5	8.8	10.6	7.3

crops, and separately the figures for industrial crops, we get the picture shown on the previous page of the development of agriculture during the period under review.

Area under Industrial Crops in the U.S.S.R.

	(In million hectares)					
	1913	1929	1930	1931	1932	1933
Cotton	0.69	1.06	1.58	2.14	2.17	2.05
Flax (long fibre)	1.02	1.63	1.75	2.39	2.51	2.40
Sugar-beet	0.65	0.77	1.04	1.39	1.54	1.21
Oil seeds	2.00	5.20	5.22	7.55	7.98	5.79

These tables reflect the two main lines in agriculture:

1) The line of the greatest possible expansion of crop areas in the period when the reorganisation of agriculture was at its height, when collective farms were being formed in tens of thousands and were driving the kulaks from the land, seizing the vacated land and taking charge of it.

2) The line of refraining from wholesale expansion of crop areas; the line of passing from wholesale expansion of crop areas to improved cultivation of the land, to the introduction of proper rotation of crops and fallow, to an increase of the harvest yield and, if shown to be necessary in practice, to a temporary reduction of crop areas.

As you know, the second line—the only correct line in agriculture—was proclaimed in 1932, when the period of reorganisation in agriculture was drawing to a close and the question of increasing the harvest yield became one of the fundamental questions of the progress of agriculture.

But the data on the growth of the crop areas cannot be regarded as a fully adequate indication of the development of agriculture. It sometimes happens that while the crop area increases, output does not increase, or even declines, because cultivation of the soil has deteriorated, and the yield per hectare has fallen. In view of this, data on crop areas must be supplemented by data on gross output.

Here is the corresponding table:

Gross Output of Grain and Industrial Crops in the U.S.S.R.

	(*In million centners*)					
	1913	*1929*	*1930*	*1931*	*1932*	*1933*
Grain crops	801.0	717.4	835.4	694.8	698.7	898.0
Raw cotton	7.4	8.6	11.1	12.9	12.7	13.2
Flax fibre	3.3	3.6	4.4	5.5	5.0	5.6
Sugar-beet	109.0	62.5	140.2	120.5	65.6	90.0
Oil seeds	21.5	35.8	36.2	51.0	45.5	46.0

It can be seen from this table that the years in which the reorganisation of agriculture was at its height, viz., 1931 and 1932, were the years of the greatest decrease in the output of grain crops.

It follows, further, from this table that in the flax and cotton areas, where the reorganisation of agriculture proceeded at a slower pace, flax and cotton hardly suffered, and progressed more or less evenly and steadily, while maintaining a high level of development.

Thirdly, it follows from this table that whereas there was only a slight fluctuation in the output of oil seeds, and a high level of development was maintained as compared with the pre-war level, in the sugar-beet districts, where the reorganisation of agriculture proceeded at the most rapid rate, sugar-beet farming, which was the last to enter the period of reorganisation, suffered its greatest decline in the last year of reorganisation, viz., in 1932, when output dropped below the pre-war level.

Lastly, it follows from this table that 1933, the first year after the completion of the reorganisation period, marks a turning-point in the development of grain and industrial crops.

This means that from now on grain crops, in the first place, and then industrial crops, will firmly and surely achieve a mighty advance.

The branch of agriculture that suffered most in the reorganisation period was livestock farming.

Here is the corresponding table:

Livestock in the U.S.S.R.

	(*Million head*)					
	1916	1929	1930	1931	1932	1933
a) Horses	35.1	34.0	30.2	26.2	19.6	16.6
b) Large cattle	58.9	68.1	52.5	47.9	40.7	38.6
c) Sheep and goats	115.2	147.2	108.8	77.7	52.1	50.6
d) Pigs	20.3	20.9	13.6	14.4	11.6	12.2

It can be seen from this table that in the period under review there was not an improvement, but a continual decline in the quantity of livestock in the country as compared with the pre-war level. It is obvious that this table reflects, on the one hand, the fact that livestock farming was most of all dominated by big kulak elements, and, on the other hand, the intense kulak agitation for the slaughter of livestock, which found favourable soil in the years of reorganisation.

Furthermore, it follows from this table that the decline in the number of livestock began in the very first year of reorganisation (1930) and continued right up to 1933. The decline was greatest in the first three years; while in 1933, the first year after the termination of the period of reorganisation, when the grain crops began to make progress, the decline in the number of livestock reached a minimum.

Lastly, it follows from this table that the reverse process has already commenced in pig breeding, and that in 1933 signs of direct progress were already seen.

This means that the year 1934 can and must mark a turning-point towards progress in all branches of livestock farming.

How did the collectivisation of peasant farms develop in the period under review?

Here is the corresponding table:

Collectivisation

	1929	1930	1931	1932	1933
Number of collective farms (thousands)	57.0	85.9	211.1	211.05	224.5

Collectivisation (cont'd)

Number of households in collective farms (millions)	1.0	6.0	13.0	14.9	15.2
Per cent of peasant farms collectivised	3.9	23.6	52.7	61.5	65.0

And what was the development as regards the areas under grain crops according to sectors?

Here is the corresponding table:

Area under Grain Crops According to Sectors

Sectors	*(In million hectares)*					*Per cent of total area in 1933*
	1929	1930	1931	1932	1933	
1. State farms	1.5	2.9	8.1	9.3	10.8	10.6
2. Collective farms	3.4	29.7	61.0	69.1	75.0	73.9
3. Individual peasant farms	91.1	69.2	35.3	21.3	15.7	15.5
Total grain crop area in the U.S.S.R.	96.0	101.8	104.4	99.7	101.5	100.0

What do these tables show?

They show that the period of reorganisation in agriculture, during which the number of collective farms and the number of their members increased at a tempestuous pace, is now ended, that it was already ended in 1932.

Hence, the further process of collectivisation is a process of the gradual absorption and re-education of the remaining individual peasant farms and farmers by the collective farms.

This means that the collective farms have triumphed completely and irrevocably. (*Stormy and prolonged applause.*)

They show also that the state farms and collective farms together control 84.5 per cent of the total area under grain in the U.S.S.R.

This means that the collective farms and state farms together have become a force which determines the fate of the whole of agriculture and of all its branches.

The tables further show that the 65 per cent of peasant

farms united in collective farms control 73.9 per cent of the total area under grain crops, whereas all the individual peasant farms that remain, representing 35 per cent of the entire peasant population, control only 15.5 per cent of the total area under grain crops.

If we add to this fact that in 1933 the various deliveries to the state made by the collective farms amounted to more than 1,000 million poods of grain, while the individual peasants, who fulfilled their plan 100 per cent, delivered only about 130,000,000 poods; whereas in 1929–30 the individual peasants delivered to the state about 780,000,000 poods, and the collective farms not more than 120,000,000 poods—then it becomes absolutely clear that during the period under review the collective farms and the individual peasants have completely exchanged roles: the collective farms during this period have become the predominant force in agriculture, whereas the individual peasants have become a secondary force and are compelled to subordinate and adapt themselves to the collective-farm system.

It must be admitted that the labouring peasantry, our Soviet peasantry, has completely and irrevocably taken its stand under the Red banner of socialism. (*Prolonged applause.*)

Let the Socialist-Revolutionary, Menshevik, and bourgeois-Trotskyist gossips chatter about the peasantry being counter-revolutionary by nature, about its mission to restore capitalism in the U.S.S.R., about its inability to serve as the ally of the working class in building socialism, and about the impossibility of building socialism in the U.S.S.R. The facts show that these gentlemen slander the U.S.S.R. and the Soviet peasantry. The facts show that our Soviet peasantry has quit the shores of capitalism for good and is going forward, in alliance with the working class, to socialism. The facts show that we have already laid the foundations of a socialist society in the U.S.S.R., and it only remains for us to erect the superstructures—a task which undoubtedly is much easier than that of laying the foundations of a socialist society.

The increase in crop area and in output is not the only thing, however, that reflects the strength of the collective farms and state farms. Their strength is reflected also in the increase in the number of tractors at their disposal, in their increasing use of machinery. There is no doubt that in this respect our collective farms and state farms have gone a long way forward.

Here is the corresponding table:

Number of Tractors Employed in Agriculture in the U.S.S.R.
(Allowance made for depreciation)

	Number of tractors in thousands				
	1929	1930	1931	1932	1933
Total number of tractors	34.9	72.1	125.3	148.5	204.1
Of which:					
a) In machine and tractor stations	2.4	31.1	63.3	74.8	122.3
b) In state farms of all systems	9.7	27.7	51.5	64.0	81.8

	Capacity in thousands of horse-power				
	1929	1930	1931	1932	1933
Total number of tractors	391.4	1,003.5	1,850.0	2,225.0	3,100.0
Of which:					
a) In machine and tractor stations	23.9	372.5	848.0	1,077.0	1,782.0
b) In state farms of all systems	123.4	483.1	892.0	1,043.0	1,318.0

Thus, we have 204,000 tractors with a total of 3,100,000 H.P. working for the collective farms and state farms. This force, as you see, is not a small one; it is a force capable of pulling up all the roots of capitalism in the countryside; it is a force twice as great as the number of tractors that Lenin once mentioned as a remote prospect.

As regards the number of agricultural machines in the machine and tractor stations and in the state farms under the People's Commissariat of State Farms, figures are given in the following tables:

In Machine and Tractor Stations

	1930	1931	1932	1933
Harvester combines (thousands)	7 (units)	0.1	2.2	11.5
Internal combustion and steam engines (thousands)	0.1	4.9	6.2	17.6
Complex and semi-complex threshers (thousands)	2.9	27.8	37.0	50.0
Electric threshing installations	168	268	551	1,283
MTS repair shops	104	770	1,220	1,933
Motor lorries (thousands)	0.2	1.0	6.0	13.5
Passenger motor-cars (units)	17	191	245	2,800

In State Farms Controlled by the People's Commissariat of State Farms

	1930	1931	1932	1933
Harvester combines (thousands)	1.7	6.3	11.9	13.5
Internal combustion and steam engines (thousands)	0.3	0.7	1.2	2.5
Complex and semi-complex threshers (thousands)	1.4	4.2	7.1	8.0
Electric installations	42	112	164	222
Repair shops:				
a) For capital repairs	72	133	208	302
b) For medium repairs	75	160	215	476
c) For running repairs	205	310	578	1,166
Motor lorries (thousands)	2.1	3.7	6.2	10.9
Passenger motor-cars (units)	118	385	625	1,890

I do not think that these figures require any explanation.

Of no little importance for the progress of agriculture was also the formation of the Political Departments of the machine and tractor stations and state farms and the sending of skilled personnel into agriculture. Everybody admits now that the personnel of the Political Departments played a tremendous role in improving the work of the collective farms and state farms. You know that during the period under review the Central Committee of the Party sent more than 23,000 Communists to the countryside to reinforce the cadres in agriculture. More than 3,000 of them were sent to work in the land organs, more than 2,000 to state farms, more than 13,000 to the Political Departments of the machine and tractor stations, and over 5,000 to the Political Departments of the state farms.

The same must be said about the provision of new engineering, technical and agronomic forces for the collective farms and state farms. As you know, more than 111,000 workers of this category were sent into agriculture during the period under review.

During the period under review, over 1,900,000 tractor drivers, harvester combine drivers and operators, and automobile drivers were trained and sent to work in the system under the People's Commissariat of Agriculture alone.

During the same period more than 1,600,000 chairmen and members of management boards of collective farms, brigade leaders for field work, brigade leaders for livestock raising, and book-keepers were trained or received additional training.

This, of course, is not enough for our agriculture. But still, it is something.

As you see, the state has done everything possible to facilitate the work of the organs of the People's Commissariat of Agriculture and of the People's Commissariat of State Farms in guiding collective-farm and state-farm development.

Can it be said that these possibilities have been properly used?

Unfortunately, it cannot.

To begin with, these People's Commissariats are more infected than others with the disease of red tape. Decisions are made, but not a thought is given to checking their fulfilment, to calling to order those who disobey the instructions and orders of the leading bodies, and to promoting honest and conscientious workers.

One would think that the existence of a huge number of tractors and machines would impose upon the land organs the obligation to keep these valuable machines in good order, to see to their timely repair, to employ them more or less efficiently. What is being done by them in this respect? Unfortunately, very little. The maintenance of tractors and machines is unsatisfactory. Repairs are also unsatisfactory, because even to this day there is a refusal to understand that the basis of repairs is running and medium repairs, and not capital repairs. As for the utilisation of tractors and machines, the unsatisfactory position in this respect is so clear and well known that it needs no proof.

One of the immediate tasks in agriculture is to introduce proper rotation of crops and to secure the extension of clean fallow and the improvement of seeds in all branches of agriculture. What is being done in this respect? Unfortunately, very little as yet. The state of affairs in regard to grain and cotton seed is so muddled that it will take a long time to put straight.

One of the effective means of increasing the yield of industrial crops is to supply them with fertilisers. What is being done in this respect? Very little as yet. Fertilisers are available, but the organs of the People's Commissariat of Agriculture fail to get them; and when they do get them they do not see to it that they are delivered on time to the places where they are required and that they are utilised properly.

In regard to the state farms, it must be said that they still fail to cope with their tasks. I do not in the least underestimate the great revolutionising role of our state farms. But if we compare the enormous sums the state has invested in the state farms with the actual results they have achieved to date, we find an enormous discrepancy to the disadvantage of the state farms. The principal reason for the discrepancy is the fact that our state grain farms are too unwieldy; the directors cannot manage such huge farms. The state farms themselves are too specialised, they have no rotation of crops and fallow land; they do not include sectors for livestock raising. Evidently, it will be necessary to split up the state farms and do away with their excessive specialisation. One might think that it was the People's Commissariat of State Farms that raised this question opportunely and succeeded in solving it. But that is not so. The question was raised and settled on the initiative of people who were not connected in any way with the People's Commissariat of State Farms.

Finally, there is the question of livestock farming. I have already reported on the serious situation with regard to livestock. One might think that our land organs would display feverish activity in an effort to put an end to the crisis of livestock farming, that they would sound the alarm, mobilise their personnel and tackle the problem of livestock farming. Unfortunately, nothing of the kind has happened, or is happening. Not only have they failed to sound the alarm about the serious livestock situation, but, on the contrary, they try to gloss over the question, and sometimes in their reports even try to conceal from the public opinion of the country the actual situation of livestock farming, which is absolutely impermissible for Bolsheviks. To hope, after this, that the land organs will be able to put livestock farming on to the right road and raise it to the proper level would be building on sand. The whole Party, all our workers, Party and non-Party, must take this matter in hand, bearing in mind that the livestock problem today is of the same prime importance as the grain problem—now successfully solved—was yesterday. There is no need to prove that our Soviet people, who have overcome many a serious obstacle in the path to the goal, will be able to overcome this obstacle as well. (*Thunderous applause.*)

Such is a brief and far from complete enumeration of the defects which must be removed, and of the tasks which must be fulfilled in the immediate future.

But the matter does not end with these tasks. There are other tasks in agriculture, concerning which a few words must be said.

First of all, we must bear in mind that the old division of our regions into industrial regions and agrarian regions has now become obsolete. We no longer have any exclusively agrarian regions that would supply grain, meat and vegetables to the industrial regions; just as we no longer have any exclusively industrial regions that would expect to obtain all necessary produce from outside, from other regions. Development is leading to the point when all our regions will be more or less industrial, and they will become increasingly so as this development proceeds. This means that the Ukraine, the North Caucasus, the Central Black Earth region, and other formerly agrarian areas can no longer supply the industrial centres with as much produce as they supplied in the past, because they have to feed their own towns and their own workers, the number of which will be increasing. But from this it follows that every region must develop its own agricultural base, so as to have its own supply of vegetables, potatoes, butter and milk, and, to some extent, grain and meat, if it does not want to get into difficulties. You know that this is quite practicable and is already being done.

The task is to pursue this line to the end at all costs.

Further, we should note the fact that the division of our regions into consuming regions and producing regions is also beginning to lose its hard and fast character. This year such "consuming" regions as the Moscow and Gorky regions delivered nearly 80,000,000 poods of grain to the state. This, of course, is no small item. In the so-called consuming zone there are about 5,000,000 hectares of virgin soil, covered with scrub. It is well known that the climate in this zone is not bad; precipitation is ample, and droughts unknown. If this land were cleared of scrub and a number of organisational measures were undertaken, it would be possible to obtain a vast area for grain crops, which with the usually high yield in these localities could supply no less market grain than is now supplied by the Lower or Middle Volga. This would be a great help for the industrial centres in the north.

Evidently, the task is to develop large tracts under grain crops in the areas of the consuming zone.

Finally, there is the question of combating drought in the Trans-Volga area. Afforestation and the planting of forest shelter belts in the eastern districts of the Trans-Volga area is of tremendous importance. As you know, this work is already taking place, although it cannot be said that it is being carried on with sufficient intensity. As regards the irrigation of the Trans-Volga area—the most important thing in combating drought—we must not allow this matter to be indefinitely postponed. It is true that this work has been held up somewhat by certain external circumstances which cause considerable forces and funds to be diverted to other purposes. But now there is no longer any reason why it should be further postponed. We cannot do without a large and absolutely stable grain base on the Volga, one which will be independent of the vagaries of the weather and will provide annually about 200,000,000 poods of marketable grain. This is absolutely necessary, in view of the growth of the towns on the Volga, on the one hand, and of the possibility of all sorts of complications in the sphere of international relations, on the other.

The task is to set to work seriously to organise the irrigation of the Trans-Volga area. (*Applause.*)

3. THE RISE IN THE MATERIAL AND CULTURAL STANDARD OF THE WORKING PEOPLE

We have thus depicted the situation of our industry and agriculture, their development during the period under review and their state at the present moment.

To sum up, we have:

a) A mighty advance in production both in industry and in the main branches of agriculture.

b) The final victory, on the basis of this advance, of the socialist system of economy over the capitalist system both in industry and in agriculture; the socialist system has become the sole system in the whole of the national economy, and the capitalist elements have been ousted from all spheres of the national economy.

c) The final abandonment of small-commodity individual farming by the overwhelming majority of the peasants; their uniting in collective farms on the basis of collective labour and collective ownership of the means of production; the complete victory of collective farming over small-commodity individual farming.

d) An ever-increasing process of expansion of the collective farms through the absorption of individual peasant farms, which are thus diminishing in number month by month and are, in fact, being converted into an auxiliary force for the collective farms and state farms.

Naturally, this historic victory over the exploiters could not but lead to a radical improvement in the material standard of the working people and in their conditions of life generally.

The elimination of the parasitic classes has led to the disappearance of the exploitation of man by man. The labour of the worker and the peasant is freed from exploitation. The incomes which the exploiters used to squeeze out of the labour of the people now remain in the hands of the working people and are used partly for the expansion of production and the enlistment of new detachments of working people in production, and partly for directly increasing the incomes of the workers and peasants.

Unemployment, that scourge of the working class, has disappeared. In the bourgeois countries millions of unemployed suffer want and privation owing to lack of work, whereas in our country there are no longer any workers who have no work and no earnings.

With the disappearance of kulak bondage, poverty in the countryside has disappeared. Every peasant, whether a collective farmer or an individual farmer, now has the opportunity of living a human existence, provided only that he wants to work conscientiously and not to be a loafer, a tramp, or a despoiler of collective-farm property.

The abolition of exploitation, the abolition of unemployment in the towns, and the abolition of poverty in the countryside are historic achievements in the material condition of the working people that are beyond even the dreams of the workers and peasants even in the most "democratic" of the bourgeois countries.

The very appearance of our large towns and industrial centres has changed. An inevitable feature of the big towns in bourgeois countries is the slums, the so-called working-class districts on the outskirts of the towns—a heap of dark, damp and dilapidated dwellings, mostly of the basement type, where usually the poor live in filth and curse their fate. The revolution in the U.S.S.R. has meant the disappearance of such slums. They have been replaced by blocks of bright and well-built workers' houses; in many cases the working-class districts of our towns present a better appearance than the centre of the town.

The appearance of the countryside has changed even more. The old type of village, with the church in the most prominent place, with the best houses—those of the police officer, the priest, and the kulaks—in the foreground, and the dilapidated huts of the peasants in the background, is beginning to disappear. Its place is being taken by the new type of village, with its public farm buildings, with its clubs, radio, cinemas, schools, libraries and crèches; with its tractors, harvester combines, threshing machines and automobiles. The former important personages of the village, the kulak-exploiter, the blood-sucking usurer, the merchant-speculator, the "little father" police officer, have disappeared. Now, the prominent personages are the leading people of the collective farms and state farms, of the schools and clubs, the senior tractor and combine drivers, the brigade leaders in field work and livestock raising, and the best men and women shock brigaders on the collective-farm fields.

The antithesis between town and country is disappearing. The peasants are ceasing to regard the town as the centre of their exploitation. The economic and cultural bond between town and country is becoming stronger. The country now receives assistance from the town and from urban industry in the shape of tractors, agricultural machinery, automobiles, workers, and funds. And the countryside itself now has its own industry, in the shape of the machine and tractor stations, repair shops, all sorts of industrial undertakings of the collective farms, small electric power stations, etc. The cultural gulf between town and country is being bridged.

Such are the principal achievements of the working people in the sphere of improving their material conditions, their everyday life, and their cultural standard.

On the basis of these achievements we have the following to record for the period under review:

a) An increase in the national income from 35,000 million rubles in 1930 to 50,000 million rubles in 1933. In view of the fact that the income of the capitalist elements, including concessionaires, at the present time constitutes less than one half of one per cent of the total national income, almost the whole of the national income is distributed among the workers and other employees, the labouring peasants, the cooperatives, and the state.

b) An increase in the population of the Soviet Union from 160,500,000 at the end of 1930 to 168,000,000 at the end of 1933.

c) An increase in the number of workers and other employees from 14,530,000 in 1930 to 21,883,000 in 1933.

The number of manual workers increased during this period from 9,489,000 to 13,797,000; the number of workers employed in large-scale industry, including transport, increased from 5,079,000 to 6,882,000; the number of agricultural workers increased from 1,426,000 to 2,519,000, and the number of workers and other employees engaged in trade increased from 814,000 to 1,497,000.

d) An increase in the total of the wages paid to workers and other employees from 13,597 million rubles in 1930 to 34,280 million rubles in 1933.

e) An increase in the average annual wages of industrial workers from 991 rubles in 1930 to 1,519 rubles in 1933.

f) An increase in the social insurance fund for workers and other employees from 1,810 million rubles in 1930 to 4,610 million rubles in 1933.

g) The adoption of a seven-hour working day in all surface industries.

h) State aid to the peasants by the organisation of 2,860 machine and tractor stations, involving an investment of 2,000 million rubles.

i) State aid to the peasants in the form of credits to the collective farms amounting to 1,600 million rubles.

j) State aid to the peasants in the form of seed and food loans amounting in the period under review to 262,000,000 poods of grain.

k) State aid to the economically weaker peasants in the shape of relief from taxation and insurance payments amounting to 370,000,000 rubles.

As regards the cultural development of the country, we have the following to record for the period under review:

a) The introduction of universal compulsory elementary education throughout the U.S.S.R., and an increase in literacy among the population from 67 per cent at the end of 1930 to 90 per cent at the end of 1933.

b) An increase in the number of pupils and students at schools of all grades from 14,358,000 in 1929 to 26,419,000 in 1933, including an increase from 11,697,000 to 19,163,000 in the number receiving *elementary* education, from 2,453,000 to 6,674,000 in the number receiving *secondary* education, and from 207,000 to 491,000 in the number receiving *higher* education.

c) An increase in the number of children receiving pre-school education from 838,000 in 1929 to 5,917,000 in 1933.

d) An increase in the number of higher educational institutions, general and special, from 91 in 1914 to 600 in 1933.

e) An increase in the number of scientific research institutes from 400 in 1929 to 840 in 1933.

f) An increase in the number of clubs and similar institutions from 32,000 in 1929 to 54,000 in 1933.

g) An increase in the number of cinemas, cinema installations in clubs, and mobile cinemas, from 9,800 in 1929 to 29,200 in 1933.

h) An increase in the circulation of newspapers from 12,500,000 in 1929 to 36,500,000 in 1933.

Perhaps it will not be amiss to point out that the proportion of workers among the students in our higher educational institutions is 51.4 per cent of the total, and that of labouring peasants 16.5 per cent; whereas in Germany, for instance, the proportion of workers among the students in higher educational institutions in 1932–33 was only 3.2 per cent of the total, and that of small peasants only 2.4 per cent.

We must note as a gratifying fact and as an indication of the progress of culture in the countryside, the increased activity of the women collective farmers in social and organisational work. We know, for example, that about 6,000 women collective farmers are chairmen of collective farms, more than 60,000 are members of management boards of collective farms, 28,000 are brigade leaders, 100,000 are team organisers, 9,000 are managers of collective-farm marketable livestock sectors, and 7,000 are tractor drivers.

Needless to say, these figures are incomplete; but even these figures quite clearly show the great progress of culture in the countryside. This fact, comrades, is of tremendous significance. It is of tremendous significance because women form half the population of our country; they constitute a huge army of workers; and they are called upon to bring up our children, our future generation, that is to say, our future. That is why we must not permit this huge army of working people to remain in darkness and ignorance! That is why we must welcome the growing social activity of the working women and their promotion to leading posts as an indubitable sign of the growth of our culture. (*Prolonged applause.*)

Finally, I must point out one more fact, but of a negative character. I have in mind the intolerable fact that our pedagogical and medical faculties are still being neglected. This is a great defect bordering on violation of the interests of the state. This defect must be remedied without fail, and the sooner the better.

4. THE PROGRESS OF TRADE TURNOVER, AND TRANSPORT

Thus we have:

a) an increase in the output of industry, including goods for mass consumption;

b) an increase in the output of agriculture;

c) a growth in the requirements and the demand for produce and manufactured goods on the part of the masses of the working people of town and country.

What more is needed to co-ordinate these conditions and to ensure that the entire mass of consumers receives the necessary goods and produce?

Some comrades think that these conditions alone are sufficient for the economic life of the country to go full steam ahead. That is a profound delusion. We can imagine a situation in which all these conditions exist; yet if the goods do not reach the consumers, economic life—far from going full steam ahead—will, on the contrary, be dislocated and disorganised to its foundations. It is high time we realised that in the last analysis goods are produced not for the sake of producing them, but for consumption. Cases have occurred where we have had quite a quantity of goods and produce, but they have not only not reached the consumer, they have continued for years to wander in the bureaucratic backwaters of our so-called commodity-distribution network, at a distance from the consumers. Naturally, under these circumstances industry and agriculture lost all stimulus to increase production; the commodity-distribution network became overstocked, while the workers and peasants had to go without these goods and produce. The result was a dislocation of the economic life of the country, despite the existence of the goods and produce. If the economic life of the country is to go full steam ahead, and industry and agriculture are to have a stimulus for further increasing their output, one more condition is necessary—namely, well-developed *trade turnover* between town and country, between the various districts and regions of the country, between the various branches of the national economy. The country must be covered with a vast network of wholesale distribution bases, shops and stores. There must be a ceaseless flow of goods through these bases, shops and stores from the producer to the consumer. The state trading system, the co-operative trading system, the local industries, the collective farms, and the individual peasants must be drawn into this work.

This is what we call fully developed *Soviet trade*, trade *without* capitalists, trade *without* speculators.

As you see, the expansion of Soviet trade is a very urgent problem, which must be solved or further progress will be rendered impossible.

And yet, in spite of the fact that this truth is perfectly obvious, in the period under review the Party has had to overcome a number of obstacles to the expansion of Soviet trade which could briefly be described as the result of an aberration of the brain among a section of Communists on questions of the necessity and importance of Soviet trade.

To begin with, there is still among a section of Communists a supercilious, disdainful attitude towards trade in general, and towards Soviet trade in particular. These Communists, so-called, look upon Soviet trade as a matter of secondary importance, not worth bothering about, and those engaged in trade as being quite hopeless. Evidently, these people do not realise that their supercilious attitude towards Soviet trade is not an expression of Bolshevik views, but rather of the views of impoverished aristocrats who are full of ambition but lack ammunition. (*Applause.*) These people do not realise that Soviet trade is our own, Bolshevik work, and that those employed in trade, including those behind the counter—if only they work conscientiously—are doing our revolutionary, Bolshevik work. (*Applause.*) It goes without saying that the Party had to give those Communists, so-called, a slight dressing down and throw their aristocratic prejudices on the rubbish heap. (*Prolonged applause.*)

Further, we had to overcome prejudices of another kind. I have in mind the Leftist chatter current among a section of our functionaries to the effect that Soviet trade is a superseded stage; that it is necessary to organise the direct exchange of products; that money will soon be abolished, because it has become mere tokens; that it is unnecessary to develop trade, since the direct exchange of products is knocking at the door. It must be observed that this Leftist petty-bourgeois chatter, which plays into the hands of the capitalist elements who are striving to sabotage the expansion of Soviet trade, is current not only among a section of our "Red professors," but also among certain of our trading personnel. Of course, it is ridiculous and funny to hear these people, who are incapable of organising the very simple business of Soviet trade, chatter about their readiness to organise the more complicated and difficult business of a direct exchange of products. But Don Quixotes are called Don Quixotes precisely because they lack the most elementary sense of reality. These people, who are as far removed from Marxism as the sky from the earth, evidently do not realise that we shall use money for a long time to come, right up to the time when the first stage of communism, i.e., the socialist stage of development, has been completed. They do not realise that money is the instrument of bourgeois economy which the Soviet Government has taken over and adapted to the interests of socialism for the purpose of expanding Soviet trade to the utmost, and so preparing the conditions necessary for the direct exchange of products. They do not realise that the direct exchange of products can replace, and be the result of, only a perfectly organised system of Soviet trade, of which we have not a trace as yet, and shall not have for some time. Naturally, in trying to organise developed Soviet trade, our Party found it necessary to give a dressing down to these "Left" freaks as well, and to scatter their petty-bourgeois chatter to the winds.

Further, we had to overcome among the people in charge of trade the unhealthy habit of distributing goods mechanically; we had to put a stop to their indifference to the demand for a greater range of goods and to the requirements of the consumers; we had to put an end to the mechanical consignment of goods, to lack of personal responsibility in trade. For this purpose, regional and inter-district wholesale distribution bases and tens of thousands of new shops and booths were opened.

Further, we had to put an end to the monopoly position of the co-operatives in the market. In this connection we instructed all the People's Commissariats to start trade in the goods manufactured by the industries under their control; and the People's Commissariat of Supplies was instructed to develop an extensive open trade in agricultural produce. This has led, on the one hand, to an improvement in co-operative trade through emulation, and, on the other hand, to a drop in market prices and to sounder conditions in the market.

A wide network of dining-rooms was established which provide food at reduced prices ("public catering"). Workers' Supply Departments were set up in the factories, and all those who had no connection with the factory were taken off the supply list; in the factories under the control of the People's Commissariat of Heavy Industry alone, no less than 500,000 such persons had to be removed from the list.

We have organised a single centralised bank for short term credit—the State Bank, with its 2,200 district branches capable of financing trade operations.

As a result of these measures we have the following to record for the period under review:

a) an increase in the number of shops and trading booths from 184,662 in 1930 to 277,974 in 1933;

b) a newly created network of regional wholesale distribution bases, numbering 1,011, and inter-district wholesale distribution bases, numbering 864;

c) a newly created network of Workers' Supply Departments, numbering 1,600;

d) an increase in the network of shops for non-rationed sale of bread, which now exist in 330 towns;

e) an increase in the number of public dining-rooms, which at the present time cater for 19,800,000 consumers;

f) an increase in state and co-operative trade turnover, including public dining-rooms, from 18,900 million rubles in 1930 to 49,000 million rubles in 1933.

It would be a mistake, however, to think that all this expansion of Soviet trade is sufficient to satisfy the requirements of our economy. On the contrary, it is now becoming clearer than ever that the present state of trade turnover cannot satisfy our requirements. Hence, the task is to develop Soviet trade still further, to draw local industry into this work, to increase collective-farm and peasant trade, and to achieve new and decisive successes in the sphere of increasing Soviet trade.

It must be pointed out, however, that we cannot restrict ourselves merely to the expansion of Soviet trade. While the development of our economy depends upon the development of the trade turnover, upon the development of Soviet trade, the development of Soviet trade, in its turn, depends upon the development of our transport, both rail and water transport, and motor transport. It may happen that goods are available, that all the possibilities exist for expanding trade turnover, but transport cannot keep up with the development of trade turnover and refuses to carry the freight. As you know, this happens rather often. Hence, transport is the weak spot which may be a stumbling-block, and indeed is perhaps already beginning to be a stumbling-block to the whole of our economy and, above all, to our trade turnover.

It is true that railway transport has increased its freight turnover from 133,900 million ton-kilometres in 1930 to 172,000 million ton-kilometres in 1933. But that is too little, far too little for us, for our economy.

Water transport has increased its freight turnover from 45,600 million ton-kilometres in 1930 to 59,900 million ton-kilometres in 1933. But that is too little, far too little for our economy.

I say nothing of motor transport, in which the number of automobiles (lorries and passenger cars) has increased from 8,800 in 1913 to 117,800 at the end of 1933. That is so little for our national economy that one is ashamed even to mention it.

There can be no doubt that all these forms of transport could work much better if the transport system did not suffer from the well-known disease called red-tape methods of management. Hence, besides the need to help transport by providing personnel and means, our task is to root out the red-tape attitude in the administration departments of the transport system and to make them more efficient.

Comrades, we have succeeded in solving correctly the main problems of industry, which is now standing firmly on its feet. We have also succeeded in solving correctly the main problems of agriculture, and we can say quite definitely that agriculture also is now standing firmly on its feet. But we are in danger of losing all these achievements if our trade turnover begins to be defective and if transport becomes a fetter on our feet. Hence, the task of expanding trade turnover and of decisively improving transport is an immediate and urgent problem which must be solved or we cannot go forward.

III. THE PARTY

I pass to the question of the Party.

The present congress is taking place under the flag of the complete victory of Leninism, under the flag of the liquidation of the remnants of the anti-Leninist groups.

The anti-Leninist group of Trotskyists has been smashed and scattered. Its organisers are now to be found in the backyards of the bourgeois parties abroad.

The anti-Leninist group of the Right deviators has been smashed and scattered. Its organisers have long ago renounced their views and are now trying in every way to expiate the sins they committed against the Party.

The groups of nationalist deviators have been smashed and scattered. Their organisers have either completely merged with the interventionist émigrés, or else they have recanted.

The majority of the adherents to these anti-revolutionary groups had to admit that the line of the Party was correct and they have capitulated to the Party.

At the Fifteenth Party Congress it was still necessary to prove that the Party line was correct and to wage a struggle against certain anti-Leninist groups; and at the Sixteenth Party Congress we had to deal the final blow to the last adherents of these groups. At this congress, however, there is nothing to prove and, it seems, no one to fight. Everyone sees that the line of the Party has triumphed. (*Thunderous applause.*)

The policy of industrialising the country has triumphed. Its results are obvious to everyone. What arguments can be advanced against this fact?

The policy of eliminating the kulaks and of complete collectivisation has triumphed. Its results are also obvious to everyone. What arguments can be advanced against this fact?

The experience of our country has shown that it is fully possible for socialism to achieve victory in one country taken separately. What arguments can be advanced against this fact?

It is evident that all these successes, and primarily the victory of the five-year plan, have utterly demoralised and smashed all the various anti-Leninist groups.

It must be admitted that the Party today is united as it has never been before. (*Stormy and prolonged applause.*)

1. QUESTIONS OF IDEOLOGICAL AND POLITICAL LEADERSHIP

Does this mean, however, that the fight is ended, and that the offensive of socialism is to be discontinued as superfluous?

No, it does not.

Does it mean that all is well in our Party; that there will be no more deviations in the Party, and that, therefore, we may now rest on our laurels?

No, it does not.

We have smashed the enemies of the Party, the opportunists of all shades, the nationalist deviators of all kinds. But remnants of their ideology still live in the minds of individual members of the Party, and not infrequently they find expression. The Party must not be regarded as something isolated from the people who surround it. It lives and works in its environment. It is not surprising that at times unhealthy moods penetrate into the Party from outside. And the ground for such moods undoubtedly exists in our country, if only for the reason that there still exist in town and country certain intermediary strata of the population who constitute a medium which breeds such moods.

The Seventeenth Conference of our Party declared that one of the fundamental political tasks in fulfilling the Second Five-

Year Plan is "to overcome the survivals of capitalism in economic life and in the minds of people." That is an absolutely correct idea. But can we say that we have already overcome all the survivals of capitalism in economic life? No, we cannot say that. Still less can we say that we have overcome the survivals of capitalism in the minds of people. We cannot say that, not only because in development the minds of people lag behind their economic position, but also because the capitalist encirclement still exists, which endeavours to revive and sustain the survivals of capitalism in the economic life and in the minds of the people of the U.S.S.R., and against which we Bolsheviks must always keep our powder dry.

Naturally, these survivals cannot but be a favourable ground for a revival of the ideology of the defeated anti-Leninist groups in the minds of individual members of our Party. Add to this the not very high theoretical level of the majority of our Party members, the inadequate ideological work of the Party bodies, and the fact that our Party functionaries are overburdened with purely practical work, which deprives them of the opportunity of augmenting their theoretical knowledge, and you will understand the origin of the confusion on a number of questions of Leninism that exists in the minds of individual Party members, a confusion which not infrequently penetrates into our press and helps to revive the survivals of the ideology of the defeated anti-Leninist groups.

That is why we cannot say that the fight is ended and that there is no longer any need for the policy of the socialist offensive.

It would be possible to take a number of questions of Leninism and demonstrate by means of them how tenaciously the survivals of the ideology of the defeated anti-Leninist groups continue to exist in the minds of certain Party members.

Take, for example, the question of building a *classless socialist society.* The Seventeenth Party Conference declared that we are advancing towards the formation of a classless socialist society. Naturally, a classless society cannot come of its own accord, as it were. It has to be achieved and built by the efforts of all the working people, by strengthening the organs of the dictatorship of the proletariat, by intensifying the class struggle, by abolishing classes, by eliminating the remnants of the capitalist classes, and in battles with enemies, both internal and external.

The point is clear, one would think.

And yet, who does not know that the enunciation of this clear and elementary thesis of Leninism has given rise to not a little confusion in the minds of a section of Party members and to unhealthy sentiments among them? The thesis that we are advancing towards a classless society—put forward as a slogan—was interpreted by them to mean a spontaneous process. And they began to reason in this way: If it is a classless society, then we can relax the class struggle, we can relax the dictatorship of the proletariat, and get rid of the state altogether, since it is fated to wither away soon in any case. And they fell into a state of foolish rapture, in the expectation that soon there would be no classes, and therefore no class struggle, and therefore no cares and worries, and therefore it is possible to lay down one's arms and go to bed—to sleep in expectation of the advent of a classless society. (*General laughter.*)

There can be no doubt that this confusion of mind and these sentiments are exactly like the well-known views of the Right deviators, who believed that the old must automatically grow into the new, and that one fine day we shall wake up and find ourselves in a socialist society.

As you see, remnants of the ideology of the defeated anti-Leninist groups are capable of revival, and are far from having lost their vitality.

Naturally, if this confusion of views and these non-Bolshevik sentiments obtained a hold over the majority of our Party, the Party would find itself demobilised and disarmed.

Let us take, further, the question of the agricultural *artel* and the agricultural *commune*. Everybody admits now that under present conditions the artel is the only correct form of the collective-farm movement. And that is quite understandable: a) the artel correctly combines the personal, everyday interests of the collective farmers with their public interests; b) the artel successfully adapts personal, everyday interests to public interests, and thereby helps to educate the individual peasants of yesterday in the spirit of collectivism.

Unlike the artel, where only the means of production are

socialised, the communes, until recently, socialised not only the means of production, but also everyday life of every member of the commune; that is to say, the members of a commune, unlike the members of an artel, did not individually own poultry, small livestock, a cow, grain, or household land. This means that in the commune the personal, everyday interests of the members have not so much been taken into account and combined with the public interests as they have been eclipsed by the latter in the interests of petty-bourgeois equalisation. It is clear that this is the weakest side of the commune. This indeed explains why communes are not widespread, why there are but a few score of them in existence. For the same reason the communes, in order to maintain their existence and save themselves from going to pieces, have been compelled to abandon the system of socialising everyday life; they are beginning to work on the basis of the workday unit, and have begun to distribute grain among their members, to permit their members to own poultry, small livestock, a cow, etc. But from this it follows that, in fact, the commune has gone over to the position of the artel. And there is nothing bad in that, because it is necessary in the interests of the sound development of the mass collective-farm movement.

This does not mean, of course, that the commune is not needed at all, and that it no longer represents a higher form of the collective-farm movement. No, the commune is needed, and it is, of course, a higher form of the collective-farm movement. This applies, however, not to the present commune, which arose on the basis of undeveloped technique and of a shortage of produce, and which is itself going over to the position of the artel; it applies to the commune of the future, which will arise on the basis of a more developed technique and of an abundance of produce. The present agricultural commune arose on the basis of an underdeveloped technique and a shortage of produce. This indeed explains why it practised equalisation and took little account of the personal, everyday interests of its members, as a result of which it is now being compelled to go over to the position of the artel, in which the personal and public interests of the collective farmers are rationally combined. The future communes will arise out of developed and prosperous artels. The future agricultural commune will arise when the fields and farms of the artel have an abundance of grain, cattle, poultry, vegetables, and all other produce; when the artels have mechanised laundries, modern kitchens and dining-rooms, mechanised bakeries, etc.; when the collective farmer sees that it is more to his advantage to get meat and milk from the collective farm's meat and dairy department than to keep his own cow and small livestock; when the woman collective farmer sees that it is more to her advantage to take her meals in the dining-room, to get her bread from the public bakery, and to have her linen washed in the public laundry, than to do all these things herself. The future commune will arise on the basis of a more developed technique and of a more developed artel, on the basis of an abundance of products. When will that be? Not soon, of course. But it will take place. It would be criminal artificially to accelerate the process of transition from the artel to the future commune. That would confuse the whole issue, and would facilitate the work of our enemies. The transition from the artel to the future commune must proceed gradually, to the extent that *all* the collective farmers become convinced that such a transition is necessary.

That is how matters stand with regard to the question of the artel and the commune.

One would think that this was clear and almost elementary.

And yet there is a fair amount of confusion on this question among a section of Party members. There are those who think that by declaring the artel to be the fundamental form of the collective-farm movement the Party has drifted away from socialism, has retreated from the commune, from the higher form of the collective-farm movement, to a lower form. Why, one may ask? Because, it is suggested, there is no equality in the artel, since differences in the requirements and in the personal, everyday life of the members of the artel are preserved; whereas in the commune there is equality, because the requirements and the personal, everyday life of its members have been made equal. But, firstly, we no longer have any communes in which there is levelling, equalisation of requirements and personal, everyday life. Practice has shown that the communes would certainly have been doomed had they not abandoned equalisation and had they not in fact gone over to the position of artels. Consequently, there is no point in referring to what no longer exists. Secondly, every Leninist knows, if he is a real Leninist, that equalisation in the sphere of requirements and personal, everyday life is a reactionary petty-bourgeois absurdity worthy of some primitive sect of ascetics, but not of a socialist society organised on Marxist lines; for we cannot expect all people to have the same requirements and tastes, and all people to mould their personal, everyday life on the same model. And, finally, are not differences in requirements and in personal, everyday life still preserved among the workers? Does that mean that workers are more remote from socialism than members of agricultural communes?

These people evidently think that socialism calls for equalisation, for levelling the requirements and personal, everyday life of the members of society. Needless to say, such an assumption has nothing in common with Marxism, with Leninism. By equality Marxism means, not equalisation of personal requirements and everyday life, but the abolition of classes, i.e., a) the equal emancipation of all working people from exploitation after the capitalists have been overthrown and expropriated; b) the equal abolition for all of private property in the means of production after they have been converted into the property of the whole of society; c) the equal duty of all to work according to their ability, and the equal right of all working people to receive in return for this according to the work performed (*socialist* society); d) the equal duty of all to work according to their ability, and the equal right of all working people to receive in return for this according to their needs (*communist* society). Moreover, Marxism proceeds from the assumption that people's tastes and requirements are not, and cannot be, identical and equal in regard to quality or quantity, whether in the period of socialism or in the period of communism.

There you have the Marxist conception of equality.

Marxism has never recognised, and does not recognise, any other equality.

To draw from this the conclusion that socialism calls for equalisation, for the levelling of the requirements of the members of society, for the levelling of their tastes and of their personal, everyday life—that according to the Marxist plan all should wear the same clothes and eat the same dishes in the same quantity—is to utter vulgarities and to slander Marxism.

It is time it was understood that Marxism is an enemy of equalisation. Already in the *Manifesto of the Communist Party* Marx and Engels scourged primitive utopian socialism and termed it reactionary because it preached "universal asceticism and social levelling in its crudest form." In his *Anti-Dühring* Engels devoted a whole chapter to a withering criticism of the "radical equalitarian socialism" put forward by Dühring in opposition to Marxist socialism.

> "The real content of the proletarian demand for equality," said Engels, "is the demand for the *abolition of classes*. Any demand for equality which goes beyond that, of necessity passes into absurdity."

Lenin said the same thing:

> "Engels was a thousand times right when he wrote that to conceive equality as meaning anything *beyond* the abolition of classes is a very stupid and absurd prejudice. Bourgeois professors have tried to make use of the concept of equality to accuse us of wanting to make all men equal to one another. They have tried to accuse the Socialists of this absurdity, which they themselves invented. But in their ignorance they did not know that the Socialists—and precisely the founders of modern scientific socialism, Marx and Engels—said: equality is an empty phrase unless equality is understood to mean the abolition of classes. We want to abolish classes, and in this respect we stand for equality. But the claim that we want to make all men equal to one another is an empty phrase and a stupid invention of intellectuals" (Lenin's speech "On Deceiving the People with Slogans about Liberty and Equality").

Clear, one would think.

Bourgeois writers are fond of depicting Marxist socialism in the shape of the old tsarist barracks, where everything is subordinated to the "principle" of equalisation. But Marxists cannot be held responsible for the ignorance and stupidity of bourgeois writers.

There can be no doubt that this confusion in the minds of some Party members concerning Marxist socialism, and their infatuation with the equalitarian tendencies of agricultural communes, are exactly like the petty-bourgeois views of our Leftist blockheads, who at one time idealised the agricultural communes to such an extent that they even tried to set up communes in mills and factories, where skilled and unskilled workers, each working at his trade, had to pool their wages in a common fund, which was then shared out equally. You know what harm these infantile equalitarian exercises of the "Left" blockheads caused our industry.

As you see, the remnants of the ideology of the defeated anti-Party groups display rather considerable tenacity.

It is obvious that if these Leftist views were to triumph in the Party, the Party would cease to be Marxist, and the collective-farm movement would be utterly disorganised.

Or take, for example, the slogan "*Make all the collective farmers prosperous.*" This slogan applies not only to collective farmers; it applies still more to the workers, for we want to make all the workers prosperous—people leading a prosperous and fully cultured life.

One would think that the point was clear. There was no point in overthrowing capitalism in October 1917 and building socialism all these years if we are not going to secure a life of plenty for our people. Socialism does not mean poverty and privation, but the abolition of poverty and privation; it means the organisation of a prosperous and cultured life for all members of society.

And yet, this clear and essentially elementary slogan has caused a good deal of perplexity, confusion and muddle among a section of our Party members. Is not this slogan, they ask, a reversion to the old slogan, "Enrich yourselves," that was rejected by the Party? If everyone becomes prosperous, they go on to say, and the poor cease to be with us, upon whom then are we Bolsheviks to rely in our work? How shall we work without the poor?

This may sound funny, but the existence of such naïve and

anti-Leninist views among a section of Party members is an undoubted fact, which we must take into account.

Evidently, these people do not understand that a wide gulf lies between the slogan "Enrich yourselves" and the slogan "Make all the collective farmers prosperous." In the first place, only *individual* persons or groups can enrich themselves; whereas the slogan concerning a prosperous life applies not to individual persons or groups, but to *all* collective farmers. Secondly, *individual* persons or groups enrich themselves for the purpose of subordinating other people to themselves and *exploiting* them; whereas the slogan concerning a prosperous life for *all* the collective farmers—with the means of production in the collective farms socialised—*precludes* all possibility of the exploitation of some persons by others. Thirdly, the slogan "Enrich yourselves" was issued in the period when the New Economic Policy was in its initial stage, when capitalism was being partly restored, when the kulak was a power, when individual peasant farming predominated in the country and collective farming was in a rudimentary state; whereas the slogan "Make all the collective farmers prosperous" was issued in the last stage of NEP, when the capitalist elements in industry had been abolished, the kulaks in the countryside crushed, individual peasant farming forced into the background and the collective farms had become the predominant form of agriculture. This is apart from the fact that the slogan "Make all the collective farmers prosperous" was issued not in isolation, but inseparably bound up with the slogan "Make the collective farms Bolshevik."

Is it not clear that in point of fact the slogan "Enrich yourselves" was a call to *restore* capitalism, whereas the slogan "Make all the collective farmers prosperous" is a call to *deal the final blow* to the last remnants of capitalism by increasing the economic power of the collective farms and by transforming all collective farmers into prosperous working people? (*Voices:* "Quite right!")

Is it not clear that there is not, and cannot be, anything in common between these two slogans? (*Voices:* "Quite right!")

As for the argument that Bolshevik work and socialism are inconceivable without the existence of the poor, it is so stupid that it is embarrassing even to talk about it. Leninists rely upon the poor when there exist both capitalist elements and the poor who are exploited by the capitalists. But when the capitalist elements have been crushed and the poor have been emancipated from exploitation, the task of Leninists is not to perpetuate and preserve poverty and the poor—the conditions for whose existence have already been eliminated—but to abolish poverty and to raise the poor to a life of prosperity. It would be absurd to think that socialism can be built on the basis of poverty and privation, on the basis of reducing personal requirements and lowering the standard of living to the level of the poor, who themselves, moreover, refuse to remain poor any longer and are pushing their way upward to a prosperous life. Who wants this sort of socialism, so-called? It would not be socialism, but a caricature of socialism. Socialism can be built only on the basis of a vigorous growth of the productive forces of society; on the basis of an abundance of produce and goods; on the basis of the prosperity of the working people, on the basis of a vigorous growth of culture. For socialism, Marxist socialism, means not the reduction of individual requirements, but their development to the utmost, to full bloom; not the restriction of these requirements or a refusal to satisfy them, but the full and all-round satisfaction of all the requirements of culturally developed working people.

There can be no doubt that this confusion in the views of certain members of the Party concerning the poor and prosperity is a reflection of the views of our Leftist blockheads, who idealise the poor as the eternal bulwark of Bolshevism under all conditions, and who regard the collective farms as an arena of fierce class struggle.

As you see, here too, on this question, the remnants of the ideology of the defeated anti-Party groups have not yet lost their tenacious hold on life.

It is obvious that had such blockheaded views triumphed in our Party, the collective farms would not have achieved the successes they have gained during the past two years, and would have disintegrated in a very short time.

Or take, for example, the *national question.* Here, too, in the sphere of the national question, just as in the sphere of other questions, there is in the views of a section of the Party a confusion which creates a certain danger. I have spoken of the tenacity of the survivals of capitalism. It should be observed that the survivals of capitalism in people's minds are much more tenacious in the sphere of the national question than in any other sphere. They are more tenacious because they are able to disguise themselves well in national costume. Many think that Skrypnik's fall from grace was an individual case, an exception to the rule. This is not true. The fall from grace of Skrypnik and his group in the Ukraine is not an exception. Similar aberrations are observed among certain comrades in other national republics as well.

What is the deviation towards nationalism—regardless whether it is a matter of the deviation towards Great-Russian nationalism or the deviation towards local nationalism? The deviation towards nationalism is the adaptation of the internationalist policy of the working class to the nationalist policy of the bourgeoisie. The deviation towards nationalism reflects the attempts of "one's own," "national" bourgeoisie to undermine the Soviet system and to restore capitalism. The source of both these deviations, as you see, is the same. It is a *departure* from Leninist internationalism. If you want to keep both deviations under fire, then aim primarily against this source, against those who depart from internationalism—regardless whether it is a matter of the deviation towards local nationalism or the deviation towards Great-Russian nationalism. (*Stormy applause.*)

There is a controversy as to which deviation represents the chief danger: the deviation towards Great-Russian nationalism, or the deviation towards local nationalism. Under present conditions, this is a formal and, therefore, a pointless controversy. It would be foolish to attempt to give ready-made recipes suitable for all times and for all conditions as regards the chief and the lesser danger. Such recipes do not exist. The chief danger is the deviation against which we have ceased to fight, thereby allowing it to grow into a danger to the state. (*Prolonged applause.*)

In the Ukraine, only very recently, the deviation towards Ukrainian nationalism did not represent the chief danger; but when the fight against it ceased and it was allowed to grow to such an extent that it linked up with the interventionists, this deviation became the chief danger. The question as to which is the chief danger in the sphere of the national question is determined not by futile, formal controversies, but by a Marxist analysis of the situation at the given moment, and by a study of the mistakes that have been committed in this sphere.

The same should be said of *the Right and "Left" deviations* in the sphere of general policy. Here, too, as in other spheres, there is no little confusion in the views of certain members of our Party. Sometimes, while fighting against the Right deviation, they turn away from the "Left" deviation and relax the fight against it, on the assumption that it is not dangerous, or hardly dangerous. This is a grave and dangerous error. It is a concession to the "Left" deviation which is impermissible for a member of the Party. It is all the more impermissible for the reason that of late the "Lefts" have completely slid over to the position of the Rights, so that there is no longer any essential difference between them.

We have always said that the "Lefts" are in fact Rights who mask their Rightness by Left phrases. Now the "Lefts" themselves confirm the correctness of our statement. Take last year's issues of the Trotskyist *Bulletin.* What do Messieurs the Trotskyists demand, what do they write about, in what does their "Left" programme find expression? They demand: *the dissolution of the state farms,* on the grounds that they do not pay; *the dissolution of the majority of the collective farms,* on the grounds that they are fictitious; *the abandonment of the policy of eliminating the kulaks; reversion to the policy of concessions, and the leasing to concessionaires of a number of our industrial enterprises,* on the grounds that they do not pay.

There you have the programme of these contemptible cowards and capitulators—their counter-revolutionary programme of restoring capitalism in the U.S.S.R.!

What difference is there between this programme and that of the extreme Rights? Clearly, there is none. It follows that the "Lefts" have openly associated themselves with the counter-revolutionary programme of the Rights in order to enter into a bloc with them and to wage a joint struggle against the Party.

How can it be said after this that the "Lefts" are not dangerous, or hardly dangerous? Is it not clear that those who talk such rubbish bring grist to the mill of the sworn enemies of Leninism?

As you see, here too, in the sphere of deviations from the line of the Party—regardless of whether we are dealing with deviations on general policy or with deviations on the national question—the survivals of capitalism in people's minds, including the minds of certain members of our Party, are quite tenacious.

There you have some of the serious and urgent problems of our ideological-political work on which there is lack of clarity, confusion, and even direct departure from Leninism in certain strata of the Party. Nor are these the only questions which could serve to demonstrate the confusion in the views of certain members of the Party.

After this, can it be said that all is well in the Party?

Clearly, it cannot.

Our tasks in the sphere of ideological and political work are:

1) To raise the theoretical level of the Party to the proper height.

2) To intensify ideological work in all the organisations of the Party.

3) To carry on unceasing propaganda of Leninism in the ranks of the Party.

4) To train the Party organisations and the non-Party active which surrounds them in the spirit of Leninist internationalism.

5) Not to gloss over, but boldly to criticise the deviations of certain comrades from Marxism-Leninism.

6) Systematically to expose the ideology and the remnants of the ideology of trends that are hostile to Leninism.

2. QUESTIONS OF ORGANISATIONAL LEADERSHIP

I have spoken of our successes. I have spoken of the victory of the Party line in the sphere of the national economy and of culture, and also in the sphere of overcoming anti-Leninist groups in the Party. I have spoken of the historic significance of our victory. But this does not mean that we have achieved victory everywhere and in all things, and that all questions have already been settled. Such successes and such victories do not occur in real life. We still have plenty of unsolved problems and defects of all sorts. Ahead of us is a host of problems demanding solution. But it does undoubtedly mean that the greater part of the urgent and immediate problems has already been successfully solved, and in this sense the very great victory of our Party is beyond doubt.

But here the question arises: how was this victory brought about, how was it actually achieved, as the result of what fight, as the result of what efforts?

Some people think that it is sufficient to draw up a correct Party line, proclaim it for all to hear, state it in the form of general theses and resolutions, and have it voted for unanimously, for victory to come of itself, automatically, as it were. That, of course, is wrong. It is a gross delusion. Only incorrigible bureaucrats and red-tapists can think so. As a matter of fact, these successes and victories did not come automatically, but as the result of a fierce struggle for the application of the Party line. Victory never comes of itself–it is usually won by effort. Good resolutions and declarations in favour of the general line of the Party are only a beginning; they merely express the desire for victory, but not the victory itself. After the correct line has been laid down, after a correct solution of the problem has been found, success depends on how the work is organised; on the organisation of the struggle for carrying out the Party line; on the proper selection of personnel; on checking the fulfilment of the decisions of the leading bodies. Otherwise the correct line of the Party and the correct solutions are in danger of being seriously prejudiced. More than that, after the correct political line has been laid down, organisational work decides everything, including the fate of the political line itself, its success or failure.

As a matter of fact, victory was achieved and won by a systematic and fierce struggle against all sorts of difficulties in the way of carrying out the Party line; by overcoming these difficulties; by mobilising the Party and the working class for the task of overcoming the difficulties; by organising the struggle to overcome the difficulties; by removing inefficient executives and choosing better ones, capable of waging the struggle against difficulties.

What are these difficulties; and where do they lie?

They are difficulties of our organisational work, difficulties of our organisational leadership. They lie in us ourselves, in our leading people, in our organisations, in the apparatus of our Party, Soviet, economic, trade-union, Young Communist League and all other organisations.

We must realise that the strength and prestige of our Party and Soviet, economic and all other organisations, and of their leaders, have grown to an unprecedented degree. And precisely because their strength and prestige have grown to an unprecedented degree, it is their work that now determines everything, or nearly everything. There can be no justification for references to so-called objective conditions. Now that the correctness of the Party's political line has been confirmed by the experience of a number of years, and that there is no longer any doubt as to the readiness of the workers and peasants to support this line, the part played by so-called objective conditions has been reduced to a minimum; whereas the part played by our organisations and their leaders has become decisive, exceptional. What does this mean? It means that from now on nine-tenths of the responsibility for the failures and defects in our work rest, not on "objective" conditions, but on ourselves, and on ourselves alone.

We have in our Party more than 2,000,000 members and candidate members. In the Young Communist League we have more than 4,000,000 members and candidate members. We have over 3,000,000 worker and peasant correspondents. The Society for the Promotion of Air and Chemical Defence has more than 12,000,000 members. The trade unions have a membership of over 17,000,000. It is to these organisations that we are indebted for our successes. And if, in spite of the existence of such organisations and of such possibilities, which facilitate the achievement of successes, we still have quite a number of shortcomings in our work and not a few failures, then it is only we ourselves, our organisational work, our bad organisational leadership, that are to blame for this.

Bureaucracy and red tape in the administrative apparatus; idle chatter about "leadership in general" instead of real and concrete leadership; the functional structure of our organisations and lack of individual responsibility; lack of personal responsibility in work, and wage equalisation; the absence of a systematic check on the fulfilment of decisions; fear of self-criticism—these are the sources of our difficulties; this is where our difficulties now lie.

It would be naïve to think that these difficulties can be overcome by means of resolutions and decisions. The bureaucrats and red-tapists have long been past masters in the art of demonstrating their loyalty to Party and Government decisions in words, and pigeon-holing them in deed. In order to overcome these difficulties it was necessary to put an end to the disparity between our organisational work and the requirements of the political line of the Party; it was necessary to raise the level of organisational leadership in all spheres of the national economy to the level of political leadership; it was necessary to see to it that our organisational work ensured the practical realisation of the political slogans and decisions of the Party.

In order to overcome these difficulties and achieve success it was necessary to *organise* the struggle to eliminate them; it was necessary to draw the masses of the workers and peasants into this struggle; it was necessary to mobilise the Party itself; it was necessary to purge the Party and the economic organisations of unreliable, unstable and degenerate elements.

What was needed for this?

We had to organise:

1) Full development of self-criticism and exposure of shortcomings in our work.

2) The mobilisation of the Party, Soviet, economic, trade-union, and Young Communist League organisations for the struggle against difficulties.

3) The mobilisation of the masses of the workers and peasants to fight for the application of the slogans and decisions of the Party and of the Government.

4) Full development of emulation and shock-brigade work among the working people.

5) A wide network of Political Departments of machine and tractor stations and state farms and the bringing of the Party and Soviet leadership closer to the villages.

6) The subdivision of the People's Commissariats, chief boards, and trusts, and the bringing of economic leadership closer to the enterprises.

7) The abolition of lack of personal responsibility in work and the elimination of wage equalisation.

8) The elimination of the "functional" system, the extension of individual responsibility, and a policy aiming at the abolition of collegium management.

9) An increase in checking the fulfilment of decisions, and a policy aiming at the reorganisation of the Central Control Commission and the Workers' and Peasants' Inspection with a view to a further increase in checking the fulfilment of decisions.

10) The transfer of skilled personnel from offices to posts closer to production.

11) The exposure and expulsion from the administrative apparatus of incorrigible bureaucrats and red-tapists.

12) The removal from their posts of people who violate the decisions of the Party and the Government, of "window-dressers" and windbags, and the promotion to their place of new people—business-like people, capable of concretely directing the work entrusted to them and of strengthening Party and Soviet discipline.

13) The purging of Soviet and economic organisations and the reduction of their staffs.

14) Lastly, the purging of the Party of unreliable and degenerate people.

These, in the main, are the measures which the Party has had to adopt in order to overcome difficulties, to raise the level of our organisational work to that of political leadership, and thus ensure the application of the Party line.

You know that it was precisely in this way that the Central Committee of the Party carried on its organisational work during the period under review.

In this the Central Committee was guided by Lenin's brilliant thought that the chief thing in organisational work is *selection of personnel and checking fulfilment.*

In regard to *selecting* the right people and dismissing those who fail to justify the confidence placed in them, I should like to say a few words.

Besides the incorrigible bureaucrats and red-tapists, as to whose removal there are no differences of opinion among us, there are two other types of executive who retard our work, hinder our work, and hold up our advance.

One of these types of executive consists of people who rendered certain services in the past, people who have become big-wigs, who consider that Party decisions and Soviet laws are not written for them, but for fools. These are the people who do not consider it their duty to fulfil the decisions of the Party and of the Government, and who thus destroy the foundations of Party and state discipline. What do they count upon when they violate Party decisions and Soviet laws? They presume that the Soviet Government will not venture to touch them, because of their past services. These overconceited big-wigs think that they are irreplaceable, and that they can violate the decisions of the leading bodies with impunity. What is to be done with executives of this kind? They must unhesitatingly be removed from their leading posts, irrespective of past services. (*Voices:* "Quite right!") They must be demoted to lower positions and this must be announced in the press. (*Voices:* "Quite right!") This is essential in order to bring those conceited big-wig bureaucrats down a peg or two, and to put them in their proper place. This is essential in order to strengthen Party and Soviet discipline in the whole of our work. (*Voices:* "Quite right!" *Applause.*)

And now about the second type of executive. I have in mind the windbags, I would say honest windbags (*laughter*), people who are honest and loyal to the Soviet power, but who are incapable of leadership, incapable of organising anything. Last year I had a conversation with one such comrade, a very respected comrade, but an incorrigible windbag, capable of drowning any live undertaking in a flood of talk. Here is the conversation.

I: How are you getting on with the sowing?

He: With the sowing, Comrade Stalin? We have mobilised ourselves. (*Laughter.*)

I: Well, and what then?

He: We have put the question squarely. (*Laughter.*)

I: And what next?

He: There is a turn, Comrade Stalin; soon there will be a turn. (*Laughter.*)

I: But still?

He: We can see an indication of some improvement. (*Laughter.*)

I: But still, how are you getting on with the sowing?

He: So far, Comrade Stalin, we have not made any headway with the sowing. (*General laughter.*)

There you have the portrait of the windbag. They have mobilised themselves, they have put the question squarely, they have a turn and some improvement, but things remain as they were.

This is exactly how a Ukrainian worker recently described the state of a certain organisation when he was asked whether that organisation had any definite line: "Well," he said, "as to a line . . . they have a line all right, but they don't seem to be doing any work." (*General laughter.*) Evidently that organisation also has its honest windbags.

And when such windbags are dismissed from their posts and are given jobs far removed from operative work, they shrug their shoulders in perplexity and ask: "Why have we been dismissed? Did we not do all that was necessary to get the work done? Did we not organise a rally of shock brigaders? Did we not proclaim the slogans of the Party and of the Government at the conference of shock brigaders? Did we not elect the whole of the Political Bureau of the Central Committee to the Honorary Presidium? (*General laughter.*) Did we not send greetings to Comrade Stalin—what more do you want of us?" (*General laughter.*)

What is to be done with these incorrigible windbags? Why, if they were allowed to remain on operative work they are capable of drowning every live undertaking in a flood of watery and endless speeches. Obviously, they must be removed from leading posts and given work other than operative work. There is no place for windbags on operative work. (*Voices:* "Quite right!" *Applause.*)

I have already briefly reported how the Central Committee

handled the selection of personnel for the state and economic organisations, and how it strengthened the checking on the fulfilment of decisions. Comrade Kaganovich will deal with this in greater detail in his report on the third item of the congress agenda.

I should like to say a few words, however, about further work in connection with increased checking on the fulfilment of decisions.

The proper organisation of checking the fulfilment of decisions is of decisive importance in the fight against bureaucracy and red tape. Are the decisions of the leading bodies carried out, or are they pigeon-holed by bureaucrats and red-tapists? Are they carried out properly, or are they distorted? Is the apparatus working conscientiously and in a Bolshevik manner, or is it working to no purpose? These things can be promptly found out only by a well-organised check on the fulfilment of decisions. A well-organised check on the fulfilment of decisions is the searchlight which helps to reveal how the apparatus is functioning at any moment and to bring bureaucrats and red-tapists into the light of day. We can say with certainty that nine-tenths of our defects and failures are due to the lack of a properly organised check on the fulfilment of decisions. There can be no doubt that with such a check on fulfilment, defects and failures would certainly have been averted.

But if checking fulfilment is to achieve its purpose, two conditions at least are required: firstly, that fulfilment is checked systematically and not spasmodically; secondly, that the work of checking fulfilment in all sections of the Party, Soviet and economic organisations is entrusted not to second-rate people, but to people with sufficient authority, to the leaders of the organisations concerned.

The proper organisation of checking fulfilment is most important of all for the central leading bodies. The organisational structure of the Workers' and Peasants' Inspection does not meet the requirements of a well-devised system for checking fulfilment. Several years ago, when our economic work was simpler and less satisfactory, and when we could count on the possibility of *inspecting* the work of all the People's Commissariats and of all the economic organisations, the

Workers' and Peasants' Inspection was adequate. But now, when our economic work has expanded and has become more complicated, and when it is no longer necessary, or possible, to *inspect* it from one centre, the Workers' and Peasants' Inspection must be reorganised. What we need now is not an inspection, but a check on the fulfilment of the decisions of the centre—what we need now is *control* over the fulfilment of the decisions of the centre. We now need an organisation that would not set itself the universal aim of inspecting everything and everybody, but which could concentrate all its attention on the work of control, on the work of checking fulfilment of the decisions of the central bodies of the Soviet power. Such an organisation can be only a Soviet Control Commission under the Council of People's Commissars of the U.S.S.R., working on assignments of the Council of People's Commissars, and having representatives in the localities who are independent of the local bodies. And in order that this organisation may have sufficient authority and be able, if necessary, to take proceedings against any responsible executive, candidates for the Soviet Control Commission must be nominated by the Party Congress and endorsed by the Council of People's Commissars and the Central Executive Committee of the U.S.S.R. I think that only such an organisation could strengthen Soviet control and Soviet discipline.

As for the Central Control Commission, it is well known that it was set up primarily and mainly for the purpose of averting a split in the Party. You know that at one time there really was a danger of a split. You know that the Central Control Commission and its organisations succeeded in averting the danger of a split. Now there is no longer any danger of a split. But, on the other hand, we are urgently in need of an organisation that could concentrate its attention mainly on checking the fulfilment of the decisions of the Party and of its Central Committee. Such an organisation can be only a Party Control Commission under the Central Committee of the C.P.S.U.(B.), working on assignments of the Party and its Central Committee and having representatives in the localities who are independent of the local organisations. Naturally, such a responsible organisation must have great authority. In order that it may have sufficient authority and be able to take proceedings against any responsible executive who has committed an offence, including members of the Central Committee, the right to elect or dismiss the members of this commission must be vested only in the supreme organ of the Party, viz., the Party congress. There can be no doubt that such an organisation will be quite capable of ensuring control over the fulfilment of the decisions of the central organs of the Party and of strengthening Party discipline.

That is how matters stand with regard to questions of organisational leadership.

Our tasks in the sphere of organisational work are:

1) To continue to adapt organisational work to the requirements of the political line of the Party;

2) To raise organisational leadership to the level of political leadership;

3) To secure that organisational leadership fully ensures the implementation of the political slogans and decisions of the Party.

* * *

I am coming to the end of my report, comrades.

What conclusions must be drawn from it?

Everybody now admits that our successes are great and extraordinary. In a relatively short space of time our country has been transferred on to the lines of industrialisation and collectivisation. The First Five-Year Plan has been successfully carried out. This arouses a feeling of pride among our workers and increases their self-confidence.

That is very good, of course. But successes sometimes have their seamy side. They sometimes give rise to certain dangers, which, if allowed to develop, may wreck the whole work. There is, for example, the danger that some of our comrades may become dizzy with successes. There have been such cases among us, as you know. There is the danger that certain of our comrades, having become intoxicated with success, will get swelled heads and begin to lull themselves with boastful songs, such as: "It's a walkover," "We can knock anybody into a cocked hat," etc. This is not precluded by any means, comrades. There is nothing more dangerous than sentiments of this kind, for they disarm the Party and demobilise its ranks. If such sentiments gain the upper hand in our Party we may be faced with the danger of all our successes being wrecked.

Of course, the First Five-Year Plan has been successfully carried out. That is true. But the matter does not and cannot end there, comrades. Before us is the Second Five-Year Plan, which we must also carry out, and successfully too. You know that plans are carried out in the course of a struggle against difficulties, in the process of overcoming difficulties. That means that there will be difficulties and there will be a struggle against them. Comrades Molotov and Kuibyshev will report to you on the Second Five-Year Plan. From their reports you will see what great difficulties we shall have to overcome in order to carry out this great plan. This means that we must not lull the Party, but sharpen its vigilance; we must not lull it to sleep, but keep it ready for action; not disarm it, but arm it; not demobilise it, but keep it in a state of mobilisation for the fulfilment of the Second Five-Year Plan.

Hence, the first conclusion: *We must not become infatuated with the successes achieved, and must not become conceited.*

We have achieved successes because we have had the correct guiding line of the Party, and because we have been able to organise the masses for putting this line into effect. Needless to say, without these conditions we should not have achieved the successes that we have achieved, and of which we are justly proud. But it is a very rare thing for ruling parties to have a correct line and to be able to put it into effect.

Look at the countries which surround us: can you find many ruling parties there that have a correct line and are putting it into effect? Actually, there are now no such parties in the world; for they are all living without prospects; they are floundering in the chaos of the crisis, and see no way of getting out of the swamp. Our Party alone knows in what direction to steer its course, and it is going forward successfully. To what does our Party owe its superiority? To the fact that it is a Marxist Party, a Leninist Party. It owes it to the fact that it is guided in its work by the teaching of Marx, Engels, Lenin. There can be no doubt that as long as we remain true to this teaching, as long as we have this compass, we shall achieve successes in our work.

It is said that in some countries in the West Marxism has already been destroyed. It is said that it has been destroyed by the bourgeois-nationalist trend known as fascism. That, of course, is nonsense. Only people who are ignorant of history can talk like that. Marxism is the scientific expression of the fundamental interests of the working class. To destroy Marxism, the working class must be destroyed. But it is impossible to destroy the working class. More than 80 years have passed since Marxism came into the arena. During this time scores and hundreds of bourgeois governments have tried to destroy Marxism. And what has happened? Bourgeois governments have come and gone, but Marxism has remained. (*Stormy applause.*) Moreover, Marxism has achieved complete victory on one-sixth of the globe; moreover, it has achieved it in the very country in which Marxism was considered to have been utterly destroyed. (*Stormy applause.*) It cannot be regarded as an accident that the country in which Marxism has achieved complete victory is now the only country in the world which knows no crises and unemployment, whereas in all other countries, including the fascist countries, crisis and unemployment have been reigning for four years now. No, comrades, that is no accident. (*Prolonged applause.*)

Yes, comrades, our successes are due to the fact that we have worked and fought under the banner of Marx, Engels, Lenin.

Hence, the second conclusion: *We must remain true to the end to the great banner of Marx, Engels, Lenin.* (*Applause.*)

The working class of the U.S.S.R. is strong not only because it has a Leninist Party that has been tried and tested in battle; further, it is strong not only because it enjoys the support of the vast masses of the labouring peasants; it is strong also because it is supported and assisted by the world proletariat. The working class of the U.S.S.R. is part of the world proletariat, its advanced detachment, and our republic is the cherished child of the world proletariat. There can be no doubt that if our working class had not had the support of the working class in the capitalist countries it would not have been able to retain power, it would not have secured the conditions for socialist construction, and, consequently, it would not have achieved the successes that it has achieved. International ties between the working class of the U.S.S.R. and the workers of the capitalist countries, the fraternal alliance between the workers of the U.S.S.R. and the workers of all countries—this is one of the cornerstones of the strength and might of the Republic of Soviets. The workers in the West say that the working class of the U.S.S.R. is the shock brigade of the world proletariat. That is very good. It means that the world proletariat is prepared to continue rendering all the support it can to the working class of the U.S.S.R. But it imposes serious duties upon us. It means that we must prove by our work that we deserve the honourable title of shock brigade of the proletarians of all countries. It imposes upon us the duty of working better and fighting better for the final victory of socialism in our country, for the victory of socialism in all countries.

Hence, the third conclusion: *We must be true to the end to the cause of proletarian internationalism, to the cause of the fraternal alliance of the proletarians of all countries.* (*Applause.*)

Such are the conclusions.

Long live the great and invincible banner of Marx, Engels, Lenin! (*Stormy and prolonged applause from the whole hall. The congress gives Comrade Stalin an ovation. The "Internationale" is sung, after which the ovation is resumed with renewed vigour. Shouts of* "Hurrah for Stalin!" "Long live Stalin!" "Long live the C.C. of the Party!")

1934

DIALECTICAL AND HISTORICAL MATERIALISM[1]

Dialectical materialism is the world outlook of the Marxist-Leninist party. It is called dialectical materialism because its approach to the phenomena of nature, its method of studying and apprehending them, is *dialectical*, while its interpretation of the phenomena of nature, its conception of these phenomena, its theory, is *materialistic*.

Historical materialism is the extension of the principles of dialectical materialism to the study of social life, an application of the principles of dialectical materialism to the phenomena of the life of society, to the study of society and its history.

When describing their dialectical method, Marx and Engels usually refer to Hegel as the philosopher who formulated the main features of dialectics. This, however, does not mean that the dialectics of Marx and Engels is identical with the dialectics of Hegel. As a matter of fact, Marx and Engels took from the Hegelian dialectics only its "rational kernel," casting aside its idealistic shell, and developed it further so as to lend it a modern scientific form.

> "My dialectic method," says Marx, "is fundamentally not only different from the Hegelian, but is its direct opposite. To Hegel, the process of thinking, which, under the name

[1] This essay by Stalin appears as a section of the book *History of the Communist Party of the Soviet Union (Short Course)*, which was written under his direct supervision and first published in 1938. Before its revision by the present rulers of the Soviet Union, the book was a standard text for Communists all over the world (it was required reading for all members of the Chinese Communist Party). Many Marxist-Leninists consider the essay itself to be the finest summary of the philosophical basis of Marxism.

of 'the Idea,' he even transforms into an independent subject, is the demiurge (creator) of the real world, and the real world is only the external, phenomenal form of 'the Idea.' With me, on the contrary, the ideal is nothing else than the material world reflected by the human mind, and translated into forms of thought." (Karl Marx, *Capital*, Vol, I).

When describing their materialism, Marx and Engels usually refer to Feuerbach as the philosopher who restored materialism to its rights. This, however, does not mean that the materialism of Marx and Engels is identical with Feuerbach's materialism. As a matter of fact, Marx and Engels took from Feuerbach's materialism its "inner kernel," developed it into a scientific-philosophical theory of materialism and cast aside its idealistic and religious-ethical encumbrances. We know that Feuerbach, although he was fundamentally a materialist, objected to the name materialism. Engels more than once declared that "in spite of the materialist foundation, Feuerbach remained bound by the traditional idealist fetters," and that "the real idealism of Feuerbach becomes evident as soon as we come to his philosophy of religion and ethics."

Dialectics comes from the Greek *dialego*, to discourse, to debate. In ancient times dialectics was the art of arriving at the truth by disclosing the contradictions in the argument of an opponent and overcoming these contradictions. There were philosophers in ancient times who believed that the disclosure of contradictions in thought and the clash of opposite opinions was the best method of arriving at the truth. This dialectical method of thought, later extended to the phenomena of nature, developed into the dialectical method of apprehending nature, which regards the phenomena of nature as being in constant movement and undergoing constant change, and the development of nature as the result of the development of the contradictions in nature, as the result of the interaction of opposed forces in nature.

In its essence, dialectics is the direct opposite of metaphysics.

1) The principal features of the Marxist *dialectical method* are as follows:

a) Contrary to metaphysics, dialectics does not regard nature as an accidental agglomeration of things, of phenomena, unconnected with, isolated from, and independent of, each other, but as a connected and integral whole, in which things, phenomena, are organically connected with, dependent on, and determined by, each other.

The dialectical method therefore holds that no phenomenon in nature can be understood if taken by itself, isolated from surrounding phenomena, inasmuch as any phenomenon in any realm of nature may become meaningless to us if it is not considered in connection with the surrounding conditions, but divorced from them; and that, vice versa, any phenomenon can be understood and explained if considered in its inseparable connection with surrounding phenomena, as one conditioned by surrounding phenomena.

b) Contrary to metaphysics, dialectics holds that nature is not a state of rest and immobility, stagnation and immutability, but a state of continuous movement and change, of continuous renewal and development, where something is always arising and developing, and something always disintegrating and dying away.

The dialectical method therefore requires that phenomena should be considered not only from the standpoint of their interconnection and interdependence, but also from the standpoint of their movement, their change, their development, their coming into being and going out of being.

The dialectical method regards as important primarily not that which at the given moment seems to be durable and yet is already beginning to die away, but that which is arising and developing, even though at the given moment it may appear to be not durable, for the dialectical method considers invincible only that which is arising and developing.

> "All nature," says Engels, "from the smallest thing to the biggest, from a grain of sand to the sun, from the protista to man, is in a constant state of coming into being and going out of being, in a constant flux, in a ceaseless state of movement and change." (F. Engels, *Dialectics of Nature.*)

Therefore, dialectics, Engels says, "takes things and their perceptual images essentially in their inter-connection, in their concatenation, in their movement, in their rise and disappearance." (*Ibid.*)

c) Contrary to metaphysics, dialectics does not regard the process of development as a simple process of growth, where quantitative changes do not lead to qualitative changes, but as a development which passes from insignificant and imperceptible quantitative changes to open, fundamental changes, to qualitative changes; a development in which the qualitative changes occur not gradually, but rapidly and abruptly, taking the form of a leap from one state to another; they occur not accidentally but as the natural result of an accumulation of imperceptible and gradual quantitative changes.

The dialectical method therefore holds that the process of development should be understood not as movement in a circle, not as a simple repetition of what has already occurred, but as an onward and upward movement, as a transition from an old qualitative state to a new qualitative state, as a development from the simple to the complex, from the lower to the higher:

> "Nature," says Engels, "is the test of dialectics, and it must be said for modern natural science that it has furnished extremely rich and daily increasing materials for this test, and has thus proved that in the last analysis nature's process is dialectical and not metaphysical, that it does not move in an eternally uniform and constantly repeated circle, but passes through a real history. Here prime mention should be made of Darwin, who dealt a severe blow to the metaphysical conception of nature by proving that the organic world of today, plants and animals, and consequently man too, is all a product of a process of development that has been in progress for millions of years." (F. Engels, *Anti-Dühring.*)

Describing dialectical development as a transition from quantitative changes to qualitative changes, Engels says:

> "In physics . . . every change is a passing of quantity

into quality, as a result of quantitative change of some form of movement either inherent in a body or imparted to it. For example, the temperature of water has at first no effect on its liquid state; but as the temperature of liquid water rises or falls, a moment arrives when this state of cohesion changes and the water is converted in one case into steam and in the other into ice. . . . A definite minimum current is required to make a platinum wire glow; every metal has its melting temperature; every liquid has a definite freezing point and boiling point at a given pressure, as far as we are able with the means at our disposal to attain the required temperatures; finally, every gas has its critical point at which, by proper pressure and cooling, it can be converted into a liquid state. . . . What are known as the constants of physics are in most cases nothing but designations for the nodal points at which a quantitative (change) increase or decrease of movement causes a qualitative change in the state of the given body, and at which, consequently, quantity is transformed into quality." (*Dialectics of Nature.*)

Passing to chemistry, Engels continues:

"Chemistry may be called the science of the qualitative changes which take place in bodies as the effect of changes of quantitative composition. This was already known to Hegel. . . . Take oxygen: if the molecule contains three atoms instead of the customary two, we get ozone, a body definitely distinct in odour and reaction from ordinary oxygen. And what shall we say of the different proportions in which oxygen combines with nitrogen or sulphur, and each of which produces a body qualitatively different from all other bodies!" (*Ibid.*)

Finally, criticizing Dühring, who scolded Hegel for all he was worth, but surreptitiously borrowed from him the well-known thesis that the transition from the insentient world to the sentient world, from the kingdom of inorganic matter to the kingdom of organic life, is a leap to a new state, Engels says:

> "This is precisely the Hegelian nodal line of measure relations, in which, at certain definite nodal points, the purely quantitative increase or decrease gives rise to a *qualitative leap*, for example, in the case of water which is heated or cooled, where boiling-point and freezing-point are the nodes at which—under normal pressure—the leap to a new aggregate state takes place, and where consequently quantity is transformed into quality." (F. Engels, *Anti-Dühring.*)

d) Contrary to metaphysics, dialectics holds that internal contradictions are inherent in all things and phenomena of nature, for they all have their negative and positive sides, a past and a future, something dying away and something developing; and that the struggle between these opposites, the struggle between the old and the new, between that which is dying away and that which is being born, between that which is disappearing and that which is developing, constitutes the internal content of the process of development, the internal content of the transformation of quantitative changes into qualitative changes.

The dialectical method therefore holds that the process of development from the lower to the higher takes place not as a harmonious unfolding of phenomena, but as a disclosure of the contradictions inherent in things and phenomena, as a "struggle" of opposite tendencies which operate on the basis of these contradictions.

> "In its proper meaning," Lenin says, "dialectics is the study of the contradiction *within the very essence of things.*"

And further:

> "Development is the 'struggle' of opposites."

Such, in brief, are the principal features of the Marxist dialectical method.

It is easy to understand how immensely important is the extension of the principles of the dialectical method to the study of social life and the history of society, and how immensely important is the application of these principles to the history of society and to the practical activities of the party of the proletariat.

If there are no isolated phenomena in the world, if all phenomena are interconnected and interdependent, then it is clear that every social system and every social movement in history must be evaluated not from the standpoint of "eternal justice" or some other preconceived idea, as is not infrequently done by historians, but from the standpoint of the conditions which gave rise to that system or that social movement and with which they are connected.

The slave system would be senseless, stupid and unnatural under modern conditions. But under the conditions of a disintegrating primitive communal system, the slave system is a quite understandable and natural phenomenon, since it represents an advance on the primitive communal system.

The demand for a bourgeois-democratic republic when tsardom and bourgeois society existed, as, let us say, in Russia in 1905, was a quite understandable, proper and revolutionary demand, for at that time a bourgeois republic would have meant a step forward. But now, under the conditions of the U.S.S.R., the demand for a bourgeois-democratic republic would be a meaningless and counter-revolutionary demand, for a bourgeois republic would be a retrograde step compared with the Soviet republic.

Everything depends on the conditions, time and place.

It is clear that without such a *historical* approach to social phenomena, the existence and development of the science of history is impossible, for only such an approach saves the science of history from becoming a jumble of accidents and an agglomeration of most absurd mistakes.

Further, if the world is in a state of constant movement and development, if the dying away of the old and the upgrowth of the new is a law of development, then it is clear that there can be no "immutable" social systems, no "eternal principles" of private property and exploitation, no "eternal ideas" of the subjugation of the peasant to the landlord, of the worker to the capitalist.

Hence the capitalist system can be replaced by the Socialist system, just as at one time the feudal system was replaced by the capitalist system.

Hence we must not base our orientation on the strata of society which are no longer developing, even though they at present constitute the predominant force, but on those strata which are developing and have a future before them, even though they at present do not constitute the predominant force.

In the eighties of the past century, in the period of the struggle between the Marxists and the Narodniks, the proletariat in Russia constituted an insignificant minority of the population, whereas the individual peasants constituted the vast majority of the population. But the proletariat was developing as a class, whereas the peasantry as a class was disintegrating. And just because the proletariat was developing as a class the Marxists based their orientation on the proletariat. And they were not mistaken, for, as we know, the proletariat subsequently grew from an insignificant force into a first-rate historical and political force.

Hence, in order not to err in policy, one must look forward, not backward.

Further, if the passing of slow quantitative changes into rapid and abrupt qualitative changes is a law of development, then it is clear that revolutions made by oppressed classes are a quite natural and inevitable phenomenon.

Hence the transition from capitalism to Socialism and the liberation of the working class from the yoke of capitalism cannot be effected by slow changes, by reforms, but only by a qualitative change of the capitalist system, by revolution.

Hence, in order not to err in policy, one must be a revolutionary, not a reformist.

Further, if development proceeds by way of the disclosure of internal contradictions, by way of collisions between opposite forces on the basis of these contradictions and so as to overcome these contradictions, then it is clear that the class struggle of the proletariat is a quite natural and inevitable phenomenon.

Hence we must not cover up the contradictions of the capitalist system, but disclose and unravel them; we must not try to check the class struggle but carry it to its conclusion.

Hence, in order not to err in policy, one must pursue an uncompromising proletarian class policy, not a reformist policy of harmony of the interests of the proletariat and the bourgeoisie, not a compromisers' policy of "the growing of capitalism into Socialism."

Such is the Marxist dialectical method when applied to social life, to the history of society.

As to Marxist philosophical materialism, it is fundamentally the direct opposite of philosophical idealism.

2) The principal features of Marxist philosophical *materialism* are as follows:

a) Contrary to idealism, which regards the world as the embodiment of an "absolute idea," a "universal spirit," "consciousness," Marx's philosophical materialism holds that the world is by its very nature *material*, that the multifold phenomena of the world constitute different forms of matter in motion, that interconnection and interdependence of phenomena, as established by the dialectical method, are a law of the development of moving matter, and that the world develops in accordance with the laws of movement of matter and stands in no need of a "universal spirit."

> "The materialist world outlook," says Engels, "is simply the conception of nature as it is, without any reservations." (MS of *Ludwig Feuerbach.*)

Speaking of the materialist views of the ancient philosopher Heraclitus, who held that "the world, the all in one, was not created by any god or any man, but was, is and ever will be a living flame, systematically flaring up and systematically dying down." Lenin comments: "A very good exposition of the rudiments of dialectical materialism."

b) Contrary to idealism, which asserts that only our mind really exists, and that the material world, being, nature, exists only in our mind, in our sensations, ideas and perceptions, the Marxist materialist philosophy holds that matter, nature, being, is an objective reality existing outside and independent of our mind; that matter is primary, since it is the source of sensations, ideas, mind, and that mind is secondary, derivative, since it is a reflection of matter, a reflection of being; that thought is a product of matter which in its development has reached a high degree of perfection, namely, of the brain, and the brain is the organ of thought; and that therefore one cannot separate thought from matter without committing a grave error. Engels says:

> "The question of the relation of thinking to being, the relation of spirit to nature is the paramount question of the whole of philosophy. . . . The answers which the philosophers gave to this question split them into two great camps. Those who asserted the primacy of spirit to nature . . . comprised the camp of *idealism.* The others, who regarded nature as primary, belong to the various schools of *materialism.*"

And further:

> "The material, sensuously perceptible world to which we ourselves belong is the only reality. . . . Our consciousness and thinking, however supra-sensuous they may seem, are the product of a material, bodily organ, the brain. Matter is not a product of mind, but mind itself is merely the highest product of matter."

Concerning the question of matter and thought, Marx says:

> "*It is impossible to separate thought from matter that thinks.* Matter is the subject of all changes."

Describing the Marxist philosophy of materialism, Lenin says:

> "Materialism in general recognizes objectively real being (matter) as independent of consciousness, sensation, experience. . . . Consciousness is only the reflection of being, at best, an approximately true (adequate, ideally exact) reflection of it."

And further:

> (a) "Matter is that which, acting upon our sense-organs, produces sensation; matter is the objective reality given to us in sensation. . . . Matter, nature, being, the physical—is primary, and spirit, consciousness, sensation, the psychical—is secondary."
>
> (b) "The world picture is a picture of how matter moves and of how '*matter thinks.*'"
>
> (c) "The brain is the organ of thought."

c) Contrary to idealism, which denies the possibility of knowing the world and its laws, which does not believe in the authenticity of our knowledge, does not recognize objective truth, and holds that the world is full of "things-in-themselves" that can never be known to science, Marxist philosophical materialism holds that the world and its laws are fully knowable, that our knowledge of the laws of nature, tested by experiment and practice, is authentic knowledge having the validity of objective truth, and that there are no things in the world which are unknowable, but only things which are still not known, but which will be disclosed and made known by the efforts of science and practice.

Criticizing the thesis of Kant and other idealists that the world is unknowable and that there are "things-in-themselves" which are unknowable, and defending the well-known materialist thesis that our knowledge is authentic knowledge, Engels writes:

> "The most telling refutation of this as of all other philosophical fancies is practice, *viz.*, experiment and industry. If we are able to prove the correctness of our conception of a natural process by making it ourselves, bringing it into being out of its conditions and using it for our own purposes into the bargain, then there is an end of the Kantian 'thing-in-itself.' The chemical substances produced in the bodies of plants and animals remained such 'things-in-themselves' until organic chemistry began to produce them one after another, whereupon the 'thing-in-itself' became a thing for us, as for instance, alizarin, the colouring matter

of the madder, which we no longer trouble to grow in the madder roots in the field, but produce much more cheaply and simply from coal tar. For three hundred years the Copernican solar system was a hypothesis, with a hundred, a thousand or ten thousand chances to one in its favour, but still always a hypothesis. But when Leverrier, by means of the data provided by this system, not only deduced the necessity of the existence of an unknown planet, but also calculated the position in the heavens which this planet must necessarily occupy, and when Galle really found this planet, the Copernican system was proved."

Accusing Bogdanov, Bazarov, Yushkevich and the other followers of Mach of fideism, and defending the well-known materialist thesis that our scientific knowledge of the laws of nature is authentic knowledge, and that the laws of science represent objective truth, Lenin says:

"Contemporary fideism does not at all reject science; all it rejects is the 'exaggerated claims' of science, to wit, its claim to objective truth. If objective truth exists (as the materialists think), if natural science, reflecting the outer world in human 'experience,' is alone capable of giving us objective truth, then all fideism is absolutely refuted."

Such, in brief, are the characteristic features of the Marxist philosophical materialism.

It is easy to understand how immensely important is the extension of the principles of philosophical materialism to the study of social life, of the history of society, and how immensely important is the application of these principles to the history of society and to the practical activities of the party of the proletariat.

If the connection between the phenomena of nature and their interdependence are laws of the development of nature, it follows, too, that the connection and interdependence of the phenomena of social life are laws of the development of society, and not something accidental.

Hence social life, the history of society, ceases to be an agglomeration of "accidents," and becomes the history of the development of society according to regular laws, and the study of the history of society becomes a science.

Hence the practical activity of the party of the proletariat must not be based on the good wishes of "outstanding individuals," not on the dictates of "reason," "universal morals," etc., but on the laws of development of society and on the study of these laws.

Further, if the world is knowable and our knowledge of the laws of development of nature is authentic knowledge, having the validity of objective truth, it follows that social life, the development of society, is also knowable, and that the data of science regarding the laws of development of society are authentic data having the validity of objective truths.

Hence the science of the history of society, despite all the complexity of the phenomena of social life, can become as precise a science as, let us say, biology, and capable of making use of the laws of development of society for practical purposes.

Hence the party of the proletariat should not guide itself in its practical activity by casual motives, but by the laws of development of society, and by practical deductions from these laws.

Hence Socialism is converted from a dream of a better future for humanity into a science.

Hence the bond between science and practical activity, between theory and practice, their unity, should be the guiding star of the party of the proletariat.

Further, if nature, being, the material world, is primary, and mind, thought, is secondary, derivative; if the material world represents objective reality existing independently of the mind of men, while the mind is a reflection of this objective reality, it follows that the material life of society, its being, is also primary, and its spiritual life secondary, derivative, and that the material life of society is an objective reality existing independently of the will of men, while the spiritual life of society is a reflection of this objective reality, a reflection of being.

Hence the source of formation of the spiritual life of society, the origin of social ideas, social theories, political views and political institutions, should not be sought for in the ideas, theories, views and political institutions themselves, but in the conditions of the material life of society, in social being, of which these ideas, theories, views, etc., are the reflection.

Hence, if in different periods of the history of society different social ideas, theories, views and political institutions are to be observed; if under the slave system we encounter certain social ideas, theories, views and political institutions, under feudalism others, and under capitalism others still, this is not to be explained by the "nature," the "properties" of the ideas, theories, views and political institutions themselves but by the different conditions of the material life of society at different periods of social development.

Whatever is the being of a society, whatever are the conditions of material life of a society, such are the ideas, theories, political views and political institutions of that society.

In this connection, Marx says:

> "It is not the consciousness of men that determines their being, but, on the contrary, their social being that determines their consciousness."

Hence, in order not to err in policy, in order not to find itself in the position of idle dreamers, the party of the proletariat must not base its activities on abstract "principles of human reason," but on the concrete conditions of the material life of society, as the determining force of social development; not on the good wishes of "great men," but on the real needs of development of the material life of society.

The fall of the utopians, including the Narodniks, Anarchists and Socialist-Revolutionaries, was due, among other things, to the fact that they did not recognize the primary role which the conditions of the material life of society play in the development of society, and, sinking to idealism, did not base their practical activities on the needs of the development of the material life of society, but, independently of and in spite of these needs, on "ideal plans" and "all-embracing projects" divorced from the real life of society.

The strength and vitality of Marxism-Leninism lie in the fact that it does base its practical activity on the needs of the development of the material life of society and never divorces itself from the real life of society.

It does not follow from Marx's words, however, that social ideas, theories, political views and political institutions are of no significance in the life of society, that they do not reciprocally affect social being, the development of the material conditions of the life of society. We have been speaking so far of the *origin* of social ideas, theories, views and political institutions, of *the way they arise*, of the fact that the spiritual life of society is a reflection of the conditions of its material life. As regards the *significance* of social ideas, theories, views and political institutions, as regards their *role* in history, historical materialism, far from denying them, stresses the role and importance of these factors in the life of society, in its history.

There are different kinds of social ideas and theories. There are old ideas and theories which have outlived their day and which serve the interests of the moribund forces of society. Their significance lies in the fact that they hamper the development, the progress of society. Then there are new and advanced ideas and theories which serve the interests of the advanced forces of society. Their significance lies in the fact that they facilitate the development, the progress of society; and their significance is the greater the more accurately they reflect the needs of development of the material life of society.

New social ideas and theories arise only after the development of the material life of society has set new tasks before society. But once they have arisen they become a most potent force which facilitates the carrying out of the new tasks set by the development of the material life of society, a force which facilitates the progress of society. It is precisely here that the tremendous organizing, mobilizing and transforming value of new ideas, new theories, new political views and new political institutions manifests itself. New social ideas and theories arise precisely because they are necessary to society, because it is *impossible* to carry out the urgent tasks of development of the material life of society without their organizing, mobilizing and transforming action. Arising out of the new tasks set by the development of the material life of society, the new social ideas and theories force their way through, become the possession of the masses, mobilize and organize them against the moribund forces of society, and thus facilitate the overthrow of these forces which hamper the development of the material life of society.

Thus social ideas, theories and political institutions, having arisen on the basis of the urgent tasks of the development of the material life of society, the development of social being, themselves then react upon social being, upon the material life of society, creating the conditions necessary for completely carrying out the urgent tasks of the material life of society, and for rendering its further development possible.

In this connection, Marx says:

> "Theory becomes a material force as soon as it has gripped the masses." (*Zur Kritik der Hegelschen Rechtsphilosophie.*)

Hence, in order to be able to influence the conditions of material life of society and to accelerate their development and their improvement, the party of the proletariat must rely upon such a social theory, such a social idea as correctly reflects the needs of development of the material life of society, and which is therefore capable of setting into motion broad masses of the people and of mobilizing them and organizing them into a great army of the proletarian party, prepared to smash the reactionary forces and to clear the way for the advanced forces of society.

The fall of the "Economists" and Mensheviks was due among other things to the fact that they did not recognize the mobilizing, organizing and transforming role of advanced theory, of advanced ideas and, sinking to vulgar materialism, reduced the role of these factors almost to nothing, thus condemning the Party to passivity and inanition.

The strength and vitality of Marxism-Leninism are derived from the fact that it relies upon an advanced theory which correctly reflects the needs of development of the material life of society, that it elevates theory to a proper level, and that it deems it its duty to utilize every ounce of the mobilizing, organizing and transforming power of this theory.

That is the answer historical materialism gives to the question of the relation between social being and social consciousness, between the conditions of development of material life and the development of the spiritual life of society.

It now remains to elucidate the following question: what, from the viewpoint of historical materialism, is meant by the "conditions of material life of society" which in the final analysis determine the physiognomy of society, its ideas, views, political institutions, etc.?

What, after all, are these "conditions of material life of society," what are their distinguishing features?

There can be no doubt that the concept "conditions of material life of society" includes, first of all, nature which surrounds society, geographical environment, which is one of the indispensable and constant conditions of material life of society and which, of course, influences the development of society. What role does geographical environment play in the development of society? Is geographical environment the chief force determining the physiognomy of society, the character of the social system of men, the transition from one system to another?

Historical materialism answers this question in the negative.

Geographical environment is unquestionably one of the constant and indispensable conditions of development of society and, of course, influences the development of society, accelerates or retards its development. But its influence is not the *determining* influence, inasmuch as the changes and development of society proceed at an incomparably faster rate than the changes and development of geographical environment. In the space of three thousand years three different social systems have been successively superseded in Europe: the primitive communal system, the slave system and the feudal system. In the eastern part of Europe, in the U.S.S.R., even four social systems have been superseded. Yet during this period geographical conditions in Europe have either not changed at all, or have changed so slightly that geography takes no note of them. And that is quite natural. Changes in geographical environment of any importance require millions of years, whereas a few hundred or a couple of thousand years are enough for even very important changes in the system of human society.

It follows from this that geographical environment cannot be the chief cause, the *determining* cause of social development, for that which remains almost unchanged in the course of tens of thousands of years cannot be the chief cause of development of that which undergoes fundamental changes in the course of a few hundred years.

Further, there can be no doubt that the concept "conditions of material life of society" also includes growth of population, density of population of one degree or another, for people are an essential element of the conditions of material life of society, and without a definite minimum number of people there can be no material life of society. Is not growth of population the chief force that determines the character of the social system of man?

Historical materialism answers this question too in the negative.

Of course, growth of population does influence the development of society, does facilitate or retard the development of society, but it cannot be the chief force of development of society, and its influence on the development of society cannot be the *determining* influence because, by itself, growth of population does not furnish the clue to the question why a given social system is replaced precisely by such and such a new system and not by another, why the primitive communal system is succeeded precisely by the slave system, the slave system by the feudal system, and the feudal system by the bourgeois system, and not by some other.

If growth of population were the determining force of social development, then a higher density of population would be bound to give rise to a correspondingly higher type of social system. But we do not find this to be the case. The density of population in China is four times as great as in the U.S.A., yet the U.S.A. stands higher than China in the scale of social development, for in China a semi-feudal system still prevails, whereas the U.S.A. has long ago reached the highest stage of development of capitalism. The density of population in Belgium is nineteen times as great as in the U.S.A., and twenty-six times as great as in the U.S.S.R. Yet the

U.S.A. stands higher than Belgium in the scale of social development; and as for the U.S.S.R., Belgium lags a whole historical epoch behind this country, for in Belgium the capitalist system prevails, whereas the U.S.S.R. has already done away with capitalism and has set up a Socialist system.

It follows from this that growth of population is not, and cannot be, the chief force of development of society, the force which *determines* the character of the social system, the physiognomy of society.

What, then, is the chief force in the complex of conditions of material life of society which determines the physiognomy of society, the character of the social system, the development of society from one system to another?

This force, historical materialism holds, is the *method of procuring the means of life* necessary for human existence, the *mode of production of material values*—food, clothing, footwear, houses, fuel, instruments of production, etc.—which are indispensable for the life of development of society.

In order to live, people must have food, clothing, footwear, shelter, fuel, etc.; in order to have these material values, people must produce them; and in order to produce them, people must have the instruments of production with which food, clothing, footwear, shelter, fuel, etc., are produced; they must be able to produce these instruments and to use them.

The *instruments of production* wherewith material values are produced, the *people* who operate the instruments of production and carry on the production of material values thanks to a certain *production experience* and *labour skill*—all these elements jointly constitute the *productive forces* of society.

But the productive forces are only one aspect of production, only one aspect of the mode of production, an aspect that expresses the relation of men to the objects and forces of nature which they make use of for the production of material values. Another aspect of production, another aspect of the mode of production, is the relation of men to each other in the process of production, men's *relations of production.* Men carry on a struggle against nature and utilize nature for the production of material values not in isolation from each other, not as separate individuals, but in common, in groups, in societies. Production, therefore, is at all times and under all conditions *social* production. In the production of material values men enter into mutual relations of one kind or another within production, into relations of production of one kind or another. These may be relations of co-operation and mutual help between people who are free from exploitation; they may be relations of domination and subordination; and, lastly, they may be transitional from one form of relations of production to another. But whatever the character of the relations of production may be, always and in every system, they constitute just as essential an element of production as the productive forces of society.

> "In production," Marx says, "men not only act on nature but also on one another. They produce only by co-operating in a certain way and mutually exchanging their activities. In order to produce, they enter into definite connections and relations with one another and only within these social connections and relations does their action on nature, does production, take place."

Consequently, production, the mode of production, embraces both the productive forces of society and men's relations of production, and is thus the embodiment of their unity in the process of production of material values.

One of the features of production is that it never stays at one point for a long time and is always in a state of change and development, and that, furthermore, changes in the mode of production inevitably call forth changes in the whole social system, social ideas, political views and political institutions—they call forth a reconstruction of the whole social and political order. At different stages of development people make use of different modes of production, or, to put it more crudely, lead different manners of life. In the primitive commune there is one mode of production, under slavery there is another mode of production, under feudalism a third mode of production, and so on. And, correspondingly, men's social system, the spiritual life of men, their views and political institutions also vary.

Whatever is the mode of production of a society, such in

the main is the society itself, its ideas and theories, its political views and institutions.

Or, to put it more crudely, whatever is man's manner of life, such is his manner of thought.

This means that the history of development of society is above all the history of the development of production, the history of the modes of production which succeed each other in the course of centuries, the history of the development of productive forces and people's relations of production.

Hence the history of social development is at the same time the history of the producers of material values themselves, the history of the labouring masses who are the chief force in the process of production and who carry on the production of material values necessary for the existence of society.

Hence, if historical science is to be a real science, it can no longer reduce the history of social development to the actions of kings and generals, to the actions of "conquerors" and "subjugators" of states, but must above all devote itself to the history of the producers of material values, the history of the labouring masses, the history of peoples.

Hence the clue to the study of the laws of history of society must not be sought in men's minds, in the views and ideas of society, but in the mode of production practised by society in any given historical period; it must be sought in the economic life of society.

Hence the prime task of historical science is to study and disclose the laws of production, the laws of development of the productive forces and of the relations of production, the laws of economic development of society.

Hence, if the party of the proletariat is to be a real party, it must above all acquire a knowledge of the laws of development of production, of the laws of economic development of society.

Hence, if it is not to err in policy, the party of the proletariat must both in drafting its program and its practical activities proceed primarily from the laws of development of production, from the laws of economic development of society.

A *second feature* of production is that its changes and development always begin with changes and development of the productive forces, and, in the first place, with changes and development of the instruments of production. Productive forces are therefore the most mobile and revolutionary element of production. First the productive forces of society change and develop, and then, *depending* on these changes and *in conformity with them,* men's relations of production, their economic relations, change. This, however, does not mean that the relations of production do not influence the development of the productive forces and that the latter are not dependent on the former. While their development is dependent on the development of the productive forces, the relations of production in their turn react upon the development of the productive forces, accelerating or retarding it. In this connection it should be noted that the relations of production cannot for too long a time lag behind and be in a state of contradiction to the growth of the productive forces, inasmuch as the productive forces can develop in full measure only when the relations of production correspond to the character, the state of the productive forces and allow full scope for their development. Therefore, however much the relations of production may lag behind the development of the productive forces, they must, sooner or later, come into correspondence with—and actually do come into correspondence with—the level of development of the productive forces, the character of the productive forces. Otherwise we would have a fundamental violation of the unity of the productive forces and the relations of production within the system of production, a disruption of production as a whole, a crisis of production, a destruction of productive forces.

An instance in which the relations of production do not correspond to the character of the productive forces, conflict with them, is the economic crises in capitalist countries, where private capitalist ownership of the means of production is in glaring incongruity with the social character of the process of production, with the character of the productive forces. This results in economic crises, which lead to the destruction of productive forces. Furthermore, this incongruity itself constitutes the economic basis of social revolution, the purpose of which is to destroy the existing relations of production and to create new relations of production corresponding to the character of the productive forces.

In contrast, an instance in which the relations of production completely correspond to the character of the productive forces is the Socialist national economy of the U.S.S.R., where the social ownership of the means of production fully corresponds to the social character of the process of production, and where, because of this, economic crises and the destruction of productive forces are unknown.

Consequently, the productive forces are not only the most mobile and revolutionary element in production, but are also the determining element in the development of production.

Whatever are the productive forces such must be the relations of production.

While the state of the productive forces furnishes an answer to the question—with what instruments of production do men produce the material values they need?—the state of the relations of production furnishes the answer to another question—who owns the *means of production* (the land, forests, waters, mineral resources, raw materials, instruments of production, production premises, means of transportation and communication, etc.), who commands the means of production, whether the whole of society, or individual persons, groups, or classes which utilize them for the exploitation of other persons, groups or classes?

Here is a rough picture of the development of productive forces from ancient times to our day. The transition from crude stone tools to the bow and arrow, and the accompanying transition from the life of hunters to the domestication of animals and primitive pasturage; the transition from stone tools to metal tools (the iron axe, the wooden plough fitted with an iron colter, etc.), with a corresponding transition to tillage and agriculture; a further improvement in metal tools for the working up of materials, the introduction of the blacksmith's bellows, the introduction of pottery, with a corresponding development of handicrafts, the separation of handicrafts from agriculture, the development of an independent handicraft industry and, subsequently, of manufacture; the transition from handicraft tools to machines and the transformation of handicraft and manufacture into machine industry; the transition to the machine system and the rise of modern large-scale machine industry—such is a general and far from complete picture of the development of the productive forces of society in the course of man's history. It will be clear that the development and improvement of the instruments of production were effected by men who were related to production, and not independently of men; and, consequently, the change and development of the instruments of production were accompanied by a change and development of men, as the most important element of the productive forces, by a change and development of their production experience, their labour skill, their ability to handle the instruments of production.

In conformity with the change and development of the productive forces of society in the course of history, men's relations of production, their economic relations also changed and developed.

Five *main* types of relations of production are known to history: primitive communal, slave, feudal, capitalist and Socialist.

The basis of the relations of production under the primitive communal system is that the means of production are socially owned. This in the main corresponds to the character of the productive forces of that period. Stone tools, and, later, the bow and arrow, precluded the possibility of men individually combating the forces of nature and beasts of prey. In order to gather the fruits of the forest, to catch fish, to build some sort of habitation, men were obliged to work in common if they did not want to die of starvation, or fall victim to beasts of prey or to neighbouring societies. Labour in common led to the common ownership of the means of production, as well as of the fruits of production. Here the conception of private ownership of the means of production did not yet exist, except for the personal ownership of certain implements of production which were at the same time means of defence against beasts of prey. Here there was no exploitation, no classes.

The basis of the relations of production under the slave system is that the slave owner owns the means of production; he also owns the worker in production—the slave, whom he can sell, purchase, or kill as though he were an animal. Such relations of production in the main correspond to the state of the productive forces of that period. Instead of stone tools, men now have metal tools at their command; instead of the wretched and primitive husbandry of the hunter, who knew neither pasturage, nor tillage, there now appear pasturage, tillage, handicrafts, and a division of labour between these branches of production. There appears the possibility of the exchange of products between individuals and between societies, of the accumulation of wealth in the hands of a few, the actual accumulation of the means of production in the hands of a minority, and the possibility of subjugation of the majority by a minority and their conversion into slaves. Here we no longer find the common and free labour of all members of society in the production process—here there prevails the forced labour of slaves, who are exploited by the non-labouring slave owners. Here, therefore, there is no common ownership of the means of production or of the fruits of production. It is replaced by private ownership. Here the slave owner appears as the prime and principal property owner in the full sense of the term.

Rich and poor, exploiters and exploited, people with full rights and people with no rights, and a fierce class struggle between them—such is the picture of the slave system.

The basis of the relations of production under the feudal system is that the feudal lord owns the means of production and does not fully own the worker in production—the serf, whom the feudal lord can no longer kill, but whom he can buy and sell. Alongside of feudal ownership there exists individual ownership by the peasant and the handicraftsman of his implements of production and his private enterprise based on his personal labour. Such relations of production in the main correspond to the state of the productive forces of that period. Further improvements in the smelting and working of iron; the spread of the iron plough and the loom; the further development of agriculture, horticulture, viniculture and dairying; the appearance of manufactories alongside of the handicraft workshops—such are the characteristic features of the state of the productive forces.

The new productive forces demand that the labourer shall display some kind of initiative in production and an inclination for work, an interest in work. The feudal lord therefore discards the slave, as a labourer who has no interest in work and is entirely without initiative, and prefers to deal with the serf, who has his own husbandry, implements of production, and a certain interest in work essential for the cultivation of the land and for the payment in kind of a part of his harvest to the feudal lord.

Here private ownership is further developed. Exploitation is nearly as severe as it was under slavery—it is only slightly mitigated. A class struggle between exploiters and exploited is the principal feature of the feudal system.

The basis of the relations of production under the capitalist system is that the capitalist owns the means of production, but not the workers in production—the wage labourers, whom the capitalist can neither kill nor sell because they are personally free, but who are deprived of means of production and, in order not to die of hunger, are obliged to sell their labour power to the capitalist and to bear the yoke of exploitation. Alongside of capitalist property in the means of production, we find, at first on a wide scale, private property of the peasants and handicraftsmen in the means of production, these peasants and handicraftsmen no longer being serfs, and their private property being based on personal labour. In place of the handicraft workshops and manufactories there appear huge mills and factories equipped with machinery. In place of the manorial estates tilled by the primitive implements of production of the peasant, there now appear large capitalist farms run on scientific lines and supplied with agricultural machinery.

The new productive forces require that the workers in production shall be better educated and more intelligent than the downtrodden and ignorant serfs, that they be able to understand machinery and operate it properly. Therefore, the capitalists prefer to deal with wage workers who are free from the bonds of serfdom and who are educated enough to be able properly to operate machinery.

But having developed productive forces to a tremendous extent, capitalism has become enmeshed in contradictions which it is unable to solve. By producing larger and larger quantities of commodities, and reducing their prices, capitalism intensifies competition, ruins the mass of small and medium private owners, converts them into proletarians and reduces their purchasing power, with the result that it becomes impossible to dispose of the commodities produced. On the other hand, by expanding production and concentrating millions of workers in huge mills and factories, capitalism lends the process of production a social character and thus undermines its own foundation, inasmuch as the social character of the process of production demands the social ownership of the means of production; yet the means of production remain private capitalist property, which is incompatible with the social character of the process of production.

These irreconcilable contradictions between the character of the productive forces and the relations of production make themselves felt in periodical crises of overproduction, when the capitalists, finding no effective demand for their goods owing to the ruin of the mass of the population which they themselves have brought about, are compelled to burn products, destroy manufactured goods, suspend production, and destroy productive forces at a time when millions of people are forced to suffer unemployment and starvation, not because there are not enough goods, but because there is an overproduction of goods.

This means that the capitalist relations of production have ceased to correspond to the state of productive forces of society and have come into irreconcilable contradiction with them.

This means that capitalism is pregnant with revolution, whose mission it is to replace the existing capitalist ownership of the means of production by Socialist ownership.

This means that the main feature of the capitalist system is a most acute class struggle between the exploiters and the exploited.

The basis of the relations of production under the Socialist system, which so far has been established only in the U.S.S.R., is the social ownership of the means of production. Here there are no longer exploiters and exploited. The goods produced are distributed according to labour performed, on the principle: "He who does not work, neither shall he eat." Here the mutual relations of people in the process of production are marked by comradely co-operation and the Socialist mutual assistance of workers who are free from exploitation.

Here the relations of production fully correspond to the state of productive forces, for the social character of the process of production is reinforced by the social ownership of the means of production.

For this reason Socialist production in the U.S.S.R. knows no periodical crises of overproduction and their accompanying absurdities.

For this reason, the productive forces here develop at an accelerated pace, for the relations of production that correspond to them offer full scope for such development.

Such is the picture of the development of men's relations of production in the course of human history.

Such is the dependence of the development of the relations of production on the development of the production forces of society, and primarily, on the development of the instruments of production, the dependence by virtue of which the changes and development of the productive forces sooner or later lead to corresponding changes and development of the relations of production.

> "The use and fabrication of instruments of labour," says Marx, "although existing in the germ among certain species of animals, is specifically characteristic of the human labour-process, and Franklin therefore defines man as a tool-making animal. Relics of bygone instruments of labour possess the same importance for the investigation of extinct economic forms of society, as do fossil bones for the determination of extinct species of animals. It is not the articles made, but how they are made, and by what instruments that enables us to distinguish different economic epochs. . . . Instruments of labour not only supply a standard of the degree of development to which human labour has attained but they are also indicators of the social conditions under which that labour is carried on." (Karl Marx, *Capital,* Vol. I).

And further:

> a) "Social relations are closely bound up with productive forces. In acquiring new productive forces men change

their mode of production; and in changing their mode of production, in changing the way of earning their living, they change all their social conditions. The hand-mill gives you society with the feudal lord; the steam-mill, society with the industrial capitalist." (*The Poverty of Philosophy*).

b) "There is a continual movement of growth in productive forces, of destruction in social relations, of formation in ideas; the only immutable thing is the abstraction of movement." (*Ibid.*)

Speaking of historical materialism as formulated in *The Communist Manifesto*, Engels says:

> "Economic production and the structure of society of every historical epoch necessarily arising therefrom constitute the foundation for the political and intellectual history of that epoch; . . . consequently ever since the dissolution of the primeval communal ownership of land all history has been a history of class struggles, of struggles between exploited and exploiting, between dominated and dominating classes at various stages of social evolution; . . . this struggle, however, has now reached a stage where the exploited and oppressed class (the proletariat) can no longer emancipate itself from the class which exploits and oppresses it (the bourgeoisie), without at the same time forever freeing the whole of society from exploitation, oppression and class struggles."

A *third feature* of production is that the rise of new productive forces and of the relations of production corresponding to them does not take place separately from the old system, after the disappearance of the old system, but within the old system; it takes place not as a result of the deliberate and conscious activity of man, but spontaneously, unconsciously, independently of the will of man. It takes place spontaneously and independently of the will of man for two reasons.

First, because men are not free to choose one mode of production or another, because as every new generation enters life it finds productive forces and relations of production already existing as the result of the work of former generations, owing to which it is obliged at first to accept and adapt itself to everything it finds ready made in the sphere of production in order to be able to produce material values.

Secondly, because, when improving one instrument of production or another, one element of the productive forces or another, men do not realize, do not understand or stop to reflect what *social* results these improvements will lead to, but only think of their everyday interests, of lightening their labour and of securing some direct and tangible advantage for themselves.

When, gradually and gropingly, certain members of primitive communal society passed from the use of stone tools to the use of iron tools, they, of course, did not know and did not stop to reflect what *social* results this innovation would lead to; they did not understand or realize that the change to metal tools meant a revolution in production, that it would in the long run lead to the slave system. They simply wanted to lighten their labour and secure an immediate and tangible advantage; their conscious activity was confined within the narrow bounds of this everyday personal interest.

When, in the period of the feudal system, the young bourgeoisie of Europe began to erect, alongside of the small guild workshops, large manufactories, and thus advanced the productive forces of society, it, of course, did not know and did not stop to reflect what *social* consequences this innovation would lead to; it did not realize or understand that this "small" innovation would lead to a regrouping of social forces which was to end in a revolution both against the power of kings, whose favours it so highly valued, and against the nobility, to whose ranks its foremost representatives not infrequently aspired. It simply wanted to lower the cost of producing goods, to throw large quantities of goods on the markets of Asia and of recently discovered America, and to make bigger profits. Its conscious activity was confined within the narrow bounds of this commonplace practical aim.

When the Russian capitalists, in conjunction with foreign capitalists, energetically implanted modern large-scale machine industry in Russia, while leaving tsardom intact and turning the peasants over to the tender mercies of the landlords, they, of course, did not know and did not stop to reflect what *social* consequences this extensive growth of productive forces would lead to, they did not realize or understand that this big leap in the realm of the productive forces of society would lead to a regrouping of social forces that would enable the proletariat to effect a union with the peasantry and to bring about a victorious Socialist revolution. They simply wanted to expand industrial production to the limit, to gain control of the huge home market, to become monopolists, and to squeeze as much profit as possible out of the national economy. Their conscious activity did not extend beyond their commonplace, strictly practical interests. Accordingly, Marx says:

> "In the social production which men carry on they enter into definite relations that are indispensable and independent of their will; these relations of production correspond to a definite stage of development of their material forces of production."

This, however, does not mean that changes in the relations of production, and the transition from old relations of production to new relations of production proceed smoothly, without conflicts, without upheavals. On the contrary, such a transition usually takes place by means of the revolutionary overthrow of the old relations of production and the establishment of new relations of production. Up to a certain period the development of the productive forces and the changes in the realm of the relations of production proceed spontaneously, independently of the will of men. But that is so only up to a certain moment, until the new and developing productive forces have reached a proper state of maturity. After the new productive forces have matured, the existing relations of production and their upholders—the ruling classes—become that "insuperable" obstacle which can only be removed by the conscious action of the new classes, by the forcible acts of these classes, by revolution. Here there stands out in bold relief the *tremendous role* of new social ideas, of new political institutions, of a new political power, whose mission it is to abolish by force the old relations of production. Out of the conflict between the new productive forces and the old relations of production, out of the new economic demands of society there arise new social ideas; the new ideas organize and mobilize the masses; the masses become welded into a new political army, create a new revolutionary power, and make use of it to abolish by force the old system of relations of production, and firmly to establish the new system. The spontaneous process of development yields place to the conscious actions of men, peaceful development to violent upheaval, evolution to revolution.

> "The proletariat," says Marx, "during its contest with the bourgeoisie is compelled, by the force of circumstances, to organize itself as a class . . . by means of a revolution, it makes itself the ruling class, and, as such, sweeps away by force the old conditions of production." (*The Communist Manifesto*)

And further:

> a) "The proletariat will use its political supremacy to wrest, by degrees, all capital from the bourgeoisie, to centralize all instruments of production in the hands of the state, *i.e.*, of the proletariat organized as the ruling class; and to increase the total of productive forces as rapidly as possible." (*Ibid.*)
>
> b) "Force is the midwife of every old society pregnant with a new one." (Karl Marx, *Capital*, Vol. I.)

Here is the brilliant formulation of the essence of historical materialism given by Marx in 1859 in his historic Preface to his famous book, *Critique of Political Economy:*

> "In the social production which men carry on they enter into definite relations that are indispensable and independent of their will; these relations of production correspond to a definite stage of development of their material forces of production. The sum total of these relations of produc-

tion constitutes the economic structure of society—the real foundation, on which rises a legal and political superstructure and to which correspond definite forms of social consciousness. The mode of production in material life determines the social, political and intellectual life process in general. It is not the consciousness of men that determines their being, but, on the contrary, their social being that determines their consciousness. At a certain stage of their development, the material forces of production in society come in conflict with the existing relations of production, or—what is but a legal expression for the same thing—with the property relations within which they have been at work before. From forms of development of the forces of production these relations turn into their fetters. Then begins an epoch of social revolution. With the change of the economic foundation the entire immense superstructure is more or less rapidly transformed. In considering such transformations a distinction should always be made between the material transformation of the economic conditions of production which can be determined with the precision of natural science, and the legal, political, religious, æsthetic or philosophic—in short, ideological forms in which men become conscious of this conflict and fight it out. Just as our opinion of an individual is not based on what he thinks of himself, so can we not judge of such a period of transformation by its own consciousness; on the contrary, this consciousness must be explained rather from the contradictions of material life, from the existing conflict between the social forces of production and the relations of production. No social order ever disappears before all the productive forces for which there is room in it have been developed; and new higher relations of production never appear before the material conditions of their existence have matured in the womb of the old society itself. Therefore, mankind always sets itself only such tasks as it can solve; since, looking at the matter more closely, we will always find that the task itself arises only when the material conditions necessary for its solution already exist or are at least in the process of formation."

Such is Marxist materialism as applied to social life, to the history of society.

Such are the principal features of dialectical and historical materialism.

REPORT TO THE EIGHTEENTH CONGRESS OF THE COMMUNIST PARTY OF THE SOVIET UNION (BOLSHEVIK) ON THE WORK OF THE CENTRAL COMMITTEE[1]

(*March 10, 1939*)

I. THE SOVIET UNION AND INTERNATIONAL AFFAIRS

Comrades, five years have elapsed since the Seventeenth Party Congress. No small period, as you see. During this period the world has undergone considerable changes. States and countries, and their mutual relations, are now in many respects totally altered.

What changes exactly have taken place in this period in the international situation? In what way exactly have the foreign and internal affairs of our country changed?

For the capitalist countries this period was one of very profound perturbations in both the economic and political spheres. In the economic sphere these were years of depression, followed, from the beginning of the latter half of 1937, by a period of new economic crisis, of a new decline of industry in the United States, Great Britain and France—consequently,

[1] This report, delivered to the first Party congress in five years, may prove to be even more important historically than the report to the Seventeenth Party Congress. Precisely at the outbreak of World War II, Stalin sums up what he sees as the strengths and weaknesses of the Soviet Union, both internally and in relation to its world-wide role. The war and its aftermath were to be the objective test of this analysis and of the achievements of Stalin's theory and practice.

these were years of new economic complications. In the political sphere they were years of serious political conflicts and perturbations. A new imperialist war is already in its second year, a war waged over a huge territory stretching from Shanghai to Gibraltar, and involving over five hundred million people. The map of Europe, Africa and Asia is being forcibly redrawn. The entire postwar system, the so-called peace regime, has been shaken to its foundations.

For the Soviet Union, on the contrary, these were years of growth and prosperity, of further economic and cultural progress, of further growth of political and military might, of struggle for the preservation of peace throughout the world.

Such is the general picture.

Let is now examine the concrete data illustrating the changes in the international situation.

1. NEW ECONOMIC CRISIS IN THE CAPITALIST COUNTRIES. INTENSIFICATION OF THE STRUGGLE FOR MARKETS AND SOURCES OF RAW MATERIAL, AND FOR A NEW REDIVISION OF THE WORLD

The economic crisis which broke out in the capitalist countries in the latter half of 1929 lasted until the end of 1933. After that the crisis passed into a depression, and was then followed by a certain revival, a certain upward trend of industry. But this upward trend of industry did not develop into a boom, as is usually the case in a period of revival. On the contrary, in the latter half of 1937 a new economic crisis began which seized the United States first of all and then England, France and a number of other countries.

The capitalist countries thus found themselves faced with a new economic crisis before they had even recovered from the ravages of the recent one.

This circumstance naturally led to an increase of unemployment. The number of unemployed in capitalist countries, which had fallen from 30,000,000 in 1933 to 14,000,000 in 1937, has now again risen to 18,000,000 as a result of the new crisis.

A distinguishing feature of the new crisis is that it differs in many respects from the preceding one, and, moreover, differs for the worse and not for the better.

Firstly, the new crisis did not begin after an industrial boom, as was the case in 1929, but after a depression and a certain revival, which, however, did not develop into a boom. This means that the present crisis will be more severe and more difficult to cope with than the previous crisis.

Further, the present crisis has broken out not in time of peace, but at a time when a second imperialist war has already begun; when Japan, already in the second year of her war with China, is disorganizing the immense Chinese market and rendering it almost inaccessible to the goods of other countries; when Italy and Germany have already placed their national economies on a war footing, squandering their reserves of raw material and foreign currency for this purpose; and when all the other big capitalist powers are beginning to reorganize themselves on a war footing. This means that capitalism will have far less resources at its disposal for a normal way out of the present crisis than during the preceding crisis.

Lastly, as distinct from the preceding crisis, the present crisis is not universal, but as yet involves chiefly the economically powerful countries which have not yet placed themselves on a war economy basis. As regards the aggressive countries, such as Japan, Germany and Italy, who have already reorganized their economies on a war footing, they, because of the intense development of their war industry, are not yet experiencing a crisis of overproduction, although they are approaching it. This means that by the time the economically powerful, nonaggressive countries begin to emerge from the phase of crisis the aggressive countries, having exhausted their reserves of gold and raw material in the course of the war fever, are bound to enter a phase of very severe crisis.

This is clearly illustrated, for example, by the figures for the visible gold reserves of the capitalist countries.

This table shows that the combined gold reserves of Germany, Italy and Japan amount to less than the reserves of Switzerland alone.

Visible Gold Reserves
of the Capitalist Countries
(In millions of former gold dollars)

	End of 1936	*September 1938*
Total	12,980	14,301
U.S.A.	6,649	8,126
Great Britain	2,029	2,396
France	1,769	1,435
Holland	289	595
Belgium	373	318
Switzerland	387	407
Germany	16	17
Italy	123	124
Japan	273	97

Here are a few figures illustrating the state of crisis of industry in the capitalist countries during the past five years and the trend of industrial progress in the U.S.S.R.

Volume of Industrial Output
Compared with 1929
(1929 = 100)

	1934	1935	1936	1937	1938
U.S.A.	66.4	75.6	88.1	92.2	72.0
Great Britain	98.8	105.8	115.9	123.7	112.0
France	71.0	67.4	79.3	82.8	70.0
Italy	80.0	93.8	87.5	99.6	96.0
Germany	79.8	94.0	106.3	117.2	125.0
Japan	128.7	141.8	151.1	170.8	165.0
U.S.S.R.	238.3	293.4	382.3	424.0	477.0

This table shows that the Soviet Union is the only country in the world where crises are unknown and where industry is continuously on the upgrade.

This table also shows that a serious economic crisis has already begun and is developing in the United States, Great Britain and France.

Further, this table shows that in Italy and Japan, who

placed their national economies on a war footing earlier than Germany, the downward course of industry already began in 1938.

Lastly, this table shows that in Germany, who reorganized her economy on a war footing later than Italy and Japan, industry is still experiencing a certain upward trend—although a small one, it is true—corresponding to that which took place in Japan and Italy until recently.

There can be no doubt that unless something unforeseen occurs, German industry must enter the same downward path as Japan and Italy have already taken. For what does placing the economy of a country on a war footing mean? It means giving industry a one-sided, war direction; developing to the utmost the production of goods necessary for war and not for consumption by the population; restricting to the utmost the production and, especially, the sale of articles of general consumption—and, consequently, reducing consumption by the population and confronting the country with an economic crisis.

Such is the concrete picture of the trend of the new economic crisis in the capitalist countries.

Naturally, such an unfavourable turn of economic affairs could not but aggravate relations among the powers. The preceding crisis had already mixed the cards and sharpened the struggle for markets and sources of raw materials. The seizure of Manchuria and North China by Japan, the seizure of Abyssinia by Italy—all this reflected the acuteness of the struggle among the powers. The new economic crisis was bound to lead, and is actually leading, to a further sharpening of the imperialist struggle. It is no longer a question of competition in the markets, of a commercial war, of dumping. These methods of struggle have long been recognized as inadequate. It is now a question of a new redivision of the world, of spheres of influence and colonies, by military action.

Japan tried to justify her aggressive actions by the argument that she had been cheated when the Nine-Power Pact was concluded and had not been allowed to extend her territory at the expense of China, whereas Britain and France possess vast colonies. Italy recalled that she had been cheated during the division of the spoils after the first imperialist war and that she must recompense herself at the expense of the spheres of influence of Britain and France. Germany, who had suffered severely as a result of the first imperialist war and the Peace of Versailles, joined forces with Japan and Italy and demanded an extension of her territory in Europe and the return of the colonies of which the victors in the first imperialist war had deprived her.

Thus the bloc of three aggressive states came to be formed.

A new redivision of the world by means of war became imminent.

2. INCREASING ACUTENESS OF THE INTERNATIONAL POLITICAL SITUATION. COLLAPSE OF THE POSTWAR SYSTEM OF PEACE TREATIES. BEGINNING OF A NEW IMPERIALIST WAR

Here is a list of the most important events during the period under review which marked the beginning of the new imperialist war. In 1935 Italy attacked and seized Abyssinia. In the summer of 1936 Germany and Italy organized military intervention in Spain, Germany entrenching herself in the north of Spain and in Spanish Morocco, and Italy in the south of Spain and in the Balearic Islands. In 1937, having seized Manchuria, Japan invaded North and Central China, occupied Peking, Tientsin and Shanghai and began to oust her foreign competitors from the occupied zone. In the beginning of 1938 Germany seized Austria, and in the autumn of 1938 the Sudeten region of Czechoslovakia. At the end of 1938 Japan seized Canton, and at the beginning of 1939 the Island of Hainan.

Thus the war, which has stolen so imperceptibly upon the nations, has drawn over five hundred million people into its orbit and has extended its sphere of action over a vast territory, stretching from Tientsin, Shanghai and Canton, through Abyssinia, to Gibraltar.

After the first imperialist war the victor states, primarily Britain, France and the United States, had set up a new regime in the relations between countries, the postwar peace regime. The main props of this regime were the Nine-Power Pact in the Far East, and the Versailles and a number of other treaties in Europe. The League of Nations was set up to regulate relations between countries within the framework of this regime, on the basis of a united front of states, of collective defence of the security of states. However, three aggressive states, and the new imperialist war launched by them, upset the entire system of this postwar peace regime. Japan tore up the Nine-Power Pact, and Germany and Italy the Versailles Treaty. In order to have their hands free, these three states withdrew from the League of Nations.

The new imperialist war became a fact.

It is not so easy in our day to suddenly break loose and plunge straight into war without regard for treaties of any kind or for public opinion. Bourgeois politicians know this quite well. So do the fascist rulers. That is why the fascist rulers decided, before plunging into war, to mould public opinion to suit their ends, that is, to mislead it, to deceive it.

A military bloc of Germany and Italy against the interests of England and France in Europe? Bless us, do you call that a bloc? "We" have no military bloc. All "we" have is an innocuous "Berlin-Rome axis"; that is, just a geometrical equation for an axis. (*Laughter.*)

A military bloc of Germany, Italy and Japan against the interests of the United States, Great Britain and France in the Far East? Nothing of the kind! "We" have no military bloc. All "we" have is an innocuous "Berlin-Rome-Tokyo triangle"; that is, a slight penchant for geometry. (*General laughter.*)

A war against the interests of Britain, France, the United States? Nonsense! "We" are waging war on the Comintern, not on these states. If you don't believe it, read the "anti-Comintern pact" concluded between Italy, Germany and Japan.

That is how Messieurs the aggressors thought to mould public opinion, although it was not hard to see how preposterous this whole clumsy game of camouflage was; for it is ridiculous to look for Comintern "hotbeds" in the deserts of Mongolia, in the mountains of Abyssinia, or in the wilds of Spanish Morocco. (*Laughter.*)

But war is inexorable. It cannot be hidden under any guise. For no "axes," "triangles" or "anti-Comintern pacts" can hide the fact that in this period Japan has seized a vast stretch of territory in China, that Italy has seized Abyssinia, that Germany has seized Austria and the Sudeten region, that Germany and Italy together have seized Spain—and all this in defiance of the interests of the nonaggressive states. The war remains a war; the military bloc of aggressors remains a military bloc; and the aggressors remain aggressors.

It is a distinguishing feature of the new imperialist war that it has not yet become universal, a world war. The war is being waged by aggressor states, who in every way infringe upon the interests of the nonaggressive states, primarily Britain, France and the U.S.A., while the latter draw back and retreat, making concession after concession to the aggressors.

Thus we are witnessing an open redivision of the world and spheres of influence at the expense of the nonaggressive states, without the least attempt at resistance, and even with a certain connivance on their part.

Incredible, but true.

To what are we to attribute this one-sided and strange character of the new imperialist war?

How is it that the nonaggressive countries, which possess such vast opportunities, have so easily and without resistance abandoned their positions and their obligations to please the aggressors?

Is it to be attributed to the weakness of the nonaggressive states? Of course not! Combined, the nonaggressive, democratic states are unquestionably stronger than the fascist states, both economically and militarily.

To what then are we to attribute the systematic concessions made by these states to the aggressors?

It might be attributed, for example, to the fear that a revolution might break out if the nonaggressive states were to go to war and the war were to assume world-wide proportions. The bourgeois politicians know, of course, that the first imperialist world war led to the victory of the revolution in one of the largest countries. They are afraid that the second imperialist world war may also lead to the victory of the revolution in one or several countries.

But at present this is not the sole or even the chief reason. The chief reason is that the majority of the nonaggressive countries, particularly England and France, have rejected the policy of collective security, the policy of collective resistance to aggressors, and have taken up a position of nonintervention, a position of "neutrality."

Formally speaking, the policy of nonintervention might be defined as follows: "Let each country defend itself against the aggressors as it likes and as best it can. That is not our affair. We shall trade both with the aggressors and with their victims." But actually speaking, the policy of nonintervention means conniving at aggression, giving free rein to war, and, consequently, transforming the war into a world war. The policy of nonintervention reveals an eagerness, a desire, not to hinder the aggressors in their nefarious work; not to hinder Japan, say, from embroiling herself in a war with China, or, better still, with the Soviet Union; not to hinder Germany, say, from enmeshing herself in European affairs, from embroiling herself in a war with the Soviet Union; to allow all the belligerents to sink deeply into the mire of war; to encourage them surreptitiously in this to allow them to weaken and exhaust one another; and then, when they have become weak enough, to appear on the scene with fresh strength, to appear, of course, "in the interests of peace," and to dictate conditions to the enfeebled belligerents.

Cheap and easy!

Take Japan, for instance. It is characteristic that before Japan invaded North China all the influential French and British newspapers shouted about China's weakness and her inability to offer resistance, and declared that Japan with her army could subjugate China in two or three months. Then the European and American politicians began to watch and wait. And then, when Japan seriously started military operations, they let her have Shanghai, the vital centre of foreign capital in China; they let her have Canton, a centre of Britain's monopoly influence in South China; they let her have Hainan, and they allowed her to surround Hongkong. Does not this look very much like encouraging the aggressor? It is as though they were saying: "Embroil yourself deeper in war; then we shall see."

Or take Germany, for instance. They let her have Austria, despite the undertaking to defend her independence; they let her have the Sudeten region; they abandoned Czechoslovakia to her fate, thereby violating all their obligations; and then they began to lie vociferously in the press about "the weakness of the Russian army," "the demoralization of the Russian air force," and "riots" in the Soviet Union, egging on the Germans to march farther east, promising them easy pickings, and prompting them: "Just start war on the Bolsheviks, and everything will be all right." It must be admitted that this too looks very much like egging on and encouraging the aggressor.

The hullabaloo raised by the British, French and American press over the Soviet Ukraine is characteristic. The gentlemen of the press there shouted until they were hoarse that the Germans were marching on Soviet Ukraine, that they now had what is called the Carpathian Ukraine, with a population of some seven hundred thousand, and that not later than this spring the Germans would annex the Soviet Ukraine, which has a population of over thirty million, to this so-called Carpathian Ukraine. It looks as if the object of this suspicious hullabaloo was to incense the Soviet Union against Germany, to poison the atmosphere and to provoke a conflict with Germany without any visible grounds.

It is quite possible, of course, that there are madmen in Germany who dream of annexing the elephant, that is, the Soviet Ukraine, to the gnat, namely, the so-called Carpathian Ukraine. If there really are such lunatics in Germany, rest assured that we shall find enough strait jackets for them in our country. (*Thunderous applause.*) But if we ignore the madmen and turn to normal people, is it not clearly absurd and foolish to seriously talk of annexing the Soviet Ukraine to this so-called Carpathian Ukraine? Imagine: The gnat comes to the elephant and says perkily: "Ah, brother, how sorry I am for you. . . . Here you are without any landlords, without any capitalists, with no national oppression, without any fascist bosses. Is that a way to live? . . . As I look at you I can't help thinking that there is no hope for you unless you annex yourself to me. . . . (*General laughter.*) Well, so be it: I allow you to annex your tiny domain to my vast territories. . . ." (*General laughter and applause.*)

Even more characteristic is the fact that certain European and American politicians and pressmen, having lost patience waiting for "the march on the Soviet Ukraine," are themselves beginning to disclose what is really behind the policy of nonintervention. They are saying quite openly, putting it down in black on white, that the Germans have cruelly "disappointed" them, for instead of marching farther east, against the Soviet Union, they have turned, you see, to the west and are demanding colonies. One might think that the districts of Czechoslovakia were yielded to Germany as the price of an undertaking to launch war on the Soviet Union, but that now the Germans are refusing to meet their bills and are sending them to Hades.

Far be it from me to moralize on the policy of nonintervention, to talk of treason, treachery and so on. It would be naive to preach morals to people who recognize no human morality. Politics are politics, as the old, case-hardened bourgeois diplomats say. It must be remarked, however, that the big and dangerous political game started by the supporters of the policy of nonintervention may end in serious fiasco for them.

Such is the true face of the now prevailing policy of nonintervention.

Such is the political situation in the capitalist countries.

3. THE SOVIET UNION AND THE CAPITALIST COUNTRIES

The war has created a new situation with regard to the relations between countries. It has enveloped them in an atmosphere of alarm and uncertainty. By undermining the postwar peace regime and overriding the elementary principles of international law, it has cast doubt on the value of international treaties and obligations. Pacifism and disarmament schemes are dead and buried. Feverish arming has taken their place. Everybody is arming, small states and big states, including primarily those which practise the policy of nonintervention. Nobody believes any longer in the unctuous speeches which claim that the Munich concessions to the aggressors and the Munich agreement opened a new era of "appeasement." They are disbelieved even by the signatories to the Munich agreement, Britain and France, who are increasing their armaments no less than other countries.

Naturally, the U.S.S.R. could not ignore these ominous developments. There is no doubt that any war, however small, started by the aggressors in any remote corner of the world constitutes a danger to the peaceable countries. All the more serious then is the danger arising from the new imperialist war, which has already drawn into its orbit over five hundred million people in Asia, Africa and Europe. In view of this, while our country is unswervingly pursuing a policy of maintaining peace, it is at the same time working very seriously to increase the preparedness of our Red Army and our Red Navy.

At the same time, in order to strengthen its international position, the Soviet Union decided to take certain other steps. At the end of 1934 our country joined the League of Nations, considering that despite its weakness the League might nevertheless serve as a place where aggressors can be exposed, and as a certain instrument of peace, however feeble, that might hinder the outbreak of war. The Soviet Union considers that in alarming times like these even so weak an international organization as the League of Nations should not be ignored. In May 1935 a treaty of mutual assistance against possible attack by aggressors was signed between France and the Soviet Union. A similar treaty was simultaneously concluded with Czechoslovakia. In March 1936 the Soviet Union concluded a treaty of mutual assistance with the Mongolian People's Republic. In August 1937 the Soviet Union concluded a pact of nonaggression with the Chinese Republic.

It was in such difficult international conditions that the Soviet Union pursued its foreign policy of upholding the cause of peace.

The foreign policy of the Soviet Union is clear and explicit.

1. We stand for peace and the strengthening of business relations with all countries. That is our position; and we shall adhere to this position as long as these countries maintain like relations with the Soviet Union, and as long as they make no attempt to trespass on the interests of our country.

2. We stand for peaceful, close and friendly relations with all the neighbouring countries which have common frontiers with the U.S.S.R. That is our position; and we shall adhere to this position as long as these countries maintain like rela-

tions with the Soviet Union, and as long as they make no attempt to trespass, directly or indirectly, on the integrity and inviolability of the frontiers of the Soviet state.

3. We stand for the support of nations which are the victims of aggression and are fighting for the independence of their country.

4. We are not afraid of the threats of aggressors, and are ready to deal two blows for every blow delivered by instigators of war who attempt to violate the Soviet borders.

Such is the foreign policy of the Soviet Union. (*Loud and prolonged applause.*)

In its foreign policy the Soviet Union relies upon:

1. Its growing economic, political and cultural might;
2. The moral and political unity of our Soviet society;
3. The mutual friendship of the nations of our country;
4. Its Red Army and Red Navy;
5. Its policy of peace;
6. The moral support of the working people of all countries, who are vitally concerned in the preservation of peace;
7. The good sense of the countries which for one reason or another have no interest in the violation of peace.

* * *

The tasks of the Party in the sphere of foreign policy are:

1. To continue the policy of peace and of strengthening business relations with all countries;
2. To be cautious and not allow our country to be drawn into conflicts by warmongers who are accustomed to have others pull the chestnuts out of the fire for them;
3. To strengthen the might of our Red Army and Red Navy to the utmost;
4. To strengthen the international bonds of friendship with the working people of all countries, who are interested in peace and friendship among nations.

II. INTERNAL AFFAIRS OF THE SOVIET UNION

Let us now pass to the internal affairs of our country.

From the standpoint of its internal situation, the Soviet Union, during the period under review, presented a picture of further progress of its entire economic life, a rise in culture, and the strengthening of the political might of the country.

In the sphere of economic development, we must regard as the most important result during the period under review the fact that the reconstruction of industry and agriculture on the basis of a new, modern technique has been completed. There are no more or hardly any more old plants in our country, with their backward technique, and hardly any old peasant farms, with their antediluvian equipment. Our industry and agriculture are now based on new, up-to-date technique. It may be said without exaggeration that from the standpoint of technique of production, from the standpoint of the degree of saturation of industry and agriculture with new machinery, our country is more advanced than any other country, where the old machinery acts as a fetter on production and hampers the introduction of new techniques.

In the sphere of the social and political development of the country, we must regard as the most important achievement during the period under review the fact that the remnants of the exploiting classes have been completely eliminated, that the workers, peasants and intellectuals have been welded into one common front of the working people, that the moral and political unity of Soviet society has been strengthened, that the friendship among the nations of our country has become closer, and that as a result of all this, the political life of our country has been completely democratized and a new Constitution created. No one will dare deny that our Constitution is the most democratic in the world, and that the results of the elections to the Supreme Soviet of the U.S.S.R., as well as to the Supreme Soviets of the Union Republics, have been the most exemplary.

The result of all this is a completely stable internal situation and a stability of government which any other government in the world might envy.

Let us examine the concrete data illustrating the economic and political situation of our country.

INDUSTRIAL PROGRESS OF THE U.S.S.R. IN 1934–38

	1933	1934	1935	1936	1937	1938	Per cent of previous year					1938 compared with 1933 (per cent)
							1934	1935	1936	1937	1938	
	In millions of rubles at 1926-27 prices											
Total output	42,030	50,477	62,137	80,929	90,166	100,375	120.1	123.1	130.2	111.4	111.3	238.8
Of which:												
1. Socialist industry	42,002	50,443	62,114	80,898	90,138	100,349	120.1	123.1	130.2	111.4	111.3	238.9
2. Private industry	28	34	23	31	28	26	121.4	67.6	134.8	90.3	92.9	92.9
	Per cent											
Total output	100.00	100.00	100.00	100.00	100.00	100.00						
Of which:												
1. Socialist industry	99.93	99.93	99.96	99.96	99.97	99.97						
2. Private industry	0.07	0.07	0.04	0.04	0.03	0.03						

1. FURTHER PROGRESS OF INDUSTRY AND AGRICULTURE

a) *Industry*. During the period under review our industry presented a picture of uninterrupted progress. This progress was reflected not only in an increase of output generally, but, and primarily, in the flourishing state of socialist industry, on the one hand, and the doom of private industry, on the other.

Opposite is a table which illustrates this.

This table shows that during the period under review the output of our industry more than doubled, and that, moreover, the whole increase in output was accounted for by socialist industry.

Further, this table shows that the only system of industry in the U.S.S.R. is the socialist system.

Lastly, this table shows that the utter doom of private industry is a fact which even a blind man cannot now deny.

The doom of private industry must not be regarded as a thing of chance. It perished, firstly, because the socialist economic system is superior to the capitalist system; and, secondly, because the socialist economic system made it possible for us to re-equip in a few years the whole of our socialist industry on new and up-to-date technical lines. This is a possibility which the capitalist economic system does not and cannot offer. It is a fact that, from the standpoint of technique of production, from the standpoint of the degree of saturation of industry with modern machinery, our industry holds first place in the world.

If we take the rate of growth of our industry, expressed in percentages of the prewar level, and compare it with the rate of growth of the industry of the principal capitalist countries, we get the following picture:

Growth of Industry in the U.S.S.R. and the Principal Capitalist Countries in 1913–38

	1913	1933	1934	1935	1936	1937	1938
U.S.S.R.	100.0	380.5	457.0	562.6	732.7	816.4	908.8
U.S.A.	100.0	108.7	112.9	128.6	149.8	156.9	120.0
Great Britain	100.0	87.0	97.1	104.0	114.2	121.9	113.3
Germany	100.0	75.4	90.4	105.9	118.1	129.3	131.6
France	100.0	107.0	99.0	94.0	98.0	101.0	93.2

This table shows that our industry has grown more than ninefold as compared with prewar, whereas the industry of the principal capitalist countries continues to mark time round about the prewar level, exceeding the latter by only 20 or 30 per cent.

This means that as regards rate of growth our socialist industry holds first place in the world.

Thus we find that as regards technique of production and rate of growth of our industry, we have already overtaken and outstripped the principal capitalist countries.

In what respect are we lagging? We are still lagging economically, that is, as regards the volume of our industrial output per head of population. In 1938 we produced about 15,000,000 tons of pig iron; Great Britain produced 7,000,000 tons. It might seem that we are better off than Great Britain. But if we divide this number of tons by the number of population we shall find that the output of pig iron per head of population in 1938 was 145 kilograms in Great Britain, and only 87 kilograms in the U.S.S.R. Or, further: in 1938 Great Britain produced 10,800,000 tons of steel and about 29,000,000,000 kilowatt-hours of electricity, whereas the U.S.S.R. produced 18,000,000 tons of steel and over 39,000,000,000 kilowatt-hours of electricity. It might seem that we are better off than Great Britain. But if we divide this number of tons and kilowatt-hours by the number of population we shall find that in 1938 in Great Britain the output of steel per head of population was 226 kilograms and of electricity 620 kilowatt-hours, whereas in the U.S.S.R. the output of steel per head of population was only 107 kilograms, and of electricity only 233 kilowatt-hours.

What is the reason for this? The reason is that our population is several times larger than that of Great Britain, and hence our requirements are greater: the Soviet Union has a population of 170,000,000, whereas Great Britain has a population of not more than 46,000,000. The economic power of a country's industry is not expressed by the volume of industrial output in general, irrespective of the size of population, but by the volume of industrial output taken in direct reference to the amount consumed per head of population. The larger a country's industrial output per head of population, the greater is its economic power; and, conversely, the smaller the output per head of population, the less is the economic power of the country and of its industry. Consequently, the larger a country's population, the greater is the need for articles of consumption, and hence the larger should be the industrial output of the country.

Take, for example, the output of pig iron. In order to outstrip Great Britain economically in respect to production of pig iron, which in 1938 amounted in that country to 7,000,000 tons, we must increase our annual output of pig iron to 25,000,000 tons. In order economically to outstrip Germany, which in 1938 produced 18,000,000 tons of pig iron in all, we must raise our annual output to 40,000,000 or 45,000,000 tons. And in order to outstrip the U.S.A. economically—not as regards the level of 1938, which was a year of crisis, and in which the U.S.A. produced only 18,800,000 tons of pig iron, but as regards the level of 1929, when the U.S.A. was experiencing an industrial boom and when it produced about 43,000,000 tons of pig iron—we must raise our annual output of pig iron to 50,000,000 or 60,000,000 tons.

The same must be said of the production of steel and rolled steel, of the machine-building industry, and so on, inasmuch as these branches of industry, and all others too, depend in the long run on the production of pig iron.

We have outstripped the principal capitalist countries as regards technique of production and rate of industrial development. That is very good, but it is not enough. We must outstrip them economically as well. We can do it, and we must do it. Only if we outstrip the principal capitalist countries economically can we reckon upon our country being fully saturated with consumers' goods, on having an abundance of products, and on being able to make the transition from the first phase of Communism to its second phase.

What do we require to outstrip the principal capitalist countries economically? First of all, we require the earnest and indomitable desire to move ahead and the readiness to make sacrifices and invest very considerable amounts of capital for the utmost expansion of our socialist industry. Have we these requisites? We undoubtedly have! Further, we require a high technique of production and a high rate of industrial development. Have we these requisites? We undoubtedly have! Lastly, we require time. Yes, comrades, time. We must build new factories. We must train new cadres for industry. But this requires time, and no little time at that. We cannot outstrip the principal capitalist countries economically in two or three years. It will require rather more than that. Take, for example, pig iron and its production. How much time do we require to outstrip the principal capitalist countries economically in regard to the production of pig iron? When the second five-year plan was being drawn up, certain members of the old personnel of the State Planning Commission proposed that the annual output of pig iron towards the end of the second five-year plan should be fixed in the amount of sixty million tons. That means that they assumed the possibility of an average annual increase in pig iron production of ten million tons. This, of course, was sheer fantasy, if not worse. Incidentally, it was not only in regard to the production of pig iron that these comrades indulged their fantasy. They considered, for example, that during the period of the second five-year plan the annual increase of population in the U.S.S.R. should amount to three or four million persons, or even more. This was also fantasy, if not worse. But if we ignore these fantastic dreamers and come down to reality, we may consider quite feasible an average annual increase in the output of pig iron of two or two and a half million tons, bearing in mind the present state of technique of iron smelting. The industrial history of the principal capitalist countries, as well as of our country, shows that such an annual rate of increase involves a great strain, but is quite feasible.

Hence, we require time, and no little time at that, in order to outstrip the principal capitalist countries economically. And the higher our productivity of labour becomes, and the more our technique of production is perfected, the more rapidly can we accomplish this cardinal economic task, the more can we reduce the period of its accomplishment.

b) *Agriculture.* Like the development of industry, the development of agriculture during the period under review has followed an upward trend. This upward trend is expressed not only in an increase of agricultural output, but, and primarily, in the growth and consolidation of socialist agriculture on the one hand, and the utter doom of individual peasant farming on the other. Whereas the grain area of the collective farms increased from 75,000,000 hectares in 1933 to 92,000,000 in 1938, the grain area of the individual peasant farmers dropped in this period from 15,700,000 hectares to 600,000 hectares, or to 0.6 per cent of the total grain area. I will not mention the area under industrial crops, a branch where individual peasant farming has been reduced to zero. Furthermore, it is well known that the collective farms now unite 18,800,000 peasant households, or 93.5 per cent of all the peasant households, aside from the collective fisheries and collective trapping and handicraft industries.

This means that the collective farms have been firmly established and consolidated, and that the socialist system of farming is now our only form of agriculture.

If we compare the areas under all crops during the period under review with the crop areas in the prerevolutionary period, we observe the following picture of growth:

AREAS UNDER ALL CROPS IN THE U.S.S.R.

	Millions of hectares						1938 compared with 1913 (per cent).
	1913	1934	1935	1936	1937	1938	
Total crop area ..	105.0	131.5	132.8	133.8	135.3	136.9	130.4
Of which:							
a) Grain	94.4	104.7	103.4	102.4	104.4	102.4	108.5
b) Industrial ...	4.5	10.7	10.6	10.8	11.2	11.0	244.4
c) Vegetable ..	3.8	8.8	9.9	9.8	9.0	9.4	247.4
d) Fodder	2.1	7.1	8.6	10.6	10.6	14.1	671.4

This table shows that we have an increase in area for all cultures, and above all for fodder, industrial crops, and vegetables.

This means that our agriculture is becoming more high-grade and productive, and that a solid foundation is being provided for the increasing application of proper crop rotation.

The wav our collective farms and state farms have been increasingly supplied with tractors, harvester-combines and other machines during the period under review is shown by the following tables:

1) TRACTORS EMPLOYED IN AGRICULTURE IN THE U.S.S.R.

	1933	1934	1935	1936	1937	1938	1938 compared with 1933 (per cent)
	a) Number of tractors (thousands)						
Total	210.9	276.4	360.3	422.7	454.5	483.5	229.3
Of which:							
a) In machine and tractor stations	123.2	177.3	254.7	328.5	365.8	394.0	319.8
b) In state farms and auxiliary agricultural undertakings	83.2	95.5	102.1	88.5	84.5	85.0	102.2
	b) Capacity (thous. hp)						
All tractors	3,209.2	4,462.8	6,184.0	7,672.4	8,385.0	9,256.2	288.4
Of which:							
a) In machine and tractor stations	1,758.1	2,753.9	4,281.6	5,856.0	6,679.2	7,137.0	423.0
b) In state farms and auxiliary agricultural undertakings	1,401.7	1,669.5	1,861.4	1,730.7	1,647.5	1,751.8	125.0

2) TOTAL HARVESTER COMBINES AND OTHER MACHINES EMPLOYED IN AGRICULTURE IN THE U.S.S.R.

(In thousands; at end of year)

	1933	1934	1935	1936	1937	1938	1938 compared with 1933 (per cent)
Harvester combines	25.4	32.3	50.3	87.8	128.8	153.5	604.3
Internal combustion and steam engines	48.0	60.9	69.1	72.4	77.9	83.8	174.6
Complex and semicomplex grain threshers	120.3	121.9	120.1	123.7	126.1	130.8	108.7
Motor trucks	26.6	40.3	63.7	96.2	144.5	195.8	736.1
Automobiles (units)	3,991	5,533	7,555	7,630	8,156	9,594	240.4

If in addition to these figures, we bear in mind that in the period under review the number of machine and tractor stations increased from 2,900 in 1934 to 6,350 in 1938, it may be safely said, on the basis of all these facts, that the reconstruction of our agriculture on the foundation of a new and up-to-date machine technique has in the main already been completed.

Our agriculture, consequently, is not only run on the largest scale, and is the most mechanized in the world, and therefore produces the largest surplus for the market, but is also more fully equipped with modern machinery than the agriculture of any other country.

If we compare the harvests of grain and industrial crops during the period under review with the prerevolutionary period, we get the following picture of growth:

Gross Production of Grain and Industrial Crops in the U.S.S.R.

	In millions of centners						1938 *compared with* 1913 *(per cent)*
	1913	1934	1935	1936	1937	1938	
Grain	801.0	894.0	901.0	827.3	1,202.9	949.9	118.6
Raw cotton	7.4	11.8	17.2	23.9	25.8	26.9	363.5
Flax fibre	3.3	5.3	5.5	5.8	5.7	5.46	165.5
Sugar beet	109.0	113.6	162.1	168.3	218.6	166.8	153.0
Oil seed	21.5	36.9	42.7	12.3	51.1	46.6	216.7

From this table it can be seen that despite the drought in the eastern and southeastern districts in 1936 and 1938, and despite the unprecedentedly large harvest in 1913, the gross production of grain and industrial crops during the period under review steadily increased as compared with 1913.

Of particular interest is the question of the amount of grain marketed by the collective farms and state farms as compared with their gross harvests. Comrade Nemchinov, the statistician, has calculated that of a gross grain harvest of 5,000,000,000 poods in prewar times, only about 1,300,000,000 poods were marketed. Thus the marketed proportion of the grain crop in those days was 26 per cent. Comrade Nemchinov computes that in the years 1926–27, for example, the proportion of marketed produce to gross harvest was about 47 per cent in the case of collective and state farming, which is large-scale farming, and about 12 per cent in the case of individual peasant farming. If we approach the matter more cautiously and assume the amount of marketed produce in the case of collective and state farming in 1938 to be 40 per cent of the gross harvest, we find that in that year our socialist grain farming was able to release, and actually did release, about 2,300,000,000 poods of grain for the market, or 1,000,000,000 poods more than was marketed in prewar times.

Consequently, the high proportion of produce marketed constitutes an important feature of state and collective farming, and is of cardinal importance for the food supply of our country.

It is this feature of the collective farms and state farms that explains the secret why our country has succeeded so easily and rapidly in solving the grain problem, the problem of producing an adequate supply of market grain for this vast country.

It should be noted that during the last three years annual grain deliveries to the state have not dropped below 1,600,000,000 poods, while sometimes, as for example in 1937, they have reached 1,800,000,000 poods. If we add to this about 200,000,000 poods or so of grain purchased annually by the state, as well as several hundred million poods sold by collective farms and farmers directly in the market, we get in all the total of grain released by the collective farms and state farms already mentioned.

Further, it is interesting to note that during the last three years the base of market grain has shifted from the Ukraine, which was formerly considered the granary of our country, to the north and the east, that is, to the R.S.F.S.R. We know that during the last two or three years grain deliveries in the Ukraine have amounted in all to about 400,000,000 poods annually, whereas in the R.S.F.S.R. the grain deliveries during these years have amounted to 1,100,000,000 or 1,200,000,000 poods annually.

That is how things stand with regard to grain farming.

As regards livestock farming, considerable advances have been made during the past few years in this, the most backward branch of agriculture, as well. True, in the number of horses and in sheep breeding we are still below the prerevolutionary level; but as regards cattle and hog breeding we have already passed the prerevolutionary level.

[See table "Total Head of Livestock in the U.S.S.R."]

There can be no doubt that the lag in horse breeding and sheep breeding will be remedied in a very short period.

c) *Trade and transport.* The progress in industry and agriculture was accompanied by an increase in the trade of the country. During the period under review the number of state and cooperative retail stores increased by 25 per cent. State and cooperative retail trade increased by 178 per cent. Trade in the collective-farm markets increased by 112 per cent. [See table "Trade."]

It is obvious that trade in the country could not have so developed without a certain increase in freight traffic. And indeed during the period under review freight traffic increased in all branches of transport, especially rail and air. There was an increase in water-borne freight, too, but with considerable fluctuations, and in 1938, it is to be regretted, there was even a drop in water-borne freight as compared with the previous year. [Table "Freight Traffic."]

Total Head of Livestock in the U.S.S.R.
(In millions)

	July							*1938 compared with*	
	1916 *according to census*	1933	1934	1935	1936	1937	1938	1916 *according to census (per cent)*	1933 *(per cent)*
Horses	35.8	16.6	15.7	15.9	16.6	16.7	17.5	48.9	105.4
Cattle	60.6	38.4	42.4	49.2	56.7	57.0	63.2	104.3	164.6
Sheep and goats	121.2	50.2	51.9	61.1	73.7	81.3	102.5	84.6	204.2
Hogs	20.9	12.1	17.4	22.5	30.5	22.8	30.6	146.4	252.9

TRADE

	1933	1934	1935	1936	1937	1938	1938 compared with 1933 (per cent)
1. State and cooperative retail stores and booths—at end of year	285,355	286,236	268,713	289,473	327,361	356,930	125.1
2. State and cooperative retail trade, including public catering (in millions of rubles)	49,789.2	61,814.7	81,712.1	106,760.9	125,943.2	138,574.3	278.3
3. Trade in collective-farm markets (in millions of rubles)	11,500.0	14,000.0	14,500.0	15,607.2	17,799.7	24,399.2	212.2
4. Regional wholesale departments of the People's Commissariats of the Food Industry, Light Industry, Heavy Industry, Timber Industry, and Local Industry of the Union Republics—at the end of year.......	718	836	1,141	1,798	1,912	1,994	277.7

Freight Traffic

	1933	1934	1935	1936	1937	1938	1938 compared with 1933 (*per cent*)
Railways (in millions of ton-kilometres)	169,500	205,700	258,100	323,400	354,800	369,100	217.7
River and marine transport (in millions of ton-kilometres)	50,200	56,500	68,300	72,300	70,100	66,000	131.5
Civil air fleet (in thousands of ton-kilometres)	3,100	6,400	9,800	21,900	24,900	31,700	1,022.6

There can be no doubt that the comparative lag in water transport in 1938 will be remedied in 1939.

2. FURTHER RISE IN THE MATERIAL AND CULTURAL STANDARD OF THE PEOPLE

The steady progress of industry and agriculture could not but lead, and has actually led, to a new rise in the material and cultural standard of the people.

The abolition of exploitation and the consolidation of the socialist economic system, the absence of unemployment, with its attendant poverty, in town and country, the enormous expansion of industry and the steady growth in the number of workers, the increase in the productivity of labour of the workers and collective farmers, the securement of the land to the collective farms in perpetuity, and the vast number of first-class tractors and agricultural machines supplied to the collective farms—all this has created effective conditions for a further rise in the standard of living of the workers and peasants. In its turn, the improvement in the standard of living of the workers and peasants has naturally led to an improvement in the standard of living of the intelligentsia, who represent a considerable force in our country and serve the interests of the workers and the peasants.

Now it is no longer a question of finding room in industry for unemployed and homeless peasants who have been set adrift from their villages and live in fear of starvation—of giving them jobs out of charity. The time has long gone by when there were such peasants in our country. And this is a good thing, of course, for it testifies to the prosperity of our countryside. If anything, it is now a question of asking the collective farms to comply with our request and to release, say, about one and a half million young collective farmers annually for the needs of our expanding industry. The collective farms, which have already become prosperous, should bear in mind that if we do not get this assistance from them it will be very difficult to continue the expansion of our industry, and that if we do not expand our industry we shall not be able to satisfy the peasants' growing demand for consumers' goods. The collective farms are quite able to meet this request of ours, since the abundance of machinery in the collective farms releases a portion of the rural workers, who, if transferred to industry, could be of immense service to our whole national economy.

As a result, we have the following indications of the improvement in the standard of living of the workers and peasants during the period under review:

1. The national income rose from 48,500,000,000 rubles in 1933 to 105,000,000,000 rubles in 1938;

2. The number of factory and office workers rose from a little over 22,000,000 in 1933 to 28,000,000 in 1938;

3. The total annual payroll rose from 34,953,000,000 rubles to 96,425,000,000 rubles;

4. The average annual wages of industrial workers, which amounted to 1,513 rubles in 1933, rose to 3,447 rubles in 1938;

5. The total monetary incomes of the collective farms rose from 5,661,900,000 rubles in 1933 to 14,180,100,000 rubles in 1937;

6. The average amount of grain received per collective-farm household in the grain-growing regions rose from 61 poods in 1933 to 144 poods in 1937, exclusive of seed, emergency seed stocks, fodder for the collectively-owned cattle, grain deliveries, and payments in kind for work performed by the machine and tractor stations;

7. State budget appropriations for social and cultural services rose from 5,839,900,000 rubles in 1933 to 35,202,500,000 rubles in 1938.

As regards the cultural standard of the people, its rise was commensurate with the rise in the standard of living.

From the standpoint of the cultural development of the people, the period under review has been marked by a veritable cultural revolution. The introduction of universal compulsory elementary education in the languages of the various nationalities of the U.S.S.R., the increasing number of schools and scholars of all grades, the increasing number of college-trained experts, and the creation and growth of a new intelligentsia, a Soviet intelligentsia—such is the general picture of the cultural advancement of our people.

Here are the figures:

1) *Rise in the Cultural Level of the People*

	Unit of measurement	1933–34	1938–39	*1938–39 compared with 1933–34*
Number of pupils and students of all grades	thousands	23,814	33,965.4	142.6%
Of which: In elementary schools	"	17,873.5	21,288.4	119.1%
In intermediate schools (general and special)	"	5,482.2	12,076.0	220.3%
In higher educational institutions	"	458.3	601.0	131.1%
Number of persons engaged in all forms of study in the U.S.S.R.	"	—	47,442.1	—
Number of public libraries	"	40.3	70.0	173.7%
Number of books in public libraries	millions	86.0	126.6	147.2%
Number of clubs	thousands	61.1	95.6	156.5%
Number of theatres	units	587	790	134.6%
Number of cinema installations (excluding narrow-film)	"	27,467	30,461	110.9%
Of which: With sound equipment	"	498	15,202	31 times
Number of cinema installations (excluding narrow-film) in rural districts	"	17,470	18,991	108.7%
Of which: With sound equipment	"	24	6,670	278 times
Annual newspaper circulation	millions	4,984.6	7,092.4	142.3%

2) *Number of Schools Built in the U.S.S.R. in 1933–38*

	In towns and hamlets	*In rural localities*	*Total*
1933	326	3,261	3,587
1934	577	3,488	4,065
1935	533	2,829	3,362
1936	1,505	4,206	5,711
1937	730	1,323	2,053
1938	583	1,246	1,829
Total (1933–38)	4,254	16,353	20,607

3) *Young Specialists Graduated From Higher Educational Institutions in 1933–38 (In thousands)*

	1933	1934	1935	1936	1937	1938
Total for U.S.S.R. (exclusive of military specialists)	34.6	49.2	83.7	97.6	104.8	106.7
1. Engineers for industry and building	6.1	14.9	29.6	29.2	27.6	25.2
2. Engineers for transport and communications	1.8	4.0	7.6	6.6	7.0	6.1
3. Agricultural engineers, agronomists, veterinarians and zootechnicians	4.8	6.3	8.8	10.4	11.3	10.6
4. Economists and jurists	2.5	2.5	5.0	6.4	5.0	5.7
5. Teachers of intermediate schools, workers' faculties, technical schools, and other educational workers, including art workers	10.5	7.9	12.5	21.6	31.7	35.7
6. Physicians, pharmacists, and physical culture instructors	4.6	2.5	7.5	9.2	12.3	13.6
7. Other specialities	4.3	11.1	12.7	14.2	9.9	9.8

As a result of this immense cultural work a numerous new, Soviet intelligentsia has arisen in our country, an intelligentsia which has emerged from the ranks of the working class, peasantry and Soviet employees, which is of the flesh and blood of our people, which has never known the yoke of exploitation, which hates exploiters, and which is ready to serve the peoples of the U.S.S.R. faithfully and devotedly.

I think that the rise of this new, socialist intelligentsia of the people is one of the most important results of the cultural revolution in our country.

3. FURTHER CONSOLIDATION OF THE SOVIET SYSTEM

One of the most important results of the period under review is that it has led to the further internal consolidation of the country, to the further consolidation of the Soviet system.

Nor could it be otherwise. The firm establishment of the socialist system in all branches of national economy, the progress of industry and agriculture, the rising material standard of the working people, the rising cultural standard of the masses and their increasing political activity—all this, accomplished under the guidance of the Soviet power, could not but lead to the further consolidation of the Soviet system.

The feature that distinguishes Soviet society today from any capitalist society is that it no longer contains antagonistic, hostile classes; that the exploiting classes have been eliminated, while the workers, peasants and intellectuals, who make up Soviet society, live and work in friendly collaboration. Whereas capitalist society is torn by irreconcilable antagonisms between workers and capitalists and between peasants and landlords—resulting in its internal instability—Soviet society, liberated from the yoke of exploitation, knows no such antagonisms, is free of class conflicts, and presents a picture of friendly collaboration between workers, peasants and intellectuals. It is this community of interest which has formed the basis for the development of such motive forces as the moral and political unity of Soviet society, the mutual friendship of the nations of the U.S.S.R., and Soviet patriotism. It has also been the basis for the Constitution of the

U.S.S.R. adopted in November 1936, and for the complete democratization of the elections to the supreme organs of the country.

As to the elections to the supreme organs, they were a magnificent demonstration of that unity of Soviet society and of that amity among the nations of the U.S.S.R. which constitute the characteristic feature of the internal situation of our country. As we know, in the elections to the Supreme Soviet of the U.S.S.R. in December 1937, nearly ninety million votes, or 98.6 per cent of the total ballot, were cast for the Communist and non-Party bloc, while in the elections to the Supreme Soviets of the Union Republics in June 1938, ninety-two million votes, or 99.4 per cent of the total ballot, were cast for the Communist and non-Party bloc.

There you have the basis of the stability of the Soviet system and the source of the inexhaustible strength of Soviet power.

This means, incidentally, that in case of war, the rear and front of our army, by reason of their homogeneity and inherent unity, will be stronger than those of any other country, a fact which people beyond our borders who are fond of military conflicts would do well to remember.

Certain foreign pressmen have been talking drivel to the effect that the purging of Soviet organizations of spies, assassins and wreckers like Trotsky, Zinoviev, Kamenev, Yakir, Tukhachevsky, Rosengoltz, Bukharin and other fiends has "shaken" the Soviet system and caused its "demoralization." All this cheap drivel deserves is laughter and scorn. How can the purging of Soviet organizations of noxious and hostile elements shake and demoralize the Soviet system? This Trotsky-Bukharin bunch of spies, assassins and wreckers, who kowtowed to the foreign world, who were possessed by a slavish instinct to grovel before every foreign bigwig and were ready to serve him as spies—this handful of people who did not understand that the humblest Soviet citizen, being free from the fetters of capital, stands head and shoulders above any high-placed foreign bigwig whose neck wears the yoke of capitalist slavery—who needs this miserable band of venal slaves, of what value can they be to the people, and whom can they "demoralize"? In 1937 Tukhachevsky, Yakir, Uborevich and other fiends were sentenced to be shot. After that, the elections to the Supreme Soviet of the U.S.S.R. were held. In these elections, 98.6 per cent of the total vote was cast for the Soviet power. At the beginning of 1938 Rosengoltz, Rykov, Bukharin and other fiends were sentenced to be shot. After that, the elections to the Supreme Soviets of the Union Republics were held. In these elections 99.4 per cent of the total vote was cast for the Soviet power. Where are the symptoms of "demoralization," we would like to know, and why was this "demoralization" not reflected in the results of the elections?

To listen to these foreign drivellers one would think that if the spies, assassins and wreckers had been left at liberty to wreck, murder and spy without let or hindrance, the Soviet organizations would have been far sounder and stronger. (*Laughter.*) Are not these gentlemen giving themselves away too soon by so insolently defending the cause of spies, assassins and wreckers?

Would it not be truer to say that the weeding out of spies, assassins and wreckers from our Soviet organizations was bound to lead, and did lead, to the further strengthening of these organizations?

What, for instance, do the events at Lake Hassan show, if not that the weeding out of spies and wreckers is the surest means of strengthening our Soviet organizations?

* * *

The tasks of the Party in the sphere of internal policy are:

1. To promote the further progress of our industry, rise of productivity of labour, and perfection of the technique of production, in order, having already outstripped the principal capitalist countries in technique of production and rate of industrial development, to outstrip them economically as well in the next ten or fifteen years.

2. To promote the further progress of our agriculture and stock breeding so as to achieve in the next three or four years an annual grain harvest of 8,000,000,000 poods, with an average yield of 12–13 centners per hectare; an average increase in the harvest of industrial crops of 30–35 per cent; and an

increase in the number of sheep and hogs by 100 per cent, of cattle by about 40 per cent, and of horses by about 35 per cent.

3. To continue to improve the material and cultural standards of the workers, peasants and intellectuals.

4. Steadfastly to carry into effect our socialist Constitution; to complete the democratization of the political life of the country; to strengthen the moral and political unity of Soviet society and fraternal collaboration among our workers, peasants and intellectuals; to promote the friendship of the peoples of the U.S.S.R. to the utmost, and to develop and cultivate Soviet patriotism.

5. Never to forget that we are surrounded by a capitalist world; to remember that the foreign espionage services will smuggle spies, assassins and wreckers into our country; and, remembering this, to strengthen our socialist intelligence service and systematically help it to defeat and eradicate the enemies of the people.

III. FURTHER STRENGTHENING OF THE C.P.S.U.(B.)

From the standpoint of the political line and day-to-day practical work, the period under review was one of complete victory for the general line of our Party. (*Loud and prolonged applause.*)

The principal achievements demonstrating the correctness of the policy of our Party and the correctness of its leadership are the firm establishment of the socialist system in the entire national economy, the completion of the reconstruction of industry and agriculture on the basis of a new technique, the fulfilment of the Second Five-Year Plan in industry ahead of time, the increase of the annual grain harvest to a level of 7,000,000,000 poods, the abolition of poverty and unemployment, and the raising of the material and cultural standard of the people.

In the face of these imposing achievements, the opponents of the general line of our Party, all the various "Left" and "Right" trends, all the Trotsky-Pyatakov and Bukharin-Rykov renegades were forced to creep into their shells, tuck away their hackneyed "platforms," and go into hiding. Lacking the manhood to submit to the will of the people, they preferred to merge with the Mensheviks, Socialist-Revolutionaries and fascists, to become the tools of foreign espionage services, to hire themselves out as spies, and to obligate themselves to help the enemies of the Soviet Union to dismember our country and to restore capitalist slavery in it.

Such was the inglorious end of the opponents of the line of our Party, who finished up as enemies of the people.

When it had smashed the enemies of the people and purged the Party and Soviet organizations of renegades, the Party became still more united in its political and organizational work and rallied even more solidly around its Central Committee. (*Stormy applause. All the delegates rise and cheer the speaker. Shouts of "Hurrah for Comrade Stalin!" "Long live Comrade Stalin!" "Hurrah for the Central Committee of our Party!"*)

Let us examine the concrete facts illustrating the development of the internal life of the Party and its organizational and propaganda work during the period under review.

1. MEASURES TO IMPROVE THE COMPOSITION OF THE PARTY. DIVISION OF ORGANIZATIONS CLOSER CONTACT BETWEEN THE LEADING PARTY BODIES AND THE WORK OF THE LOWER BODIES

The strengthening of the Party and of its leading bodies during the period under review proceeded chiefly along two lines: along the line of regulating the composition of the Party, ejecting unreliable elements and selecting the best elements, and along the line of dividing up the organizations, reducing their size, and bringing the leading bodies closer to the concrete, day-to-day work of the lower bodies.

There were 1,874,488 Party members represented at the Seventeenth Party Congress. Comparing this figure with the number of Party members represented at the preceding congress, the Sixteenth Party Congress, we find that in the interval between these two congresses 600,000 new members joined the Party. The Party could not but feel that such a mass influx into its ranks in the conditions prevailing in 1930–33 meant an unhealthy and undesirable expansion of its membership. The Party knew that not only honest and loyal people were joining its ranks, but also chance elements and careerists, who were seeking to utilize the badge of the Party for their own personal ends. The Party could not but know that its strength lay not only in the size of its membership, but, and above all, in the quality of its members. The question accordingly rose of regulating the composition of the Party. It was decided to continue the purge of Party members and candidate members begun in 1933; and the purge actually was continued until May 1935. It was further decided to suspend the admission of new members into the Party; and it actually was suspended until September 1936, the admission of new members being resumed only on November 1, 1936. Further, in connection with the dastardly murder of Comrade Kirov, which showed that there were quite a number of suspicious elements in the Party, it was decided to undertake a verification of the records of Party members and an exchange of old Party cards for new ones, both these measures being completed only in September 1936. Only after this was the admission of new members and candidate members into the Party resumed. As a result of all these measures, the Party succeeded in weeding out chance, passive, careerist and directly hostile elements, and in culling the staunchest and most loyal. It cannot be said that the purge was not accompanied by grave mistakes. There were unfortunately more mistakes than might have been expected. Undoubtedly, we shall have no need to resort to the method of mass purges any more. Nevertheless, the purge of 1933–36 was unavoidable and its results, on the whole, were beneficial. The number of Party members represented at this, the Eighteenth Congress, is about 1,600,000, which is 270,000 less than were represented at the Seventeenth Congress. But there is nothing bad in that. On the contrary, it is all to the good, for the Party strengthens itself by clearing its ranks of dross. Our Party is now somewhat smaller in membership, but on the other hand it is better in quality.

That is a big achievement.

As regards improvement of the day-to-day leadership of the Party by bringing it closer to the work of the lower bodies and by making it more concrete, the Party came to the conclusion that the best way to make it easier for the Party bodies to guide the organizations and to make the leadership itself concrete, alive and practical was to divide up the organizations, to reduce their size. People's Commissariats as well as the administrative organizations of the various territorial divisions, that is, the Union Republics, territories, regions, districts, etc., were divided up. The result of the measures adopted is that instead of 7 Union Republics, we now have 11; instead of 14 People's Commissariats of the U.S.S.R. we have 34; instead of 70 territories and regions we have 110; instead of 2,559 urban and rural districts we have 3,815. Correspondingly, within the system of leading Party bodies, we now have 11 central committees, headed by the Central Committee of the C.P.S.U.(B.), 6 territorial committees, 104 regional committees, 30 area committees, 212 city committees, 336 city district committees, 3,479 rural district committees, and 113,060 primary Party organizations.

It cannot be said that the division of organizations is already over. Most likely it will be carried further. But, however that may be, it is already yielding good results both in the improvement of the day-to-day leadership of the work and in bringing the leadership itself closer to the concrete work of the lower bodies. I need not mention that the division of organizations has made it possible to promote hundreds and thousands of new people to leading posts.

That, too, is a big achievement.

2. SELECTION, PROMOTION AND ALLOCATION OF CADRES

Regulating the composition of the Party and bringing the leading bodies closer to the concrete work of the lower bodies was not, and could not be, the only means of further strengthening the Party and its leadership. Another means adopted in the period under review was a radical improvement in the training of cadres, in the work of selecting, promoting and allocating cadres and of testing them in the process of work.

The Party cadres constitute the commanding staff of the Party; and since our Party is in power, they also constitute the commanding staff of the leading organs of state. After a correct political line has been worked out and tested in practice, the Party cadres become the decisive force in the leadership exercised by the Party and the state. A correct political line is, of course, the primary and most important thing. But that in itself is not enough. A correct political line is not needed as a declaration, but as something to be carried into effect. But in order to carry a correct political line into effect, we must have cadres, people who understand the political line of the Party, who accept it as their own line, who are prepared to carry it into effect, who are able to put it into practice and are capable of answering for it, defending it and fighting for it. Failing this, a correct political line runs the risk of being purely nominal.

And here arises the problem of properly selecting cadres and fostering them, of promoting new people, of correctly allocating cadres, and testing them by work accomplished.

What is meant by properly selecting cadres?

Properly selecting cadres does not mean just gathering around one a lot of assistants and subs, setting up an office and issuing order after order. (*Laughter.*) Nor does it mean abusing one's powers, switching scores and hundreds of people back and forth from one job to another without rhyme or reason and conducting endless "reorganizations." (*Laughter.*)

Proper selection of cadres means:

Firstly, valuing cadres as the gold reserve of the Party and the state, treasuring them, respecting them.

Secondly, knowing cadres, carefully studying their individual merits and shortcomings, knowing in what post the capacities of a given worker are most likely to develop.

Thirdly, carefully fostering cadres, helping every promising worker to advance, not grudging time on patiently "bothering" with such workers and accelerating their development.

Fourthly, boldly promoting new and young cadres in time, so as not to allow them to stagnate in their old posts and grow stale.

Fifthly, allocating workers to posts in such a way that each feels he is in the right place, that each may contribute to our common cause the maximum his personal capacities enable him to contribute, and that the general trend of the work of allocating cadres may fully answer to the demands of the political line for the carrying out of which this allocation of cadres is designed.

Particularly important in this respect is the bold and timely promotion of new and young cadres. It seems to me that our people are not quite clear on this point yet. Some think that in selecting people we must chiefly rely on the old cadres. Others, on the contrary, think that we must chiefly rely on young cadres. It seems to me that both are mistaken. The old cadres, of course, represent a valuable asset to the Party and the state. They possess what the young cadres lack, namely, tremendous experience in leadership, a schooling in Marxist-Leninist principles, knowledge of affairs, and a capacity for orientation. But, firstly, there are never enough old cadres, there are far less than required, and they are already partly going out of commission owing to the operation of the laws of nature. Secondly, part of the old cadres are sometimes inclined to keep a too persistent eye on the past, to cling to the past, to stay in the old rut and fail to observe the new in life. This is called losing the sense of the new. It is a very serious and dangerous shortcoming. As to the young cadres, they, of course, have not the experience, the schooling, the knowledge of affairs and the capacity of orientation of the old cadres. But, firstly, the young cadres constitute the vast majority; secondly, they are young, and as yet are not subject to the danger of going out of commission; thirdly, they possess in abundance the sense of the new, which is a valuable quality in every Bolshevik worker; and, fourthly, they develop and acquire knowledge so rapidly, they press upward so eagerly, that the time is not far off when they will overtake the old fellows, take their stand side by side with them, and become worthy of replacing them. Consequently, the thing is not whether to rely on the old cadres or on the new cadres, but to steer for a combination, a union of the old and the young cadres in one common symphony of leadership of the Party and the state. (*Prolonged applause.*)

That is why we must boldly and in good time promote young cadres to leading posts.

One of the important achievements of the Party during the period under review in the matter of strengthening the Party leadership is that, when selecting cadres, it has successfully pursued, from top to bottom, just this course of combining old and young workers.

Data in the possession of the Central Committee of the Party show that during the period under review the Party succeeded in promoting to leading state and Party posts over five hundred thousand young Bolsheviks, members of the Party and people standing close to the Party, over twenty per cent of whom were women.

What is our task now?

Our task now is to concentrate the work of selecting cadres, from top to bottom, in the hands of one body and to raise it to a proper, scientific, Bolshevik level.

This entails putting an end to the division of the work of studying, promoting and selecting cadres among various departments and sectors and concentrating it in one body.

This body should be the Cadres Administration of the Central Committee of the C.P.S.U.(B.) and a corresponding cadres department in each of the republican, territorial and regional Party organizations.

3. PARTY PROPAGANDA. MARXIST-LENINIST TRAINING OF PARTY MEMBERS AND PARTY CADRES

There is still another sphere of Party work, a very important and very responsible one, in which the work of strengthening the Party and its leading bodies has been carried on during the period under review. I am referring to Party propaganda and agitation, oral and printed, the work of training the Party members and Party cadres in the spirit of Marxism-Leninism, the work of raising the political and theoretical level of the Party and its workers.

There is hardly need to dwell on the cardinal importance of Party propaganda, of the Marxist-Leninist training of our people. I am referring not only to Party functionaries. I am also referring to the workers in the Young Communist League, trade union, trade, cooperative, economic, state, educational, military and other organizations. The work of regulating the composition of the Party and of bringing the leading bodies closer to the activities of the lower bodies may be organized satisfactorily; the work of promoting, selecting and allocating cadres may also be organized satisfactorily; but, with all this, if our Party propaganda for some reason or other goes lame, if the Marxist-Leninist training of our cadres begins to languish, if our work of raising the political and theoretical level of these cadres flags, and the cadres themselves cease on account of this to show interest in the prospect of our further progress, cease to understand the truth of our cause and are transformed into narrow plodders with no outlook, blindly and mechanically carrying out instructions from above—then our entire state and Party work must inevitably languish. It must be accepted as an axiom that the higher the political level and the Marxist-Leninist knowledge of the workers in any branch of state or Party work, the better and more fruitful will be the work itself, and the more effective the results of the work; and, vice versa, the lower the political level of the workers, and the less they are imbued with the knowledge of Marxism-Leninism, the greater will be the likelihood of disruption and failure in the work, of the workers themselves becoming shallow and deteriorating into paltry plodders, of their degenerating altogether. It may be confidently stated that if we succeeded in training the cadres in all branches of our work ideologically and in schooling them politically to such an extent as to enable them easily to orientate themselves in the internal and international situation; if we succeeded in making them quite mature Marxists-Leninists capable of solving the problems involved in the guidance of the country without serious error, we would have every reason to consider nine-tenths of our problems already settled. And we certainly can accomplish this, for we have all the means and opportunities for doing so.

The training and moulding of our young cadres usually proceeds in each particular branch of science or technology along the line of specialization. This is necessary and desirable. There is no reason why a man who specializes in medicine should at the same time specialize in physics or botany, or vice versa. But there is one branch of science which Bolsheviks in all branches of science are in duty bound to know, and that is the Marxist-Leninist science of society, of the laws of social development, of the laws of development of the proletarian revolution, of the laws of development of socialist construction, and of the victory of Communism. For a man who calls himself a Leninist cannot be considered a real Leninist if he shuts himself up in his speciality, in mathematics, botany or chemistry, let us say, and sees nothing beyond that speciality. A Leninist cannot be just a specialist in his favourite science; he must also be a political and social worker, keenly interested in the destinies of his country, acquainted with the laws of social development, capable of applying these laws, and striving to be an active participant in the political guidance of the country. This, of course, will be an additional burden on specialists who are Bolsheviks. But it will be a burden more than compensated for by its results.

The task of Party propaganda, the task of the Marxist-Leninist training of cadres, is to help our cadres in all branches of work to become versed in the Marxist-Leninist science of the laws of social development.

Measures for improving the work of propaganda and of the Marxist-Leninist training of cadres have been discussed many times by the Central Committee of the C.P.S.U.(B.) jointly with propagandists from various regional Party organizations. The publication, in September 1938, of the *History of the C.P.S.U.(B.)—Short Course* was taken into account in this connection. It was ascertained that the publication of the *History of the C.P.S.U.(B.)* had given a new impetus to Marxist-Leninist propaganda in our country. The results of the work of the Central Committee of the C.P.S.U.(B.) have been published in its decision, "On the Organization of Party Propaganda in Connection with the Publication of the *History of the C.P.S.U.(B.)—Short Course.*"

On the basis of this decision and with due reference to the decisions of the Plenum of the Central Committee of the C.P.S.U.(B.) of March 1937, "On Defects in Party Work," the Central Committee of the C.P.S.U.(B.) has outlined the following major measures for eliminating the defects in Party propaganda and improving the work of the Marxist-Leninist training of Party members and Party cadres:

1. To concentrate the work of Party propaganda and agitation in one body and to merge the propaganda and agitation departments and the press departments into a single Propaganda and Agitation Administration of the Central Commit-

tee of the C.P.S.U.(B.), and to organize corresponding propaganda and agitation departments in each republican, territorial and regional Party organization;

2. Recognizing as incorrect the infatuation for the system of propaganda through study circles, and considering the method of individual study of the principles of Marxism-Leninism by Party members to be more expedient, to centre the attention of the Party on propaganda through the press and on the organization of a system of propaganda by lectures;

3. To organize one-year Courses of Instruction for our lower cadres in each regional centre;

4. To organize two-year Lenin Schools for our middle cadres in various centres of the country;

5. To organize a Higher School of Marxism-Leninism under the auspices of the Central Committee of the C.P.S.U.(B.) with a three-year course for the training of highly-qualified Party theoreticians;

6. To set up one-year Courses of Instruction for propagandists and journalists in various centres of the country;

7. To set up in connection with the Higher School of Marxism-Leninism six-month Courses of Instruction for teachers of Marxism-Leninism in the higher educational establishments.

There can be no doubt that the realization of these measures, which are already being carried out, although not yet sufficiently, will soon yield beneficial results.

4. SOME QUESTIONS OF THEORY

Another of the defects of our propagandist and ideological work is the absence of full clarity among our comrades on certain theoretical questions of vital practical importance, the existence of a certain amount of confusion on these questions. I refer to the question of the state in general, and of our socialist state in particular, and to the question of our Soviet intelligentsia.

It is sometimes asked: "We have abolished the exploiting classes; there are no longer any hostile classes in the country; there is nobody to suppress; hence there is no more need for the state; it must die away.—Why then do we not help our socialist state to die away? Why do we not strive to put an end to it? Is it not time to throw out all this rubbish of a state?"

Or again: "The exploiting classes have already been abolished in our country; Socialism has in the main been built; we are advancing towards Communism. Now, the Marxist doctrine of the state says that there is to be no state under Communism.—Why then do we not help our socialist state to die away? Is it not time we relegated the state to the museum of antiquities?"

These questions show that those who ask them have conscientiously memorized certain tenets of the doctrine of Marx and Engels about the state. But they also show that these comrades have not grasped the essential meaning of this doctrine; that they do not realize in what historical conditions the various tenets of this doctrine were elaborated; and, what is more, that they do not understand present-day international conditions, have overlooked the capitalist encirclement and the dangers it entails for the socialist country. These questions not only betray an underestimation of the capitalist encirclement, but also an underestimation of the role and significance of the bourgeois states and their organs, which send spies, assassins and wreckers into our country and are waiting for a favourable opportunity to attack it by armed force. They likewise betray an underestimation of the role and significance of our socialist state and of its military, punitive and intelligence organs, which are essential for the defence of the Land of Socialism from foreign attack. It must be confessed that the comrades mentioned are not the only ones guilty of this underestimation. All the Bolsheviks, all of us without exception, to a certain extent sin in this respect. Is it not surprising that we learned about the espionage and conspiratorial activities of the Trotskyite and Bukharinite ringleaders only quite recently, in 1937 and 1938, although, as the evidence shows, these gentry were in the service of foreign espionage organizations and carried on conspiratorial activities from the very first days of the October Revolution? How could we have failed to notice so grave a matter? How are we to explain this blunder? The usual answer to this question is that we could not possibly have assumed that these people could have fallen so low. But that is no explanation, still less is it a justification: for the blunder was a blunder. How is this blunder to be explained? It is to be explained by an underestimation of the strength and significance of the mechanism of the bourgeois states surrounding us and of their espionage organs, which endeavour to take advantage of people's weaknesses, their vanity, their slackness of will, to enmesh them in their espionage nets and use them to surround the organs of the Soviet state. It is to be explained by an underestimation of the role and significance of the mechanism of our socialist state and of its intelligence service, by an underestimation of the importance of this intelligence service, by the twaddle that an intelligence service in a Soviet state is an unimportant trifle, and that the Soviet intelligence service and the Soviet state itself will soon have to be relegated to the museum of antiquities.

What could have given rise to this underestimation?

It arose owing to the fact that certain of the general tenets of the Marxist doctrine of the state were incompletely elaborated and were inadequate. It received currency owing to our unpardonably heedless attitude to matters pertaining to the theory of the state, in spite of the fact that we have had twenty years of practical experience in state affairs which provides rich material for theoretical generalizations, and in spite of the fact that, given the desire, we have every opportunity of successfully filling this gap in theory. We have forgotten Lenin's highly important injunction about the theoretical duties of Russian Marxists, that it is their mission to further develop the Marxist theory. Here is what Lenin said in this connection:

> "We do not regard Marxist theory as something completed and inviolable; on the contrary, we are convinced that it has only laid the cornerstone of the science which Socialists *must* further advance in all directions if they wish to keep pace with life. We think that an *independent* elaboration of the Marxist theory is especially essential for Russian Socialists, for this theory provides only general *guiding* principles, which, *in particular*, are applied in Eng-

land differently from France, in France differently from Germany, and in Germany differently from Russia."

Consider, for example, the classical formulation of the theory of the development of the socialist state given by Engels:

"As soon as there is no longer any class of society to be held in subjection; as soon as, along with class domination and the struggle for individual existence based on the former anarchy of production, the collisions and excesses arising from these have also been abolished, there is nothing more to be repressed which would make a special repressive force, a state, necessary. The first act in which the state really comes forward as the representative of society as a whole—the taking possession of the means of production in the name of society—is at the same time its last independent act as a state. The interference of the state power in social relations becomes superfluous in one sphere after another, and then ceases of itself. The government of persons is replaced by the administration of things and the direction of the process of production. The state is not 'abolished,' *it withers away.*" (F. Engels, *Anti-Dühring.*)

Is this proposition of Engels' correct?

Yes, it is correct, but only on one of two conditions: (1) *if* we study the socialist state only from the angle of the internal development of a country, abstracting ourselves in advance from the international factor, isolating, for the convenience of investigation, the country and the state from the international situation; or (2) *if* we assume that Socialism is already victorious in all countries, or in the majority of countries, that a socialist encirclement exists instead of a capitalist encirclement, that there is no more danger of foreign attack, and that there is no more need to strengthen the army and the state.

Well, but what if Socialism has been victorious only in one, separate country, and if, in view of this, it is quite impossible to abstract oneself from international conditions—

what then? Engels' formula does not furnish an answer to this question. As a matter of fact, Engels did not set himself this question, and therefore could not have given an answer to it. Engels proceeds from the assumption that Socialism has already been victorious more or less simultaneously in all countries, or in a majority of countries. Consequently, Engels is not here investigating any specific socialist state of any particular country, but the development of the socialist state in general, on the assumption that Socialism has been victorious in a majority of countries—according to the formula: "Assuming that Socialism is victorious in a majority of countries, what changes must the proletarian, socialist state undergo?" Only this general and abstract character of the problem can explain why in his investigation of the question of the socialist state Engels completely abstracted himself from such a factor as international conditions, the international situation.

But it follows from this that Engels' general formula about the destiny of the socialist state in general cannot be extended to the partial and specific case of the victory of Socialism in one country only, a country which is surrounded by a capitalist world, is subject to the menace of foreign military attack, cannot therefore abstract itself from the international situation, and must have at its disposal a well-trained army, well-organized punitive organs, and a strong intelligence service, consequently, must have its own state, strong enough to defend the conquests of Socialism from foreign attack.

We cannot expect the Marxian classics, separated as they were from our day by a period of forty-five or fifty-five years, to have foreseen each and every zigzag of history in the distant future in every separate country. It would be ridiculous to expect that the Marxian classics should have elaborated for our benefit ready-made solutions for each and every theoretical problem that might arise in any particular country fifty or one hundred years afterwards, so that we, the descendants of the Marxian classics, might calmly doze at the fireside and munch ready-made solutions. (*General laughter.*) But we can and should expect of the Marxists-Leninists of our day that they do not confine themselves to learning by rote a few general tenets of Marxism; that they delve deeply into the essence of Marxism; that they learn to take account of the experience gained in the twenty years of existence of the socialist state in our country; that, lastly, they learn, with the use of this experience and with knowledge of the essence of Marxism, to apply the various general tenets of Marxism concretely, to lend them greater precision and improve them. Lenin wrote his famous book, *The State and Revolution,* in August 1917, that is, a few months before the October Revolution and the establishment of the Soviet state. Lenin considered it the main task of this book to defend Marx's and Engels' doctrine of the state from distortion and vulgarization by the opportunists. Lenin was preparing to write a second volume of *The State and Revolution,* in which he intended to sum up the principal lessons of the experience of the Russian revolutions of 1905 and 1917. There can be no doubt that Lenin intended in the second volume of his book to elaborate and to further develop the theory of the state on the basis of the experience gained during the existence of Soviet power in our country. Death, however, prevented him from carrying this task into execution. But what Lenin did not manage to do should be done by his disciples. (*Loud applause.*)

The state arose because society split up into antagonistic classes; it arose in order to keep in restraint the exploited majority in the interests of the exploiting minority. The instruments of state authority became concentrated mainly in the army, the punitive organs, the espionage service, the prisons. Two basic functions characterize the activity of the state: at home (the main function), to keep in restraint the exploited majority; abroad (not the main function), to extend the territory of its class, the ruling class, at the expense of the territory of other states, or to defend the territory of its own state from attack by other states. Such was the case in slave society and under feudalism. Such is the case under capitalism.

In order to overthrow capitalism it was not only necessary to remove the bourgeoisie from power, not only to expropriate the capitalists, but also to smash entirely the bourgeois state machine, its old army, its bureaucratic officialdom and its police force, and to substitute for it a new, proletarian form of state, a new, socialist state. And that, as we know, is exactly what the Bolsheviks did. But it does not follow that the new, proletarian state may not retain certain functions of the old state, modified to suit the requirements of the proletarian state. Still less does it follow that the forms of our socialist state must remain unchanged, that all the original functions of our state must be fully retained in future. As a matter of fact, the forms of our state are changing and will continue to change in line with the development of our country and with the changes in the international situation.

Lenin was absolutely right when he said:

> "The forms of bourgeois states are extremely varied, but their essence is the same: whatever their form, all these states, in the final analysis, are inevitably the *dictatorship of the bourgeoisie.* The transition from capitalism to Communism certainly cannot but yield a great abundance and variety of political forms, but the essence will inevitably be the same: *the dictatorship of the proletariat.*"

Since the October Revolution, our socialist state has passed through two main phases in its development.

The first phase was the period from the October Revolution to the elimination of the exploiting classes. The principal task in that period was to suppress the resistance of the overthrown classes, to organize the defence of the country against the attack of the interventionists, to restore industry and agriculture, and to prepare the conditions for the elimination of the capitalist elements. Accordingly, in this period our state performed two main functions. The first function was to suppress the overthrown classes within the country. In this respect our state bore a superficial resemblance to previous states whose functions had also been to suppress recalcitrants, with the fundamental difference, however, that our state suppressed the exploiting minority in the interests of the labouring majority, while previous states had suppressed the exploited majority in the interests of the exploiting minority. The second function was to defend the country from foreign attack. In this respect it likewise bore a superficial resemblance to previous states, which also undertook the armed defence of their countries, with the fundamental difference, however, that our state defended from foreign attack the gains of the labouring majority, while previous states in such cases defended the wealth and privileges of the exploiting minority. Our state had yet a third function: this was the work of economic organization and cultural education performed by our state bodies with the purpose of developing the infant shoots of the new, socialist economic system and re-educating the people in the spirit of Socialism. But this new function did not attain to any considerable development in that period.

The second phase was the period from the elimination of the capitalist elements in town and country to the complete victory of the socialist economic system and the adoption of the new Constitution. The principal task in this period was to establish the socialist economic system all over the country and to eliminate the last remnants of the capitalist elements, to bring about a cultural revolution, and to form a thoroughly modern army for the defence of the country. And the functions of our socialist state changed accordingly. The function of military suppression within the country ceased, died away; for exploitation had been abolished, there were no more exploiters left, and so there was no one to suppress. In place of this function of suppression the state acquired the function of protecting socialist property from thieves and pilferers of the property of the people. The function of armed defence of the country from foreign attack fully remained; consequently, the Red Army and the Navy also fully remained, as did the punitive organs and the intelligence service, which are indispensable for the detection and punishment of the spies, assassins and wreckers sent into our country by foreign espionage services. The function of economic organization and cultural education by the state organs also remained, and was developed to the full. Now the main task of our state within the country is peaceful economic organization and cultural education. As for our army, punitive organs, and intelligence service, their edge is no longer turned to within the country but to without, against external enemies.

As you see, we now have an entirely new, socialist state, one without precedent in history and differing considerably in form and functions from the socialist state of the first phase.

But development cannot stop there. We are moving ahead, towards Communism. Will our state remain in the period of Communism also?

Yes, it will, unless the capitalist encirclement is liquidated, and unless the danger of foreign military attack has been eliminated, although naturally, the forms of our state will again change in conformity with the change in the situation at home and abroad.

No, it will not remain and will wither away if the capitalist encirclement is liquidated and is replaced by a socialist encirclement.

That is how the question stands with regard to the socialist state.

The second question is that of the Soviet intelligentsia.

On this question, too, as on the question of the state, there is a certain unclearness and confusion among Party members.

In spite of the fact that the position of the Party on the question of the Soviet intelligentsia is perfectly clear, there are still current in our Party views hostile to the Soviet intelligentsia and incompatible with the Party position. As you know, those who hold these false views practise a disdainful and contemptuous attitude to the Soviet intelligentsia and regard it as a force alien and even hostile to the working class and the peasantry. True, during the period of Soviet development the intelligentsia has undergone a radical change both in composition and status. It has become closer to the people and is honestly collaborating with it, in which respect it differs fundamentally from the old, bourgeois intelligentsia. But this apparently means nothing to these comrades. They go on harping on the old tune and wrongly apply to the Soviet intelligentsia views and attitudes which were justified in the old days when the intelligentsia was in the service of the landlords and capitalists.

In the old prerevolutionary days, under capitalism, the intelligentsia consisted primarily of members of the propertied classes—noblemen, manufacturers, merchants, kulaks and so on. Some members of the intelligentsia were sons of small tradesmen, petty officials, and even of peasants and workingmen, but they did not and could not play a decisive part. The intelligentsia as a whole depended for their livelihood on the propertied classes and ministered to them. Hence it is easy to understand the mistrust, often bordering on hatred, with which the revolutionary elements of our country and above all the workers regarded the intellectuals. True, the old intelligentsia produced some courageous and revolutionary individuals or handfuls of individuals who adopted the standpoint of the working class and completely threw in their lot with the working class. But such people were all too few among the intelligentsia, and they could not change the complexion of the intelligentsia as a whole.

But the position with regard to the intelligentsia has radically changed since the October Revolution, since the defeat of the foreign armed intervention, and especially since the victory of industrialization and collectivization, when the abolition of exploitation and the firm establishment of the socialist economic system made it effectively possible to give the country a new Constitution and to put it into effect. The most influential and highly-qualified section of the old intelligentsia broke away from the main body in the very first days of the October Revolution, proclaimed war on the Soviet government, and joined the ranks of the saboteurs. They met with well-deserved punishment for this; they were smashed and dispersed by the organs of Soviet power. Subsequently the majority of those that survived were recruited by the enemies of our country as wreckers and spies, and thus expunged themselves by their own deeds from the ranks of the intellectuals. Another section of the old intelligentsia, less qualified but more numerous, continued for a long time to temporize, waiting for "better days"; but then, apparently giving up hope, decided to go and serve and live in harmony with the Soviet government. The greater part of this group of the old intelligentsia are getting well on in years and are beginning to go out of commission. A third section of the old intelligentsia, mainly comprising its rank and file, and still less qualified than the section just mentioned, joined forces with the people and supported the Soviet government.

They needed to perfect their education, and they set about doing so in our universities. But parallel with this painful process of differentiation and break-up of the old intelligentsia there was going on a rapid process of formation, mobilization and mustering of forces of a new intelligentsia. Hundreds of thousands of young people from the ranks of the working class, the peasantry and the working intelligentsia entered the universities and technical colleges, from which they emerged to reinforce the attenuated ranks of the intelligentsia. They infused fresh blood into it and animated it with a new, Soviet spirit. They radically changed the whole aspect of the intelligentsia, moulding it in their own form and image. The remnants of the old intelligentsia were dissolved in the new, Soviet intelligentsia, the intelligentsia of the people. There thus arose a new, Soviet intelligentsia, intimately bound up with the people and, for the most part, ready to serve them faithfully and loyally.

As a result, we now have a numerous, new, popular, socialist intelligentsia, fundamentally different from the old, bourgeois intelligentsia both in composition and in social and political character.

The old theory about the intelligentsia, which taught that it should be distrusted and combated, fully applied to the old, prerevolutionary intelligentsia, which served the landlords and capitalists. This theory is now out-of-date and does not fit our new, Soviet intelligentsia. A new theory is needed for our new intelligentsia, one teaching the necessity for a cordial attitude towards it, solicitude and respect for it, and cooperation with it in the interests of the working class and the peasantry.

That is clear, I should think.

It is therefore all the more astonishing and strange that after all these fundamental changes in the status of the intelligentsia, there should be people in our Party who attempt to apply the old theory, which was directed against the bourgeois intelligentsia, to our new, Soviet intelligentsia, which is basically a socialist intelligentsia. These people, it appears, assert that workers and peasants who until recently were working in Stakhanov fashion in the factories and collective farms and who were then sent to universities to be educated, thereby ceased to be real people and became second-rate people. So we are to conclude that education is a pernicious and dangerous thing. (*Laughter.*) We want all our workers and peasants to be cultured and educated, and we shall achieve this in time. But in the opinion of these queer comrades, this purpose harbours a grave danger; for after the workers and peasants become cultured and educated they may face the danger of being classified as second-rate people. (*Loud laughter.*) The possibility is not precluded that these queer comrades may in time sink to the level of extolling backwardness, ignorance, benightedness and obscurantism. It would be quite in the nature of things. Theoretical vagaries have never led, and never can lead, to any good.

Such is the position with regard to our new, socialist intelligentsia.

* * *

Our tasks in respect to the further strengthening of the Party are:

1. To systematically improve the composition of the Party, raising the ideological level of its membership, and admitting into its ranks, by a process of individual selection, only tried and tested comrades who are loyal to the cause of Communism.

2. To establish closer contact between the leading bodies and the work of the lower bodies, so as to make their work of leadership more practical and specific and less confined to meetings and offices.

3. To centralize the work of selecting cadres, to train them carefully and foster them, to study the merits and demerits of workers thoroughly, to promote young workers boldly and adapt the selection and allocation of cadres to the requirements of the political line of the Party.

4. To centralize Party propaganda and agitation, to extend the propaganda of the ideas of Marxism-Leninism, and to raise the theoretical level and improve the political schooling of our cadres.

* * *

Comrades, I am now about to conclude my report.

I have sketched in broad outline the path traversed by our Party during the period under review. The results of the work of the Party and of its Central Committee during this period are well known. There have been mistakes and shortcomings in our work. The Party and the Central Committee did not conceal them and strove to correct them. There have also been important successes and big achievements, which must not however be allowed to turn our heads.

The chief conclusion to be drawn is that the working class of our country, having abolished the exploitation of man by man and firmly established the socialist system, has proved to the world the truth of its cause. That is the chief conclusion, for it strengthens our faith in the power of the working class and in the inevitability of its ultimate victory.

The bourgeoisie of all countries asserts that the people cannot get along without capitalists and landlords, without merchants and kulaks. The working class of our country has proved in practice that the people can get along perfectly well without exploiters.

The bourgeosie of all countries asserts that the working class, having destroyed the old bourgeois system, will be incapable of building anything new to replace the old. The working class of our country has proved in practice that it is quite capable not only of destroying the old system but of building a new and better system, a socialist system, a system, moreover, to which crises and unemployment are unknown.

The bourgeoisie of all countries asserts that the peasantry is incapable of taking the path of Socialism. The collective-farm peasants of our country have proved in practice that they can do so quite successfully.

The chief endeavour of the bourgeoisie of all countries and of its reformist hangers-on is to kill in the working class faith in its own strength, faith in the possibility and inevitability of its victory, and thus to perpetuate capitalist slavery. For the bourgeoisie knows that if capitalism has not yet been overthrown and still continues to exist, it owes this not to its own merits, but to the fact that the proletariat still has not enough faith in the possibility of its victory. It cannot be said that the efforts of the bourgeoisie in this respect have been altogether unsuccessful. It must be confessed that the bourgeoisie and its agents among the working class have to some extent succeeded in poisoning the minds of the working class with the virus of doubt and disbelief. If the successes of the working class of our country, if its fight and victory serve to rouse the spirit of the working class in the capitalist countries and to strengthen its faith in its own power and in its victory, then our Party may say that its work has not been in vain. And there need be no doubt that this will be the case. (*Loud and prolonged applause.*)

Long live our victorious working class! (*Applause.*)

Long live our victorious collective-farm peasantry! (*Applause.*)

Long live our socialist intelligentsia! (*Applause.*)

Long live the great friendship of the nations of our country! (*Applause.*)

Long live the Communist Party of the Soviet Union! (*Applause.*)

(*The delegates rise and hail Comrade Stalin with loud and stormy cheers. Cries of: "Long live Comrade Stalin!" "Hurrah for our great Stalin!" "Hurrah for our beloved Stalin!"*)

THE TWENTY-SIXTH ANNIVERSARY OF THE OCTOBER REVOLUTION[1]

Comrades! Today the peoples of the Soviet Union celebrate the twenty-sixth anniversary of the great October Socialist Revolution. For the third time our country marks the anniversary of her people's revolution in the conditions of the Patriotic War.

In October, 1941, our motherland lived through hard days. The enemy approached the capital. He surrounded Leningrad from the land. Our troops were compelled to retreat. Enormous efforts of the army and the exertion of all the forces of the people were necessary to check the enemy and to strike a serious blow at him at Moscow.

By October, 1942, the danger to our motherland had become even greater. The enemy stood then barely one hundred and twenty kilometers from Moscow, had broken into Stalingrad, and entered the foothills of the Caucasus.

But even in those grave days the army and the people did not lose heart, but stanchly bore all trials. They found strength to check the enemy and to deal him a retaliating blow. True to the behests of our great Lenin, they defended the achievements of the October Revolution without sparing their strength and their lives.

As is well known, those efforts of the army and the people were not in vain. Shortly after the October days of last year our troops passed over to the offensive and struck a fresh powerful blow at the Germans, first at Stalingrad, in the Caucasus, in the area of the middle reaches of the Don, and then, at the beginning of 1943, at Velikie Luki, at Leningrad, and in the area of Rhzev and Vyazma. Since then the Red Army has never let the initiative out of its hands. Its blows through-

[1] Speech delivered at Moscow, November 6, 1943.

out the summer of this year became increasingly strong, its military mastery grew with every month. Since then our troops have won big victories and the Germans have suffered one defeat after another.

No matter how hard the enemy tried he still failed to score any success on the Soviet-German front that was of the least importance.

I. A YEAR OF RADICAL TURN IN THE COURSE OF THE WAR

The past year, between the twenty-fifth and twenty-sixth anniversaries of the October Revolution, marked a turn in the Patriotic War. This year marked a turn, in the first place, because in this year the Red Army, for the first time during the course of the war, succeeded in carrying through a big summer offensive against the German troops, and under the blows of our forces the German fascist troops were compelled to abandon hurriedly the territory they had seized, not infrequently saving themselves from encirclement by flight and abandoning on the battlefield huge quantities of equipment, stores of armaments and ammunition, and large numbers of wounded officers and men.

Thus the successes of our summer campaign in the second half of this year followed up and completed the successes of our winter campaign at the beginning of this year.

Now, when the Red Army is developing the successes of the winter campaign and has dealt a powerful blow at German troops in summer, it is possible to consider as finally dead and buried the fairy tale that the Red Army is allegedly incapable of conducting a successful offensive in the summertime. The past year has shown that the Red Army can advance in summer just as well as in winter.

As a result of these offensive operations in the course of the past year our troops were able to fight their way forward from 500 kilometers in the central part of the front up to 1,300 kilometers in the south and to liberate nearly 1,000,000 square kilometers of territory—that is, almost two-thirds of the Soviet land temporarily seized by the enemy.

Along with this the enemy troops have been hurled back

from Vladikavkaz to Kherson, from Elista to Krivoi Rog, from Stalingrad to Kiev, from Voronezh to Gomel, from Vyazma and Rzhev to the approaches of Orsha and Vitebsk.

Having no faith in the stability of their earlier successes on the Soviet-German front, the Germans had been building powerful defense lines for a long time beforehand, especially along the big rivers. But in this year's battles neither rivers nor powerful fortifications saved the Germans. Our troops shattered the Germans' defense and within only three months of the summer of 1943 skillfully forced four very serious water barriers—the Northern Donets, the Desna, the Sozh, and the Dnieper. I do not speak even about such barriers as the Germans' defense in the area of the Mius River—west of Rostov—and the defense in the area of the Molochnaya River —near Melitopol. At present the Red Army is battering the enemy successfully on the other side of the Dnieper.

This year also marked a turn, because the Red Army within a comparatively short time was able to annihilate and grind down the most experienced old cadres of German fascist troops, and at the same time to steel and multiply its own cadres in successful offensive battles in the course of the year.

In the battles on the Soviet-German front during the past year the German-fascist army lost more than 4,000,000 officers and men, including not less than 1,800,000 killed. During this year the Germans also lost more than 14,000 aircraft, over 25,000 tanks, and not less than 40,000 guns.

The German fascist army now is not what it was at the outbreak of war. While at the outbreak of war it had sufficient numbers of experienced cadres, now it has been diluted with newly baked, young, inexperienced officers whom the Germans are hurriedly throwing onto the front, as they have neither the necessary reserves of officers nor the time to train them.

The picture presented today by the Red Army is quite different. Its cadres have grown and been tempered in successful offensive battles in the course of the past year. The numbers of its fighting cadres are growing and will grow further as the existence of the necessary officer reserve gives it time and opportunity to train young officer cadets and promote them to responsible posts.

It is characteristic that instead of the 240 divisions which faced our front last year, 179 of which were German divisions, this year the Red Army at the front is faced with 257 divisions, of which 207 are German. The Germans evidently count upon compensating for the lower quality of their divisions by increasing their numbers. However, the defeat of the Germans in the past year shows that it is impossible to compensate for deterioration in the quality of divisions by increasing their numbers.

From a purely military point of view the defeat of the German troops on our front at the close of this year was predetermined by two major events: the battle of Stalingrad and the battle of Kursk.

The battle of Stalingrad ended in the encirclement of a German army 300,000 strong, its rout and the capture of about one-third of the surrounded troops. To form an idea of the scale of that slaughter unparalleled in history which took place on the fields of Stalingrad, one should know that after the battle of Stalingrad was over, there were found and buried 147,200 dead German officers and men and 46,700 dead Soviet officers and men.

Stalingrad signified the decline of the German fascist army. As is well known, the Germans were unable to recover after the Stalingrad slaughter.

As to the battle of Kursk, it ended in the rout of the two main advancing groups of German fascist troops, and in our troops launching a counter-offensive which turned subsequently into the powerful summer offensive of the Red Army.

The battle of Kursk began with the offensive of the Germans on Kursk from the north and south. That was the last attempt of the Germans to carry out a big summer offensive and in the event of its success to redeem their losses. As is well known, the offensive ended in failure. The Red Army not only repulsed the German offensive, but passed over to the offensive itself and by a series of consecutive blows in the course of the summer period hurled back the German fascist troops beyond the Dnieper. If the battle of Stalingrad foreshadowed the decline of the German fascist army, the battle of Kursk confronted it with disaster.

Finally, this year marked a turn, because the successful offensive of the Red Army radically aggravated the economic and military-political situation of fascist Germany and confronted her with a profound crisis. The Germans counted on carrying out in the summer of this year a successful offensive on the Soviet-German front to redeem their losses and to bolster their shaken prestige in Europe. But the Red Army upset the Germans' calculations, repulsed their offensive, launched an offensive itself, and proceeded to drive the Germans westward and thereby crushed the prestige of German arms.

The Germans counted on taking the line of prolonging the war, started building defense lines and "walls," and proclaimed for all to hear that their new positions were impregnable. But the Red Army again upset the Germans' calculations, broke through their defense lines and "walls," and continues to advance successfully, giving them no time to drag out the war.

The Germans counted on rectifying the situation at the front by "total" mobilization. But here, too, events upset the Germans' calculations. The summer campaign has already consumed two-thirds of the "totally" mobilized men; however, it does not look as if this circumstance has brought about any improvement in the position of the German fascist army.

It may prove necessary to proclaim another "total" mobilization, and there is no reason why a repetition of such a measure should not result in the "total" collapse of a certain state.

The Germans counted on retaining a firm hold on the Ukraine in order to avail themselves of the Ukrainian agricultural produce for their army and population, and of the Donbas coal for the factories and railways serving the German army. But here, too, they miscalculated. As a result of the successful offensive of the Red Army the Germans have lost not only the Donbas coal but also the richest grain-growing regions of the Ukraine, and there is no reason to think that they will not lose the rest of the Ukraine, too, in the nearest future.

Naturally all these miscalculations could not but impair and in fact did impair radically the economic and military-political situation of fascist Germany. Fascist Germany experiences a profound crisis. She faces disaster.

II. NATIONWIDE ASSISTANCE TO THE FRONT

The successes of the Red Army would have been impossible without the support of the people, without the selfless work of the Soviet people in the factories and plants, collieries and mines, in transport and agriculture.

In hard wartime conditions the Soviet people proved able to insure its army everything most necessary and constantly perfected its fighting equipment. Never during the whole course of the war has the enemy been able to surpass our army as regards quality of armaments. At the same time, our industry has supplied the front with ever greater quantities of fighting equipment.

The past year marked a turn not only in the progress of hostilities, but also in the work of our rear. We were no longer confronted with such tasks as evacuating enterprises to the east and of switching industry to the production of armaments. The Soviet state now has an efficient and rapidly expanding war economy.

Thus all the efforts of the people could be concentrated on the increase of production and on the further improvement of armaments, especially of tanks, aircraft, guns, and self-propelling artillery. In this we have gained big successes. Supported by the entire people, the Red Army received uninterrupted supplies of fighting equipment, rained millions of bombs, mines, and shells upon the enemy, brought thousands of tanks and aircraft into battle.

There is every ground to say that the selfless labor of Soviet people in the rear will go down in history along with the heroic struggle of the Red Army as an unexampled feat of people in defense of their motherland. The workers of the Soviet Union who in the years of peaceful construction built up a highly developed, powerful socialist industry, have during this Patriotic War been working with a real fury of energy to help the front, displaying true labor heroism.

Everyone knows that in the war against the U.S.S.R. the Hitlerites had at their disposal not only the highly developed industry of Germany, but also the rather powerful industries of the vassal and occupied countries. Nevertheless the Hitlerites failed to maintain the quantitative superiority in military equipment which they had at the outbreak of the war against the Soviet Union. Now the former superiority of the enemy as regards the number of tanks, aircraft, mortars, and automatic rifles has been eliminated. If our army now experiences no serious shortage of arms, ammunition, and equipment, credit for this goes in the first place to our working class.

The peasants of the Soviet Union who during the year of peaceful construction, on the basis of the collective farming system, transformed backward farming into up-to-date agriculture, have displayed during the Patriotic War a high degree of understanding of the common national interest which has no parallel in the history of the countryside. By selfless labor to help the front they have shown that the Soviet peasantry considers this war against the Germans its own cause, a war for its own life and liberty.

It is well known that as a result of its invasion by the fascist hordes our country was deprived temporarily of the important agricultural districts of the Ukraine, of the Don and the Kuban valleys. Nevertheless, our collective and state farms supplied the army and the country with food without any serious interruptions.

Naturally, without the collective farming system, without the selfless labor of the men and women collective farmers, we could not have coped with this most difficult task. If in the third year of the war our army experiences no shortage of food, if the population is supplied with food, and industry with raw materials, this is evidence of the strength and vitality of our collective farming system and of the patriotism of our collective farm peasantry.

A great part in helping the front has been played by our transport, by railway transport in the first place, and also by river, sea, and motor transport. As is known, transport is a vital means of communication between the rear and the front. One may manufacture great quantities of arms and ammunition, but if transport does not deliver them to the front in time they may remain a dead weight as far as the front is concerned. It must be said that transport plays a decisive part in the timely delivery to the front of arms, ammunition, food, clothing, etc.

And if in spite of wartime difficulties and shortages of fuel, we have been able to supply the front with everything necessary, this should be credited in the first place to our transport workers and employees.

Nor does our intelligentsia lag behind the working class and peasantry in helping the front. The Soviet intelligentsia is working with devotion for the defense of our country, constantly improving the armaments of the Red Army, and the technology and organization of production. It helps the workers and collective farmers to expand industry and agriculture, and promotes Soviet science and culture in the conditions of war. This does credit to our intelligentsia.

All the peoples of the Soviet Union have risen as one to defend their motherland, rightly considering the present Patriotic War the common cause of all working people, irrespective of nationality or religion.

By now the Hitlerite politicians have themselves seen how hopelessly stupid were their hopes of discord and strife among the peoples of the Soviet Union. The friendship of the peoples of our country has withstood all hardships and trials of war and has become tempered still further in the common struggle of all Soviet people against the fascist invaders.

This is a source of the strength of the Soviet Union.

As in the years of peaceful construction, so in the days of war, the leading and guiding force of the Soviet people has been the party of Lenin, the party of the Bolsheviks. No other party has ever enjoyed or enjoys such prestige among the masses of the people as our Bolshevik Party.

And this is natural. Under the leadership of the party of the Bolsheviks the workers, peasants, and intelligentsia of our country have won their freedom and built a socialist society. In this Patriotic War the party stood before us as the inspirer and organizer of the nationwide struggle against the fascist invaders.

The organizational work of the party has united and directed toward a common goal all the efforts of the Soviet people, subordinating all our forces and means to the cause of the enemy's defeat. During the war the party has cemented still further its kinship with the people, has established still closer connections with the broad masses of the working people. This is a source of strength for our state.

The present war has forcefully confirmed Lenin's well-known statement that war is an all-around test of a nation's material and spiritual forces. The history of wars teaches that only those states stood this test which proved stronger than their adversaries as regards the development and organization of their economy, as regards the experience, skill, and fighting spirit of their troops, and as regards the fortitude and unity of their people throughout the war.

Ours is just such a state. The Soviet state was never so stable and solid as now in the third year of the Patriotic War. The lessons of the war show that the Soviet system proved not only the best form of organizing the economic and cultural development of the country in the years of peaceful construction, but also the best form of mobilizing all the forces of the people for resistance to the enemy in time of war.

The Soviet power set up twenty-six years ago has transformed our country within a short historical period into an impregnable fortress. The Red Army has the most stable and reliable rear of all the armies in the world. This is a source of the strength of the Soviet Union.

There is no doubt that the Soviet state will emerge from the war even stronger and even more consolidated. The German invaders are desolating and devastating our lands in an endeavor to undermine the power of our state. To an even greater extent than before, the offensive of the Red Army has exposed the barbarous bandit nature of the Hitlerite army. In the districts they seized the Germans have exterminated hundreds of thousands of our civilians. Like the medieval barbarians of Attila's hordes, the German fiends trample the fields, burn down villages and towns, and demolish industrial enterprises and cultural institutions.

The German crimes are evidence of the weakness of the fascist invaders, for only usurpers who themselves do not believe in their victory act in this way. And the more hopeless the position of the Hitlerites becomes, the more viciously they rage in their atrocities and plunder.

Our people will not forgive the German fiends for these crimes. We shall make the German criminals answer for all their misdeeds.

In areas where the fascist cutthroats have for a time been masters we shall have to restore the demolished towns and villages, industry, transport, agriculture, and cultural institutions; we shall have to create normal living conditions for the Soviet people delivered from fascist slavery. The work of the restoration of the economy and culture is already going full blast in the districts liberated from the enemy. But this is only the beginning.

We must completely eliminate the consequences of the Germans' domination in the districts liberated from German occupation. This is the great national task. We can and must cope with this difficult task within a short time.

III. CONSOLIDATION OF THE ANTI-HITLER COALITION. DISINTEGRATION OF THE FASCIST BLOC

The past year has marked a turn not only in the Patriotic War of the Soviet Union but in the whole World War. The changes which have taken place during this year in the military and international situation have been favorable to the U.S.S.R. and the Allied countries friendly to it, and detrimental to Germany and her accomplices in brigandage in Europe.

The victories of the Red Army have had results and consequences far beyond the limits of the Soviet-German front; they have changed the whole further course of the World War and acquired great international significance. The victory of the Allied countries over the common enemy has come nearer, while the relations among the Allies, the fighting partnership of their armies, far from weakening have, contrary to the expectations of their enemies, grown stronger and more enduring.

Eloquent evidence of this also are the historic decisions of the Moscow conference of representatives of the Soviet Union, Great Britain and the United States of America recently published in the press. Now our united countries are filled with determination to deal the enemy common blows which will result in final victory over him.

This year the Red Army's blows at the German fascist troops were supported by the combat operations of our Allies in North Africa, in the Mediterranean Basin and in southern Italy. At the same time the Allies subjected and are still subjecting important industrial centers of Germany to substantial bombing and thus considerably weakening the enemy's military power. If to all this is added the fact that the Allies are regularly supplying us with various munitions and raw materials, it can be said without exaggeration that by all this they considerably facilitated the successes of our summer campaign.

Of course the present actions of the Allied armies in the south of Europe cannot as yet be regarded as a second front. But still this is something like a second front. Obviously the opening of a real second front in Europe, which is not so distant, will considerably hasten the victory over Hitlerite Germany and will consolidate even more the fighting partnership of the Allied countries.

Thus the events of the past year show that the anti-Hitler coalition is a firm association of peoples, and rests on a solid foundation.

By now it is obvious to everyone that by unleashing this war the Hitlerite clique has led Germany and her flunkeys into a hopeless impasse. The defeats of the fascist troops on the Soviet-German front and the blows of our Allies at the Italo-German troops have shaken the whole edifice of the fascist bloc, and it is crumbling now before our very eyes. Italy has dropped out of the Hitlerite coalition never to return. Mussolini can change nothing because he is in fact a prisoner of the Germans.

Next in line are the other partners in the coalition. Finland, Hungary, Rumania, and other vassals of Hitler, discouraged by Germany's military defeats, have now finally lost faith in an outcome of the war favorable for them, and are anxious to find a way out of the bog into which Hitler has dragged them. Now, when the time has come to answer for their brigandage, Hitlerite Germany's accomplices in plunder but recently so obedient to their master are in search of a vent, looking for an opportune moment to slip out of the bandit gang unnoticed.

In entering the war the partners in the Hitlerite bloc counted on a quick victory. They had already allotted beforehand who would get what: who would get buns and pies and who bumps and black eyes. They naturally meant the bumps and black eyes for their adversaries, and the buns and pies for themselves. But now it is obvious that Germany and her flunkeys will get no buns and pies, but will have to share the bumps and black eyes.

Anticipating this unattractive prospect, Hitler's accomplices are now racking their brains for a way to get out of the war with as few bumps and black eyes as possible. Italy's example shows Hitler's vassals that the longer they postpone their inevitable break with the Germans and permit them to lord it in their states, the greater the devastation in store for their countries, the more suffering their peoples will have to bear. Italy's example also shows that Hitlerite Germany has no intention of defending her vassal countries, but means to convert them into a scene of devastating war if only she can stave off the hour of her own defeat.

The cause of German fascism is lost, and the sanguinary "new order" it has set up is on the way to collapse. An outburst of the people's wrath against the fascist enslavers is brewing in the occupied countries of Europe. Germany's former prestige in the countries of her Allies and in the neutral countries is lost beyond recovery, and her economic and political ties with neutral states have been undermined. The time is long past when the Hitlerite clique clamored boisterously about the Germans winning world domination. Now, as is well known, the Germans have other matters than world domination to worry about, they have to think about keeping body and soul together.

Thus the course of the war has shown that the alliance of fascist states did not and does not rest on a reliable foundation. The Hitlerite coalition was formed on the basis of the predatory, rapacious ambitions of its members. As long as the Hitlerites were scoring military successes, the fascist coalition seemed to be a stable association. But the very first defeats of the fascist troops resulted in the actual disintegration of the bandit bloc.

Hitlerite Germany and her vassals stand on the verge of disaster.

The victory of the Allied countries over Hitlerite Germany will put on the agenda the important questions of the organizing and rebuilding of the state, economic and cultural life of the European peoples. The policy of our government in these questions remains unchanging. Together with our Allies we shall have to:

1. Liberate the peoples of Europe from the fascist invaders and help them rebuild their national states dismembered by the fascist enslavers; the peoples of France, Belgium, Yugoslavia, Czechoslovakia, Poland, Greece, and other states now under the German yoke must again become free and independent;

2. Grant the liberated peoples of Europe the full right and freedom to decide for themselves the question of their form of government;

3. Take measures that all fascist criminals responsible for this war and the sufferings of the peoples bear stern punishment and retribution for all the crimes they committed, no matter in what country they may hide;

4. Establish such an order in Europe as will completely preclude the possibility of new aggression on the part of Germany;

5. Establish lasting economic, political, and cultural collaboration among the peoples of Europe based on mutual confidence and mutual assistance for the purpose of rehabilitating the economic and cultural life destroyed by the Germans.

During the past year the Red Army and the Soviet people have achieved great successes in the struggle against the German invaders. We achieved a radical turning point in the war in favor of our country, and now the war is heading for its final outcome.

But it is not like the Soviet people to rest on their achievements, to exult in their successes. Victory may elude us if complacency appears in our ranks. Victory cannot be won without struggle and strain. It is won in battle. Victory is near now, but to win it a fresh exertion of strength is needed, selfless work throughout the rear, skillful and resolute actions of the Red Army at the front.

It would be a crime against the motherland, against the Soviet people who have fallen temporarily under the fascist yoke, against the peoples of Europe languishing under German oppression, if we failed to use all opportunities to hasten the enemy's defeat. The enemy must not be given any respite. That is why we must exert all our strength to finish off the enemy.

The Soviet people and the Red Army clearly see the difficulties of the coming struggle. But now it is already clear that the day of our victory is approaching. The war has entered that stage when it is a question of driving the invaders completely from Soviet soil and liquidating the fascist "new order in Europe." The time is not far distant when we shall completely clear the enemy from the Ukraine and Byelorussia and the Leningrad and Kalinin Regions, liberate from the German invaders the peoples of the Crimea, Lithuania, Latvia, Estonia, Moldavia, and the Karelo-Finnish Republic.

Comrades! For the victory of the Anglo-Soviet-American fighting alliance! For the liberation of the peoples of Europe from the fascist yoke! For the complete expulsion of the German fiends from our land!

Long live our Red Army!
Long live our Navy!
Long live our gallant men and women guerrillas!
Long live our great motherland!
Death to the German invaders!

(1943)

MARXISM AND LINGUISTICS[1]

I. CONCERNING MARXISM IN LINGUISTICS

A group of comrades of the younger generation have asked me to give my opinion in the press on questions relating to the science of language, particularly in reference to Marxism in linguistics. I am not a linguist and cannot of course satisfy these comrades fully. But as to Marxism in linguistics, as well as in other social sciences, this is a subject with which I have a direct connection. I have therefore consented to answer a number of questions put by these comrades.

QUESTION: *Is it true that language is a superstructure on the base?*

ANSWER: No, it is not true.

The base is the economic structure of society at a given stage of its development. The superstructure consists of the political, legal, religious, artistic, and philosophical views of society and the political, legal, and other institutions corresponding to them.

Every base has its own superstructure corresponding to it. The base of the feudal system has its superstructure—its political, legal, and other views and the corresponding institutions; the capitalist base has its own superstructure, and so has the socialist base. If the base changes or is eliminated, then following this its superstructure changes or is eliminated; if a

[1] These five letters, all published in the summer of 1950, represent part of Stalin's offensive against some of the "authorities" dominating Soviet thought. The first letter is a polemic against the disciples of N. Y. Marr, a Soviet scholar whose ideas had long ruled the field of linguistics in the U.S.S.R.

new base arises, then following this a superstructure arises corresponding to it.

In this respect language radically differs from superstructure. Take, for example, Russian society and the Russian language. During the past thirty years the old, capitalist base was eliminated in Russia and a new, socialist base was built. Correspondingly, the superstructure on the capitalist base was eliminated and a new superstructure created corresponding to the socialist base. The old political, legal, and other institutions were consequently supplanted by new, socialist institutions. But in spite of this the Russian language has remained essentially what it was before the October Revolution.

What has changed in the Russian language in this period? To a certain extent the vocabulary of the Russian language has changed, in the sense that it has been supplemented by a large number of new words and expressions, which have arisen in connection with the rise of a new socialist production, of a new state, a new socialist culture, a new public spirit and ethics, and lastly, in connection with the development of technology and science; a number of words and expressions have changed their meaning; a number of obsolete words have fallen out of the vocabulary. As to the basic vocabulary and grammatical structure of the Russian language, which constitute the foundation of the language, they, after the elimination of the capitalist base, far from having been eliminated and supplanted by a new basic vocabulary and a new grammatical system of the language, have been preserved in their entirety and have not undergone any serious changes—have been preserved precisely as the foundation of modern Russian.

Further, the superstructure is a product of the base; but this does not mean that it merely reflects the base, that it is passive, neutral, indifferent to the fate of its base, to the fate of the classes, to the character of the system. On the contrary, no sooner does it arise than it becomes an exceedingly active force, actively assisting its base to take shape and consolidate itself, and doing everything it can to help the new system finish off and eliminate the old base and the old classes.

It cannot be otherwise. The base creates the superstructure precisely in order that it may serve it, that it may actively help it to take shape and consolidate itself, that it may actively strive for the elimination of the old, moribund base and its old superstructure. The superstructure has only to renounce its role of auxiliary, it has only to pass from a position of active defense of its base to one of indifference toward it, to adopt the same attitude to all classes, and it loses its virtue and ceases to be a superstructure.

In this respect language radically differs from superstructure. Language is not a product of one or another base, old or new, within the given society, but of the whole course of the history of society and the history of bases throughout centuries. It was created not by any class, but by all society, by all the classes of society, by the efforts of hundreds of generations. It was created for the satisfaction of the needs not of only one class, but of all society, of all the classes of society. Precisely for this reason it was created as a single language for society, common to all members of that society, as the common language of its people. Hence the role of language as an auxiliary, as a means of intercourse between people, consists not in serving one class to the detriment of other classes, but in equally serving all society, all classes of society. This, in fact, explains why a language may equally serve both the old, moribund system and the new, nascent system; both the old base and the new base, both the exploiters and the exploited.

It is no secret to anyone that the Russian language served Russian capitalism and Russian bourgeois culture before the October Revolution just as well as it now serves the socialist system and the socialist culture of Russian society.

The same must be said of the Ukrainian, Byelorussian, Uzbek, Kazakh, Georgian, Armenian, Estonian, Latvian, Lithuanian, Moldavian, Tatar, Azerbaijan, Bashkir, Turkmen, and other languages of the Soviet nations; they served the old, bourgeois systems of these nations just as well as they serve the new, socialist system.

It could not be otherwise. Language exists, and it has been created precisely in order to serve society as a whole, as a means of intercourse between people, in order to be common to the members of society and the single language of society, serving members of society equally, irrespective of their class status. A language has only to depart from this position of being the common language of the people and to give preference and support to any one social group to the detriment of other social groups of that society, and it loses its virtue, ceases to be a means of intercourse between the people of that society, and becomes the jargon of some social group, degenerates, and is doomed to disappear.

In this respect, while it differs in principle from the superstructure, language does not differ from the implements of production, from machines, let us say, which may equally serve a capitalist system and a socialist system.

Further, the superstructure is the product of one epoch, an epoch in which the given economic base exists and operates. The superstructure is therefore short-lived; it is eliminated and disappears with the elimination and disappearance of the given base.

Language, on the contrary, is the product of a whole number of epochs, in the course of which it takes shape, is enriched, develops, and is polished. A language therefore exists immeasurably longer than any base or any superstructure. This in fact explains why the rise and disappearance not only of one base and its superstructure, but of several bases and their corresponding superstructures have not led in history to the elimination of a given language, to the elimination of its structure, and to the rise of a new language with a new vocabulary and a new grammatical system.

It is more than one hundred years since Pushkin died. In this period the feudal system and the capitalist system were eliminated in Russia, and the third, a socialist, system has arisen. Hence two bases, with their superstructures, have been eliminated, and a new, socialist base has arisen, with its new superstructure. Yet if we take the Russian language, for example, it has not in this great length of time undergone any fundamental change, and the modern Russian language differs very little in structure from the language of Pushkin.

What has changed in the Russian language in this period? In this period the Russian vocabulary has been much enlarged; a great number of obsolete words have dropped out of the vocabulary; the meaning of a large number of words has changed; the grammatical system of the language has improved. As to the general structure of Pushkin's language, with its grammatical system and its basic vocabulary, it has been preserved in all essentials as the basis of modern Russian.

And this is quite understandable. Indeed, what necessity is there, after every revolution, for the existing structure of the language, its grammatical construction and basic vocabulary to be destroyed and supplanted by new ones, as is usually the case with the superstructure? Who would benefit if "water," "earth," "mountain," "forest," "fish," "man," "to walk," "to do," "to produce," "to trade," etc., were called not water, earth, mountain, etc., but something else? Who would benefit from the change of words in a language and the combination of words in sentences following not the existing, but some entirely different grammar? What would be the use to the revolution of such an upheaval in language? History, generally, never does anything of moment without some particular necessity. What, one asks, can be the necessity for such a language upheaval, when it is demonstrated that the existing language and its structure are fundamentally quite suitable for the needs of the new system? The old superstructure can and should be destroyed and replaced by a new one in the course of a few years, in order to give free scope for the development of the productive forces of society; but how can an existing language be destroyed and a new one built in its place in the course of a few years without causing anarchy in social life and without creating the threat of the collapse of society? Who but Don Quixotes could set themselves such a task?

Lastly, there is one other radical distinction between superstructure and language. The superstructure is not directly connected with production, with man's productive activity. It is connected with production only indirectly through the economy, through the base. The superstructure therefore does not reflect changes of development of the productive forces immediately and directly, but only after changes in the base, through the prism of changes wrought in the base by the changes in production. This means that the sphere of action of the superstructure is narrow and restricted.

Language, on the contrary, is connected with man's productive activity directly, and not only with man's productive activity, but with all his other activities in all spheres of work, from production to the base and from the base to the superstructure. That is why language reflects changes in production immediately and directly, without waiting for changes in the base. That is why the sphere of action of language, which embraces all spheres of man's activity, is far broader and more varied than the sphere of action of the superstructure. More, it is practically unlimited.

It is this which primarily explains why language, or rather its vocabulary, is in an almost constant state of change. The continuous development of industry and agriculture, of trade and transport, of technology and science, demands that language should supplement its vocabulary with new words and expressions, needed for their operation. And language, directly reflecting these needs, does replenish its vocabulary with new words, and perfects its grammatical system.

Hence:

a) A Marxist cannot regard language as a superstructure on the base;

b) To confuse language and superstructure is a serious error.

QUESTION: *Is it true that language always was and is of a class character, that there is no such thing as a non-class language common and uniform to all the people of a society?*

ANSWER: No, it is not true.

It is not difficult to understand that in a society which has no classes there can be no such thing as a class language. There were no classes in the primitive communal clan system, and consequently there could be no class language—the language was then the common and single language of the whole collective body. The objection that the word class should be taken as covering every human collective, including the primitive communal collective, is not an objection but a play on words that is not worth refuting.

As to the subsequent development from clan languages to tribal languages, from tribal languages to the languages of nationalities, and from languages of nationalities to national languages—everywhere and at all stages of development, language, as a means of intercourse between the people of a society, was the common and single language of that society, serving its members equally, irrespective of their social standing.

I am not referring here to the empires of the slave and medieval periods, the empires of Cyrus or Alexander the Great, let us say, or of Caesar or of Charles the Great, which had no economic base of their own and were transitory and unstable military and administrative associations. These empires not only did not have, but they could not have a single language common to the whole empire and understood by all the members of the empire. They were conglomerations of tribes and nationalities, each of which lived its own life and had its own language. Consequently, it is not these or similar empires I have in mind, but the tribes and nationalities forming part of an empire which had their own economic base and their own languages, formed in the distant past. History tells us that the languages of these tribes and nationalities were not class languages, but general languages of the people, common languages for tribes and nationalities, used and understood by all people.

Side by side with this, of course, there were dialects, vernaculars, but they were dominated by, and subordinated to the single and common language of the tribe or nationality.

Later, with the appearance of capitalism, the elimination of feudal division, and the formation of national markets, nationalities developed into nations, and the languages of nationalities into national languages. History tells us that the national languages are not class, but common languages, common to the members of each nation and constituting the single language of the nation.

It was said above that, as a means of intercourse between the people of a society, language serves all classes of that society equally, and in this respect displays what may be called an indifference to classes. But people, the individual social groups, the classes, are far from indifferent to language. They strive to utilize the language in their own interests, to impose their own special vocabulary, special terms, and special expressions upon it. The upper strata of the propertied classes, who are divorced from and detest the people—the aristocratic nobility, the upper strata of the bourgeoisie—particularly distinguished themselves in this respect. "Class" dialects, jargons, drawing-room "languages" are created. These dialects and jargons are often incorrectly referred to in literature as the "aristocratic language" or "bourgeois language" in contradistinction to "proletarian language" or "peasant language." For this reason, strange as it may seem, some of our comrades have come to the conclusion that national language is a fiction, and that in reality, only class languages exist.

There is nothing, I think, more erroneous than this conclusion. Can these dialects and jargons be regarded as languages? Certainly not. They cannot, firstly, because these dialects and jargons have no grammatical system or basic vocabularies of their own—they borrow them from the national language. They cannot, secondly, because these dialects and jargons are confined to a narrow sphere of members of the upper strata of a given class and are entirely unsuitable as a means of intercourse for society as a whole. What, then, do they have? They have a collection of specific words reflecting the specific tastes of the aristocracy or the upper strata of the bourgeoisie; a certain number of expressions and turns of speech distinguished by refinement and gallantry, and free of the "coarse" expressions and turns of speech of the national language; lastly, a certain number of foreign words. However, the bulk, that is, the overwhelming majority, of the words and the grammatical system are borrowed from the common national language. Dialects and jargons are therefore offshoots of the common national language, possessing no linguistic independence of any kind and doomed to stagnation. Anyone who believes that dialects and jargons can develop into independent languages, that they are capable of ousting and supplanting the national language, has lost all sense of historical perspective and has abandoned the Marxist position.

References are made to Marx, and the passage from his article, *St. Max*,[2] is quoted where it is said that the bourgeois have "their own language," that this language "is a product of the bourgeoisie," that it is permeated with the spirit of mer-

[2] The second section of the joint philosophical work by Marx and Engels, *The German Ideology*, of which only the first and third sections have been published in English. St. Max is a satirical reference to Max Stirner (1806–56), philosophical anarchist and author of *The Ego and His Own*.

cantilism and sale and purchase. Certain comrades cite this passage with the idea of proving that Marx believes in the "class character" of language and denied the existence of a single national language. If these comrades were impartial, they should have cited another passage from this same article, *St. Max,* where Marx, touching on the way common national languages arose, speaks of "the concentration of dialects into a single national language as the result of economic and political concentration."

Marx, consequently, did recognize the necessity of a *single* national language, as the highest form, to which dialects, as lower forms, are subordinate.

What, then, can this bourgeois language be which, according to Marx, is "a product of the bourgeoisie"? Did Marx consider it as much a language as the national language, with its own specific linguistic structure? Could he have considered it such a language? Of course not. Marx merely wanted to say that the bourgeois had polluted the common national language with their huckster vocabulary, that the bourgeois, in other words, have their huckster jargon.

It thus appears that these comrades have misrepresented Marx. And they misrepresented him because they quoted Marx, not like Marxists, but like dogmatists, without delving into the essence of the matter.

References are made to Engels, and the words from his *Condition of the Working Class in England* are cited where he says that "the English working class has with the course of time become a different people from the English bourgeoisie," that "the working men speak a different dialect, have different ideas and concepts, different morals and moral principles, different religion and politics from the bourgeoisie." Certain comrades conclude from this passage that Engels denied the necessity for a common, national language, that he believed, consequently, in the "class character" of language. True, Engels speaks here of a dialect, not of a language, fully realizing that, being an offshoot of the national language, a dialect cannot supplant the national language. But these comrades, apparently, do not regard with sympathy the existence of a difference between language and dialect. . . .

It is obvious that the quotation is inappropriate, because

Engels here speaks, not of "class languages" but chiefly of class ideas, concepts, morals, moral principles, religion, and politics. It is perfectly true that the ideas, concepts, morals, moral principles, religion, and politics of the bourgeois and proletarian are directly antithetic. But where does national language or the "class character" of language come in here? Can the existence of class contradictions in society serve as an argument in favor of the "class character" of language, or against the necessity of a common national language? Marxism says that a common language is one of the most important earmarks of a nation, although knowing very well that there are class contradictions within the nation. Do the comrades referred to recognize this Marxist thesis?

References are made to Lafargue,[3] and it is said that in his pamphlet, *Language and Revolution*, he recognized the "class character" of language, and that he denied the necessity of a common, national language. This is not true. Lafargue does indeed speak of a "noble" or "aristocratic language" and of the "jargons" of various strata of society. But these comrades forget that Lafargue is not interested in the differences between languages and jargons and that, referring to dialects now as "artificial speech," now as "jargon," he definitely says in this pamphlet that "the artificial speech of the aristocracy . . . arose out of the common language of the people, which was spoken by bourgeois and artisan, town and country."

Consequently, Lafargue recognizes the existence and necessity of a common national language, and fully realizes that the "aristocratic language" and other dialects and jargons are subordinate to and dependent on a common national language.

It follows that the reference to Lafargue misses the mark.

References are made to the fact that at one time in England the feudal lords talked "for centuries" in French, while the English people spoke English, and this is alleged to be an argument in favor of the "class character" of language and against the necessity of a common national language. This is not an argument, it is more like a joke. Firstly, not all the feudal lords spoke French at that time, but only a small upper

[3] Paul Lafargue (1842–1911), a member of the Paris Commune, Marx's son-in-law, and one of the founders of French socialism.

stratum of English feudal lords attached to the court and in the counties. Secondly, it was not some "class language" they spoke, but the ordinary national language of the French. Thirdly, we know that in the course of time this French language had disappeared without trace, yielding to the common national language of the English. Do these comrades think that the English feudal lords "for centuries" held intercourse with the English people through interpreters, that they did not use the English language, that there was no common national language of the English at that time, and that the French language in England was then anything more serious than a drawing-room language current only within the narrow circle of the upper English aristocracy? How can one possibly deny the existence and the necessity of a common national language on the basis of laughable "arguments" like this?

There was a time when Russian aristocrats also toyed with the French language at the tsar's court and in the drawing rooms. They prided themselves on the fact that when they spoke Russian they stumbled into French, that they could only speak Russian with a French accent. Does this mean that there was no common national Russian language at that time in Russia, that the common national language was a fiction, and the "class language" a reality?

Our comrades are here making at least two mistakes.

The first mistake is that they confuse language with superstructure. They think that since superstructure has a class character, language must be a class, and not a common, national, language. But I have already said that language and superstructure are two different concepts, and that a Marxist must not confuse them.

The second mistake of these comrades is that they conceive the opposing interests of the bourgeoisie and the proletariat, the fierce class struggle between them, as meaning the disintegration of society, as a break of all ties between the hostile classes. They believe that, since society has split and there is no longer a single society but only classes, a common language of society, a national language, is unnecessary. If society is split and there is no longer a common national language, what remains? There remain classes and "class languages."

Naturally, every "class language" will have its "class" grammar —a "proletarian" grammar or a "bourgeois" grammar. True, such grammars do not exist in nature. But this does not worry these comrades; they believe that such grammars will appear in due course.

There used to be "Marxists" in our country who asserted that the railways left to us after the October Revolution were bourgeois railways, that it would be unseemly for us, Marxists, to utilize them, that they should be torn up and new, "proletarian" railways be built. For this they were nicknamed "troglodytes." . . .

It is obvious that such a primitive anarchist view of society, classes, and language has nothing in common with Marxism. But it undoubtedly exists and continues to prevail in the minds of certain of our muddled comrades.

It is of course wrong to say that because of the existence of a fierce class struggle society has split into classes which are no longer economically connected one with another in one society. On the contrary, as long as capitalism exists, the bourgeois and proletarians will be bound together by every economic thread as parts of one capitalist society. The bourgeois cannot live and grow rich unless they have hired laborers; the proletarians cannot exist unless they hire themselves to the capitalists. If the economic ties between them were to cease, it would mean the entire cessation of production, and the entire cessation of production would mean the doom of society, and the doom of the classes themselves. Naturally, no class wants to incur self-destruction. Consequently, however sharp the class struggle may be, it cannot lead to the disintegration of society. Only ignorance of Marxism and complete failure to understand the nature of language could have suggested to some of our comrades the fairy tale about the disintegration of society, "class" languages, and "class" grammars.

Reference is further made to Lenin, and it is said that Lenin recognized the existence of two cultures under capitalism, bourgeois and proletarian, and that the slogan of national culture under capitalism is a nationalist slogan. All this is true, and Lenin is absolutely right in this. But where does the "class character" of language come in? When these comrades refer to what Lenin said about two cultures under capitalism, it is evidently with the idea of suggesting to the reader that the existence of two cultures, bourgeois and proletarian, in society means that there must also be two languages, inasmuch as language is linked with culture and, consequently, that Lenin denies the necessity of a common national language, and consequently, that Lenin believes in "class" languages. The mistake of these comrades is that they identify and confuse language with culture. But culture and language are two different things. Culture may be either bourgeois or socialist, but language, as a means of intercourse, is always a common national language and can serve both bourgeois and socialist culture. Is it not a fact that the Russian, Ukrainian, and Uzbek languages are now serving the socialist culture of these nations just as well as they served their bourgeois cultures before the October Revolution? Consequently, these comrades are profoundly mistaken when they assert that the existence of two different cultures leads to the formation of two different languages and to the negation of the necessity of a common language.

When Lenin spoke of two cultures, he proceeded precisely from the precept that the existence of two cultures cannot lead to the negation of a common language and the formation of two languages, that the language must be a common one. When the Bundists accused Lenin of denying the necessity of a national language and regarding culture as "non-national," Lenin, as we know, vigorously protested and declared that he was fighting bourgeois culture and not a national language, the necessity for which he regarded as indisputable. It is strange that some of our comrades have followed in the footsteps of the Bundists.

As to a common language, the necessity of which Lenin allegedly denies, it would be well to pay attention to the following words of Lenin:

> "Language is a most important means of human intercourse; a common language and its unhampered development is one of the most important conditions of really free and broad trade, commensurate with modern capitalism, of the free and broad grouping of the population in all the separate classes."

It follows that our respected comrades misrepresented the views of Lenin.

Reference, lastly, is made to Stalin. The passage from Stalin is quoted where he says that "the bourgeoisie and its nationalist parties were and remain in this period the chief directing force of such nations." This is all true. The bourgeoisie and its nationalist party really do direct bourgeois culture, just as the proletariat and its internationalist party direct proletarian culture. But where does the "class character" of the language come in? Do not these comrades know that national language is a form of national culture, that national language may serve both bourgeois and socialist culture? Are not our comrades familiar with the well-known formula of the Marxists that the present Russian, Ukrainian, Byelorussian, and other cultures are socialist in content and national in form, *i.e.*, in language? Do they agree to this Marxist formula?

The mistake of our comrades is that they do not see the difference between culture and language, and do not understand that culture changes in content with every new period in the development of society, whereas language remains basically the same throughout a number of periods, equally serving both the new culture and the old.

Hence:

a) Language, as a means of intercourse, always was and remains the single language of a society, common to all its members;

b) The existence of dialects and jargons does not negate but confirms the existence of a common national language, of which they are offshoots and to which they are subordinate;

c) The formula about "the class character" of language is erroneous and non-Marxist.

QUESTION: *What are the characteristic features of language?*

ANSWER: Language is one of those social phenomena which operate throughout the existence of society. It arises and develops with the rise and development of a society. It dies when the society dies. Without society there is no language. Accordingly, language and its laws of development may be understood only if studied in inseparable connection with the history of society, with the history of the people to whom the language under study belongs, and who are its creators and repositories.

Language is a medium, an instrument with the help of which people communicate with one another, exchange thoughts, and seek mutual understanding. Being directly connected with thought, language registers and records in words and in words combined into sentences the results of thought and man's successes in his quest for knowledge, and thus makes possible the exchange of ideas in human society.

Exchange of ideas is a constant and vital necessity, for without it, it is impossible to co-ordinate the actions of people in the struggle against the forces of nature, in the effort to produce essential material values; without it, it is impossible to ensure the success of society's productive activity, and, hence, the very existence of social production becomes impossible. Consequently, without a language understood by a society and common to all its members, that society must cease to produce, must disintegrate and cease to exist as a society. In this sense, language, while it is a medium of communication, is at the same time an instrument of struggle and development of society.

As we know, all the words in a language together constitute its vocabulary. The chief thing in a language's vocabulary is its basic word stock which includes all the root words as its nucleus. It is less extensive than the language's vocabulary, but it persists for a very long time, for centuries, and provides the language with a basis for building new words. The vocabulary reflects the state of the language: the richer and more varied the vocabulary, the richer and more developed the language.

However, by itself the vocabulary does not constitute the language—it is rather the building material of the language. Just as in construction work the building materials do not constitute the building, although the latter cannot be constructed without them, so too a language's vocabulary does not constitute the language itself, although no language is conceivable without it. But the vocabulary of a language assumes a tremendous significance when it falls under the charge of its grammar, which determines the rules governing the modification of words and the grouping of words into sentences, and thus lends language a harmonious and intelligible character. Grammar (morphology and syntax) is the collection of rules governing the modification of words and their combination into sentences. It is, therefore, thanks to grammar that language acquires the ability to invest man's thoughts in a material linguistic integument.

The distinguishing feature of grammar is that it determines the rules of modification of words—not particular concrete words, but words in general, without any concreteness; it also determines the rules for the formation of sentences, not particular concrete sentences—with, let us say, a concrete subject, a concrete predicate, etc.—but all sentences in general, irrespective of the concrete form of any sentence in particular. Hence, abstracting itself, as regards both words and sentences, from the particular and concrete, grammar takes that which is general and basic in the modification of words and their combination into sentences, and builds it into grammatical rules, grammatical laws. Grammar is the outcome of a prolonged work of abstraction of human thought; it is a gauge of the tremendous achievement of thought.

In this respect grammar resembles geometry, which creates its laws by a process of abstraction from concrete objects, regarding objects as bodies without any concreteness, and defining the relations between them, not as the concrete relations of concrete objects, but as the relations of bodies in general, without any concreteness.

Unlike the superstructure, which is not connected with production directly but through the economy, language is directly connected with man's productive activity, as well as with all his other activity in all his spheres of work without exception. That is why a language's vocabulary, being the most sensitive to change, is in a state of almost constant change, and unlike the superstructure, language does not have to wait until the base is eliminated; it makes changes in its vocabulary before the base is eliminated and irrespective of the state of the base.

However, a language's vocabulary does not change in the way the superstructure does, that is, by abolishing the old and building something new, but by replenishing the existing vocabulary with new words which have arisen with changes in the social system, with the development of production, of culture, science, etc. At the same time, although a certain number of obsolescent words keep falling out of a language's vocabulary, a far larger number of new words are added. As to the basic stock of words, it continues to persist in all its fundamentals and is used as the basis for the language's vocabulary.

This is quite understandable. There is no necessity to destroy the basic word stock when it can be effectively used through the course of several historical periods; not to speak of the fact that, it being impossible to create a new basic word stock in a short period, the destruction of the basic word stock accumulated in the course of centuries would result in the paralysis of the language, the complete disruption of intercourse between people.

The grammatical structure of language changes even more slowly than its basic word stock. Elaborated in the course of epochs, and having become part of the flesh and blood of the language, the grammatical system changes still more slowly than the basic word stock. Of course, it undergoes change with the lapse of time, becomes more perfected, improves and gives greater definition to its rules, and acquires new rules; but the fundamentals of the grammatical system persist for a very long time, since, as history shows, they are able to render effective service to society throughout a succession of epochs.

Hence the grammatical system of a language and its basic word stock constitute its foundation, the specific nature of the language.

History shows that languages possess great stability and a tremendous power of resistance to forcible assimilation. Some historians, instead of explaining this phenomenon, confine themselves to expressing their surprise at it. But there is absolutely no reason for surprise. Languages owe their stability to their grammatical system and their basic word stock. The Turkish assimilators strove for hundreds of years to mutilate, shatter, and destroy the language of the Balkan peoples. During this period the vocabulary of the Balkan languages underwent considerable change; many Turkish words and expressions were absorbed; there were "convergencies" and "divergencies." Nevertheless, the Balkan languages stood firm and survived.

Why? Because their grammatical system and basic word stocks were preserved in the main.

It follows from this that a language, its structure, cannot be regarded as the product of only one epoch. The structure, grammatical system, and basic word stock of a language are the product of a number of epochs.

It is to be presumed that the rudiments of modern language arose in hoary antiquity, before the epoch of slavery. It was a rather simple language with a very meager stock of words but with a grammatical system, although, it is true, a primitive one, but a grammatical system nonetheless.

The subsequent development of production, the appearance of classes, the appearance of writing, the rise of states, which needed a more or less well-regulated correspondence for their administration, the development of trade, which needed a well-regulated correspondence even more, the invention of the printing press, the development of literature—all these were the causes of very great changes in the development of language. During this period tribes and nationalities broke up and scattered, intermingled and crossed; later there arose national languages and states, revolutions took place, and old social systems were replaced by new. All this caused even greater changes in language and its development.

However, it would be a profound mistake to think that language developed in the way superstructure developed—by destroying that which existed and building something new in its place. In actual fact, language did not develop by destroying existing languages and creating new ones, but by extending and perfecting the basic elements of the existing language. At the same time, the transition of language from one quality to another did not take the form of an explosion, of the destruction at one blow of the old and the creation of something new, but by the gradual and prolonged accumulation of the elements of the new quality, of the new language structure, and the gradual dying away of the elements of the old quality.

It is said that the theory that languages developed by stages is a Marxist theory, since it recognizes the necessity of sudden explosions as a condition for the transition of the languages from an old quality to a new one. This is, of course, untrue, for it is difficult to find anything Marxist in this theory. And if the theory of stages really does recognize sudden explosions in the history of the development of language, so much the worse for it. Marxism does not recognize sudden explosions in the development of languages, the sudden death of an existing language and the sudden creation of a new language. Lafargue was wrong when he spoke of a "sudden linguistic revolution between 1789 and 1794" in France (see Lafargue's pamphlet, *Language and Revolution*). There was no linguistic revolution, let alone a sudden one, in France at that time. True enough, the vocabulary of the French language was replenished during that period with new words and expressions, a certain number of obsolete words disappeared, and the meaning of certain words changed—but that was all. Changes of this nature, however, do not determine the destiny of a language. The chief thing in a language is its grammatical system and basic word stock. But far from disappearing in the period of the French bourgeois revolution, the grammatical system and basic word stock of the French language were preserved without substantial change, and not only were they preserved, but they continue to live to this day in the modern French language. I need hardly say that a period of five or six years is a ridiculously small period for the elimination of an existing language and the building of a new national language ("a sudden linguistic revolution!"). Centuries are needed for this.

Marxism holds that the transition of a language from an old quality to a new does not take place by way of an explosion, by the destruction of an existing language and the creation of a new one, but by the gradual accumulation of the elements of the new quality, and, hence, by the gradual dying away of the elements of the old quality.

It should be said in general for the benefit of comrades who have an infatuation for such explosions that the law of transition from an old quality to a new by means of an explosion is inapplicable not only to the history of the development of languages; it is not always applicable to some other social phenomena of a basal or superstructural character. It is compulsory for a society divided into hostile classes. But it is not at all compulsory for a society which has no hostile classes. In a period of eight to ten years we effected a transition in the agriculture of our country from the bourgeois individual-peasant system to the socialist, collective-farm system. This was a revolution which eliminated the old bourgeois economic system in the countryside and created a new, socialist system. But this revolution did not take place by means of an explosion, that is, by the overthrow of the existing power and the creation of a new power, but by a gradual transition from the old bourgeois system of the countryside to a new system. And we succeeded in doing this because it was a revolution from above, because the revolution was accomplished on the initiative of the existing power with the support of the overwhelming mass of the peasantry.

It is said that the numerous instances of mixture of languages in the past furnish reason to believe that when languages mix, a new language is formed by means of an explosion, by the sudden transition from an old quality to a new. This is absolutely untrue.

The mixing of languages cannot be regarded as an instantaneous and decisive blow the results of which became manifest within a few years. The mixing of languages is a prolonged process which continues for hundreds of years. Therefore, there can be no question of explosion in such cases.

Further, it would be absolutely wrong to think that the result of the mixture of, say, two languages is a new, third language, which does not resemble either of the mixed languages and differs qualitatively from both of them. As a matter of fact one of the languages usually emerges victorious from the mixture, retains its grammatical system, its basic word stock, and continues to advance in accordance with its inherent laws of development, while the other language loses its quality and gradually dies out.

Consequently, mixing does not result in a new, third language; rather, one of the languages persists, retains its grammatical system and basic word stock and is able to advance in accordance with the inherent laws of its development.

True, the vocabulary of the victorious language is somewhat enriched at the expense of the vanquished language, but this strengthens, rather than weakens, it.

Such was the case, for instance, with the Russian language,

with which the languages of a number of other peoples mixed in the course of historical development, and which always emerged the victor.

Of course, the vocabulary of the Russian language was enlarged in the process from the vocabularies of the other languages but this not only did not weaken, but on the contrary enriched and strengthened the Russian language.

And the national individuality of the Rusian language did not suffer in the slightest, because the Russian language preserved its grammatical system and basic word stock and continued to advance and perfect itself in accordance with the inherent laws of its development.

Undoubtedly, Soviet linguistics has nothing valuable to gain from the theory of mixture. If it is true that the chief task of linguistics is to study the inherent laws of language development, it has to be admitted that the theory of mixture does not even set itself this task, let alone accomplish it—it simply does not notice it or does not understand it.

QUESTION: *Did* Pravda *act correctly in inaugurating an open discussion on questions of linguistics?*

ANSWER: It did.

In what way these linguistic questions will be settled will become clear when the discussion ends. But it may already be said that the discussion has been very useful.

It has brought out, in the first place, that in linguistic bodies both in the capital and in the republics a regime has prevailed which is alien to science and men of science. The slightest criticism of the state of affairs in Soviet linguistics, even the most timid attempts to criticize the so-called "new doctrine" in linguistics, were persecuted and suppressed by the leading linguistic circles. Valuable workers and researchers in linguistics were dismissed from their posts or demoted for being critical of N. Y. Marr's legacy or expressing the slightest disapproval of his teachings. Linguists were appointed to responsible posts, not on their merits, but because of their unqualified acceptance of N. Y. Marr's theories.

It is generally recognized that no science can develop and flourish without a battle of opinions, without freedom of criticism. But this generally recognized rule was ignored and flouted in the most outrageous fashion. A tight group of infallible leaders, having insured themselves against all possible criticism, began to act arbitrarily and highhandedly.

To give one example: The so-called "Baku Course" (lectures delivered by N. Y. Marr in Baku) which the author himself had rejected and had forbidden to be republished, was republished nevertheless by order of this leading caste (Comrade Meshchaninov calls them "disciples" of N. Y. Marr) and unreservedly included in the list of manuals recommended to students. This means that the students were deceived by having a rejected "course" presented to them as a first-class textbook. If I were not convinced of the integrity of Comrade Meshchaninov and the other linguistic leaders, I would say that such conduct is tantamount to sabotage.

How could this have happened? It happened because the Arakcheyev[4] regime prevailing in linguistics cultivates irresponsibility and encourages such highhanded actions.

The discussion has been useful above all because it brought this Arakcheyev regime into the light of day and smashed it to smithereens.

But this has not been the only use of the discussion. It not only smashed the old regime in linguistics, but it also brought out the incredible confusion of ideas on cardinal questions of linguistics which prevails among the leading circles in this branch of science. Before the discussion they hushed up and glossed over the unhealthy state of affairs in linguistics. But after the discussion began, silence became impossible and they were compelled to come out in the pages of the press. And what did we find? It turned out that in N. Y. Marr's teachings there are many shortcomings, errors, undefined problems, and unelaborated tenets. Why, one asks, have N. Y. Marr's "disciples" begun to talk about this only now, after the discussion began? Why did they not see to it before? Why did they not speak about it in due time openly and honestly, as befits scientists?

Having admitted "some" of N. Y. Marr's errors, his "disci-

[4] Meaning an arbitrary and cruel regime. Count Alexei Arakcheyev (1769–1834) was a court favorite under the tsars Paul I and Alexander I.

ples," it appears, think that Soviet linguistics can only be advanced on the basis of a "rectified" version of N. Y. Marr's theory, which they consider a Marxist one. No, save us from N. Y. Marr's "Marxism"! N. Y. Marr did indeed want to be, and endeavored to be, a Marxist, but he could not become one. He was nothing but a simplifier and vulgarizer of Marxism, like the "Proletcultists" or the "Rappists."[5]

N. Y. Marr introduced into linguistics the incorrect, non-Marxist formula that language is a superstructure, and got himself into a muddle and put linguistics into a muddle. Soviet linguistics cannot be advanced on the basis of an incorrect formula.

N. Y. Marr introduced into linguistics another and also incorrect and non-Marxist formula regarding the "class character" of language, and got himself into a muddle and put linguistics into a muddle. Soviet linguistics cannot be advanced on the basis of an incorrect formula which is contrary to the course of the history of peoples and languages.

N. Y. Marr intoduced into linguistics an immodest, boastful, arrogant tone alien to Marxism and tending toward a crass and frivolous negation of everything done in linguistics prior to N. Y. Marr.

N. Y. Marr shrilly abused the comparative-historical method as "idealistic." Yet it must be said that, despite all its serious shortcomings, the comparative-historical method was nevertheless better than N. Y. Marr's really idealistic four-element analysis, because the former gives a stimulus to work, to a study of languages, while the latter gives a stimulus only to lie on one's back and tell fortunes from teacups with the help of the celebrated four elements.

N. Y. Marr haughtily discountenanced every attempt to study groups (families) of languages as a manifestation of the "ancestral language" theory. Yet it cannot be denied that the linguistic affinity of the Slav nations, say, is beyond question, and that a study of the linguistic affinity of those nations might be of great value to linguistics in the study of the laws

[5] Soviet cultural and writers' organizations of the early years following the Russian Revolution. They were severely criticized for their extremely sectarian policies and activities.

of language development. The "ancestral language" theory, of course, has nothing to do with the matter.

Listening to N. Y. Marr, and especially to his "disciples," one might think that prior to N. Y. Marr there was no such thing as linguistics, that linguistics appeared with N. Y. Marr's "new teachings." Marx and Engels were much more modest: They held that their dialectical materialism was a product of the development of the sciences, including philosophy, in preceding periods.

Thus the discussion was also useful in bringing to light ideological shortcomings in Soviet linguistics.

I think that the sooner our linguistics is rid of N. Y. Marr's errors, the sooner will it be possible to extricate it from its present crisis.

Elimination of the Arakcheyev regime in linguistics, rejection of N. Y. Marr's errors, and the introduction of Marxism into linguistics are, in my opinion, the way in which Soviet linguistics may be put on a sound basis.

June 20, 1950

II. REPLY TO KRASHENINNIKOVA

Comrade Krasheninnikova,

I am answering your questions.

QUESTION 1: *Your article convincingly shows that language is neither the base nor the superstructure. Would it be right to consider that language is a phenomenon peculiar to both the base and the superstructure, or would it be more correct to regard language as an intermediate phenomenon?*

ANSWER: Of course, peculiar to language, as a social phenomenon, is that which is common to all social phenomena, including the base and the superstructure, namely: It serves society in the same manner as society is served by all the other social phenomena, including the base and the superstructure. But this, essentially speaking, exhausts that which is common to and inherent in all social phenomena. Further on, serious distinctions begin between social phenomena.

The point is that social phenomena have, in addition to this common feature, their own specific peculiarities which distinguish them from each other and which are above all important for science. The specific peculiarities of the base consist in that it serves society economically. The specific peculiarities of the superstructure consist in that it serves society by means of political, legal, esthetic, and other ideas and creates for society the corresponding political, legal, and other institutions. Of what then do the specific peculiarities of language consist, the peculiarities distinguishing it from other social phenomena? They consist in that language serves society as a means of intercourse between people, as a means for exchanging thoughts in society, as a means enabling people to understand each other and to organize joint work in all spheres of human activity, both in the sphere of production and in the sphere of economic relations, in the sphere of politics and in the sphere of culture, in public and in everyday life. These peculiarities belong only to language, and precisely because they belong only to language, language constitutes the object of study of an independent science—linguistics. Without these peculiarities of language, linguistics would lose its right to independent existence.

Briefly, language cannot be ranked either among bases or among superstructures.

Neither can it be ranked among "intermediate" phenomena between the base and the superstructure, as such "intermediate" phenomena do not exist.

But perhaps language could be ranked among the productive forces of society, among, let us say, the implements of production? Indeed, there does exist a certain analogy between language and implements of production: Implements of production, as does language, manifest a kind of indifference toward classes and can equally serve different classes of society, both old and new. Does this circumstance provide ground for ranking language among implements of production? No, it does not.

At one time, N. Y. Marr, seeing that his formula—"language is a superstructure on the base"—was encountering objections, decided to "readjust" himself and announced that "language is an implement of production." Was N. Y. Marr right in ranking language among implements of production? No, he certainly was not.

The point is that the similarity between language and implements of production ends with that analogy of which I have just spoken. But, on the other hand, there is a radical difference between language and implements of production. This difference is that while implements of production produce material wealth, language produces nothing or "produces" words only. To be more exact, people possessing implements of production can produce material wealth, but those very same people, while having a language, but not having the implements of production, cannot produce material wealth. It is not difficult to understand that were language capable of the production of material wealth, windbags would be the richest men on earth.

QUESTION 2: *Marx and Engels define language as "the direct reality of thought," as "practical . . . actual consciousness." "Ideas," Marx says, "do not exist divorced from language." To what extent, in your opinion, should linguistics occupy itself with the semantic aspect of language, semantics and historical semasiology and stylistics, or should the subject of linguistics be form only?*

ANSWER: Semantics (semasiology) is one of the important sections of linguistics. The semantic aspect of words and expressions is of serious importance for the study of language. Therefore semantics (semasiology) must be assured a fitting place in linguistics.

However, in developing problems of semantics and in utilizing its data, its significance must in no way be overestimated, and still more its use must not be abused. I have in mind certain philologists, who, indulging excessively in semantics, disregard language as "the direct reality of thought" inseparably connected with thinking, who divorce thinking from language and maintain that language is outliving its age and that it is possible to get along without language.

Listen to what N. Y. Marr says: "Language exists only inasmuch as it expresses itself in sounds; the action of thinking occurs also without revealing itself. . . . Language (vocal language) has now already begun to yield its functions to the latest inventions which are unreservedly conquering space, while thinking is on the upgrade, departing from its unutilized accumulations in the past and its new acquisitions, and it is to oust and fully replace language. The future language is thinking which is developing in technique free of natural matter. No language, even vocal language, which is nonetheless connected with the standards of nature, will succeed in standing up against it."

If we interpret this "labor-magic" gibberish into simple human language, the conclusion may be drawn that:

a) N. Y. Marr divorces thinking from language;

b) N. Y. Marr considers that intercourse between people can be achieved without language, with the help of thinking itself, of thinking free of the "natural matter" of language, free of "the standards of nature";

c) In divorcing thinking from language and "having freed" it from "the natural matter" of language, N. Y. Marr lands in the swamp of idealism.

It is said that thoughts arise in the mind of man prior to their being expressed in speech, that they arise without language material, without the language shell, in, so to speak, a naked form. But this is absolutely wrong. Whatever the thoughts that may arise in the mind of man, they can arise and exist only on the basis of the language material, on the basis of language terminology and phrases. Bare thoughts, free of the language material, free of the "natural matter" of language—do not exist. "Language is the direct reality of thought" (Marx). The reality of thought manifests itself in language. Only idealists can speak of thinking as not connected with the "natural matter" of language, of thinking without language.

In brief: An overestimation of semantics and abuse of the latter led N. Y. Marr to idealism.

Consequently, if semantics (semasiology) is safeguarded from exaggerations and abuses, similar to those N. Y. Marr and some of his "disciples" indulge in, it can greatly benefit linguistics.

QUESTION 3: *You quite justly say that the bourgeoisie and the proletariat have ideas, concepts, customs, and moral principles that are diametrically opposed. The class character of these phenomena certainly affected the semantic aspect of language (and at times its form—the vocabulary—too, as is correctly pointed out in your article). In analyzing concrete language material and, first of all, the semantic aspect of language, can we speak of the class essence of the concepts they express, particularly in those cases when the matter concerns the language expression not only of the thought of man but also of his attitude toward reality, where his class affinity manifests itself especially clearly?*

ANSWER: In brief, you want to know whether classes influence language, whether they contribute their specific words and expressions to language, whether there are cases when people attach a different meaning, in accordance with the class to which they belong, to one and the same words and expressions?

Yes, classes do influence language, contribute their own specific words and expressions to language, and at times understand one and the same words and expressions differently. That is unquestionably so.

From this, however, it does not follow that specific words and expressions, as well as the difference in semantics, can be of serious importance for the development of a single language common to the whole people, that they are capable of debilitating its significance or of changing its character.

Firstly, such specific words and expressions, as well as cases of difference in semantics, are so few in language that they hardly make up one percent of the entire language material. Consequently, all the remaining preponderant mass of words and expressions, as well as their semantics, are *common* to all classes of society.

Secondly, specific words and expressions having a class shade are used in speech not according to rules of some sort of "class" grammar, which does not exist in reality, but according to rules of the grammar of the existing common language of the whole people.

Hence, the presence of specific words and expressions and the facts of differences in the semantics of language do not refute, but, on the contrary, confirm the presence of, and need for, a single language common to all the people.

QUESTION 4: *In your article you quite correctly qualify Marr as a vulgarizer of Marxism. Does this mean that linguists, including us, the young generation, should discard* the whole *of the linguistic legacy of Marr, who nonetheless has a number of valuable linguistic research works (Comrades Chikobava, Sanzheyev and others wrote about them during the discussion)? Can we, in approaching Marr critically, take from him nonetheless what is useful and valuable?*

ANSWER: Of course, the works of N. Y. Marr do not consist only of errors. N. Y. Marr made the crassest mistakes when he introduced into linguistics elements of Marxism in a distorted form, when he tried to create an independent theory of language. But N. Y. Marr has certain good works, written with talent, wherein, forgetting his theoretical claims, he conscientiously and, one must say, capably studies individual languages. In such works one may find no little that is valuable and instructive. It stands to reason that what is valuable and instructive should be taken from N. Y. Marr and used.

QUESTION 5: *Many linguists consider* formalism *as one of the main reasons for the stagnation in Soviet linguistics. We would very much like to know your opinion on what formalism in linguistics consists of and how it should be overcome.*

ANSWER: N. Y. Marr and his "disciples" accuse of "formalism" all linguists who do not accept N. Y. Marr's "new doctrine." This of course is frivolous and foolish.

N. Y. Marr held grammar to be an empty "formality," and the people considering the grammatical system as the foundation of language as formalists. This is altogether foolish.

I think that "formalism" was invented by the authors of the "new doctrine" to make it easier for them to struggle against their opponents in linguistics.

The reason for the stagnation in Soviet linguistics is not the "formalism" invented by N. Y. Marr and his "disciples" but the Arakcheyev regime and the theoretical gaps in linguistics.

The Arakcheyev regime was set up by N. Y. Marr's "disciples." It was N. Y. Marr and his closest colleagues who put linguistics in a theoretical muddle. To get rid of the stagnation, both the one and the other must be eliminated. The elimination of these plagues will cure Soviet linguistics, lead it out onto a broad highway, and enable Soviet linguistics to occupy the first place in world linguistics.

June 29, 1950

III. REPLY TO SANZHEYEV

To Comrade Sanzheyev

Esteemed Comrade Sanzheyev,

My answer to your letter has been long delayed, since your letter was forwarded to me only yesterday from the offices of the Central Committee.

You are unquestionably correct in your interpretation of my standpoint on the question of dialects.

"Class" dialects, which would be more correctly called jargons, serve a limited upper stratum of society and not the masses of the people. Moreover, they lack their own grammatical system and basic word stocks. In view of this, they can by no means develop into independent languages.

On the other hand, local ("territorial") dialects serve the masses of the people, and they have their own grammatical systems and basic word stocks. In view of this, some local dialects may, in the process of the formation of nations, become the basis of national languages and develop into independent national languages. Such was the case, for example, with the Kursk-Orel dialect (Kursk-Orel "speech") of the Russian language, which became the basis of the Russian national language. The same should be said of the Poltava-Kiev dialect of the Ukrainian language, which became the basis of the Ukrainian national language. As for the other dialects of such languages they lose their original character, become fused with these languages, and disappear within them.

There are also reverse processes, when the single language of a nationality which had not yet developed into a nation, owing to the absence of the necessary economic conditions of development, collapses as a result of the state disintegration of this nationality, while the local dialects, which were not yet digested in a single language, come to life and give birth to the formation of separate independent languages. This probably was the case with the single Mongolian language, for example.

July 11, 1950

IV. REPLY TO D. BELKIN AND S. FURER

I have received your letters.

Your mistake is that you have confused two different things and substituted a different subject for the subject treated in my reply to Comrade Krasheninnikova.

1. In this reply I criticize N. Y. Marr, who, speaking of language (phonetic) and thought, separates language from thought and thus lapses into idealism. Consequently, my reply applies to normal people possessing a language. And I maintain that ideas can originate in these people only on the basis of language material, that bare ideas not connected with language material do not exist in people possessing a language.

Instead of accepting or rejecting this proposition, you put up anomalous, tongueless people, deaf mutes who lack a language, and whose thoughts cannot of course originate on the basis of language material. As you see, it is an entirely different theme which I have not dwelt upon and could not dwell upon, since linguistics treats of normal people possessing a language, and not of anomalous deaf mutes who lack a language.

You have substituted another topic which was not discussed for the topic under discussion.

2. From Comrade Belkin's letter it appears that he places on the same level the "language of words" (the phonetic language) and the "language of gestures" (the "hand" language in N. Y. Marr's terms). He apparently thinks that the language of gestures and the language of words are equivalent, that at one time human society lacked a language of words,

and that at that time the "hand" language substituted for the language of words which appeared later.

But if this is really what Comrade Belkin thinks, he is making a serious mistake. The phonetic language, or the language of words, has always been the only language of human society capable of serving as a fully valid means of human intercourse. History does not know of a single human society, even the most backward, which did not have its own phonetic language. Ethnography does not know of any backward nationality, even if it was as primitive as or even more primitive than the Australians or the Tierra del Fuegans of the last century, that did not possess its own phonetic language. The phonetic language is one of those forces in the history of mankind which helped people to detach themselves from the animal kingdom, to unite in societies, develop their thinking, organize social production, conduct a successful struggle against the forces of nature, and achieve the progress we have at the present time.

In this respect, the significance of the so-called language of gestures is negligible owing to its extreme poverty and limitations. This, precisely speaking, is not a language, and not even a surrogate language which may in one way or another substitute for the phonetic language, but an auxiliary medium with extremely limited means used by man sometimes for emphasizing this or that point in his speech. The language of gestures cannot be placed on a level with the phonetic language, just as the primitive wooden hoe cannot be placed on a level with the modern caterpillar tractor with a quintuple plow and tractor-drawn drill.

3. You are apparently interested primarily in deaf mutes and only then in problems of linguistics. Apparently, this very circumstance has prompted you to address a number of questions to me. Well, if you insist, I am not averse to granting your request. And so, how do matters stand with regard to the deaf mutes? Does their thought function, do ideas originate? Yes, their thought functions, ideas do originate. It is clear that since the deaf mutes lack a language, their ideas cannot originate on the basis of language material. But does this mean that the ideas of deaf mutes are bare, not connected with the "rules of nature" (N. Y. Marr's expression)? No, it does not

mean that. The ideas of deaf mutes originate and can exist only on the basis of the images, perceptions, and conceptions formed in practice about objects of the exterior world and their relations among themselves, thanks to the senses of sight, touch, taste, and smell. Outside of these images, perceptions, and conceptions, thought is empty, devoid of any content whatever, *i.e.*, it does not exist.

July 22, 1950

V. REPLY TO A. KHOLOPOV

I have received your letter.

My answer has been slightly delayed owing to my preoccupation with work.

Your letter tacitly proceeds from two assumptions: from the assumption that it is possible to quote the works of one author or another *apart* from the historical period treated by the quotation, and, secondly, from the assumption that this or that conclusion or formula of Marxism, obtained as a result of studying one period of historical development, is correct for all periods of development and must therefore remain *unchanged*.

I must say that both these assumptions are deeply erroneous.

A few examples.

1. In the forties of the past century, when monopoly capitalism did not yet exist, when capitalism was developing more or less smoothly along an ascending line, spreading to new territories it had not occupied, and the law of uneven development could not yet be fully effective, Marx and Engels arrived at the conclusion that the socialist revolution could not triumph in any single country, that it could triumph only as a result of a general blow in all or in the majority of the civilized countries. This conclusion subsequently became the guiding principle for all Marxists.

But at the beginning of the twentieth century, especially in the period of the first World War, when it became evident to everybody that pre-monopoly capitalism had clearly grown into monopoly capitalism, when ascending capitalism was transformed into moribund capitalism, when the war disclosed the incurable weaknesses of the world imperialist front, and the law of uneven development predetermined differing periods of duration for the maturing of the proletarian revolution in different countries, Lenin, proceeding from the Marxist theory, arrived at the conclusion that under the new conditions of development the socialist revolution could well triumph in one particular country, that the simultaneous victory of the socialist revolution in all countries or in the majority of the civilized countries was impossible owing to the uneven maturing of the revolution in these countries, that the old formula of Marx and Engels no longer corresponded to the new historical conditions.

It appears that we have here two different conclusions on the question of the victory of socialism, which are not only mutually contradictory, but also mutually exclusive.

Some textualists and Talmudists, who quote formally, without delving into the substance of the matter and in isolation from historical conditions, may say that one of these conclusions should be rejected as absolutely wrong, and the second conclusion should be extended to all periods of development as absolutely correct. However, Marxists cannot but know that textualists and Talmudists err; they cannot but know that both these conclusions are correct, not absolutely, but each for its time: the conclusion of Marx and Engels for the period of pre-monopoly capitalism, and Lenin's conclusion for the period of monopoly capitalism.

2. In his *Anti-Dühring*, Engels wrote that the state must wither away after the victory of the socialist revolution. On this basis, the textualists and Talmudists in our party began to demand, after the victory of the socialist revolution in our country, that the Communist Party should take steps to bring about the speedy withering away of our state, to dissolve state institutions, to give up a permanent army.

But the Soviet Marxists, on the basis of the study of the world situation in our time, came to the conclusion that, under conditions of capitalist encirclement, when the victory of the socialist revolution has taken place in only one country, while capitalism rules in all the other countries, the country of the victorious revolution must not weaken, but in every way strengthen its state, the state institutions, the intelligence organs, and the army, if this country does not wish to be crushed by the capitalist encirclement. The Russian Marxists came to the conclusion that Engels' formula implies the victory of socialism in all countries or in the majority of countries, that it is inapplicable to the case when socialism triumphs in one particular country, while capitalism rules in all the other countries.

Obviously we have here two different, mutually exclusive formulas on the destinies of the socialist state.

The textualists and Talmudists may say that this circumstance creates an impossible situation, that one of the formulas should be rejected as absolutely wrong, and the other should be extended to all periods of development of the socialist state as absolutely correct. However, Marxists cannot but know that textualists and Talmudists err, for these two formulas are correct, not absolutely, but each for its own time: the formula of the Soviet Marxists, for the period of the victory of socialism in one or several countries, and Engels' formula, for the period when the consecutive victory of socialism in separate countries will lead to the victory of socialism in the majority of countries and when the necessary conditions will thus be created for the application of Engels' formula.

Many more such examples could be cited.

The same should be said of the two different formulas on the question of language taken from different works by Stalin and cited by Comrade Kholopov in his letter.

Comrade Kholopov refers to Stalin's work, *Concerning Marxism in Linguistics*, where the conclusion is drawn that, as a result of the crossing of two languages, let us say, one of the languages usually comes out the victor, whereas the other dies away, that consequently this cross does not yield some new, third language, but preserves one of the languages. He further refers to another conclusion taken from Stalin's report to the Sixteenth Congress of the Communist Party of the Soviet Union, where it is said that in the period of the victory of socialism on a world scale, when socialism has been consolidated and has become a matter of everyday life, the national languages must inevitably fuse into one common language, which, of course, will be neither Great Russian no German, but something new. Comparing these two formulas and seeing that far from coinciding, they exclude each other, Comrade Kholopov is driven to despair. "From your article," he writes in his letter, "I understand that the crossing of languages can *never* result in some new language, whereas before the article I was firmly convinced that, according to your speech at the Sixteenth Congress of the Communist Party of the Soviet Union, languages will fuse into one common language under *communism.*"

Obviously, having discovered a contradiction between these two formulas, and believing deeply that this contradiction must be eliminated, Comrade Kholopov considers it necessary to get rid of one of the formulas as the incorrect one and to clutch at the other formula as the correct one for all times and countries, but he does not know exactly which formula to clutch at. It seems like a hopeless situation. Comrade Kholopov does not even guess that both formulas may be correct—each for its time.

This is always the case with textualists and Talmudists who, quoting formally without penetrating into the substance of the matter and irrespective of the historical conditions treated in the quotations, invariably land in a hopeless situation.

And yet, if the essence of the question is analyzed, there are no grounds for a hopeless situation. The point is that Stalin's pamphlet *Concerning Marxism in Linguistics* and Stalin's speech at the Sixteenth Party Congress have in mind two entirely different epochs, as a result of which the formulas too are different.

Stalin's formula in the part of his pamphlet relating to the crossing of languages refers to the epoch *before the victory of socialism* on a world scale, when the exploiting classes are the dominating force in the world, when national and colonial oppression remains in effect, when the national isolation and mutual distrust of the nations are reinforced by state differences, when there is as yet no national equality, when the crossing of languages takes place in the course of a struggle for the domination of one of the languages, when the conditions are as yet lacking for peaceful and friendly co-operation of nations and languages, when not co-operation and mutual enrichment of the languages but the assimilation of some and the victory of other languages are on the order of the day. It is understandable that under such conditions there can only be victorious and defeated languages. Precisely these conditions are presupposed in Stalin's formula when it says that the crossing of two languages, let us say, will result not in the formation of a new language, but in the victory of one of these languages and the defeat of the other.

As regards Stalin's other formula, taken from the speech at the Sixteenth Party Congress, in the section relating to the fusion of languages into one common language, it has in mind an entirely different epoch, namely, the epoch *after the victory of socialism* on a world scale, when world imperialism will no longer exist, the exploiting classes will be overthrown, national and colonial oppression will be eliminated, the national isolation and mutual distrust of nations will be replaced by mutual confidence and the rapprochement of nations, national equality will be put into practice, the policy of oppression and assimilation of languages will be eliminated, co-operation among nations will be organized, and national languages will have the opportunity freely to enrich one another on the basis of co-operation. It is understandable that the suppression and defeat of some languages and the victory of other languages are out of the question under such conditions. In this case we will have not two languages, one of which is suffering defeat while the other emerges victorious from the struggle, but hundreds of national languages from which at first the most enriched single zonal languages will emerge as a result of lengthy economic, political, and cultural co-operation of nations, and subsequently the zonal languages will fuse into one common international language, which will of course be neither German, nor Russian, nor English, but a new language which has absorbed the best elements of the national and zonal languages.

Consequently, the two different formulas correspond to two different epochs in the development of society, and precisely because they correspond to them, the two formulas are correct, each for its own epoch.

To demand that these formulas should not be mutually contradictory, that they should not exclude each other, is just as absurd as it would be to demand that there should be no contradiction between the epoch of the domination of capitalism and the epoch of the domination of socialism, that socialism and capitalism should not exclude each other.

Textualists and Talmudists regard Marxism, the separate deductions and formulas of Marxism, as a collection of dogmas which "never" change, regardless of the changes in the condition of development of society. They think that if they memorize these deductions and formulas by heart and begin to cite them in every manner, they will be able to solve any problem, calculating that the memorized deductions and formulas will be useful to them for all times and countries, for all cases in life. But this can be the reasoning only of those people who see the letter of Marxism, but do not see its essence, who memorize the texts of deductions and formulas of Marxism, but do not understand their content.

Marxism is the science of the laws of development of nature and society, the science of the revolution of the oppressed and exploited masses, the science of the victory of socialism in all countries, the science of the building of communist society. Marxism as a science cannot stand still; it develops and perfects itself. In the course of its development Marxism cannot but be enriched by new experience, by new knowledge; consequently, its separate formulas and deductions cannot but change in the course of time, cannot but be replaced by new formulas and deductions corresponding to the new historical tasks. Marxism does not recognize any immutable deductions and formulas, applicable to all epochs and periods. Marxism is an enemy of all dogmatism.

July 28, 1950

ECONOMIC PROBLEMS OF SOCIALISM IN THE U.S.S.R.[1]

To the Participants in the Economic Discussion

I. REMARKS ON ECONOMIC QUESTIONS CONNECTED WITH THE NOVEMBER 1951 DISCUSSION

I have received all the materials on the economic discussion arranged to assess the draft textbook on political economy. The material received includes the "Proposals for the Improvement of the Draft Textbook on Political Economy," "Proposals for the Elimination of Mistakes and Inaccuracies" in the draft, and the "Memorandum on Disputed Issues."

On all these materials, as well as on the draft textbook, I consider it necessary to make the following remarks.

1. CHARACTER OF ECONOMIC LAWS UNDER SOCIALISM

Some comrades deny the objective character of laws of science, and of the laws of political economy particularly, under socialism. They deny that the laws of political economy reflect law-governed processes which operate independently of the will of man. They believe that in view of the specific role assigned to the Soviet state by history, the Soviet state and its leaders can abolish existing laws of political economy and can "form," "create," new laws.

[1] Stalin surely intended this treatise, which appeared in the spring of 1952, to serve as a basis for discussion in the Nineteenth Party Congress, the first held since 1939, set to convene in October. It is a theoretical work of major importance (see Introduction).

These comrades are profoundly mistaken. It is evident that they confuse laws of science, which reflect objective processes in nature or society, processes which take place independently of the will of man, with the laws which are issued by governments, which are made by the will of man, and which have only juridical validity. But they must not be confused.

Marxism regards laws of science—whether they be laws of natural science or laws of political economy—as the reflection of objective processes which take place independently of the will of man. Man may discover these laws, get to know them, study them, reckon with them in his activities and utilize them in the interests of society, but he cannot change or abolish them. Still less can he form or create new laws of science.

Does this mean, for instance, that the results of the action of the laws of nature, the results of the action of the forces of nature, are generally inavertible, that the destructive action of the forces of nature always and everywhere proceeds with an elemental and inexorable power that does not yield to the influence of man? No, it does not. Leaving aside astronomical, geological and other similar processes, which, even if he has come to know the laws of their development, man really is powerless to influence, in many other cases man is very far from powerless, in the sense of being able to influence the processes of nature. In all such cases, having come to know the laws of nature, reckoning with them and relying on them, and intelligently applying and utilizing them, man can restrict their sphere of action, and can impart a different direction to the destructive forces of nature and convert them to the use of society.

To take one of numerous examples. In olden times the overflow of big rivers, flood, and the resulting destruction of homes and crops, was considered an inavertible calamity, against which man was powerless. But with the lapse of time and the development of human knowledge, when man had learned to build dams and hydro-power stations, it became possible to protect society from the calamity of flood which had formerly seemed to be inavertible. More, man learned to curb the destructive forces of nature, to harness them, so to speak, to convert the force of water to the use of society and to utilize it for the irrigation of fields and the generation of power.

Does this mean that man has thereby abolished laws of nature, laws of science, and has created new laws of nature, new laws of science? No, it does not. The fact is that all this procedure of averting the action of the destructive forces of water and of utilizing them in the interests of society takes place without any violation, alteration or abolition of scientific laws or the creation of new scientific laws. On the contrary, all this procedure is effected in precise conformity with the laws of nature and the laws of science, since any violation, even the slightest, of the laws of nature would only upset matters and render the procedure futile.

The same must be said of the laws of economic development, the laws of political economy—whether in the period of capitalism or in the period of socialism. Here, too, the laws of economic development, as in the case of natural science, are objective laws, reflecting processes of economic development which take place independently of the will of man. Man may discover these laws, get to know them and, relying upon them, utilize them in the interests of society, impart a different direction to the destructive action of some of the laws, restrict their sphere of action, and allow fuller scope to other laws that are forcing their way to the forefront; but he cannot destroy them or create new economic laws.

One of the distinguishing features of political economy is that its laws, unlike those of natural science, are impermanent, that they, or at least the majority of them, operate for a definite historical period, after which they give place to new laws. However, these laws are not abolished, but lose their validity owing to the new economic conditions and depart from the scene in order to give place to new laws, laws which are not created by the will of man, but which arise from the new economic conditions.

Reference is made to Engels' *Anti-Dühring*, to his formula which says that, with the abolition of capitalism and the socialization of the means of production, man will obtain control of his means of production, that he will be set free from the yoke of social and economic relations and become the "master" of his social life. Engels calls this freedom "appreciation of necessity." And what can this "appreciation of necessity" mean? It means that, having come to know objective laws ("necessity"), man will apply them with full consciousness in the interests of society. That is why Engels says in the same book:

"The laws of his own social activity, which have hitherto confronted him as extraneous laws of nature dominating him, will then be applied by man with complete understanding, and hence will be dominated by man."

As we see, Engels' formula does not speak at all in favour of those who think that under socialism economic laws can be abolished and new ones created. On the contrary, it demands, not the abolition, but the understanding of economic laws and their intelligent application.

It is said that economic laws are elemental in character, that their action is inavertible and that society is powerless against them. That is not true. It is making a fetish of laws, and oneself the slave of laws. It has been demonstrated that society is not powerless against laws, that, having come to know economic laws and relying upon them, society can restrict their sphere of action, utilize them in the interests of society and "harness" them, just as in the case of the forces of nature and their laws, just as in the case of the overflow of big rivers cited in [the] illustration above.

Reference is made to the specific role of Soviet government in building socialism, which allegedly enables it to abolish existing laws of economic development and to "form" new ones. That also is untrue.

The specific role of Soviet government was due to two circumstances: first, that what Soviet government had to do was not to replace one form of exploitation by another, as was the case in earlier revolutions, but to abolish exploitation altogether; second, that in view of the absence in the country of any ready-made rudiments of a socialist economy, it had to create new, socialist forms of economy, "starting from scratch," so to speak.

That was undoubtedly a difficult, complex and unprecedented task. Nevertheless, the Soviet government accomplished this task with credit. But it accomplished it not because it supposedly destroyed the existing economic laws and "formed" new ones, but only because it relied on the economic law that the relations of production *must necessarily conform* with the character of the productive forces. The productive forces of our country, especially in industry, were social in character, the form of ownership, on the other hand, was private, capitalistic. Relying on the economic law that the relations of production must necessarily conform with the character of the productive forces, the Soviet government socialized the means of production, made them the property of the whole people, and thereby abolished the exploiting system and created socialist forms of economy. Had it not been for this law, and had the Soviet government not relied upon it, it could not have accomplished its mission.

The economic law that the relations of production must necessarily conform with the character of the productive forces has long been forcing its way to the forefront in the capitalist countries. If it has failed so far to force its way into the open, it is because it is encountering powerful resistance on the part of obsolescent forces of society. Here we have another distinguishing feature of economic laws. Unlike the laws of natural science, where the discovery and application of a new law proceeds more or less smoothly, the discovery and application of a new law in the economic field, affecting as it does the interests of obsolescent forces of society, meets with the most powerful resistence on their part. A force, a social force, capable of overcoming this resistance, is therefore necessary. In our country, such a force was the alliance of the working class and the peasantry, who represented the overwhelming majority of society. There is no such force yet in other, capitalist countries. This explains the secret why the Soviet government was able to smash the old forces of society, and why in our country the economic law that the relations of production must necessarily conform with the character of the productive forces received full scope.

It is said that the necessity for balanced (proportionate) development of the national economy in our country enables the Soviet government to abolish existing economic laws and to create new ones. That is absolutely untrue. Our yearly and five-yearly plans must not be confused with the objective economic law of balanced, proportionate development of the national economy. The law of balanced development of the national economy arose in opposition to the law of competition and anarchy of production under capitalism. It arose from the socialization of the means of production, after the law of competition and anarchy of production had lost its validity. It became operative because a socialist economy can be conducted only on the basis of the economic law of balanced development of the national economy. That means that the law of balanced development of the national economy makes it *possible* for our planning bodies to plan social production correctly. But *possibility* must not be confused with *actuality*. They are two different things. In order to turn the possibility into actuality, it is necessary to study this economic law, to master it, to learn to apply it with full understanding, and to compile such plans as fully reflect the requirements of this law. It cannot be said that the requirements of this economic law are fully reflected by our yearly and five-yearly plans.

It is said that some of the economic laws operating in our country under socialism, including the law of value, have been "transformed," or even "radically transformed," on the basis of planned economy. That is likewise untrue. Laws cannot be "transformed," still less "radically" transformed. If they can be transformed, then they can be abolished and replaced by other laws. The thesis that laws can be "transformed" is a relic of the incorrect formula that laws can be "abolished" or "formed." Although the formula that economic laws can be transformed has already been current in our country for a long time, it must be abandoned for the sake of accuracy. The sphere of action of this or that economic law may be restricted, its destructive action—that is, of course, if it is liable to be destructive—may be averted, but it cannot be "transformed" or "abolished."

Consequently, when we speak of "subjugating" natural forces or economic forces, of "dominating" them, etc., this does not mean that man can "abolish" or "form" scientific laws. On the contrary, it only means that man can discover laws, get to know them and master them, learn to apply them with full understanding, utilize them in the interests of society, and thus subjugate them, secure mastery over them.

Hence, the laws of political economy under socialism are

objective laws, which reflect the fact that the processes of economic life are law-governed and operate independently of our will. People who deny this postulate are in point of fact denying science, and, by denying science, they are denying all possibility of prognostication—and, consequently, are denying the possibility of directing economic activity.

It may be said that all this is correct and generally known; but that there is nothing new in it, and that it is therefore not worth spending time reiterating generally-known truths. Of course, there really is nothing new in this; but it would be a mistake to think that it is not worth spending time reiterating certain truths that are well known to us. The fact is that we, the leading core, are joined every year by thousands of new and young forces who are ardently desirous of assisting us and ardently desirous of proving their worth, but who do not possess an adequate Marxist education, are unfamiliar with many truths that are well known to us, and are therefore compelled to grope in the darkness. They are staggered by the colossal achievements of Soviet government, they are dazzled by the extraordinary successes of the Soviet system, and they begin to imagine that Soviet government can "do anything," that "nothing is beyond it," that it can abolish scientific laws and form new ones. What are we to do with these comrades? How are we to educate them in Marxism-Leninism? I think that systematic reiteration and patient explanation of so-called "generally-known" truths is one of the best methods of educating these comrades in Marxism.

2. COMMODITY PRODUCTION UNDER SOCIALISM

Certain comrades affirm that the Party acted wrongly in preserving commodity production after it had assumed power and nationalized the means of production in our country. They consider that the Party should have banished commodity production there and then. In this connection they cite Engels, who says:

"The seizure of the means of production by society puts an end to commodity production, and therewith to the domination of the product over the producer." (See *Anti-Dühring.*)

These comrades are profoundly mistaken.

Let us examine Engels' formula. Engels' formula cannot be considered fully clear and precise, because it does not indicate whether it is referring to the seizure by society of *all* or only part of the means of production, that is, whether *all* or only part of the means of production are converted into public property. Hence, *this* formula of Engels' may be understood either way.

Elsewhere in *Anti-Dühring* Engels speaks of mastering "*all* the means of production," of taking possession of "*all* means of production." Hence, in this formula Engels has in mind the nationalization not of part, but of all the means of production, that is, the conversion into public property of the means of production not only of industry, but also of agriculture.

It follows from this that Engels has in mind countries where capitalism and the concentration of production have advanced far enough both in industry and in agriculture to permit the expropriation of *all* the means of production in the country and their conversion into public property. Engels, consequently, considers that in *such* countries, parallel with the socialization of *all* the means of production, commodity production should be put an end to. And that, of course, is correct.

There was only one such country at the close of the last century, when *Anti-Dühring* was published—Britain. There the development of capitalism and the concentration of production both in industry and in agriculture had reached such a point that it would have been possible, in the event of the assumption of power by the proletariat, to convert *all* the country's means of production into public property and to put an end to commodity production.

I leave aside in this instance the question of the importance of foreign trade to Britain and the vast part it plays in her national economy. I think that only after an investigation of this question can it be finally decided what would be the future of commodity production in Britain after the proletariat had assumed power and *all* the means of production had been nationalized.

However, not only at the close of the last century, but today too, no country has attained such a degree of development of capitalism and concentration of production in agriculture as is to be observed in Britain. As to the other countries, notwithstanding the development of capitalism in the countryside, they still have a fairly numerous class of small and medium rural owner-producers, whose future would have to be decided if the proletariat should assume power.

But here is a question: what are the proletariat and its party to do in countries, ours being a case in point, where the conditions are favourable for the assumption of power by the proletariat and the overthrow of capitalism, where capitalism has so concentrated the means of production in industry that they may be expropriated and made the property of society, but where agriculture, notwithstanding the growth of capitalism, is divided up among numerous small and medium owner-producers to such an extent as to make it impossible to consider the expropriation of these producers?

To this question Engels' formula does not furnish an answer. Incidentally, it was not supposed to furnish an answer to it, since it arose from another question, namely, what should be the fate of commodity production after *all* the means of production had been socialized.

And so, what is to be done if *not all*, but only part of the means of production have been socialized, yet the conditions are favourable for the assumption of power by the proletariat —should the proletariat assume power and should commodity production be abolished immediately after this?

We cannot, of course, consider an answer the opinion of certain half-baked Marxists who believe that under such conditions the thing to do is to refrain from taking power and to wait until capitalism has succeeded in ruining the millions of small and medium producers and converting them into farm labourers and in concentrating the means of production in agriculture, and that only after this would it be possible to consider the assumption of power by the proletariat and the socialization of *all* the means of production. Naturally, this is a "solution" which Marxists cannot accept if they do not want to disgrace themselves completely.

Nor can we consider an answer the opinion of other half-baked Marxists, who think that the thing to do would be to assume power and to expropriate the small and medium rural producers and to socialize their means of production. Marxists cannot adopt this senseless and criminal course either, because it would destroy all chances of victory for the socialist revolution, and would throw the peasantry into the camp of the enemies of the proletariat for a long time.

The answer to this question was given by Lenin in his writings on the "tax in kind" and in his celebrated "cooperative plan."

Lenin's answer may be briefly summed up as follows:

a) Favourable conditions for the assumption of power should not be missed—the proletariat should assume power without waiting until capitalism succeeded in ruining the millions of small and medium individual producers;

b) The means of production in industry should be expropriated and converted into public property;

c) As to the small and medium individual producers, they should be gradually united in producers' cooperatives, i.e., in large agricultural enterprises, collective farms;

d) Industry should be developed to the utmost and the collective farms should be placed on the modern technical basis of large-scale production, not expropriating them, but on the contrary generously supplying them with first-class tractors and other machines;

e) In order to ensure an economic bond between town and country, between industry and agriculture, commodity production (exchange through purchase and sale) should be preserved for a certain period, it being the form of economic tie with the town which is *alone acceptable* to the peasants, and Soviet trade—state, cooperative, and collective-farm—should be developed to the full and the capitalists of all types and descriptions ousted from trading activity.

The history of socialist construction in our country has shown that this path of development, mapped out by Lenin, has fully justified itself.

There can be no doubt that in the case of all capitalist countries with a more or less numerous class of small and medium producers, this path of development is the only possible and expedient one for the victory of socialism.

It is said that commodity production must lead, is bound

to lead, to capitalism all the same, under all conditions. That is not true. Not always and not under all conditions! Commodity production must not be identified with capitalist production. They are two different things. Capitalist production is the highest form of commodity production. Commodity production leads to capitalism only *if* there is private ownership of the means of production, *if* labour power appears in the market as a commodity which can be bought by the capitalist and exploited in the process of production, and *if*, consequently, the system of exploitation of wageworkers by capitalists exists in the country. Capitalist production begins when the means of production are concentrated in private hands, and when the workers are bereft of means of production and are compelled to sell their labour power as a commodity. Without this there is no such thing as capitalist production.

Well, and what is to be done if the conditions for the conversion of commodity production into capitalist production do not exist, if the means of production are no longer private but socialist property, if the system of wage labour no longer exists and labour power is no longer a commodity, and if the system of exploitation has long been abolished—can it be considered then that commodity production will lead to capitalism all the same? No, it cannot. Yet ours is precisely such a society, a society where private ownership of the means of production, the system of wage labour, and the system of exploitation have long ceased to exist.

Commodity production must not be regarded as something sufficient unto itself, something independent of the surrounding economic conditions. Commodity production is older than capitalist production. It existed in slave-owning society, and served it, but did not lead to capitalism. It existed in feudal society and served it, yet, although it prepared some of the conditions for capitalist production, it did not lead to capitalism. Why then, one asks, cannot commodity production similarly serve our socialist society for a certain period without leading to capitalism, bearing in mind that in our country commodity production is not so boundless and all-embracing as it is under capitalist conditions, being confined within strict bounds thanks to such decisive economic conditions as social ownership of the means of production, the abolition of the system of wage labour, and the elimination of the system of exploitation?

It is said that, since the domination of social ownership of the means of production has been established in our country, and the system of wage labour and exploitation has been abolished, commodity production has lost all meaning and should therefore be done away with.

That is also untrue. Today there are two basic forms of socialist production in our country: state, or publicly-owned production, and collective-farm production, which cannot be said to be publicly owned. In the state enterprises, the means of production and the product of production are national property. In the collective farm, although the means of production (land, machines) do belong to the state, the product of production is the property of the different collective farms, since the labour, as well as the seed, is their own, while the land, which has been turned over to the collective farms in perpetual tenure, is used by them virtually as their own property, in spite of the fact that they cannot sell, buy, lease or mortgage it.

The effect of this is that the state disposes only of the product of the state enterprises, while the product of the collective farms, being their property, is disposed of only by them. But the collective farms are unwilling to alienate their products except in the form of commodities, in exchange for which they desire to receive the commodities they need. At present the collective farms will not recognize any other economic relation with the town except the commodity relation —exchange through purchase and sale. Because of this, commodity production and trade are as much a necessity with us today as they were thirty years ago, say, when Lenin spoke of the necessity of developing trade to the utmost.

Of course, when instead of the two basic production sectors, the state sector and the collective-farm sector, there will be only one all-embracing production sector, with the right to dispose of all the consumer goods produced in the country, commodity circulation, with its "money economy," will disappear, as being an unnecessary element in the national economy. But so long as this is not the case, so long as the two basic production sectors remain, commodity production and commodity circulation must remain in force, as a necessary and very useful element in our system of national economy. How the formation of a single and united sector will come about, whether simply by the swallowing up of the collective-farm sector by the state sector—which is hardly likely (because that would be looked upon as the expropriation of the collective farms)—or by the setting up of a single *national* economic body (comprising representatives of state industry and of the collective farms), with the right at first to keep account of all consumer product in the country, and eventually also to distribute it, by way, say, of products-exchange—is a special question which requires separate discussion.

Consequently, *our* commodity production is not of the ordinary type, but is a special kind of commodity production, commodity production without capitalists, which is concerned mainly with the goods of associated socialist producers (the state, the collective farms, the cooperatives), the sphere of action of which is confined to items of personal consumption, which obviously cannot possibly develop into capitalist production, and which, together with its "money economy," is designed to serve the development and consolidation of socialist production.

Absolutely mistaken, therefore, are those comrades who allege that, since socialist society has not abolished commodity forms of production, we are bound to have the reappearance of all the economic categories characteristic of capitalism: labour power as a commodity, surplus value, capital, capitalist profit, the average rate of profit, etc. These comrades confuse commodity production with capitalist production, and believe that once there is commodity production there must also be capitalist production. They do not realize that our commodity production radically differs from commodity production under capitalism.

More, I think that we must also discard certain other concepts taken from Marx's *Capital*—where Marx was concerned with an analysis of capitalism—and artificially pasted on to our socialist relations. I am referring to such concepts, among others, as "necessary" and "surplus" labour, "necessary" and "surplus" product, "necessary" and "surplus" time. Marx analyzed capitalism in order to elucidate the source of exploitation of the working class—surplus value—and to arm the working class, which was bereft of means of production, with an intellectual weapon for the overthrow of capitalism. It is natural that Marx used concepts (categories) which fully corresponded to capitalist relations. But it is strange, to say the least, to use these concepts now, when the working class is not only not bereft of power and means of production, but, on the contrary, is in possession of the power and controls the means of production. Talk of labour power being a commodity, and of "hiring" of workers sounds rather absurd now, under our system: as though the working class, which possesses means of production, hires itself and sells its labour power to itself. It is just as strange to speak now of "necessary" and "surplus" labour: as though, under our conditions, the labour contributed by the workers to society for the extension of production, the promotion of education and public health, the organization of defence, etc., is not just as necessary to the working class, now in power, as the labour expended to supply the personal needs of the worker and his family.

It should be remarked that in his *Critique of the Gotha Program*, where it is no longer capitalism that he is investigating, but, among other things, the first phase of communist society, Marx recognizes labour contributed to society for extension of production, for education and public health, for administrative expenses, for building up reserves, etc., to be just as necessary as the labour expended to supply the consumption requirements of the working class.

3. THE LAW OF VALUE UNDER SOCIALISM

I think that our economists should put an end to this incongruity between the old concepts and the new state of affairs in our socialist country, by replacing the old concepts with new ones that correspond to the new situation.

We could tolerate this incongruity for a certain period, but the time has come to put an end to it.

It is sometimes asked whether the law of value exists and operates in our country, under the socialist system.

Yes, it does exist and does operate. Wherever commodities

and commodity production exist, there the law of value must also exist.

In our country, the sphere of operation of the law of value extends, first of all, to commodity circulation, to the exchange of commodities through purchase and sale, the exchange, chiefly, of articles of personal consumption. Here, in this sphere, the law of value preserves, within certain limits, of course, the function of a regulator.

But the operation of the law of value is not confined to the sphere of commodity circulation. It also extends to production. True, the law of value has no regulating function in our socialist production, but it nevertheless influences production, and this fact cannot be ignored when directing production. As a matter of fact, consumer goods, which are needed to compensate the labour power expended in the process of production, are produced and realized in our country as commodities coming under the operation of the law of value. It is precisely here that the law of value exercises its influence on production. In this connection, such things as cost accounting and profitableness, production costs, prices, etc., are of actual importance in our enterprises. Consequently, our enterprises cannot, and must not, function without taking the law of value into account.

Is this a good thing? It is not a bad thing. Under present conditions, it really is not a bad thing, since it trains our business executives to conduct production on rational lines and disciplines them. It is not a bad thing because it teaches our executives to count production magnitudes, to count them accurately, and also to calculate the real things in production precisely, and not to talk nonsense about "approximate figures," spun out of thin air. It is not a bad thing because it teaches our executives to look for, find and utilize hidden reserves latent in production, and not to trample them underfoot. It is not a bad thing because it teaches our executives systematically to improve methods of production, to lower production costs, to practise cost accounting, and to make their enterprises pay. It is a good practical school which accelerates the development of our executive personnel and their growth into genuine leaders of socialist production at the present stage of development.

The trouble is not that production in our country is influenced by the law of value. The trouble is that our business executives and planners, with few exceptions, are poorly acquainted with the operations of the law of value, do not study them, and are unable to take account of them in their computations. This, in fact, explains the confusion that still reigns in the sphere of price-fixing policy. Here is one of many examples. Some time ago it was decided to adjust the prices of cotton and grain in the interest of cotton growing, to establish more accurate prices for grain sold to the cotton growers, and to raise the prices of cotton delivered to the state. Our business executives and planners submitted a proposal on this score which could not but astound the members of the Central Committee, since it suggested fixing the price of a ton of grain at practically the same level as a ton of cotton, and, moreover, the price of a ton of grain was taken as equivalent to that of a ton of baked bread. In reply to the remarks of members of the Central Committee that the price of a ton of bread must be higher than that of a ton of grain, because of the additional expense of milling and baking, and that cotton was generally much dearer than grain, as was also borne out by their prices in the world market, the authors of the proposal could find nothing coherent to say. The Central Committee was therefore obliged to take the matter into its own hands and to lower the prices of grain and raise the prices of cotton. What would have happened if the proposal of these comrades had received legal force? We should have ruined the cotton growers and would have found ourselves without cotton.

But does this mean that the operation of the law of value has as much scope with us as it has under capitalism, and that it is the regulator of production in our country too? No, it does not. Actually, the sphere of operation of the law of value under our economic system is strictly limited and placed within definite bounds. It has already been said that the sphere of operation of commodity production is restricted and placed within definite bounds by our system. The same must be said of the sphere of operation of the law of value. Undoubtedly, the fact that private ownership of the means of production does not exist, and that the means of production both in town and country are socialized, cannot but restrict the sphere of operation of the law of value and the extent of its influence on production.

In this same direction operates the law of balanced (proportionate) development of the national economy, which has superseded the law of competition and anarchy of production.

In this same direction, too, operate our yearly and five-yearly plans and our economic policy generally, which are based on the requirements of the law of balanced development of the national economy.

The effect of all this, taken together, is that the sphere of operation of the law of value in our country is strictly limited, and that the law of value cannot under our system function as the regulator of production.

This, indeed, explains the "striking" fact that whereas in our country the law of value, in spite of the steady and rapid expansion of our socialist production, does not lead to crises of overproduction, in the capitalist countries this same law, whose sphere of operation is very wide under capitalism, does lead, in spite of the low rate of expansion of production, to periodical crises of overproduction.

It is said that the law of value is a permanent law, binding upon all periods of historical development, and that if it does lose its function as a regulator of exchange relations in the second phase of communist society, it retains at this phase of development its function as a regulator of the relations between the various branches of production, as a regulator of the distribution of labour among them.

That is quite untrue. Value, like the law of value, is a historical category connected with the existence of commodity production. With the disappearance of commodity production, value and its forms and the law of value also disappear.

In the second phase of communist society, the amount of labour expended on the production of goods will be measured not in a roundabout way, not through value and its forms, as is the case under commodity production, but directly and immediately—by the amount of time, the number of hours, expended on the production of goods. As to the distribution of labour, its distribution among the branches of production will be regulated not by the law of value, which will have ceased to function by that time, but by the growth of society's demand for goods. It will be a society in which production will be regulated by the requirements of society, and computation of the requirements of society will acquire paramount importance for the planning bodies.

Totally incorrect, too, is the assertion that under our present economic system, in the first phase of development of communist society, the law of value regulates the "proportions" of labour distributed among the various branches of production.

If this were true, it would be incomprehensible why our light industries, which are the most profitable, are not being developed to the utmost, and why preference is given to our heavy industries, which are often less profitable, and sometimes altogether unprofitable.

If this were true, it would be incomprehensible why a number of our heavy industry plants which are still unprofitable and where the labour of the worker does not yield the "proper returns," are not closed down, and why new light industry plants, which would certainly be profitable and where the labour of the workers might yield "big returns," are not opened.

If this were true, it would be incomprehensible why workers are not transferred from plants that are less profitable, but very necessary to our national economy, to plants which are more profitable—in accordance with the law of value, which supposedly regulates the "proportions" of labour distributed among the branches of production.

Obviously, if we were to follow the lead of these comrades, we should have to cease giving primacy to the production of means of production in favour of the production of articles of consumption. And what would be the effect of ceasing to give primacy to the production of the means of production? The effect would be to destroy the possibility of the continuous expansion of our national economy, because the national economy cannot be continuously expanded without giving primacy to the production of means of production.

These comrades forget that the law of value can be a regulator of production only under capitalism, with private ownership of the means of production, and competition, anarchy of production, and crises of overproduction. They forget that in our country the sphere of operation of the law of value is limited by the social ownership of the means of production, and by the law of balanced development of the national economy, and is consequently also limited by our yearly and five-yearly plans, which are an approximate reflection of the requirements of this law.

Some comrades draw the conclusion from this that the law of balanced development of the national economy and economic planning annul the principle of profitableness of production. That is quite untrue. It is just the other way round. If profitableness is considered not from the standpoint of individual plants or industries, and not over a period of one year, but from the standpoint of the entire national economy and over a period of, say, ten or fifteen years, which is the only correct approach to the question, then the temporary and unstable profitableness of some plants or industries is beneath all comparison with that higher form of stable and permanent profitableness which we get from the operation of the law of balanced development of the national economy and from economic planning, which save us from periodical economic crises disruptive to the national economy and causing tremendous material damage to society, and which ensure a continuous and high rate of expansion of our national economy.

In brief, there can be no doubt that under our present socialist conditions of production, the law of value cannot be a "regulator of the proportions" of labour distributed among the various branches of production.

4. ABOLITION OF THE ANTITHESIS BETWEEN TOWN AND COUNTRY, AND BETWEEN MENTAL LABOUR AND PHYSICAL LABOUR, AND ELIMINATION OF DISTINCTIONS BETWEEN THEM

This heading covers a number of problems which essentially differ from one another. I combine them in one section, not in order to lump them together, but solely for brevity of exposition.

Abolition of the antithesis between town and country, between industry and agriculture, is a well-known problem which was discussed long ago by Marx and Engels. The economic basis of this antithesis is the exploitation of the country by the town, the expropriation of the peasantry and the ruin of the majority of the rural population by the whole course of development of industry, trade and credit under capitalism. Hence, the antithesis between town and country under capitalism must be regarded as an antagonism of interests. This it was that gave rise to the hostile attitude of the country towards the town and towards "townfolk" in general.

Undoubtedly, with the abolition of capitalism and the exploiting system in our country, and with the consolidation of the socialist system, the antagonism of interests between town and country, between industry and agriculture, was also bound to disappear. And that is what happened. The immense assistance rendered by the socialist town, by our working class, to our peasantry in eliminating the landlords and kulaks strengthened the foundation for the alliance between the working class and the peasantry, while the systematic supply of first-class tractors and other machines to the peasantry and its collective farms converted the alliance between the working class and the peasantry into friendship between them. Of course, the workers and the collective-farm peasantry do represent two classes differing from one another in status. But this difference does not weaken their friendship in any way. On the contrary, their interests lie along one common line, that of strengthening the socialist system and attaining the victory of communism. It is not surprising, therefore, that not a trace remains of the former distrust, not to speak of the former hatred, of the country for the town.

All this means that the ground for antithesis between town and country, between industry and agriculture, has already been eliminated by our present socialist system.

This, of course, does not mean that the effect of the abolition of the antithesis between town and country will be that "the great towns will perish" (Engels, *Anti-Dühring*). Not only will the great towns not perish, but new great towns will appear as centres of the maximum development of culture, and as centres not only of large-scale industry, but also of the processing of agricultural produce and of powerful development of all branches of the food industry. This will facilitate the cultural progress of the nation and will tend to even up conditions of life in town and country.

We have a similar situation as regards the problem of the abolition of the antithesis between mental and physical labour. This too is a well-known problem which was discussed by Marx and Engels long ago. The economic basis of the antithesis between mental and physical labour is the exploitation of the physical workers by the mental workers. Everyone is familiar with the gulf which under capitalism divided the physical workers of enterprises from the managerial personnel. We know that this gulf gave rise to a hostile attitude on the part of the workers towards managers, foremen, engineers and other members of the technical staff, whom the workers regarded as their enemies. Naturally, with the abolition of capitalism and the exploiting system, the antagonism of interests between physical and mental labour was also bound to disappear. And it really has disappeared in our present socialist system. Today, the physical workers and the managerial personnel are not enemies, but comrades and friends, members of a single collective body of producers who are vitally interested in the progress and improvement of production. Not a trace remains of the former enmity between them.

Of quite a different character is the problem of the disappearance of distinctions between town (industry) and country (agriculture), and between physical and mental labour. This problem was not discussed by the Marxian classics. It is a new problem, one that has been raised practically by our socialist construction.

Is this problem an imaginary one? Has it any practical or theoretical importance for us? No, this problem cannot be considered an imaginary one. On the contrary, it is for us a problem of the greatest seriousness.

Take, for instance, the distinction between agriculture and industry. In our country it consists not only in the fact that the conditions of labour in agriculture differ from those in industry, but, mainly and chiefly, in the fact that whereas in industry we have public ownership of the means of production and of the product of industry, in agriculture we have not public, but group, collective-farm ownership. It has already been said that this fact leads to the preservation of commodity circulation, and that only when this distinction between industry and agriculture disappears, can commodity production with all its attendant consequences also disappear. It therefore cannot be denied that the disappearance of this essential distinction between agriculture and industry must be a matter of paramount importance for us.

The same must be said of the problem of the abolition of the essential distinction between mental labour and physical labour. It, too, is a problem of paramount importance for us. Before the socialist emulation movement assumed mass proportions, the growth of our industry proceeded very haltingly, and many comrades even suggested that the rate of industrial development should be retarded. This was due chiefly to the fact that the cultural and technical level of the workers was too low and lagged far behind that of the technical personnel. But the situation changed radically when the socialist emulation movement assumed a mass character. It was from that moment on that industry began to advance at accelerated speed. Why did socialist emulation assume the character of a mass movement? Because among the workers whole groups of comrades came to the fore who had not only mastered the minimum requirements of technical knowledge, but had gone further and risen to the level of the technical personnel; they began to correct technicians and engineers, to break down the existing norms as antiquated, to introduce new and more up-to-date norms, and so on. What should we have had if not only isolated groups, but the majority of the workers had raised their cultural and technical level to that of the engineering and technical personnel? Our industry would have risen to a height unattainable by industry in other countries. It therefore cannot be denied that the abolition of the essential distinction between mental and physical labour by raising the cultural and technical level of the workers to that of the technical personnel cannot but be of paramount importance for us.

Some comrades assert that in the course of time not only will the essential distinction between industry and agriculture, and between physical and mental labour, disappear, but so will *all* distinction between them. That is not true. Abolition of the essential distinction between industry and agriculture cannot lead to the abolition of all distinction between them. Some distinction, even if inessential, will certainly remain, owing to the difference between the conditions of work in industry and in agriculture. Even in industry the conditions of labour are not the same in all its branches: the conditions of labour, for example, of coal miners differ from those of the workers of a mechanized shoe factory, and the conditions of labour of ore miners from those of engineering workers. If that is so, then all the more must a certain distinction remain between industry and agriculture.

The same must be said of the distinction between mental and physical labour. The essential distinction between them, the difference in their cultural and technical levels, will certainly disappear. But some distinction, even if inessential, will remain, if only because the conditions of labour of the managerial staffs and those of the workers are not identical.

The comrades who assert the contrary do so presumably on the basis of the formulation given in some of my statements, which speaks of the abolition of the distinction between industry and agriculture, and between mental and physical labour, without any reservation to the effect that what is meant is the abolition of the *essential* distinction, not of all distinction. That is exactly how the comrades understood my formulation, assuming that it implied the abolition of all distinction. But this indicates that the formulation was unprecise, unsatisfactory. It must be discarded and replaced by another formulation, one that speaks of the abolition of essential distinctions and the persistence of inessential distinctions between industry and agriculture, and between mental and physical labour.

5. DISINTEGRATION OF THE SINGLE WORLD MARKET AND DEEPENING OF THE CRISIS OF THE WORLD CAPITALIST SYSTEM

The disintegration of the single, all-embracing world market must be regarded as the most important economic sequel of the Second World War and of its economic consequences. It has had the effect of further deepening the general crisis of the world capitalist system.

The Second World War was itself a product of this crisis.

Each of the two capitalist coalitions which locked horns in the war calculated on defeating its adversary and gaining world supremacy. It was in this that they sought a way out of the crisis. The United States of America hoped to put its most dangerous competitors, Germany and Japan, out of action, seize foreign markets and the world's raw material resources, and establish its world supremacy.

But the war did not justify these hopes. It is true that Germany and Japan were put out of action as competitors of the three major capitalist countries: the U.S.A., Great Britain and France. But at the same time China and other, European, people's democracies broke away from the capitalist system and, together with the Soviet Union, formed a united and powerful socialist camp confronting the camp of capitalism. The economic consequences of the existence of two opposite camps was that the single all-embracing world market disintegrated, so that now we have two parallel world markets, also confronting one another.

It should be observed that the U.S.A., and Great Britain and France, themselves contributed—without themselves desiring it, of course—to the formation and consolidation of the new, parallel world market. They imposed an economic blockade on the U.S.S.R., China and the European people's democracies, which did not join the "Marshall plan" system, thinking thereby to strangle them. The effect, however, was not to strangle, but to strengthen the new world market.

But the fundamental thing, of course, is not the economic blockade, but the fact that since the war these countries have joined together economically and established economic cooperation and mutual assistance. The experience of this cooperation shows that not a single capitalist country could have rendered such effective and technically competent assistance to the People's Democracies as the Soviet Union is rendering them. The point is not only that this assistance is the cheapest possible and technically superb. The chief point is that at the bottom of this cooperation lies a sincere desire to help one another and to promote the economic progress of all. The result is a fast pace of industrial development in these countries. It may be confidently said that, with this pace of industrial development, it will soon come to pass that these countries will not only be in no need of imports from capitalist countries, but will themselves feel the necessity of finding an outside market for their surplus products.

But it follows from this that the sphere of exploitation of the world's resources by the major capitalist countries (U.S.A., Britain, France) will not expand, but contract; that their opportunities for sale in the world market will deteriorate, and that their industries will be operating more and more below capacity. That, in fact, is what is meant by the deepening of the general crisis of the world capitalist system in connection with the disintegration of the world market.

This is felt by the capitalists themselves, for it would be difficult for them not to feel the loss of such markets as the U.S.S.R. and China. They are trying to offset these difficulties with the "Marshall plan," the war in Korea, frantic rearmament, and industrial militarization. But that is very much like a drowning man clutching at a straw.

This state of affairs has confronted the economists with two questions:

a) Can it be affirmed that the thesis expounded by Stalin before the Second World War regarding the relative stability of markets in the period of the general crisis of capitalism is still valid?

b) Can it be affirmed that the thesis expounded by Lenin in the spring of 1916—namely, that, in spite of the decay of capitalism, "on the whole, capitalism is growing far more rapidly than before"—is still valid?

I think that it cannot. In view of the new conditions to which the Second World War has given rise, both these theses must be regarded as having lost their validity.

6. INEVITABILITY OF WARS BETWEEN CAPITALIST COUNTRIES

Some comrades hold that, owing to the development of new international conditions since the Second World War, wars between capitalist countries have ceased to be inevitable. They consider that the contradictions between the socialist camp and the capitalist camp are more acute than the contradictions among the capitalist countries; that the U.S.A. has brought the other capitalist countries sufficiently under its sway to be able to prevent them going to war among themselves and weakening one another; that the foremost capitalist minds have been sufficiently taught by the two world wars and the severe damage they caused to the whole capitalist world not to venture to involve the capitalist countries in war with one another again—and that, because of all this, wars between capitalist countries are no longer inevitable.

These comrades are mistaken. They see the outward phenomena that come and go on the surface, but they do not see those profound forces which, although they are so far operating imperceptibly, will nevertheless determine the course of developments.

Outwardly, everything would seem to be "going well": the U.S.A. has put Western Europe, Japan and other capitalist countries on rations; Germany (Western), Britain, France, Italy and Japan have fallen into the clutches of the U.S.A. and are meekly obeying its commands. But it would be mistaken to think that things can continue to "go well" for "all eternity," that these countries will tolerate the domination and oppression of the United States endlessly, that they will not endeavour to tear loose from American bondage and take the path of independent development.

Take, first of all, Britain and France. Undoubtedly, they are imperialist countries. Undoubtedly, cheap raw materials and secure markets are of paramount importance to them. Can it be assumed that they will endlessly tolerate the present situation, in which, under the guise of "Marshall plan aid," Americans are penetrating into the economies of Britain and France and trying to convert them into adjuncts of the United States economy, and American capital is seizing raw materials and markets in the British and French colonies and thereby plotting disaster for the high profits of the British and French capitalists? Would it not be truer to say that capitalist Britain, and, after her, capitalist France, will be compelled in the end to break from the embrace of the U.S.A. and enter into conflict with it in order to secure an independent position and, of course, high profits?

Let us pass to the major vanquished countries, Germany (Western) and Japan. These countries are now languishing in misery under the jackboot of American imperialism. Their industry and agriculture, their trade, their foreign and home policies, and their whole life are fettered by the American occupation "regime." Yet only yesterday these countries were great imperialist powers and were shaking the foundations of the domination of Britain, the U.S.A. and France in Europe and Asia. To think that these countries will not try to get on their feet again, will not try to smash the U.S. "regime," and force their way to independent development, is to believe in miracles.

It is said that the contradictions between capitalism and socialism are stronger than the contradictions among the capitalist countries. Theoretically, of course, that is true. It is not only true now, today; it was true before the Second World War. And it was more or less realized by the leaders of the capitalist countries. Yet the Second World War began not as a war with the U.S.S.R., but as a war between capitalist countries. Why? Firstly, because war with the U.S.S.R., as a socialist land, is more dangerous to capitalism than war between capitalist countries; for whereas war between capitalist countries puts in question only the supremacy of certain capitalist countries over others, war with the U.S.S.R. must certainly put in question the existence of capitalism itself. Secondly, because the capitalists, although they clamour, for "propaganda" purposes, about the aggressiveness of the Soviet Union, do not themselves believe that it is aggressive, because they are aware of the Soviet Union's peaceful policy and know that it will not itself attack capitalist countries.

After the First World War it was similarly believed that Germany had been definitely put out of action, just as certain comrades now believe that Japan and Germany have been definitely put out of action. Then, too, it was said and clamoured in the press that the United States had put Europe on rations; that Germany would never rise to her feet again, and that there would be no more wars between capitalist countries. In spite of this, Germany rose to her feet again as a great power within the space of some fifteen or twenty years after her defeat, having broken out of bondage and taken the path of independent development. And it is significant that it was none other than Britain and the United States that helped Germany to recover economically and to enhance her economic war potential. Of course, when the United States and Britain assisted Germany's economic recovery, they did so with a view to setting a recovered Germany against the Soviet Union, to utilizing her against the land of socialism. But Germany directed her forces in the first place against the Anglo-French-American bloc. And when Hitler Germany declared war on the Soviet Union, the Anglo-French-American bloc, far from joining with Hitler Germany, was compelled to enter into a coalition with the U.S.S.R. against Hitler Germany.

Consequently, the struggle of the capitalist countries for markets and their desire to crush their competitors proved in practice to be stronger than the contradictions between the capitalist camp and the socialist camp.

What guarantee is there, then, that Germany and Japan will not rise to their feet again, will not attempt to break out of American bondage and live their own independent lives? I think there is no such guarantee.

But it follows from this that the inevitability of wars between capitalist countries remains in force.

It is said that Lenin's thesis that imperialism inevitably generates war must now be regarded as obsolete, since powerful popular forces have come forward today in defence of peace and against another world war. That is not true.

The object of the present-day peace movement is to rouse the masses of the people to fight for the preservation of peace and for the prevention of another world war. Consequently, the aim of this movement is not to overthrow capitalism and establish socialism—it confines itself to the democratic aim of preserving peace. In this respect, the present-day peace movement differs from the movement of the time of the First World War for the conversion of the imperialist war into civil war, since the latter movement went farther and pursued socialist aims.

It is possible that in a definite conjuncture of circumstances the fight for peace will develop here or there into a fight for socialism. But then it will no longer be the present-day peace movement; it will be a movement for the overthrow of capitalism.

What is most likely is that the present-day peace movement, as a movement for the preservation of peace, will, if it succeeds, result in preventing a *particular* war, in its temporary postponement, in the temporary preservation of a *particular* peace, in the resignation of a bellicose government and its supersession by another that is prepared temporarily to keep the peace. That, of course, will be good. Even very good. But, all the same, it will not be enough to eliminate the inevitability of wars between capitalist countries generally. It will not be enough, because, for all the successes of the peace movement, imperialism will remain, continue in force—and, consequently, the inevitability of wars will also continue in force.

To eliminate the inevitability of war, it is necessary to abolish imperialism.

7. THE BASIC ECONOMIC LAWS OF MODERN CAPITALISM AND OF SOCIALISM

As you know, the question of the basic economic laws of capitalism and of socialism arose several times in the course of the discussion. Various views were expressed on this score, even the most fantastic. True, the majority of the participants in the discussion reacted feebly to the matter, and no decision on the point was indicated. However, none of the participants denied that such laws exist.

Is there a basic economic law of capitalism? Yes, there is. What is this law, and what are its characteristic features? The basic economic law of capitalism is such a law as determines not some particular aspect or particular processes of the development of capitalist production, but all the principal aspects and all the principal processes of its development—one, consequently, which determines the essence of capitalist production, its essential nature.

Is the law of value the basic economic law of capitalism? No. The law of value is primarily a law of commodity production. It existed before capitalism, and, like commodity production, will continue to exist after the overthrow of capitalism, as it does, for instance, in our country, although, it is true, with a restricted sphere of operation. Having a wide sphere of operation in capitalist conditions, the law of value, of course, plays a big part in the development of capitalist production. But not only does it not determine the essence of capitalist production and the principles of capitalist profit; it does not even pose these problems. Therefore, it cannot be the basic economic law of modern capitalism.

For the same reasons, the law of competition and anarchy of production, or the law of uneven development of capitalism in the various countries cannot be the basic economic law of capitalism either.

It is said that the law of the average rate of profit is the basic economic law of modern capitalism. That is not true. Modern capitalism, monopoly capitalism, cannot content itself with the average profit, which moreover has a tendency to decline, in view of the decreasing organic composition of capital. It is not the average profit, but the maximum profit that modern monopoly capitalism demands, which it needs for more or less regular extended reproduction.

Most appropriate to the concept of a basic economic law of capitalism is the law of surplus value, the law of the origin and growth of capitalist profit. It really does determine the basic features of capitalist production. But the law of surplus value is too general a law; it does not cover the problem of the highest rate of profit, the securing of which is a condition for the development of monopoly capitalism. In order to fill this hiatus, the law of surplus value must be made more concrete and developed further in adaptation to the conditions of monopoly capitalism, at the same time bearing in mind that monopoly capitalism demands not any sort of profit, but precisely the maximum profit. That will be the basic economic law of modern capitalism.

The main features and requirements of the basic economic law of modern capitalism might be formulated roughly in this way: the securing of the maximum capitalist profit through the exploitation, ruin and impoverishment of the majority of the population of the given country, through the enslavement and systematic robbery of the peoples of other countries, especially backward countries, and, lastly, through wars and militarization of the national economy, which are utilized for the obtaining of the highest profits.

It is said that the average profit might nevertheless be

regarded as quite sufficient for capitalist development under modern conditions. That is not true. The average profit is the lowest point of profitableness, below which capitalist production becomes impossible. But it would be absurd to think that, in seizing colonies, subjugating peoples and engineering wars, the magnates of modern monopoly capitalism are striving to secure only the average profit. No, it is not the average profit, nor yet superprofit—which, as a rule, represents only a slight addition to the average profit—but precisely the maximum profit that is the motor of monopoly capitalism. It is precisely the necessity of securing the maximum profits that drives monopoly capitalism to such risky undertakings as the enslavement and systematic plunder of colonies and other backward countries, the conversion of a number of independent countries into dependent countries, the organization of new wars—which to the magnates of modern capitalism is the "business" best adapted to the extraction of the maximum profit—and, lastly, attempts to win world economic supremacy.

The importance of the basic economic law of capitalism consists, among other things, in the circumstance that, since it determines all the major phenomena in the development of the capitalist mode of production, its booms and crises, its victories and defeats, its merits and demerits—the whole process of its contradictory development—it enables us to understand and explain them.

Here is one of many "striking" examples.

We are all acquainted with facts from the history and practice of capitalism illustrative of the rapid development of technology under capitalism, when the capitalists appear as the standard-bearers of the most advanced techniques, as revolutionaries in the development of the technique of production. But we are also familiar with facts of a different kind, illustrative of a halt in technical development under capitalism, when the capitalists appear as reactionaries in the development of new techniques and not infrequently resort to hand labour.

How is this howling contradiction to be explained? It can only be explained by the basic economic law of modern capitalism, that is, by the necessity of obtaining the maximum profit. Capitalism is in favour of new techniques when they promise it the highest profit. Capitalism is against new techniques, and for resort to hand labour, when the new techniques do not promise the highest profit.

That is how matters stand with the basic economic law of modern capitalism.

Is there a basic economic law of socialism? Yes, there is. What are the essential features and requirements of this law? The essential features and requirements of the basic law of socialism might be formulated roughly in this way: the securing of the maximum satisfaction of the constantly rising material and cultural requirements of the whole of society through the continuous expansion and perfection of socialist production on the basis of higher techniques.

Consequently: instead of maximum profits—maximum satisfaction of the material and cultural requirements of society; instead of development of production with breaks in continuity from boom to crisis and from crisis to boom—unbroken expansion of production; instead of periodic breaks in technical development, accompanied by destruction of the productive forces of society—an unbroken process of perfecting production on the basis of higher techniques.

It is said that the law of the balanced, proportionate development of the national economy is the basic economic law of socialism. That is not true. Balanced development of the national economy, and, hence, economic planning, which is a more or less faithful reflection of this law, can yield nothing by themselves, if it is not known for what purpose economic development is planned, or if that purpose is not clear. The law of balanced development of the national economy, can yield the desired result only if there is a purpose for the sake of which economic development is planned. This purpose the law of balanced development of the national economy cannot itself provide. Still less can economic planning provide it. This purpose is inherent in the basic economic law of socialism, in the shape of its requirements, as expounded above. Consequently, the law of balanced development of the national economy can operate to its full scope only if its operation rests on the basic economic law of socialism.

As to economic planning, it can achieve positive results

only if two conditions are observed: a) if it correctly reflects the requirements of the law of balanced development of the national economy, and b) if it conforms in every way to the requirements of the basic economic law of socialism.

8. OTHER QUESTIONS

1) Extra-economic coercion under feudalism.

Of course, extra-economic coercion did play a part in strengthening the economic power of the feudal landlords; however, not it, but feudal ownership of the land was the basis of feudalism.

2) Personal property of the collective-farm household.

It would be wrong to say, as the draft textbook does, that "every household in a collective farm has in personal use a cow, small livestock and poultry." Actually, as we know, it is not in personal use, but as personal *property* that the collective-farm household has its cow, small livestock, poultry, etc. The expression "in personal use" has evidently been taken from the Model Rules of the Agricultural Artel. But a mistake was made in the Model Rules of the Agricultural Artel. The Constitution of the U.S.S.R., which was drafted more carefully, puts it differently, viz.:

"Every household in a collective farm . . . has as its personal property a subsidiary husbandry on the plot, a dwelling house, livestock, poultry and minor agricultural implements."

That, of course, is correct.

It would be well, in addition, to state more particularly that every collective farmer has as his personal property from one to so-many cows, depending on local conditions, so-many sheep, goats, pigs (also from-to, depending on local conditions), and an unlimited quantity of poultry (ducks, geese, hens, turkeys).

Such detailed particulars are of great importance for our comrades abroad, who want to know what exactly has remained as the personal property of the collective-farm household now that agriculture in our country has been collectivized.

3) Total rent paid by the peasants to the landlords; also total expenditure on the purchase of land.

The draft textbook says that as a result of the nationalization of the land, "the peasantry were released from paying rent to the landlords to a total of about 500 million rubles annually" (it should be "gold" rubles). This figure should be verified, because it seems to me that it does not include the rent paid over the whole of Russia, but only in a majority of the Russian gubernias. It should also be borne in mind that in some of the border regions of Russia rent was paid in kind, a fact which the authors of the draft textbook have evidently overlooked. Furthermore, it should be remembered that the peasants were released not only from the payment of rent, but also from annual expenditure for the purchase of land. Was this taken into account in the draft textbook? It seems to me that it was not; but it should have been.

4) Coalescence of the monopolies with the state machine.

The word "coalescence" is not appropriate. It superficially and descriptively notes the process of merging of the monopolies with the state, but it does not reveal the economic import of this process. The fact of the matter is that the merging process is not simply a process of coalescence, but the subjugation of the state machine to the monopolies. The word "coalescence" should therefore be discarded and replaced by the words "subjugation of the state machine to the monopolies."

5) Use of machines in the U.S.S.R.

The draft textbook says that "in the U.S.S.R. machines are used in all cases when they economize the labour of society." That is by no means what should be said. In the first place, machines in the U.S.S.R. always economize the labour of society, and we accordingly do not know of any cases when, in the U.S.S.R., they have not economized the labour of society. In the second place, machines not only economize labour; they also lighten the labour of the worker, and accordingly, in our conditions, in contradistinction to the conditions of capitalism, the workers use machines in the processes of labour with the greatest eagerness.

It should therefore be said that nowhere are machines used so willingly as in the U.S.S.R., because they economize the labour of society and lighten the labour of the worker, and, as there is no unemployment in the U.S.S.R., the workers use machines in the national economy with the greatest eagerness.

6) Living standards of the working class in capitalist countries.

Usually, when speaking of the living standards of the working class, what is meant is only the standards of employed workers, and not of what is known as the reserve army of unemployed. Is such an attitude to the question of the living standards of the working class correct? I think it is not. If there is a reserve army of unemployed, whose members cannot live except by the sale of their labour power, then, the unemployed must necessarily form part of the working class; and if they do form part of the working class, then their destitute condition cannot but influence the living standards of the workers engaged in production. I therefore think that when describing the living standards of the working class in capitalist countries, the condition of the reserve army of unemployed workers should also be taken into account.

7) National income.

I think it *absolutely* necessary to add a chapter on national income to the draft textbook.

8) Should there be a special chapter in the textbook on Lenin and Stalin as the founders of the political economy of socialism?

I think that the chapter, "The Marxist Theory of Socialism. Founding of the Political Economy of Socialism by V. I. Lenin and J. V. Stalin," should be excluded from the textbook. It is entirely unnecessary, since it adds nothing, and only colourlessly reiterates what has already been said in greater detail in earlier chapters of the textbook.

As regards the other questions, I have no remarks to make on the "Proposals" of Comrades Ostrovityanov, Leontyev, Shepilov, Gatovsky, etc.

9. INTERNATIONAL IMPORTANCE OF A MARXIAN TEXTBOOK ON POLITICAL ECONOMY

I think that the comrades do not appreciate the importance of a Marxist textbook on political economy as fully as they should. It is needed not only by our Soviet youth. It is particularly needed by Communists and communist sympathizers in all countries. Our comrades abroad want to know how we broke out of capitalist slavery; how we rebuilt the economy of our country on socialist lines; how we secured the friendship of the peasantry; how we managed to convert a country which was only so recently poverty-stricken and weak into a rich and mighty country; what are the collective farms; why, although the means of production are socialized, we do not abolish commodity production, money, trade, etc. They want to know all this, and much else, not out of mere curiosity, but in order to learn from us and to utilize our experience in their own countries. Consequently, the appearance of a good Marxian textbook on political economy is not only of political importance at home, but also of great international importance.

What is needed, therefore, is a textbook which might serve as a reference book for the revolutionary youth not only at home, but also abroad. It must not be too bulky, because an over-bulky textbook cannot be a reference book and is difficult to assimilate, to master. But it must contain everything fundamental relating both to the economy of our country and to the economy of capitalism and the colonial system.

During the discussion, some comrades proposed the inclusion in the textbook of a number of additional chapters: the historians—on history, the politicians—on politics, the philosophers—on philosophy, the economists—on economics. But the effect of this would be to swell the textbook to unwieldy dimensions. That, of course, must not be done. The textbook employs the historical method to illustrate problems of political economy, but that does not mean that we must turn a textbook on political economy into a history of economic relations.

What we need is a textbook of 500, at most 600 pages—not more. That will be a reference book on Marxian political economy—and an excellent gift to the young Communists of all countries.

Incidentally, in view of the inadequate level of Marxist development of the majority of the Communist parties abroad, such a textbook might also be of great use to communist cadres abroad who are no longer young.

10. WAYS OF IMPROVING THE DRAFT TEXTBOOK ON POLITICAL ECONOMY

During the discussion some comrades "ran down" the draft textbook much too assiduously, berated its authors for errors and oversights, and claimed that the draft was a failure. That is unfair. Of course, there are errors and oversights in the textbook—they are to be found in practically every big undertaking. Be that as it may, the overwhelming majority of the participants in the discussion were nevertheless of the opinion that the draft might serve as a basis for the future textbook and only needed certain corrections and additions. Indeed, one has only to compare the draft with the textbooks on political economy already in circulation to see that the draft stands head and shoulders above them. For that the authors of the draft deserve great credit.

I think that in order to improve the draft textbook, it would be well to appoint a small committee which would include not only the authors of the textbook, and not only supporters, but also opponents of the majority of the participants in the discussion, out-and-out critics of the draft textbook.

It would also be well to include in the committee a competent statistician to verify the figures and to supply additional statistical material for the draft, as well as a competent jurist to verify the accuracy of the formulations.

The members of the committee should be temporarily relieved of all other work and should be well provided for, so that they might devote themselves entirely to the textbook.

Furthermore, it would be well to appoint an editorial committee, of three persons, say, to take care of the final editing of the textbook. This is necessary also in order to achieve unity of style, which, unfortunately, the draft textbook lacks.

Time limit for presentation of the finished textbook to the Central Committee—one year.

February 1, 1952

REPLY TO COMRADE ALEXANDER ILYICH NOTKIN

Comrade Notkin,

I was in no hurry to reply, because I saw no urgency in the questions you raised. All the more that there are other questions which are urgent, and which naturally deflected attention from your letter.

I shall answer point by point.

The first point.

There is a statement in the "Remarks" to the effect that society is not powerless against the laws of science, that man, having come to know economic laws, can utilize them in the interests of society. You assert that this postulate cannot be extended to other social formations, that it holds good only under socialism and communism, that the elemental character of the economic processes under capitalism, for example, makes it impossible for society to utilize economic laws in the interests of society.

That is not true. At the time of the bourgeois revolution in France, for instance, the bourgeoisie utilized against feudalism the law that relations of production must necessarily conform with the character of the productive forces, overthrew the feudal relations of production, created new, bourgeois relations of production, and brought them into conformity with the character of the productive forces which had arisen in the bosom of the feudal system. The bourgeoisie did this not because of any particular abilities it possessed, but because it was vitally interested in doing so. The feudalists put up resistance to this not from stupidity, but because they were vitally interested in preventing this law from becoming effective.

The same must be said of the socialist revolution in our country. The working class utilized the law that the relations of production must necessarily conform with the character of the productive forces, overthrew the bourgeois relations of production, created new, socialist relations of production and brought them into conformity with the character of the productive forces. It was able to do so not because of any particular abilities it possessed, but because it was vitally interested in doing so. The bourgeoisie, which from an advanced force at the dawn of the bourgeois revolution had already become a counterrevolutionary force, offered every resistance to the implementation of this law—and it did so not because it lacked organization, and not because the elemental nature of economic processes drove it to resist, but chiefly because it was to its vital interest that the law should not become operative.

Consequently:

1. Economic processes, economic laws are in one degree or another utilized in the interests of society not only under socialism and communism, but under other formations as well;

2. The utilization of economic laws in class society always and everywhere has a class background to it, and, moreover, always and everywhere the champion of the utilization of economic laws in the interests of society is the advanced class, while the obsolescent classes resist it.

The difference in this matter between the proletariat and the other classes which at any time in the course of history revolutionized the relations of production consists in the fact that the class interests of the proletariat merge with the interests of the overwhelming majority of society, because proletarian revolution implies the abolition not of one or other form of exploitation, but of all exploitation, while the revolutions of other classes, which abolished only one or other form of exploitation, were confined within the limits of their narrow class interests, which conflicted with the interests of the majority of society.

The "Remarks" speak of the class background of the utilization of economic laws in the interests of society. It is stated there that "unlike the laws of natural science, where the discovery and application of a new law proceeds more or less smoothly, the discovery and application of a new law in the economic field, affecting as it does the interests of obsolescent forces of society, meets with the most powerful resistance on their part." This point you missed.

The second point.

You assert that complete conformity of the relations of production with the character of the productive forces can be achieved only under socialism and communism, and that under other formations the conformity can only be partial.

That is not true. In the epoch following the bourgeois revolution, when the bourgeoisie had shattered the feudal relations of production and established bourgeois relations of production, there undoubtedly were periods when the bourgeois production relations did fully conform with the character of the productive forces. Otherwise, capitalism could not have developed as swiftly as it did after the bourgeois revolution.

Further, the words "full conformity" must not be understood in the absolute sense. They must not be understood as meaning that there is no lagging of the relations of production behind the growth of the productive forces under socialism. The productive forces are the most mobile and revolutionary forces of production. They undeniably move in advance of the relations of production even under socialism. Only after a certain lapse of time do the relations of production change in line with the character of the productive forces.

How, then, are the words "full conformity" to be understood? They are to be understood as meaning that under socialism things do not usually go to the length of a conflict between the relations of production and the productive forces, that society is in a position to take timely steps to bring the lagging relations of production into conformity with the character of the productive forces. Socialist society is in a position to do so because it does not include obsolescent classes that might organize resistance. Of course, even under socialism there will be backward, inert forces that do not realize the necessity for changing the relations of production; but they, of course, will not be difficult to overcome without bringing matters to a conflict.

The third point.

It appears from your argument that you regard the means of production, and, in the first place, the implements of production produced by our nationalized enterprises, as commodities.

Can means of production be regarded as commodities in our socialist system? In my opinion they certainly cannot.

A commodity is a product which may be sold to any purchaser, and when its owner sells it, he loses ownership of it and the purchaser becomes the owner of the commodity, which he may resell, pledge or allow to rot. Do means of production come within this category? They obviously do not. In the first place, means of production are not "sold" to any purchaser, they are not "sold" even to collective farms; they are only allocated by the state to its enterprises. In the second place, when transferring means of production to any enterprise, their owner—the state—does not at all lose the ownership of them; on the contrary, it retains it fully. In the third place, directors of enterprises who receive means of production from the Soviet state, far from becoming their owners, are deemed to be the agents of the state in the utilization of the means of production in accordance with the plans established by the state.

It will be seen, then, that under our system means of production can certainly not be classed in the category of commodities.

Why, in that case, do we speak of the value of means of production, their cost of production, their price, etc.?

For two reasons.

Firstly, this is needed for purposes of calculation and settlement, for determining whether enterprises are paying or running at a loss, for checking and controlling the enterprises. But that is only the formal aspect of the matter.

Secondly, it is needed in order, in the interests of our foreign trade, to conduct sales of means of production to foreign countries. Here, in the sphere of foreign trade, but *only in this sphere*, our means of production really are commodities, and really are sold (in the direct meaning of the term).

It therefore follows that in the sphere of foreign trade the means of production produced by our enterprises retain the properties of commodities both essentially and formally, but that in the sphere of domestic economic circulation, means of production lose the properties of commodities, cease to be commodities and pass out of the sphere of operation of the law of value, retaining only the outward integument of commodities (calculation, etc.).

How is this peculiarity to be explained?

The fact of the matter is that in our socialist conditions economic development proceeds not by way of upheavals, but by way of gradual changes, the old not simply being abolished out of hand, but changing its nature in adaptation to the new, and retaining only its form; while the new does not simply destroy the old, but infiltrates into it, changes its nature and its functions, without smashing its form, but utilizing it for the development of the new. This, in our economic circulation, is true not only of commodities, but also of money, as well as of banks, which, while they lose their old functions and acquire new ones, preserve their old form, which is utilized by the socialist system.

If the matter is approached from the formal angle, from the angle of the processes taking place on the surface of phenomena, one may arrive at the incorrect conclusion that the categories of capitalism retain their validity under our economy. If, however, the matter is approached from the standpoint of Marxist analysis, which strictly distinguishes between the substance of an economic process and its form, between the deep processes of development and the surface phenomena, one comes to the only correct conclusion, namely, that it is chiefly the form, the outward appearance, of the old categories of capitalism that have remained in our country, but that their essence has radically changed in adaptation to the requirements of the development of the socialist economy.

The fourth point.

You assert that the law of value exercises a regulating influence on the prices of the "means of production" produced by agriculture and delivered to the state at the procurement prices. You refer to such "means of production" as raw materials—cotton, for instance. You might have added flax, wool and other agricultural raw materials.

It should first of all be observed that in this case it is not "means of production" that agriculture produces, but only one of the means of production—raw materials. The words "means of production" should not be juggled with. When Marxists speak of the production of means of production, what they primarily have in mind is the production of implements of production, what Marx calls "the instruments of labour, those of a mechanical nature, which, taken as a whole, we may call the bone and muscles of production," which constitute the "characteristics of a given epoch of production." To equate a part of the means of production (raw materials) with the means of production, including the implements of production, is to sin against Marxism, because Marxism considers that the implements of production play a decisive role compared with all other means of production. Everyone knows that, by themselves, raw materials cannot produce implements of production, although certain kinds of raw material are necessary for the production of implements of production, while no raw material can be produced without implements of production.

Further: is the influence of the law of value on the price of raw materials produced by agriculture a *regulating* influence, as you, Comrade Notkin, claim? It would be a regulating one, if prices of agricultural raw materials had "free" play in our country, if the law of competition and anarchy of production prevailed, if we did not have a planned economy, and if the production of raw materials were not regulated by plan. But since all these "ifs" are missing in our economic system, the influence of the law of value on the price of agricultural raw materials cannot be a regulating one. In the first place, in our country prices of agricultural raw materials are fixed, established by plan, and are not "free." In the second place, the quantities of agricultural raw materials produced are not determined spontaneously or by chance elements, but by plan. In the third place, the implements of production needed for the producing of agricultural raw materials are concentrated not in the hands of individuals, or groups of individuals, but in the hands of the state. What then, after this, remains of the regulating function of the law of value? It appears that the law of value is itself regulated by the above-mentioned factors characteristic of socialist production.

Consequently, it cannot be denied that the law of value does influence the formation of prices of agricultural raw materials, that it is one of the factors in this process. But still less can it be denied that its influence is not, and cannot be, a regulating one.

The fifth point.

When speaking, in my "Remarks," of the profitableness of the socialist national economy, I was controverting certain comrades who allege that, by not giving great preference to profitable enterprises, and by tolerating the existence side by side with them of unprofitable enterprises, our planned economy is killing the very principle of profitableness of economic undertakings. The "Remarks" say that profitableness considered from the standpoint of individual plants or industries is beneath all comparison with that higher form of profitableness which we get from our socialist mode of production, which saves us from crises of overproduction and ensures us a continuous expansion of production.

But it would be mistaken to conclude from this that the profitableness of individual plants and industries is of no particular value and is not deserving of serious attention. That, of course, is not true. The profitableness of individual plants and industries is of immense value for the development of our industry. It must be taken into account both when planning construction and when planning production. It is an elementary requirement of our economic activity at the present stage of development.

The sixth point.

It is not clear how your words "extended production in strongly deformed guise" in reference to capitalism are to be understood. It should be said that such production, and extended production at that, does not occur in nature.

It is evident that, after the world market has split, and the sphere of exploitation of the world's resources by the major capitalist countries (U.S.A., Britain, France) has begun to contract, the cyclical character of the development of capitalism—expansion and contraction of production—must continue to operate. However, expansion of production in these countries will proceed on a narrower basis, since the volume of production in these countries will diminish.

The seventh point.

The general crisis of the world capitalist system began in the period of the First World War, particularly due to the falling away of the Soviet Union from the capitalist system. That was the first stage in the general crisis. A second stage in the general crisis developed in the period of the Second World War, especially after the European and Asian people's democracies fell away from the capitalist system. The first crisis, in the period of the First World War, and the second crisis, in the period of the Second World War, must not be regarded as separate, unconnected and independent crises, but as stages in the development of the general crisis of the world capitalist system.

Is the general crisis of world capitalism only a political, or only an economic crisis? Neither the one, nor the other. It is a general, i.e., all-round crisis of the world capitalist system, embracing both the economic and the political spheres. And it is clear that at the bottom of it lies the ever-increasing decay of the world capitalist economic system, on the one hand, and the growing economic might of the countries which have fallen away from capitalism—the U.S.S.R., China and the other people's democracies—on the other.

April 21, 1952

From: CONCERNING THE ERRORS OF COMRADE L. D. YAROSHENKO

Some time ago the members of the Political Bureau of the C.C., C.P.S.U.(B.) received a letter from Comrade Yaroshenko, dated March 20, 1952, on a number of economic questions which were debated at the November discussion. The author of the letter complains that the basic documents summing up the discussion, and Comrade Stalin's "Remarks," "contain no reflection whatever of the opinion" of Comrade Yaroshenko. Comrade Yaroshenko also suggests in his note that he should be allowed to write a "Political Economy of Socialism," to be completed in a year or a year and a half, and that he should be given two assistants to help him in the work.

I think that both Comrade Yaroshenko's complaint and his proposal need to be examined on their merits.

Let us begin with the complaint.

Well, then, what is the "opinion" of Comrade Yaroshenko which has received no reflection whatever in the abovementioned documents?

I. COMRADE YAROSHENKO'S CHIEF ERROR

To describe Comrade Yaroshenko's opinion in a couple of words, it should be said that it is un-Marxian—and, hence, profoundly erroneous.

Comrade Yaroshenko's chief error is that he forsakes the Marxist position on the question of the role of the productive forces and of the relations of production in the development of society, that he inordinately overrates the role of the productive forces, and just as inordinately underrates the role of the relations of production, and ends up by declaring that under socialism the relations of production are a component part of the productive forces.

Comrade Yaroshenko is prepared to grant the relations of production a certain role under the conditions of "antagonistic class contradictions," inasmuch as there the relations of production "run counter to the development of the productive forces." But he confines it to a purely negative role, the role of a factor which retards the development of the productive forces, which fetters their development. Any other functions, positive functions, of the relations of production, Comrade Yaroshenko fails to see.

As to the socialist system, where "antagonistic class contradictions" no longer exist, and where the relations of production "no longer run counter to the development of the productive forces," here, according to Comrade Yaroshenko, the relations of production lose every vestige of an independent role, they cease to be a serious factor of development, and are absorbed by the productive forces, becoming a component part of them. Under socialism, Comrade Yaroshenko says, "men's production relations become part of the organization of the productive forces, as a means, an element of their organization." (Comrade Yaroshenko's letter to the Political Bureau of the C.C.)

If that is so, what is the chief task of a Political Economy of Socialism? Comrade Yaroshenko replies: "The chief problem of the Political Economy of Socialism, therefore, *is not* to investigate the relations of production of the members of socialist society; *it is* to elaborate and develop a scientific theory of the organization of the productive forces in social production, a theory of the planning of economic development." (Comrade Yaroshenko's speech at the Plenary Discussion.)

That, in fact, explains why Comrade Yaroshenko is not interested in such economic questions of the socialist system as the existence of different forms of property in our economy, commodity circulation, the law of value, etc., which he believes to be minor questions that only give rise to scholastic disputes. He plainly declares that in his Political Economy of Socialism "disputes as to the role of any particular category of socialist political economy—value, commodity, money, credit, etc.,—which very often with us are of a scholastic character, *are replaced* by a healthy discussion of the rational organization of the productive forces in social production, by a scientific demonstration of the validity of such organization." (Comrade Yaroshenko's speech in the Discussion Working Panel.)

In short, political economy without economic problems.

Comrade Yaroshenko thinks that it is enough to arrange a "rational organization of the productive forces," and the transition from socialism to communism will take place without any particular difficulty. He considers that this is quite sufficient for the transition to communism. He plainly declares that "under socialism, the basic struggle for the building of a communist society reduces itself to a struggle for the proper organization of the productive forces and their rational utilization in social production." (Speech at the Plenary Discussion.) Comrade Yaroshenko solemnly proclaims that "Communism is the highest scientific organization of the productive forces in social production."

It appears, then, that the essence of the communist system begins and ends with the "rational organization of the productive forces."

From all this, Comrade Yaroshenko concludes that there cannot be a single Political Economy for all social formations, that there must be two political economies: one for pre-socialist social formations, the subject of investigation of which is men's relations of production, and the other for the socialist system, the subject of investigation of which should be not the production, i.e., the economic, relations, but the rational organization of the productive forces.

Such is the opinion of Comrade Yaroshenko.

What can be said of this opinion?

It is not true, in the first place, that the role of the relations of production in the history of society has been confined to that of a brake, a fetter on the development of the productive forces. When Marxists speak of the retarding role of the relations of production, it is not all relations of production they have in mind, but only the old relations of production, which no longer conform to the growth of the productive forces and, consequently, retard their development. But, as we know, besides the old, there are also new relations of production, which supersede the old. Can it be said that the role of the new relations of production is that of a brake on the productive forces? No, it cannot. On the contrary, the new relations of production are the *chief* and decisive force, the one which in fact determines the further, and, moreover, powerful, development of the productive forces, and without which the latter would be doomed to stagnation, as is the case today in the capitalist countries.

Nobody can deny that the development of the productive forces of our Soviet industry has made tremendous strides in the period of the five-year plans. But this development would not have occurred if we had not, in October 1917, replaced the old, capitalist relations of production by new, socialist relations of production. Without this revolution in the production, the economic, relations of our country, our productive forces would have stagnated, just as they are stagnating today in the capitalist countries.

Nobody can deny that the development of the productive forces of our agriculture has made tremendous strides in the past twenty or twenty-five years. But this development would not have occurred if we had not in the 'thirties replaced the old, capitalist production relations in the countryside by new, collectivist production relations. Without this revolution in production, the productive forces of our agriculture would have stagnated, just as they are stagnating today in the capitalist countries.

Of course, new relations of production cannot, and do not, remain new forever; they begin to grow old and to run counter to the further development of the productive forces; they begin to lose their role of principal mainspring of the productive forces, and become a brake on them. At this point, in place of these production relations which have become antiquated, new production relations appear whose role it is to be the principal mainspring spurring the further development of the productive forces.

This peculiar development of the relations of production from the role of a brake on the productive forces to that of the principal mainspring impelling them forward, and from the role of principal mainspring to that of a brake on the productive forces, constitutes one of the chief elements of the

Marxian materialist dialectics. Every novice in Marxism knows that nowadays. But Comrade Yaroshenko, it appears, does not know it.

It is not true, in the second place, that the production, i.e., the economic, relations lose their independent role under socialism, that they are absorbed by the productive forces, that social production under socialism is reduced to the organization of the productive forces. Marxism regards social production as an integral whole which has two inseparable sides: the productive forces of society (the relation of society to the forces of nature, in contest with which it secures the material values it needs), and the relations of production (the relations of men to one another in the process of production). These are two different sides of social production, although they are inseparably connected with one another. And just because they constitute different sides of social production, they are able to influence one another. To assert that one of these sides may be absorbed by the other and be converted into its component part, is to commit a very grave sin against Marxism.

Marx said:

"In production men not only act on nature but also on one another. They produce only by cooperating in a certain way and mutually exchanging their activities. In order to produce, they enter into definite connections and relations with one another and only within these social connections and relations does their action on nature, does production, take place."

Consequently, social production consists of two sides, which, although they are inseparably connected, reflect two different categories of relations: the relations of men to nature (productive forces), and the relations of men to one another in the process of production (production relations). Only when both sides of production are present do we have social production, whether it be under the socialist system or under any other social formation.

Comrade Yaroshenko, evidently, is not quite in agreement with Marx. He considers that this postulate of Marx is not applicable to the socialist system. Precisely for this reason he reduces the problem of the Political Economy of Socialism to the rational organization of the productive forces, discarding the production, the economic, relations and severing the productive forces from them.

If we followed Comrade Yaroshenko, therefore, what we would get is, instead of a Marxian Political Economy, something in the nature of Bogdanov's "Universal Organizing Science."

Hence, starting from the right idea that the productive forces are the most mobile and revolutionary forces of production, Comrade Yaroshenko reduces the idea to an absurdity, to the point of denying the role of the production, the economic, relations under socialism; and instead of a full-blooded social production, what he gets is a lopsided and scraggy technology of production—something in the nature of Bukharin's "technique of social organization."

Marx says:

"In the social production of their life [that is, in the production of the material values necessary to the life of men—*J. St.*], men enter into definite relations that are indispensable and independent of their will, relations of production which correspond to a definite stage of development of their material productive forces. The sum total of these relations of production constitute the economic structure of society, the real foundation, on which rises a legal and political superstructure and to which correspond definite forms of social consciousness." (*A Contribution to the Critique of Political Economy*, Preface.)

This means that every social formation, socialist society not excluded, has its economic foundation, consisting of the sum total of men's relations of production. What, one asks, happens to the economic foundation of the socialist system with Comrade Yaroshenko? As we know, Comrade Yaroshenko has already done away with relations of production under socialism as a more or less independent sphere, and has included the little that remains of them in the organization of the productive forces. Has the socialist system, one asks, its own economic foundation? Obviously, seeing that the relations of production have disappeared as a more or less independent factor under socialism, the socialist system is left without an economic foundation.

In short, a socialist system without an economic foundation. A rather funny situation . . .

Is a social system without an economic foundation possible at all? Comrade Yaroshenko evidently believes that it is. Marxism, however, believes that such social systems do not occur in nature.

It is not true, lastly, that communism means the rational organization of the productive forces, that the rational organization of the productive forces is the beginning and end of the communist system, that it is only necessary to organize the productive forces rationally, and the transition to communism will take place without particular difficulty. There is in our literature another definition, another formula of communism —Lenin's formula: "Communism is Soviet rule plus the electrification of the whole country." Lenin's formula is evidently not to Comrade Yaroshenko's liking, and he replaces it with his own homemade formula: "Communism is the highest scientific organization of the productive forces in social production."

In the first place, nobody knows what this "higher scientific" or "rational" organization of the productive forces which Comrade Yaroshenko advertises represents, what its concrete import is. In his speeches at the Plenum and in the working panels of the discussion, and in his letter to the members of the Political Bureau, Comrade Yaroshenko reiterates this mythical formula dozens of times, but nowhere does he say a single word to explain how the "rational organization" of the productive forces, which supposedly constitutes the beginning and end of the essence of the communist system, should be understood.

In the second place, if a choice must be made between the two formulas, then it is not Lenin's formula, which is the only correct one, that should be discarded, but Comrade Yaroshenko's pseudo formula, which is so obviously chimerical and un-Marxian, and is borrowed from the arsenal of Bogdanov, from his "Universal Organizing Science."

Comrade Yaroshenko thinks that we have only to ensure a rational organization of the productive forces, and we shall be able to obtain an abundance of products and to pass to communism, to pass from the formula, "to each according to his work," to the formula, "to each according to his needs." That is a profound error, and reveals a complete lack of understanding of the laws of economic development of socialism. Comrade Yaroshenko's conception of the conditions for the transition from socialism to communism is far too rudimentary and puerile. He does not understand that neither an abundance of products, capable of covering all the requirements of society, nor the transition to the formula, "to each according to his needs," can be brought about if such economic factors as collective-farm, group, property, commodity circulation, etc., remain in force. Comrade Yaroshenko does not understand that before we can pass to the formula, "to each according to his needs," we shall have to pass through a number of stages of economic and cultural re-education of society, in the course of which work will be transformed in the eyes of society from only a means of supporting life into life's prime want, and social property into the sacred and inviolable basis of the existence of society.

In order to pave the way for a real, and not declaratory transition to communism, at least three main preliminary conditions have to be satisfied.

1. It is necessary, in the first place, to ensure, not a mythical "rational organization" of the productive forces, but a continuous expansion of all social production, with a relatively higher rate of expansion of the production of means of production. The relatively higher rate of expansion of production of means of production is necessary not only because it has to provide the equipment both for its own plants and for all the other branches of the national economy, but also because reproduction on an extended scale becomes altogether impossible without it.

2. It is necessary, in the second place, by means of gradual transitions carried out to the advantage of the collective farms, and, hence, of all society, to raise collective-farm property to the level of public property, and, also by means of gradual transitions, to replace commodity circulation by a system of products-exchange, under which the central government, or some other social-economic centre, might control the whole product of social production in the interests of society.

Comrade Yaroshenko is mistaken when he asserts that

there is no contradiction between the relations of production and the productive forces of society under socialism. Of course, our present relations of production are in a period when they fully conform to the growth of the productive forces and help to advance them at seven-league strides. But it would be wrong to rest easy at that and to think that there are no contradictions between our productive forces and the relations of production. There certainly are, and will be, contradictions, seeing that the development of the relations of production lags, and will lag, behind the development of the productive forces. Given a correct policy on the part of the directing bodies, these contradictions cannot grow into antagonisms, and there is no chance of matters coming to a conflict between the relations of production and the productive forces of society. It would be a different matter if we were to conduct a wrong policy, such as that which Comrade Yaroshenko recommends. In that case conflict would be inevitable, and our relations of production might become a serious brake on the further development of the productive forces.

The task of the directing bodies is therefore promptly to discern incipient contradictions, and to take timely measures to resolve them by adapting the relations of production to the growth of the productive forces. This, above all, concerns such economic factors as group, or collective-farm, property and commodity circulation. At present, of course, these factors are being successfully utilized by us for the promotion of the socialist economy, and they are of undeniable benefit to our society. It is undeniable, too, that they will be of benefit also in the near future. But it would be unpardonable blindness not to see at the same time that these factors are already beginning to hamper the powerful development of our productive forces, since they create obstacles to the full extension of government planning to the whole of the national economy, especially agriculture. There is no doubt that these factors will hamper the continued growth of the productive forces of our country more and more as time goes on. The task therefore is to eliminate these contradictions by gradually converting collective-farm property into public property, and by introducing—also gradually—products-exchange in place of commodity circulation.

3. It is necessary, in the third place, to ensure such a cultural advancement of society as will secure for all members of society the all-round development of their physical and mental abilities, so that the members of society may be in a position to receive an education sufficient to enable them to be active agents of social development, and in a position freely to choose their occupations and not be tied all their lives, owing to the existing division of labour, to some one occupation.

What is required for this?

It would be wrong to think that such a substantial advance in the cultural standard of the members of society can be brought about without substantial changes in the present status of labour. For this, it is necessary, first of all, to shorten the working day at least to six, and subsequently to five hours. This is needed in order that the members of society might have the necessary free time to receive an all-round education. It is necessary, further, to introduce universal compulsory polytechnical education, which is required in order that the members of society might be able freely to choose their occupations and not be tied to some one occupation all their lives. It is likewise necessary that housing conditions should be radically improved, and that real wages of workers and employees should be at least doubled, if not more, both by means of direct increases of wages and salaries, and, more especially, by further systematic reductions of prices for consumer goods.

These are the basic conditions required to pave the way for the transition to communism.

Only after *all* these preliminary conditions are satisfied in their entirety may it be hoped that work will be converted in the eyes of the members of society from a nuisance into "life's prime want" (Marx), that "labour will become a pleasure instead of a burden" (Engels), and that social property will be regarded by all members of society as the sacred and inviolable basis of the existence of society.

Only after *all* these preliminary conditions have been satisfied in their entirety will it be possible to pass from the socialist formula, "from each according to his ability, to each according to his work," to the communist formula, "from each according to his ability, to each according to his needs."

This will be a radical transition from one form of economy, the economy of socialism, to another, higher form of economy, the economy of communism.

As we see, the transition from socialism to communism is not such a simple matter as Comrade Yaroshenko imagines. To attempt to reduce this complex and multiform process, which demands deep-going economic changes, to the "rational organization of the productive forces," as Comrade Yaroshenko does, is to substitute Bogdanovism for Marxism.

II. OTHER ERRORS OF COMRADE YAROSHENKO

1. From his incorrect opinion, Comrade Yaroshenko draws incorrect conclusions relative to the character and province of political economy.

Comrade Yaroshenko denies the necessity for a single political economy for all social formations, on the grounds that every social formation has its specific economic laws. But he is absolutely wrong there, and is at variance with such Marxists as Engels and Lenin.

Engels says that political economy is "the science of the conditions and forms under which the *various human societies* have produced and exchanged and on this basis have distributed their products." (*Anti-Dühring.*) Hence, political economy investigates the laws of economic development not of any one social formation, but of the various social formations.

With this, as we know, Lenin was in full agreement. In his critical comments on Bukharin's *Economics of the Transition Period,* he said that Bukharin was wrong in restricting the province of political economy to commodity production, and above all to capitalist production, observing that in doing so Bukharin was taking "a step backward from Engels."

Fully in conformity with this is the definition of political economy given in the draft textbook, when it says that political economy is the science which studies "the laws of the social production and distribution of material values *at the various stages* of development of human society."

That is understandable. The various social formations are governed in their economic development not only by their own specific economic laws, but also by the economic laws that are common to all formations, such as, for instance, the law that the productive forces and the relations of production are united in one integral social production, and the law governing the relations between the productive forces and the relations of production in the process of development of all social formations. Hence, social formations are not only divided from one another by their own specific laws, but also connected with one another by the economic laws common to all formations.

Engels was quite right when he said:

"In order to carry out this critique of bourgeois economy completely, an acquaintance with the capitalist form of production, exchange and distribution did not suffice. The forms which had preceded it or those which still exist alongside it in less developed countries had also, at least in their main features, to be examined and compared." (*Anti-Dühring.*)

It is obvious that here, on this question, Comrade Yaroshenko is in tune with Bukharin.

Further, Comrade Yaroshenko declares that in his "Political Economy of Socialism," "the categories of political economy—value, commodity, money, credit, etc.,—*are replaced* by a healthy discussion of the rational organization of the productive forces in social production," that, consequently, the subject of investigation of *this* political economy will *not* be the production relations of socialism, *but* "the elaboration and development of a scientific theory of the organization of the productive forces, theory of economic planning, etc.," and that, under socialism, the relations of production lose their independent significance and are absorbed by the productive forces as a component part of them.

It must be said that never before has any retrograde "Marxist" delivered himself of such unholy twaddle. Just imagine a political economy of socialism without economic, production problems! Does such a political economy exist anywhere in creation? What is the effect, in a political economy of socialism, of replacing economic problems by problems of organization of the productive forces? The effect is to abolish the political economy of socialism. And that is just what Comrade Yaroshenko does—he abolishes the political economy of socialism. In this, his position fully coincides with that of Bukharin. Bukharin *said* that with the elimination of capitalism, political economy would also be eliminated. Comrade Yaroshenko does not say this, but he *does* it; he does abolish the political economy of socialism. True, he pretends that he is not in full agreement with Bukharin; but that is only a trick, and a penny-ha'penny trick. In actual fact he is doing what Bukharin preached and what Lenin rose up in arms against. Comrade Yaroshenko is following in the footsteps of Bukharin.

Further, Comrade Yaroshenko reduces the problems of the political economy of socialism to problems of the rational organization of the productive forces, to problems of economic planning, etc. But he is profoundly in error. The rational organization of the productive forces, economic planning, etc., are not problems of political economy, but problems of the economic policy of the directing bodies. They are two different provinces, which must not be confused. Comrade Yaroshenko has confused these two different things, and has made a terrible mess of it. Political economy investigates the laws of development of men's relations of production. Economic policy draws practical conclusions from this, gives them concrete shape, and builds its day to day work on them. To foist upon political economy problems of economic policy is to kill it as a science.

The province of political economy is the production, the economic, relations of men. It includes: a) the forms of ownership of the means of production; b) the status of the various social groups in production and their interrelations that follow from these forms, or what Marx calls: "mutual exchange of their activities"; c) the forms of distribution of products, which are entirely determined by them. All these together constitute the province of political economy.

This definition does not contain the word "exchange," which figures in Engels' definition. It is omitted because "exchange" is usually understood by many to mean exchange of commodities, which is characteristic not of all, but only of some social formations, and this sometimes gives rise to misunderstanding, even though the word "exchange" with Engels did not mean only commodity exchange. As will be seen, however, that which Engels meant by the word "exchange" has been included, as a component part, in the above definition. Hence, this definition of the province of political economy fully coincides in content with Engels' definition.

2. When speaking of the basic economic law of some particular social formation, the presumption usually is that the latter cannot have several basic economic laws, that it can have only some one basic economic law, which precisely for that reason is the *basic* law. Otherwise we should have several basic economic laws for each social formation, which would be contrary to the very concept of a basic law. But Comrade Yaroshenko does not agree with this. He thinks that it is possible to have not one, but several basic economic laws of socialism. It is incredible, but a fact. At the Plenary Discussion, he said:

"The magnitudes and correlations of the material funds of social production and reproduction are determined by the available labour power engaged in social production and its prospective increase. This is the basic economic law of socialist society, and it determines the structure of socialist social production and reproduction."

That is one basic economic law of socialism.

In this same speech Comrade Yaroshenko declared:

"In socialist society, the correlations between Departments I and II are determined by the fact that production must have means of production in quantities sufficient to enlist all the able-bodied members of the population in social production. This is the basic economic law of socialism, and it is at the same time a demand of our Constitution, following from the right to work enjoyed by Soviet citizens."

That, so to speak, is a second basic economic law of socialism.

Lastly, in his letter to the members of the Political Bureau, Comrade Yaroshenko declares:

"Accordingly, the essential features and requirements of the basic economic law of socialism may, it seems to me, be roughly formulated as follows: the continuous expansion and perfection of the production of the material and cultural conditions of life of society."

Here we have a third basic economic law of socialism.

Whether all these laws are basic economic laws of socialism, or only one of them, and if only one of them, which exactly—to these questions Comrade Yaroshenko gives no answer in his last letter addressed to the members of the Political Bureau. When formulating the basic economic law of socialism in his letter to the members of the Political Bureau he "forgot," it is to be presumed, that in his speech at the Plenary Discussion three months earlier he had already formulated two other basic economic laws of socialism, evidently believing that nobody would notice this dubious manoeuvre, to say the least of it. But, as we see, he miscalculated.

Let us assume that the first two basic economic laws of socialism formulated by Comrade Yaroshenko no longer exist, and that from now on he regards as the basic economic law of socialism the third one, which he formulated in his letter to the members of the Political Bureau. Let us turn to this letter.

Comrade Yaroshenko says in this letter that he does not agree with the definition of the basic economic law of socialism which Comrade Stalin gave in his "Remarks." He says:

"The chief thing in this definition is 'the securing of the maximum satisfaction of . . . the requirements of the whole of society.' Production is presented here as the means of attaining this principal aim—satisfaction of requirements. Such a definition furnishes grounds for assuming that the basic economic law of socialism formulated by you is based not on the primacy of production, but on the primacy of consumption."

It is evident that Comrade Yaroshenko has completely failed to understand the essence of the problem, and does not see that talk about the primacy of consumption or of production has absolutely nothing to do with the case. When speaking of the primacy of any social process over another, it is usually assumed that the two processes are more or less homogeneous in character. One may, and should, speak of the primacy of the production of means of production over the production of means of consumption, because production is involved in both cases, and they are therefore more or less homogeneous. But one cannot speak, and it would be wrong to speak, of the primacy of consumption over production, or of production over consumption, because production and consumption are two entirely different spheres, which, it is true, are connected with one another, but which are different spheres all the same. Comrade Yaroshenko obviously fails to realize that what we are speaking of here is not the primacy of consumption or of production, but of what *aim* society sets social production, to what *purpose* it subordinates social production—under socialism, say. So that when Comrade Yaroshenko says that "the basis of the life of socialist society, as of all other society, is production," it is entirely beside the point. Comrade Yaroshenko forgets that men produce not for production's sake, but in order to satisfy their needs. He forgets that production divorced from the satisfaction of the needs of society withers and dies.

Can we speak in general of the aims of capitalist or socialist production, of the purposes to which capitalist or socialist production are subordinated? I think that we can and should.

Marx says:

"The direct aim of capitalist production is not the production of goods, but the production of surplus value, or of profit in its developed form; not the product, but the surplus product. From this standpoint, labour itself is productive only in so far as it creates profit or surplus product for capital. In so far as the worker does not create it, his labour is unproductive. Consequently, the sum-total of applied productive labour is of interest to capital only to the extent that through it—or in relation to it—the sum-total of surplus labour increases. Only to that extent is what is called necessary labour time necessary. To the extent that it does not produce this result, it is superfluous and has to be discontinued.

"It is the constant aim of capitalist production to produce the maximum surplus value or surplus product with the minimum of capital advanced; in so far as this result is not attained by overworking the labourer, it is a tendency of capital to seek to produce a given product with the least expenditure—economizing labour power and costs . . .

"The labourers themselves figure in this conception as what they actually are in capitalist production—only means of production; not an aim in themselves and not the aim of production." (*Theory of Surplus Value*, Vol. II, Part 2.)

These words of Marx are remarkable not only because they concisely and precisely define the aim of capitalist production, but also because they indicate the basic aim, the principal purpose, which socialist production should be set.

Hence, the aim of capitalist production is profit-making. As to consumption, capitalism needs it only in so far as it ensures the making of profit. Outside of this, consumption means nothing to capitalism. Man and his needs disappear from its field of vision.

What is the aim of socialist production? What is that main purpose to which social production should be subordinated under socialism?

The aim of socialist production is not profit, but man and his needs, that is, the satisfaction of his material and cultural requirements. As is stated in Comrade Stalin's "Remarks," the aim of socialist production is "the securing of the maximum satisfaction of the constantly rising material and cultural requirements of the whole of society."

Comrade Yaroshenko thinks that what he is confronted with here is the "primacy" of consumption over production. That, of course, is a misapprehension. Actually, what we have here is not the primacy of consumption, but the *subordination* of socialist production to its principal aim of securing the maximum satisfaction of the constantly rising material and cultural requirements of the whole of society.

Consequently, maximum satisfaction of the constantly rising material and cultural requirements of the whole of society is the *aim* of socialist production; continuous expansion and perfection of socialist production on the basis of higher techniques is the *means* for the achievement of the aim.

Such is the basic economic law of socialism.

Desiring to preserve what he calls the "primacy" of production over consumption, Comrade Yaroshenko claims that the "basic economic law of socialism" consists in "the continuous expansion and perfection of the production of the material and cultural conditions of society." That is absolutely wrong. Comrade Yaroshenko grossly distorts and vitiates the formula given in Comrade Stalin's "Remarks." With him, production is converted from a means into an end, and the maximum satisfaction of the constantly rising material and cultural requirements of society is thrown out. What we get is expansion of production for the sake of expansion of production, production as an aim in itself; man and his requirements disappear from Comrade Yaroshenko's field of vision.

It is therefore not surprising that, with the disappearance of man as the aim of socialist production, every vestige of Marxism disappears from Comrade Yaroshenko's "conception."

And so, what Comrade Yaroshenko arrives at is not the "primacy" of production over consumption, but something like the "primacy" of bourgeois ideology over Marxist ideology. . . .

May 22, 1952

SPEECH TO THE NINETEENTH CONGRESS OF THE COMMUNIST PARTY OF THE SOVIET UNION[1]

(*October 14, 1952*)

Comrades!

Allow me, in the name of our Congress, to express our gratitude to all the fraternal parties and groups whose representatives have honored our Congress with their presence or who have sent to our Congress welcoming salutations—gratitude for your friendly greetings, for your wishes of success, for your confidence.

For us this confidence is especially valuable, as it signifies readiness to support our Party in its struggle for a bright future for the peoples of the world, in its struggle against war, in its struggle for the preservation of peace.

It would be a mistake to think that our Party, being now a mighty power, is no longer in need of support. This is untrue. Our Party and our country always were and always will be in need of the trust, sympathy, and support of fraternal peoples abroad.

What is special about this support is that any support of the peaceful aspirations of our Party by a fraternal Party also means at the same time support of their own people in their struggle for the preservation of peace. At the time of the armed aggression against the Soviet Union in 1918–19, when English workers organized a struggle against the war under the slogan "Hands off Russia," that was support—support, first of all, of their own people's struggle for peace, and then, sec-

[1] Translated from *Pravda,* October 15, 1952, by Kathleen Kerr. This is Stalin's last-known major public address.

ond, support of the Soviet Union. When Comrade Thorez and Comrade Togliatti declare that their people will not make war against the peoples of the Soviet Union, then that is support —support, first of all, for the workers and peasants of France and Italy in their struggle for peace, and then support for the peaceful aspirations of the Soviet Union. This special characteristic of mutual support is accounted for by the fact that the interests of our Party not only do not contradict, but, on the contrary, merge with the interests of all peace-loving peoples. The interests of the Soviet Union in general are inseparable from the cause of peace throughout the world.

Clearly, our Party must not remain in debt to its fraternal parties, but rather must in turn render them support in their struggle for the liberation of their peoples and in their struggle for the preservation of peace. As is well known, that is exactly what our Party does. After our Party seized power in 1917 and began the actual liquidation of the oppression of the capitalist and landlord systems, representatives of fraternal parties, admiring the bravery and success of our Party, conferred upon it the title "shock brigade" of the world-wide revolutionary and workers' movement. In this way they expressed their hope that the victories of the "shock brigade" would advance the cause of the peoples still languishing under the oppression of capitalism. I think that our Party has justified these hopes, especially during the period of the Second World War, when the Soviet Union, crushing the German and Japanese military tyranny, delivered the nations of Europe and Asia from the menace of fascist slavery.

Of course it was quite hard to fulfill this esteemed role while the "shock brigade" was still the only one of its kind, carrying out its vanguard role almost in solitude. That's how things used to be. Now—it's a completely different matter. Now, when from China and Korea to Czechoslovakia and Hungary new "shock brigades" have emerged in the form of people's democracies, now it has become easier for our Party to carry out its tasks—and the work has gone more cheerfully.

Special attention must be given to those Communist, democratic, or worker-peasant parties that have not yet come to power and still labor beneath the harsh heel of Draconic bourgeois rule. It's harder for them to work, of course.

But it's not as hard for them to work as it was for us Russian Communists during the czarist period, when the smallest movement forward was proclaimed a most serious crime. However, the Russian Communists stood firm, were not frightened by the difficulty, and attained victory. The same shall be with these parties.

Why will it not be as hard for these parties to work, in comparison with the Russian Communists of the czarist period?

Because, in the first place, they have before their eyes the examples of struggle and success presented by the Soviet Union and the peoples' democracies. Consequently, they can learn from the mistakes and successes of these countries and thus lighten their labor.

Because, secondly, the bourgeoisie itself—the major enemy of the liberation movement—has become different, has changed in a significant way, has become more reactionary, has lost contact with the people, and thus has weakened itself. Clearly this situation also must lighten the work of the revolutionary and democratic parties.

Formerly, the bourgeoisie presumed to play the liberal, defending bourgeois-democratic freedoms, and thereby gained some popularity for itself among the people. Now not a trace of this liberalism remains. There are no longer any so-called "personal freedoms"—the rights of individuality are recognized now only for those who have capital, and all the rest of the citizens are treated as human raw material, fit only for exploitation. The principle of equality of peoples and nations is trampled underfoot, replaced by the principle of equal rights for the exploiting minority and total absence of rights for the exploited majority of citizens. The banner of bourgeois-democratic freedoms has been thrown overboard. In my opinion, it has fallen upon you, representatives of Communist and democratic parties, to pick up this banner and carry it forward if you wish to gather around yourselves the majority of the people. There is no one else to raise it.

Formerly, the bourgeoisie was considered the leader of nations; it maintained the rights and independence of nations, putting them "before all else." Now not a trace of this national principle remains. Now the bourgeoisie will sell the rights and independence of their nations for dollars. The banner of national independence and national sovereignty has been thrown overboard. There is no doubt that it has fallen upon you, representatives of Communist and democratic parties, to pick it up and carry it forward, if you wish to be patriots of your countries, if you wish to become the leaders of nations. There is no one else to raise it.

Thus stands the matter in the present time. Certainly all these circumstances must lighten the work of Communist and democratic parties that have not yet come into power. It follows that these are all reasons to count on success and victory for our fraternal parties in countries still under the rule of capital.

Long live our fraternal parties!

Long life to the leaders of our fraternal parties!

Long live peace among nations!

Down with the makers of war!

(The speech is repeatedly punctuated by storms of applause, and ends with a tumultuous ovation and enthusiastic cheers for Stalin as leader of the world revolution and the forces of peace among nations.)